THE ENTERPRISE OF LAW

JUSTICE WITHOUT THE STATE

By
Bruce L. Benson

PACIFIC RESEARCH INSTITUTE FOR PUBLIC POLICY
San Francisco, California

ISBN 0-936488-30-1

Printed in the United States of America.

Pacific Research Institute for Public Policy
177 Post Street
San Francisco, CA 94108
(415) 989-0833

Library of Congress Cataloging-in-Publication Data

Benson, Bruce, 1949–
    The enterprise of law : justice without the state / by Bruce L.
Benson.
        p.   cm.
    Includes bibliographical references and index.
    ISBN 0-936488-29-8 : $39.95 — ISBN 0-936488-30-1 (pbk.) : $14.95
    1. Rules of law—United States.   2. Law enforcement—United States.
3. Justice Administration of—United States..   4. Privatization—Law
and legislation—United States.   I. Title.
    KF382.846   1990
    340'11—dc20   90-7381
                                                                        CIP

CONTENTS

ACKNOWLEDGEMENTS

This project has taken several years to complete, and a large number of people have either been significantly affected by it or had significant effects on it. I would like to acknowledge as many of them as I can recall. First, I must thank my wife Terrie and daughter Lacey for their ongoing support. They put up with me as I tried to juggle an over-committed research agenda that ate up many of the weekends and evenings I should have spent with them.

The secretaries at Montana State University and Florida State University typed several very different drafts of the book, transferred various drafts from one word processing system to another twice, and finally, one of them taught me to do my own word processing. But some of the secretaries also got interested in what I was writing and began to comment on it and ask questions about it. Three deserve special thanks in this regard: Anne Phillips, Vickie Garland, and Carol Bullock.

Over the course of its evolution, this manuscript benefited greatly from a number of reviews. In particular, Randy Barnett reviewed the first draft of the book, and from the perspective of a legal scholar, he recommended much of the literature on legal theory and history that I have since drawn on extensively. Furthermore, from the perspective of a former prosecuting attorney, Professor Barnett corrected numerous misperceptions I had about the criminal justice process. Finally his extensive comments and organizational suggestions were invaluable.

Several other reviewers were also very helpful in guiding this book's development, including Terry Anderson, Gordon Tullock, Marshall Fritz, Harold Berman, and C. S. Cockburn. Terry Anderson, in his capacity as the Pacific Research Institute's economic advisor, was particularly instrumental in determining the book's final form and content. With his help and advice, and with Marianne Keddington's editing of the final draft, the book was made considerably more readable (and much shorter). Other people affiliated with the Pacific Research Institute provided me with useful comments and reference material, including Chip Mellor, Charles Baird, David Theroux, and Greg Christainsen. In addition, correspondence and conversations with Leonard Liggio (and several other people affiliated with the Institute for Humane Studies), Murray Rothbard, Lawrence Sherman, and Chuck Logan led me to explore useful references that I probably would have missed. Encouraging comments by P. J. Hill and others (again including Gordon Tullock and Charles Baird) on a chapter I wrote for a Pacific Research Institute book ("Guns for Protection and Other Private Sector Responses to the Fear of Violent Crime," in *Firearms and Violence: Issues of Regulation,* Don Kates, Jr., ed. [Cambridge, Mass.: Ballinger Press, 1984]) actually led to my further investigation of the issues examined in this book. Many discussions with colleagues at Montana State and Florida State, such as Ron Johnson, Merle Faminow, Terry Anderson, Rick Stroup, Dick Wagner, Larry Wollen, Tom McCaleb, Randy Holcombe, Dave Rasmussen, and others I apologize for forgetting to mention, also helped me formulate and sharpen my arguments. Parts of the book were presented at the Legal Studies Workshop and the Political Economy Seminar Series at Florida State University, as well as the Public Choice Seminar Series at George Mason University, the Austrian Economics Colloquium at New York University, the Public Choice Society meetings, and the Southern Economic Association meetings. Discussion following those presentations was very beneficial. The Liberty Fund also sponsored a conference organized by the Pacific Research Institute on "Law, Liberty, and Responsible Individuals" in June of 1989. That conference provided me with an opportunity to subject part of my work to critical evaluation by a gathering of eminent legal and economic scholars.

Indeed, much of the book has undergone considerable indirect peer review. Certain sections draw on earlier publications of mine in the *Journal of Libertarian Studies,* the *Antitrust Bulletin,* the *Southern Economic Journal,* the *Journal of Legal Studies* (written with John Baden), the Pacific

Research Institute sponsored book *Firearms and Violence: Issues of Regulation*, edited by Don Kates, Jr., and in a chapter (written with M. L. Greenhut) for *Antitrust and Regulation*, edited by Ronald Grieson (Lexington Books, 1986). In addition, materials developed and written for this book have already been published in the *Madison Papers Series*, the *Harvard Journal of Law and Public Policy*, the *Journal of Libertarian Studies*, the *International Review of Law and Economics*, the *Cato Journal*, the *Journal of Institutional and Theoretical Economics*, and the *Southern Economic Journal*. I thank all of these book publishers and journals, their editors and referees, and my coauthors for their contributions. The *Southern Economic Journal*'s choice of my paper drawn from this book ("The Spontaneous Evolution of Commercial Law") to receive the Georgescu-Roegen Prize as the best article published in the journal during 1988–1989 is a particularly pleasing recognition by my peers that my work on this subject might be worthy of attention.

Several institutions must also be acknowledged. My departments and department chairmen at both Montana State and Florida State were always very supportive. The Institute for Humane Studies provided financial support in the form of an F. Leroy Hill Summer Fellowship, that allowed me to explore a number of related issues much more deeply than I might have, and much of the work they supported ultimately found its way into the book. The Political Economy Research Center also supported the development of several papers that I have drawn upon for the book. Finally, and most significantly, I wish to explicitly acknowledge the vital contributions made by people affiliated with the Pacific Research Institute. I have already mentioned the valuable reviews and comments on the book from Institute associates, but their contributions go far beyond that. To start with, the Institute's willingness to fund the book was what convinced me that it was a project worth pursuing. The Institute's continued support of the project over what turned out to be a much longer period than anyone anticipated has involved many people. In particular: Chip Mellor's behind the scenes efforts to keep the project on track, and to provide the kind of technical and intellectual inputs I needed, were clearly essential (he also proposed, organized, and ran the Liberty Fund Conference mentioned above); Terry Anderson saw to it that the book was written and packaged in a fashion that would maximize its chances of being marketable (subject to the constraints arising from the limited abilities of the author); Pam Riley prepared the market to receive the book; and Linda Clumeck prepared the book for the market. I am sure that I am unaware of the full extent and importance of the efforts made by these individuals and others at the Institute. Thank you all for your invaluable contributions.

Bruce L. Benson
Department of Economics
Florida State University

1

INTRODUCTION

Anyone who would even question the "fact" that law and order are necessary functions of government is likely to be considered a ridiculous, uninformed radical by most observers. Bernard Herber, in a typical public finance textbook, for example, wrote

> The...function...of providing domestic stability in the form of law and order and the protection of property...could be logically opposed only by an avowed anarchist. Since...[law and order is] not [a] controversial function of government,...[it does] not require a lengthy analysis in the effort to construct an economic case for the existence of a public sector for resource allocation purposes.[1]

But even though most academics do not question the logic of government domination of law and the maintenance of order, large segments of the population do. Surveys and polls indicate growing dissatisfaction with all aspects of government law enforcement in the United States, particularly with the courts and the corrections system. More importantly, citizens are turning to the private sector in ever increasing numbers for services which presumably are "not controversial functions of government." Privately produced crime detection and prevention, arbitration, and mediation are growth industries in the United States.

This study will use economic theory to compare institutions and incentives that influence public and private performance in the provision of law and its enforcement. Some critics may contend that law is not an appropriate subject for "economic analysis," because it is not produced and allocated in exchange markets. To be certain, economics has a great deal to say about market institutions, but its relevance and scope are not so narrowly limited. Economic theory requires only that scarce resources be allocated among competing uses. Clearly, the enterprise of law—the use of police services, court time, and all other inputs in the process of making law and establishing order—requires scarce resources that must be allocated. Beyond that, economic theory explains human behavior by considering how individuals react to incentives and constraints.

Using economic theory, then, it can be convincingly demonstrated that private-sector (i.e., market or voluntary) institutions are capable of establishing strong incentives that lead to effective law making and law enforcement. The resulting legal constraints facilitate interaction and support social order by inducing cooperation and reducing violent confrontation. It can also be shown that public-sector institutions create incentives that can lead to substantial inefficiencies in the provision of these same functions. In fact, our modern reliance on government to make law and establish order is not the historical norm. Public police forces were not imposed on the populace until the middle of the nineteenth century in the United States and Great Britian, for instance, and then only in the face of considerable citizen resistance.[2] Crime victims played the prosecutors' role in England until almost the turn of the century, and they did not yield to public prosecution without a struggle.[3] The foundation of commercial law was developed by the European merchant community and enforced through merchant courts.[4] To this day, international trade is "governed" to a large extent by merchants, as they make, arbitrate, and enforce their own law; and in the United States, at least 75 percent of commercial disputes are settled through private arbitration or mediation with decisions based on business custom and practice (customary commercial law).[5] Arbitration services, particularly for commercial disputes, have been increasingly used for some time, but the last few years have witnessed the development of a new industry—private for-profit courts competing with public courts for a wide spectrum of civil disputes.[6] Furthermore, there are now over twice as many private police as public police in the United States, as citizens hire more and more watchmen, guards, and highly trained security experts.[7] Between 1964 and 1981, employment by private firms offering protective and detective services increased by 432.9 percent, and the number of firms offering such services grew by 285.5 percent over the same period (see Table 9.3).

Individuals are also increasingly supplementing government protection with efforts of their own.[8] More and more citizens are buying firearms for personal protection; burglar alarms are being installed and guard dogs purchased. Citizens are barring their windows, learning self-defense, carrying whistles and other noisemakers, and buying self-protection devices. There is a growing business in providing bullet-proof cars and security systems for the powerful and wealthy who fear assassination or kidnapping. There are also less costly activities, such as neighborhood or tenant watches and patrols, and escort groups. A Gallup poll found that during the early 1980s, 17 percent of those surveyed reported at least one of these voluntary crime prevention efforts in their neighborhood.[9]

People turn to the private sector when public police and courts are presumably available because there is a growing dissatisfaction with public-sector efforts to maintain social order. Citizens' dissatisfaction arises in part because of a growing belief that the government is not adequately controlling crime. In 1982, the *Figgie Report on Fear of Crime* found that "most people perceive crime rates as continually increasing and look at any decline as an aberration, a temporary ebb in the inexorably rising tide of petty theft, armed robbery, murder, and international terror." The report also pointed out that crime statistics understate the true level of crime. According to the report, an estimated 60 percent of all personal larceny cases where there is no contact between the thief and his victim go unreported; and less than 50 percent of all assaults, less than 60 percent of all household burglaries, less than 30 percent of household larcenies, and only a little more than half of all robberies and rapes are reported.[10] Thus, the *Figgie Report* concluded: "These striking statistics are either a measure of the lack of public confidence in the ability of the police to solve crimes or a more realistic appraisal of what is possible. . . ."[11] After all, in 1980 less than 20 percent of reported crimes were cleared by arrest (down from 26 percent in 1960), and in at least one California county only 12 percent of those arrested as felons in 1977 were actually convicted.[12] The U.S. Department of Justice report on crime victimization in 1979 found that approximately 10 percent of unreported crimes were not reported because people believed that the police "do not want to be bothered."[13]

Dissatisfaction with the public criminal law apparatus extends to the courts as well. Since 1965 more and more people have come to believe that the courts have not been harsh enough in criminal cases, rising from 48.9 percent in 1965 to 84.9 in 1978 (see Table 1.1);[14] from 1980 to 1986, this percentage held fairly steady in the 82 to 86 percent range.[15] A 1972 study found that

Table 1.1   Trends in Attitude Toward the Courts.

Survey	Date	Percentage Saying Courts Are Not Harsh Enough
Gallup	3 / 1965	48.9
Gallup	9 / 1965	59.3
Gallup	1 / 1968	63.1
Gallup	1 / 1969	74.4
GSS	3 / 1972	74.4
Gallup	12 / 1972	66.3
GSS	3 / 1973	73.1
GSS	3 / 1974	77.9
GSS	3 / 1975	79.2
GSS	3 / 1976	81.0
GSS	3 / 1977	83.0
GSS	3 / 1978	84.9

SOURCE: A. L. Stinchcombe et al., *Crime and Punishment—Changing Attitudes in America* (San Francisco: Jossey-Bass Publishers, 1980), p. 31.

82 percent of its survey respondents agreed "somewhat" or "a great deal" that "recent Supreme Court decisions have made it more difficult to punish criminals."[16]

The *Figgie Report* also found that 80 percent of the study's sample believed that the courts and prison system were ineffective in rehabilitating criminals. More than half of those surveyed (52 percent) thought that the prison sentences currently given do not discourage crime and that the "revolving door policy in the justice system makes a prison term a mere inconvenience for the experienced criminal."[17] Plea bargaining now leads to approximately 90 percent of criminal convictions, implying to many that criminals are getting off with light sentences; beyond that, criminals serve, on average, less than half their sentences in jail (down from 61 percent in 1965).[18] Many also believe that prisons do not fulfill their functions of deterrence and rehabilitation, but instead serve as "schools" for the study of crime. Indeed, a nationwide follow-up study of 78,143 offenders who were released from prison in 1972 found that 74 percent were rearrested.[19]

The courts receive low marks from citizens in the area of civil law as well. A 1978 survey found that only 23 percent of those interviewed had a high degree of confidence in state and local courts, while over a third of the sample expressed little or no confidence. Moreover, 57 percent believed that "efficiency in the courts" was a serious national problem.[20] After all, court backlogs can delay a civil trial for more than five years in some states.[21]

Why is delay in the public courts such a problem when most criminal cases are settled by plea bargaining and most commercial disputes are settled by private arbitration? Why, for that matter, does the system rely so heavily on plea bargaining and private arbitration? Why do citizens think they must spend billions of dollars to hire private police officers and establish private security systems when the government is already spending billions on a public police force? Why are local, state, and federal authorities spending taxpayers' dollars to contract with private firms to build, staff, and maintain prisons when the public prison system already costs billions of dollars? Why do victims of crimes choose not to report a significant portion of all crimes committed? These questions and others like them can only be answered by comparing the institutions associated with public-sector law creation and enforcement with private-sector counterparts. Neither system is perfect, but the growing dissatisfaction with the public sector's performance and increasing reliance on private-sector alternatives indicates that it is time to question the *presumption* that law and order must be governmentally provided.

In the analysis that follows, I consider such topics as the characteristics of primitive legal systems and the evolution of common law and other legal systems. I explore modern law enforcement; the behavior of public police, prosecutors and judges; and political corruption. I also examine current trends in government "contracting" with private firms for police and prison services, and trends in private-sector provision of arbitration, mediation, and crime prevention. Issues in legal theory are discussed, such as the role of custom in law and the question of how "law" should be defined. Throughout the analysis, I liberally use others' thoughts and research findings, demonstrating that many of the relatively broad conclusions reached using an economic perspective have been reached by others in their complementary, yet relatively more narrow, approaches. But more importantly, drawing from a large and seemingly dispersed literature can lead to a more complete understanding of the potential for private-sector maintenance of social order. In this way we can achieve a more accurate comparison of the effectiveness of the public and private sector in this vital public policy area.

ENDNOTES

1. Bernard P. Herber, *Modern Public Finance: The Study of Public Sector Economics* (Homewood, Ill.: Richard D. Irwin, Inc., 1975), p. 22.
2. Truett A. Ricks, Bill G. Tillett and Clifford W. Van Meter, *Principles of Security* (Cincinnati: Criminal Justice Studies, Anderson Publishing Co.,

1981), p. 5; and Frank Morn, *The Eye that Never Sleeps* (Bloomington, Ind.: University Press, 1982), p. 8.

3. Juan Cardenas, "The Crime Victim in the Prosecutorial Process," *Harvard Journal of Law and Public Policy* 9 (Spring 1986): 361.

4. Leon Trakman, *The Law Merchant: The Evolution of Commercial Law* (Littleton, Colo.: Fred B. Rothman and Co., 1983); Harold J. Berman, *Law and Revolution: The Formation of Western Legal Tradition* (Cambridge, Mass.: Harvard University Press, 1983); and Bruce L. Benson, "The Spontaneous Evolution of Commercial Law," *Southern Economic Journal* 55 (January 1989).

5. Jerold S. Auerbach, *Justice Without Law* (New York: Oxford University Press, 1983), p. 113.

6. Benson, "The Spontaneous Evolution of Commercial Law"; Gary Pruitt, "California's Rent-a-Judge Justice," *Journal of Contemporary Studies* 5 (Spring 1982): 49–57; and Richard Koenig, "More Firms Turn to Private Courts to Avoid Expensive Legal Fights," *Wall Street Journal* (January 4, 1984).

7. Ricks, et al., *Principles of Security*, p. 13, and Norman K. Bottom and John Kostanoski, *Security and Loss Control* (New York: Macmillan Publishing Co., 1983), pp. 31–32.

8. See for example, Research and Forecasts, Inc., *America Afraid: How Fear of Crime Changes the Way We Live, Based on the Widely Publicized Figgie Report* (New York: New America Library, 1983). Such actions by individuals are discussed at length in Chapter 9.

9. Lawrence Sherman, "Patrol Strategies for Police," in *Crime and Public Policy,* James Q. Wilson, ed. (San Francisco: Institute for Contemporary Studies Press, 1983), p. 145.

10. Research and Forecasts, Inc., *America Afraid: How Fear of Crime Changes the Way We Live,* p. 105. These kinds of estimates have been made by many others, including government sources. See for example, President's Commission on Law Enforcement and Administration of Justice, *The Challenge of Crime in a Free Society* (New York: Arno Press, 1967), p. 22.

11. Research and Forecasts, Inc., ibid., p. 105.

12. U.S. Department of Justice, *Uniform Crime Reports,* for various years (see table 12.1); Robert W. Poole, Jr., *Cutting Back City Hall* (New York: Universe Books, 1978), p. 52.

13. Research and Forecasts, Inc., *America Afraid: How Fear of Crime Changes the Way We Live,* p. 105.

14. A. L. Stinchcombe, et al., *Crime and Punishment—Changing Attitudes in America* (San Francisco: Jossey-Bass Publishers, 1980), p. 31.

15. U.S. Department of Justice, *Source Book of Criminal Justice Statistics—1986* (Washington, D.C.: Bureau of Justice Statistics, 1987), pp. 86–87.

16. M. Blumenthal, et al., *Justifying Violent Crime: Attitudes of American Men* (Ann Arbor, Mich.: Institute for Social Research, 1972), p. 83.

17. Research and Forecasts, Inc., *America Afraid: How Fear of Crime Changes the Way We Live,* p. 102.
18. U.S. Department of Justice, *Sourcebook of Criminal Justice Statistics—1976* (Washington, D.C.: Bureau of Justice Statistics, 1977).
19. J. L. Barkas, *Protecting Yourself Against Crime,* Public Affairs Pamphlet No. 564 (New York: The Public Affairs Committee, Inc., 1978), p. 20.
20. Yankelovich, Skely and White, Inc., *The Public Image of Courts: Highlights of a National Survey of the General Public, Judges, Lawyers and Community Leaders* (Williamsburg, Va.: National Center for State Courts, 1978), Table III.6, p. 25 and Table IV.1, p. 29.
21. For example, see discussion in Robert W. Poole, Jr., "Can Justice Be Privatized?" *Fiscal Watchdog* 49 (November 1980), p. 2; and William C. Wooldridge, *Uncle Sam, the Monopoly Man* (New Rochelle, N.Y.: Arlington House, 1970), p. 1.

PART I

FROM VOLUNTARY TO AUTHORITARIAN LAW

2

CUSTOMARY LEGAL SYSTEMS WITH VOLUNTARY ENFORCEMENT

It is a widely held belief that state governments and law develop together and, therefore, that law and order could not exist in a society without the organized, authoritarian institutions of the state. One means of dispelling this perception is to illustrate that a nation-state is not a prerequisite for law. First, however, it is necessary to understand just what is meant by "law," and how systems of law work.

THE ENTERPRISE OF CUSTOMARY LAW

If law is simply represented by any system of rules, as some have suggested,[1] then "morality" and law would appear to be synonymous. Lon Fuller contended that "law," when more appropriately ". . .viewed as a direction of purposive human effort, consists in the enterprise of subjecting human conduct to the governance of rules."[2] Law consists of both rules of conduct and the mechanisms or processes for applying those rules. Individuals must have incentives to recognize rules of conduct or the rules become irrelevant, so institutions for enforcement are necessary. Similarly, when the implications of existing rules are unclear, dispute resolution institutions are required. As conditions change, mechanisms for development of new rules and changes in old rules must exist. So, legal systems display very similar structural characteristics.[3] Fuller's definition of law is accepted here, in part because it allows the analysis of law to focus on the institutions involved in the production and enforcement of legal rules, and on the incentives which both lead to the development of and arise as a consequence of those institutions. That is, it lends itself to an economic analysis of the enterprise of law.

Law can be imposed from above by some coercive authority, such as a king, a legislature, or a supreme court, or law can develop "from the ground" as customs and practice evolve.[4] Law imposed from the top—authoritarian law—typically requires the support of a powerful minority; law developed from the bottom up—customary law—requires widespread acceptance. Hayek explained that many issues of law are not

> whether the parties have abused anybody's will, but whether their actions have conformed to expectations which other parties had reasonably formed because they corresponded to the practices on which the everyday conduct of the members of the group was based. The significance of customs here is that they give rise to expectations that guide people's actions, and what will be regarded as binding will therefore be those practices that everybody counts on being observed and which thereby condition the success of most activities.[5]

Customary law is recognized, not because it is backed by the power of some strong individual or institution, but because each individual recognizes the benefits of behaving in accordance with other individuals' expectations, *given* that others also behave as he expects. Alternatively, if a minority coercively imposes law from above, then that law will require much more force to maintain social order than is required when law develops from the bottom through mutual recognition and acceptance.

Reciprocities are the basic source both of the recognition of duty to obey law and of law enforcement in a customary law system. That is, individuals must "exchange" recognition of certain behavioral rules for their mutual benefit. Fuller suggested three conditions that make a duty clear and acceptable to those affected:

> *First,* the relationship of reciprocity out of which the duty arises must result from a voluntary agreement between the parties immediately affected; they themselves "create" the duty. *Second,* the reciprocal performances of the parties must in some sense be equal in value. . . . We cannot here speak of an exact identity, for it makes no sense at all to exchange, say, a book or idea in return for exactly the same book or idea. The bond of reciprocity unites men, not simply in spite of their differences but because of their differences. . . . *Third,* the relationships within the society must be sufficiently fluid so that the same duty you owe me today, I may owe you tomorrow—in other words, the relationship of duty must in theory and in practice be reversible.[6]

Because the source of recognition of customary law is reciprocity, private property rights and the rights of individuals are likely to constitute the most important primary rules of conduct in such legal systems. After all, voluntary recognition of laws and participation in their enforcement is likely to arise only when substantial benefits from doing so can be internalized by each individual. Punishment is frequently the threat that induces recognition of law imposed from above, but incentives must be largely positive when customary law prevails. Individuals must expect to gain as much or more than the costs they bear from voluntary involvement in the legal system. Protection of personal property and individual rights is a very attractive benefit.

Under customary law, offenses are treated as torts (private wrongs or injuries) rather than crimes (offenses against the state or the "society"). A potential action by one person has to affect someone else before any question of legality can arise; any action that does not, such as what a person does alone or in voluntary cooperation with someone else but in a manner that clearly harms no one, is not likely to become the subject of a rule of conduct under customary law. Fuller proposed that "customary law" might best be described as a "language of interaction." [7] Facilitating interaction can only be accomplished with recognition of clear (although not necessarily written) codes of conduct enforced through reciprocally acceptable, well established adjudication arrangements accompanied by effective legal sanctions.

James Buchanan asked, if government is dismantled "how do rights re-emerge and come to command respect? How do 'laws' emerge that carry with them general respect for their 'legitimacy'?" [8] He contended that collective action would be necessary to devise a "social contract" or "constitution" to define rights and to establish the institutions to enforce those rights. But collective action can be achieved through individual agreements, with useful rules spreading to other members of a group. Demsetz explained that property rights will be defined when the benefits of doing so cover the costs of defining and enforcing such rights.[9] Such benefits may become evident because a dispute arises, implying that existing rules do not adequately cover some new situation. The parties involved must expect the benefits from resolving the dispute (e.g., avoiding a violent confrontation), and of establishing a new rule, to outweigh the cost of resolving the dispute and enforcing the resulting judgment, or they would not take it to the adjudication system.

Dispute resolution can be a major source of legal change since an adjudicator will often make more precise those rules about which differences of opinion exist, and even supply new rules because no generally recognized rules cover a new situation.[10] If the relevant group accepts the ruling it becomes part of customary law, but not because it is coercively imposed on a group by some authority backing the court. Thus, good rules that facilitate interaction tend to be selected over time, while bad decisions are ignored.

Dispute resolution is not the only source of legal evolution under customary law. Individuals may observe others behaving in a particular way in a new situation and adopt similar behavior themselves, recognizing the benefit of avoiding confrontation. Institutions for enforcement similarly evolve due to recognition of reciprocal benefits.

Consider the development of dispute resolution procedures. No state-like coercive authority exists in a customary system to force disputants into a court. Because rules of customary law are in the nature of torts, the aggrieved party must pursue prosecution. Under such circumstances, individuals have strong reciprocal incentives to form mutual support groups for legal matters. The makeup of such groups may reflect family (as it frequently did in primitive societies),[11] religion (as in some primitive groups),[12] geographic proximity (as in Anglo-Saxon England),[13] functional similarity (as with commercial law),[14] or contractual arrangements (e.g., as in medieval Ireland and in medieval Iceland).[15] The group members are obligated to aid any other member in a valid dispute, given that the member has fulfilled his obligations in the past. Thus, ability to obtain support in a dispute depends on reciprocal loyalty.[16]

Should a dispute arise, reciprocal support groups give individuals a position of strength. This does not necessarily mean, however, that disputes are settled by warfare between groups. Violence is a costly means of solving a dispute: if the accuser and his support group attack the accused, the accused's group is obliged to avenge the attack. Consequently, arrangements and procedures for non-violent dispute resolution should evolve very quickly in customary law systems.

The impetus for accepting adjudication in a customary legal system (as well as in an authoritarian system) is the omnipresent threat of force, but use of such force is certainly not likely to be the norm. Rather, an agreement between the parties must be negotiated. Frequently, a mutually acceptable arbitrator or mediator is chosen to consider the dispute, but this individual (or group) will have no vested authority to impose a solution on disputants. The ruling, therefore, must be acceptable to the groups to which both parties in the dispute belong. The only real power an arbitrator or mediator holds under such a system is that of persuasion.[17]

If the accused offender is found guilty, the "punishment" tends to be economic in nature: restitution in the form of a fine or indemnity to be paid to the plaintiff. Liability, intent, the value of the damages, and the status of the offended person all may be considered in determining the indemnity. Every invasion of person or property is generally valued in terms of property.

A judgment under customary law is typically enforceable because of an effective threat of total ostracism by the community (e.g., the primitive tribe, the merchant community). Reciprocities between the groups, recognizing the high cost of refusal to accept good judgments, takes those who refuse such a judgment outside their support group and they become outcasts or "outlaws." The adjudicated solutions tend to be accepted due to fear of this severe boycott sanction.

Carl Menger proposed that the origin, formation, and ultimate process of all social institutions (including law) is essentially the same as the spontaneous order Adam Smith described for markets.[18] Markets coordinate interactions, as does customary law. Both develop as they do because the actions they are intended to coordinate are performed more effectively under one system or process than another. The more effective institutional arrangement replaces the less effective one.

The evolutionary process is not one of deliberate design. In the case of primitive societies, for example, early kinship or neighborhood groups were effective social arrangements for internalizing reciprocal legal benefits—as well as other benefits arising out of cooperative production, defense, religious practices, and so on—*relative* to previously existing arrangements. Others saw some of those benefits and either joined existing groups or copied their successful characteristics and formed new groups. Neither the members of the earliest groups nor those who followed had to understand what particular aspect of the contract actually facilitated interactions that led to an improved social order. One example of a primitive legal system is revealed in Leopold Popisil's work with the Kapauku Papuans of West New Guinea.

THE KAPAUKU PAPUANS OF WEST NEW GUINEA

In 1954, Popisil began conducting research among the Kapauku Papuans, a primitive linguistic group of about 45,000 people living by means of horticulture in the western part of the central highlands of West New Guinea. He discovered that their reciprocal arrangements for support and protection were based on kinship. Members of two or more patrilineages, however, typically joined together for defensive and legal purpose, even though they often belonged to different sibs. These "confederations" generally encompassed from three to nine villages, with each village consisting of about fifteen households.

The Kapauku had no formal governmental authority with coercive power. Most observers concluded that there was a lack of leadership among those people, but one Dutch administrator noted that "there is a man who seems to have some influence upon the others. He is referred to by the name *tonowi* which means 'the rich one.' Nevertheless, I would hesitate to call him a chief or a leader at all; *primus inter pares* [the first among equals] would be a more proper designation for him."[19] Popisil suggested that to understand the role and prestige of the *tonowi* one must recognize two "basic values" of the Kapauku: individualism and physical freedom. For instance, a detailed system of private property rights was evident, and there was no common ownership.

> A house, boat, bow and arrows, field, crops, patches of second-growth forest, or even a meal shared by a family or household is always owned by one person. Individual ownership. . . is so extensive in the Kamu Valley that we find the virgin forests divided into tracts which belong to single individuals. Relatives, husbands and wives do not own anything in common. Even an eleven-year-old boy can own his field and his money and play the role of debtor and creditor as well.[20]

The paramount role of individual rights also was evident in the position of the *tonowi*, typically "a healthy man in the prime of life" who had accumulated a good deal of wealth. He was, Popisil reported, "an individual who has a great amount of cowrie-shell money, extensive credit, several wives, approximately twenty pigs, a reasonably large house, and many cultivated fields."[21] Individual wealth almost always depended on work effort and skill, so a *tonowi* was generally a mature, skilled individual with considerable physical and intellectual abilities. But not all *tonowi* achieved the respect necessary to assume leadership. "The way in which capital is acquired and how it is used make a great difference," Popisil concluded; "the natives favor rich candidates who are generous and honest. These two attributes are greatly valued by the culture."[22]

Each individual in the society could choose to contract with any available *tonowi* (availability generally involved kinship). Typically, followers became debtors to a *tonowi* in exchange for agreeing to perform certain duties in support of the *tonowi*. The followers got much more than a loan, however: "The expectation of future favors and advantages is probably the most potent motivation for most of the headman's followers. . . . Even individuals from neighboring confederations may yield to the wishes of a *tonowi* in case his help may be needed in the future."[23] Thus, *tonowi* leadership was given, not taken, and reflected to a great extent an ability to "persuade the unit to support a man in a dispute or to fight for his cause."[24] Thus, this position of leadership was achieved through reciprocal exchange of support between a *tonowi* and his followers, support that could be freely withdrawn by either party (e.g., upon payment of debt or demand for repayment).[25] The informality and contractual characteristics of Kapauku leadership led many Western observers to conclude that Kapauku society lacked law, but there is clear evidence that law was recognized, and that processes for adjudication and change existed in the Kapauku's legal system.

Recognition. Recognition of law was based on kinship and contractual reciprocities motivated by the benefits of individual rights and private property. Indeed, a "mental codification of abstract rules" existed, so that legal decisions were part of a "going order."[26] Grammatical phrases or references to specific customs, precedents, or rules were present in all adjudication decisions that Popisil observed. He concluded: "not only does a legal decision solve a specific case, but it also formulates an ideal—a solution intended to be utilized in a similar situation in the future. The ideal component binds all other members of the group who did not participate in the case under consideration. The [adjudicator] himself turns to his previous decisions for consistency. In a way, they also bind him. Lawyers speak in such a case about the binding force of the precedent."[27]

Adjudication. The Kapauku "process of law" appears to have been highly standardized, almost to the point of ritual. It typically started with a loud quarrel where the plaintiff accused the defendant of committing a harmful act while the defendant responded with denials or justification. The quarrel involved loud shouting in order to attract other people, including one or more *tonowi*. Close relatives and friends of those involved in the dispute presented opinions and testimony in loud, emotional speeches. The *tonowi* generally listened until the exchange approached violence, whereupon he began his argument. If he waited too long, "stick fighting" or even war could occur, but this was rare (Popisil observed 176 dispute resolutions involving "difficult cases"; only five led to stick fights and one resulted in war).[28] The *tonowi* began by "admonishing" the disputants to have patience and then proceeded to question the accused and various witnesses. He searched the scene of the offense or the defendant's house for evidence.

Popisil reported: "Having secured the evidence and made up his mind about the factual background of the dispute, the authority starts the activity called by natives *boko duwai,* the process of making a decision and inducing the parties to the dispute to follow it."[29] The *tonowi* then summed up the evidence, appealed to the relevant rules and precedents, and suggested what should be done.

When judged to be guilty, a Kapauku was punished. Sanctions varied considerably depending on the offense. Despite the use of a wide array of sanctions, however, the Kapauku's paramount concern for individual freedom precluded imprisonment, and neither torture nor physical harm was permitted. As with primitive societies in general, "economic sanctions are by far the most preferred ones among the Kapauku."[30] Popisil observed several cases where the defendant was simply ordered to pay the sum stipulated in a broken contract or to make monetary restitution. Defendants were sometimes asked to return loans to their *tonowi,* thus losing their reciprocal arrangement for protection.

The Kapauku did resort to physical punishment at times, but in a sense, their use of physical punishment actually reflected the paramount role of individual rights. Defendants often had a *choice* between an economic sanction and a physical sanction, and could weigh the personal and family costs of the alternatives. One form of physical sanction was beating the offender's head and shoulders with a stick. The offenders were not constrained, so they could fight back; but in each instance Popisil observed, they submitted without raising a defense.

Economic payment was apparently considered an insufficient sanction for a few offenses, but even in these instances, "a heinous criminal or a captured enemy would be killed but never tortured or deprived of liberty."[31] In keeping with the emphasis on individual freedom, the killing generally took place in an ambush with bow and arrow: "A culprit. . .would always have the chance to run or fight back."[32]

Ostracism took one of two general forms. First, "the most dreaded and feared of the psychological and social sanctions of the Kapauku is the *public reprimand.*"[33] Similarly, punishment by sorcery or through the shaman's helping spirits could also be employed, with "disease and death [being] the ultimate (psychosomatic) effect of this 'supernatural' punishment."[34] Second, when the offender would not accept a judgment that the group considered to be just, the offender could be declared an outlaw. His reciprocal arrangements for protection were no longer in force, so anyone in the confederation was obligated to pursue him, either killing him or driving him from the area (which presumably would also lead to his death).

What if a *tonowi* was ineffective or dishonest in his legal role? Clearly, change in leadership was possible; indeed, one purpose of the Kapauku procedure that involved articulation of relevant laws by the *tonowi* was to achieve public acceptance of his ruling. After all, one source of "the affinity between legality and justice consisted simply in the fact that a rule articulated and made known permits the public to judge its fairness."[35]

Within the Kapauku, "every functioning subgroup...has its own legal system which is necessarily different in some respects from those of the other subgroups. ... Because an individual...is simultaneously a member of several subgroups of different inclusiveness (for example, a Kapauku is a member of his household, sublineage, lineage, and political confederacy...) he is subject to all the different legal systems of the subgroups of which he is a member."[36] There were also differences between the laws of these legal systems so an individual was subject to several legal systems with different laws. It might seem that jurisdictional conflicts would arise under such circumstances. Note, however, that a multiplicity of legal systems is the norm in both primitive and modern state-dominated societies,[37] because the spectrum of interactions ranges from intimacy at one end (e.g., family relations) through interactions of friendly strangers (e.g., commercial transactions) to hostility at the other (e.g., enemies, or hostile nations). The nature of the interaction substantially changes from one level to another, so efficient facilitation of these various types of interaction *demands* different laws and procedures.[38]

Among the Kapauku, an individual could be tried only by a *tonowi* of a group to which he belonged. Thus, a dispute was considered by the *tonowi* of the *least inclusive group* that included both litigants as its members.[39] The status of the *tonowi* was cumulative, and the designation of *tonowi* of a relatively inclusive group (e.g., a confederacy) was accorded to the *tonowi* of the largest constituent subgroup. If two litigants were in the same family, jurisdiction for the dispute was at the family level; two parties from different families but the same sublineage were judged by a *tonowi* from that sublineage; and so on. The *tonowi* of a confederacy might be viewed as a sort of "chief justice," but there was no appeal from one level to the next so he only judged cases where the disputants were not from the same lineage.[40]

The types of law adjudicated and the kinds of sanctions that could be employed varied from level to level.[41] Disputes over refusal of economic cooperation, breaches of etiquette, and verbal quarreling, for instance, were adjudicated only at the family level; war crimes and disloyalty were tried only at the confederacy level. Thus, rules of adjudication among the Kapauku included clearly specified detailed jurisdictional delineations.

Change. Kapauku law was not static, and Popisil documented two ways that "legislation" could occur. First, law could change as custom changed. For example, before 1954 an adulterous woman was executed by her husband. But as the price for wives increased, men—particularly relatively poor men—came to realize that the sanction was too costly and the punishment was changed to beating or perhaps wounding the adulteress. The new customary sanction was upheld by *tonowi* in four adultery cases observed by Popisil during 1954–1955: "Thus what started as a more economical practice among the poorer husbands became customary law by being incorporated into legal decisions."[42] In a similar fashion, a law can lose its popular support and be abolished.

A second procedure for legal change was observed when a change in one lineage's incest laws resulted from "successful legislation" by a sublineage *tonowi*. Popisil reported: "He succeeded in changing an old rule of sib exogamy into a new law that permitted intrasib marriages as close as between second cousins."[43] This legislation did not force compliance by others, but its acceptance spread as individuals voluntarily adopted it. First it was adopted by the *tonowi,* then by young men in his sublineage, and ultimately by *tonowi* of other sublineages within the same lineage. The head of the confederacy also ultimately accepted the new law, but other lineages in the same confederacy did not. Thus, incest laws varied across lineages within the same confederacy. This legal change was an intentional legal innovation *initiated* by a *tonowi,* although its adoption was voluntary.

Law in Primitive Societies: Some Generalizations. Because many social scientists and legal scholars believe that physical sanctions administered by a coercive authority are the basic criterion of law, many primitive societies have been held to be "lawless." The example of law among the Kapauku clearly denies this view—and it is only one example among many.[44] As Hoebel explained, in virtually all primitive societies

> the community group, although it may be ethnologically a segment of a tribe, is autonomous and politically independent. There is no tribal state. Leadership resides in family or local group headmen who have little coercive authority and are hence lacking in both the means to exploit and the means to judge. They are not explicitly elected to office; rather, they lead by the tacit consent of their followers, and they lose their leadership when their people begin no longer to accept their suggestions. . . . As it is, their leadership is confined to action in routine matters. The patriarchal tyrant of the primitive horde is nothing but a figment of nineteenth-century speculation. . . . But primitive anarchy does not mean disorder.[45]

The legal system evident in Kapauku culture—and in many other primitive societies—exhibits several characteristics: 1) primary rules characterized by a predominant concern for *individual rights and private property;* 2) responsibility of law enforcement falling to the victim backed by *reciprocal arrangements for protection and support in a dispute;* 3) standard *adjudicative procedures* established in order to *avoid violent forms of dispute resolution;* 4) *offenses treated as torts* and typically punishable by *economic payments in restitution;* 5) strong *incentives to yield to prescribed punishment* when guilty of an offense due to the reciprocally established *threat of social ostracism;* and 6) legal change arising through an *evolutionary process of developing customs and norms.*[46]

By studying the incentives and institutions of primitive law, it becomes evident that precisely the same kinds of customary legal systems have existed in more complex societies, ranging from medieval Iceland, Ireland, and Anglo-Saxon England to the development of the medieval Law Merchant, and even to the western frontier of the United States during the 1800s.[47]

THE BEGINNINGS OF COMMON LAW

Anglo-Saxon law prior to the Norman invasion had virtually all the characteristics of primitive legal systems. Evidence of the nature of early English law comes primarily from a few "codes" compiled by kings who rose to power during the late Anglo-Saxon period. In addition, a number of tracts or custumals were written after the Norman conquest in an effort to compile the customary law of the time, much of which was Anglo-Saxon in origin.[48] Sir James Stephen concluded in 1883 that "the general impression which [one such compilation] makes is that [the Anglo-Saxons] had an abundance of customs and laws sufficiently well established for practical purposes."[49] Similarly, Sir Frederick Pollock and Frederick Maitland surmised that "written Anglo-Saxon laws. . .are mere super-structures on a much larger base of custom."[50]

The early codes did not define crimes, but they did define as illegal a large proportion of the offenses that appear in a modern criminal code.[51] Indeed, Anglo-Saxon laws were very concerned with protection of individuals and their property. In particular, offenses against individuals are minutely provided for by the laws which delineate the economic payment appropriate for homicide, various kinds of wounds, rape, and indecent assaults. Similarly, theft was extensively treated in the codes. The law of property was unwritten so little specific detail can be found, but right of possession was clearly the primary concept of property law:

> it is possession that has to be defended or recovered, and to possess without dispute, or by judicial award after a dispute real or feigned is the only sure foundation of title and end of strife. A right to possess, distinct from actual possession, must be admitted if there is any rule of judicial redress at all; but it is only through the conception of that specific right that ownership finds any place in pure Germanic [and, therefore, Anglo-Saxon] law. Those who have studied the modern learning of possessory rights and remedies are aware that our common law has never really abandoned this point of view.[52]

Note the striking similarity in emphasis on individual harm and property between the Anglo-Saxon and Germanic customary law and the laws of primitive societies.

The primitive German tribes from which the Anglo-Saxons descended had kinship as the basis for reciprocal recognition and enforcement of law.[53] The kindred was reciprocally responsible for protection and for pursuit when an offense occurred, and successful pursuit resulted in payment of restitution defined by a system of *wergeld* or man-price (*wer*).[54] These were more than just reciprocal policing arrangements, however; they clearly involved a surety responsibility as well. As Lyon noted, the kindred had a "duty to make amends" for the offenses of one of its members.[55] The Anglo-Saxons carried this system to England, and there can be little doubt that "the kindred is one of the principal bonds of Anglo-Saxon society and one of the foundations of its law. . . . [T]he kindred was a group so powerful and so entrenched by custom and tradition that it never completely yielded priority to government."[56]

When the Anglo-Saxons moved into Britain after about A.D. 450, they were generally led by tribal war chiefs. German tribes were divided into *pagi,* each of which was made up of *vici.* Lyon suggested that a *pagus* might have consisted of one hundred men or households, while the *vici* was a subdivision of the *pagus* responsible for law enforcement.[57] Conceivably, these *vici* were bound by kinship. As J. H. Baker explained, public meetings were held to

> . . .encourage the parties to settle their differences or at least submit them to arbitration. The parties can air their grievances before their fellows, and with communal advice perhaps reach a compromise. If the parties cannot agree, the community does not act as a judge or jury, but may agree on the test which the parties, or one of them, should perform to establish the truth of the matter.

Procedures of this sort do not evolve through coercion, but parties who do not cooperate may be put outside the protection of the community.[58]

By the tenth century, in much of Anglo-Saxon Britain, there was a clearly recognized legal institution called the "hundred." The primary purposes of the organizations were rounding up stray cattle and dispensing justice.[59] One member of the hundred, the *hundredsmann,* was recognized as a chief official who was informed when a theft occurred and who informed the men of the several "tithings" that made up the hundred and had a reciprocal duty to pursue the thief. A tithing was not obviously based on kinship (as the *vici* may have been); it was apparently a group of neighbors, many of whom probably were kin. As kinship reciprocities broke down, perhaps due to increased mobility, neighborhood groups were probably organized. These voluntary groups were clearly designed as cooperative protection and law enforcement associations. Stephen characterized them as "the police system of the country, and in that capacity [their members] had various duties, of which the most important was that of raising in case of need the hue and cry, and tracking thieves and stolen cattle." But their role went well beyond policing; they also "made everyone accountable for all his neighbors."[60] The tithing took on the legal functions of the *vici.*

An individual who was not bonded by such a group was effectively an outcast, forced to be self-sufficient, so individuals had strong incentives to join a group. Because others in the group provided insurance (credit) for all members, however, they would not accept or keep someone who was not of good character. Consequently, members of a surety organization could disclaim someone who committed an egregious wrong,[61] providing strong incentives to abide by the law.

> This healthy system tended to reduce or prevent the introduction into any society of anyone who did not have credentials transferred from a previous peaceful participation in a surety association. . . . Thus, social relations were maintained only with people who shared surety protection.[62]

In effect, everyone who wanted to participate in and benefit from the social order was bonded.

The tithings and hundreds organizations also performed the local judicial function.[63] Four members of a tithing served as "suitors" of a hundred court, along with four members of all the other tithings within the court's jurisdiction. "The court consisted of the suitors collectively, but a representative body of twelve seem to have been instituted as a judicial committee of the court."[64] This committee served as an arbitrator in disputes between members of tithing groups in the area. Disputes between individuals who were not in the same hundred jurisdiction were handled by a shire court. All the suitors in the hundred courts within a shire were also suitors in the shire court, but again a twelve-man committee served the judicial arbitration function. Above the shire court there was apparently a third court to handle disputes between individuals who did not reside within the jurisdiction of one shire.[65]

The hundreds organization has been characterized as a major innovation implemented by Anglo-Saxon kings before the tenth century, because the hundreds were described in some of the king's early codes. Lyon has argued, for instance, that as their kingdoms grew, kings needed a way to organize local government, so they supplemented "the duties of the kindred in protection and policing by introducing. . .the tithing."[66] According to this view, authoritarian royal legislation "forced" freemen to join in a surety arrangement and to exercise the tithings' policing function. As Blair pointed out, however, this interpretation "mistake[s] the nature of Anglo-Saxon legal codes which were not so much concerned with promulgation of new law as with codification of established custom. There is little doubt that the hundred [and tithing] was functioning as a unit" before they appeared in any code.[67]

There are several other reasons to believe that Anglo-Saxon reciprocal arrangements correspond to those in primitive societies (and in more advanced ones like Iceland and Ireland). A primary reason for recognizing reciprocal duty in these systems was that offenses were treated as torts with economic restitution as the major form of punishment. Thus, potential victims recognized that in order to recoup their losses when an offense occurred, they would probably require community support. As a consequence, they were obliged to back others' claims in a reciprocal fashion.

A well-established set of rules arose some centuries before there were written records.[68] When a dispute arose, it was subject to arbitration ending in a prescribed payment to the winner.[69] Monetary payments could be made for any offense if it was the first offense committed by the aggressor.[70] "A deed of homicide," for example, "can be paid for by money. . .the offender could buy back the peace he had broken."[71] Refusal to submit to arbitration would result in a legal right for the accuser to take the life of the accused.[72] Likewise, refusing to accept the monetary fine put the accuser outside the law.[73] Refusal by either party to yield to the court's decision, thus, led to outlawry and the potential of a "blood-feud."

Some historians have viewed outlawry and the blood-feud as the primary legal sanctions prior to efforts by kings to force acceptance of economic restitution.[74] In all likelihood, however, given the incentives arising in customary legal systems and the resulting institutions of primitive law, the blood-feud was a valid recourse only after an attempt had been made to go to trial, long before kings became active in law. In this way, the potential for such violence was used to force compliance with the monetary sanction set forth by the courts.[75] Furthermore, because the earliest written codes were articulations of existing customs, the *wergeld* system probably preceded their appearance. As with primitive law in general, the threat of violence was used to create incentives that could lead to a peaceful settlement. In addition, an outlaw was ostracized by the society in general and physical retribution became the responsibility of the entire community. The threat of social ostracism would seem to have been quite severe, providing very strong incentives to submit to and abide by the rulings of arbitration.

Institutions were developed to avoid violence even when a person was unable to pay his fine. For certain offenses involving especially large fines, for example, an offender was apparently given up to a year to pay.[76] But there was another option as well. "Slavery was a recognized penalty when the thief was unable to make restitution. This...might be regarded as handing over the debtor's person by way of compensation rather than a punishment in the modern sense."[77]

By the time laws began to be recorded, ealdormen (later called earls) had become a king's appointed representatives in a shire, and by the ninth century, part of the aristocracy. The appointed position probably evolved from a tribal or kinship arrangement involving a well-respected individual (elder) whose opinion carried particular weight in the community (e.g., like a *tonowi* among the Kapauku).[78] Early codes make it clear that "the ealdorman, and the king at need, may be called in if the plaintiff is not strong enough himself; in other words the contumacious denier of justice may be dealt with as an enemy of the commonwealth."[79] Thus, the ostracism process by which an offender was made an outlaw was backed by the most powerful members of Anglo-Saxon society. A strong offender might resist if he had little to fear from his neighbors, but when his entire society backed the ostracism it was probably a very significant threat. In fact, if a victim had to call upon an elder (and ultimately an ealdorman or king), the monetary cost to the offender would increase considerably. He would not only have to pay monetary restitution (*wer*) to the victim or his kin, but also to the individual (*wite*) who used his power to bring about a settlement. Once kingship evolved, there were actually three kinds of fines:

> The fines were called *wer, bot* and *wite.* The *wer* was a price set upon a man according to his rank in life. If he was killed the *wer* was to be paid to his relations. If he was convicted of theft he had in some cases to pay the amount of his *wer* to his lord, or the king. If he was outlawed his sureties (*borhs*) might have to pay his *wer.*
>   *Bot* was compensation to a person injured by a crime. It might be either a fixed rate (*angild*); or at the market price of the stolen goods (*ceaf-gild*).
>   *Wite* was a fine paid to the king or other lord in respect of an offense.[80]

It should be stressed that kings and ealdormen had no sovereign powers to coerce compliance. The king's "business is not to see justice done in his name in an ordinary course, but to exercise a special reserved power which a man must not invoke unless he has failed to get his cause heard in the jurisdiction of his own hundred."[81] This institutionalization of a king's role in the justice process, and in particular a *payment* to the king for performing his role (*wite*), was one of the first steps in what would soon be a rapid extension of the king's role in law.

By the ninth and tenth centuries, England was a kingdom (or at times several kingdoms) and Anglo-Saxon kings were clearly recognized, but these institutions did not develop initially for the purpose of seeing justice done.

Around A.D. 450 Saxon or Jutish chieftains led the first of the Germanic raiding parties into Britain; others quickly followed. Chieftains were war leaders whom freemen *chose* to follow,[82] and their tenure was temporary unless warfare was continuous. For those Anglo-Saxons who moved into Britain, however, warfare apparently became virtually permanent, as efforts were continually being made to expand landholdings. Thus, successful war chiefs became more or less permanent leaders and their land holdings expanded. Of course, the primary reason for voluntarily following a war leader was the anticipation of gains, partly in the form of land. Whenever *voluntary* associations arise, reciprocal benefits must be significant.

The word "king" derives from the old English work *cyninge,* and the earliest historical records refer to *ceosan* as *cyninge,* which means "choose as king."[83] The "office" of kings was not necessarily hereditary, and appointment of a successor was not automatic; nor was a kingship considered a position for life. Kings apparently tried to establish a system of life tenure and hereditary succession very early in the Anglo-Saxon period, but these efforts were never completely successful.[84]

Kingship required reciprocal recognition of duty, reflecting the solid contractual foundation of leadership during earlier periods. War chiefs provided followers with battle equipment, food, and war booty (including land) in exchange for their support in war. Anglo-Saxon kings were expected to help protect the rights and property of the citizens of their kingdoms in exchange for their loyalty.[85] Interestingly, it was not until the tenth century that there was a clear expression of a requirement that freemen had to swear an oath of fealty to their king; kings' oaths to their subjects are recorded for much earlier periods.

Through shifting contractual arrangements, the land area associated with a particular lord could change, and at some earlier time when many kingdoms existed, freemen could probably shift from one king to another when a particular king proved to be a poor leader.[86] Significantly, the rights and well-being of freemen declined considerably as the power of kingship increased. Blair noted that "the one generalization about the Anglo-Saxon agrarian community upon which all seem to agree is that the condition of the peasantry was markedly worse in the later part of the period [of Anglo-Saxon rule] than it had been in the earlier. . . . [I]t should be recognized that the position of the seventh-century ceorl [agrarian freeman] as an independent freeman of some substance is mainly derived from the position he held in the law."[87]

Why did freemen's freedoms and well-being gradually diminish as the powers of kings expanded? Because the Anglo-Saxons were virtually in a constant state of war, they required strong war chiefs. Military ability won a small group of war chiefs prestige *and* land, and their accumulated wealth allowed some to set themselves apart as kings. If a king's successor was endowed with military ability, his kingdom would last; and if the king could establish a blood descendant as his successor and that descendant had similar skills in warfare, precedent for a hereditary dynasty would be established. As long as a hereditary descendant was a good leader, followers had little reason to dispute his "right" to be king.

Between 450 and 600, the number of kingdoms declined until reasonably well established dynasties existed in seven fairly well defined regions of Britain. Throughout this period, the primary function of kings was in warfare. They apparently did not presume to be law-makers, and law enforcement remained in the hands of local reciprocally established groups. The next 250 years saw further consolidation, with three kingdoms (Northumbria, Mercia, and Wessex) moving to positions of dominance. During most of this period, warfare was between the various Anglo-Saxon kingdoms. In the late eighth century, however, Vikings began to raid the English coast.

None of the Anglo-Saxon kingdoms was prepared to meet the Viking attacks. The English seaboard was simply too long to defend without a greater concentration of military force than any of the kingdoms controlled, and the Scandinavian invaders ultimately destroyed the dynasties of all the kingdoms except Wessex. Alfred, King of Wessex, fortified south England, and began the gradual unification process by retaking London from the Danes. His son, Edward the Elder, continued the reconquest of Danish holdings and by 917 had recovered the former kingdoms of Mercia and East Anglia. During the next three years he established himself as the most powerful ruler in all of Britain. By 937, "the older political system had perished through the disintegration or destruction of several once independent kingdoms upon which that system had rested and its place had been taken by the single kingdom of England."[88]

By the early eleventh century, many of the relatively localized functions of ealdormen (e.g., within a shire) had been taken over by royal appointees (sheriffs). The earls who remained, by now clearly designated as royal appointees, were lords over much larger areas (several shires) than the typical ealdorman of earlier times. Thus, the aristocracy that survived the long period of warfare was quite strong and relatively concentrated.

At the same time, the well-being of non-noble freemen in England declined considerably. In the ebb and flow of the wars, crops were constantly destroyed and farms burned. Men frequently left their lands to protect their area from raids and invading armies. "These and other factors, including the growth of powerful families among the nobility, tended towards the depression of many of the less fortunate, especially in the later part of the period. . .[and] had produced semi-servile communities in many parts of the country."[89]

Events occurred during the late tenth century that hastened the decline of the non-noble classes of freemen. In 980, the Danes began raiding England again, and local areas were left to their own defenses. Some lords paid the Danes to spare their lands and the king followed their lead, paying the raiders a large tribute (Danegeld) to leave his kingdom alone. During the next few years, large sums were raised through taxation to pay more Danegeld. The burden of these taxes further reduced the well-being of the English peasantry.

A Dane, Canute, took the throne in 1016. He appeased the Anglo-Saxons by confirming their customary laws, establishing a close rapport with the

Anglo-Saxon aristocracy, and supporting their church, actually ruling as an Anglo-Saxon.[90] While Canute's reign (1016–1035) was a peaceful one, his sons viewed England as a foreign source of revenues. They extracted as much from the English as they could, further reducing the status of Anglo-Saxon freemen. In 1042, the crown fell to Edward the Confessor, who surrounded himself with Norman advisors and appointed Normans to rich ecclesiastic positions. Actual control of England fell to the most powerful of the Anglo-Saxon earls, who possessed vast land holdings.[91] In 1066 when Edward died, Harold, the dominant member of aristocracy, was chosen as his successor, despite stronger hereditary claims to the throne. It was Harold who was killed on September 28, 1066, at the Battle of Hastings.

This very brief discussion of the development of the Anglo-Saxon kingdom emphasizes that the reason for the development of the institution of kingship was not a need for establishment of law or maintenance of *internal* order. Rather, government evolved due to external conflict (warfare). Throughout the decades of warfare and the growing power of the aristocracy, kingship as an engine of war also acquired important legal ramifications. Anglo-Saxon kings saw the justice process as a source of revenue, and violations of certain laws began to be referred to as violations of the "king's peace."[92] Well before the Norman conquest, outlawry began to involve not only liability to be killed with impunity but "forfeiture of goods to the king."[93] The codes of the later kings indicate that the attractiveness of such revenues was apparently quite strong. As Pollock and Maitland stressed, one of the

> bad features of pecuniary mulcts was the introduction of a fiscal element into the administration of criminal law. Criminal jurisdiction became a source of revenue; "pleas and forfeitures" were among profitable rights which the king could grant to prelates and thegns. A double process was at work; on the one hand the king was becoming supreme judge in all causes; on the other hand he was granting out jurisdiction as though it were so much land.[94]

The stage was being set for the king to take over many aspects of law production and enforcement.

The concept of the "king's peace" traces directly to Anglo-Saxon law in the sense that every freeman's house had a "peace"; if it was broken, the violator had to pay. Initially, the king's peace simply referred to the peace of the king's house, but as royal power expanded, the king declared that his peace extended to other places. First it was applied to places where the king traveled, then to churches, monasteries, highways, and bridges.

Eventually, it would be "possible for royal officers such as sheriffs to proclaim the king's peace wherever suitable. Even included were festivals and special occasions of the year such as Christmas, Lent, Easter, and Whitsuntide."[95]

Violations of the king's peace required payment to the king. The expansion in places and times protected by the king's peace meant greater potential for revenue. Kings also gradually added offenses against others that required payment of *wite* to the king. As revenues grew from such operations, the king could "buy" additional support for such arrangements by granting the right to parts of those revenues to others (e.g., earls and sheriffs). The populace did not always accept these changes gracefully, because they meant that the true victim of an offense claimed as a crime against the king received little or no restitution.[96] As Pollock and Maitland indicated: "There is a constant tendency to conflict between the old customs of the family and the newer laws of the State; the family preserves archaic habits and claims which clash at every turn with the development of a law-abiding commonwealth of the modern time."[97]

CUSTOMARY LAW FOR THE COMMERCIAL REVOLUTION

Although Anglo-Saxon customary law was giving way to authoritarian law, the development of medieval commercial law, *lex mercatoria*, or the "Law Merchant," effectively shatters the myth that government must define and enforce "the rules of the game." Because the Law Merchant developed outside the constraints of political boundaries and escaped the influence of political rulers for longer than many other Western legal systems, it provides the best example of what a system of customary law can achieve.

With the fall of the Roman Empire, commercial activities in Europe drastically declined.[98] From the sixth to the tenth centuries, commercial trade was almost nonexistent. But by the eleventh and twelfth centuries, rapid expansion in agricultural productivity meant that less labor was needed to produce sufficient food and clothing to sustain the population. Agricultural commodities were produced at levels that stimulated greater trade, and the population began to move into towns.

One consequence of (and one impetus for) the increased agricultural productivity and urbanization was the re-emergence of a class of professional merchants to facilitate trade. Customary law had traditionally been the source of the rules of trade and commerce, but by the tenth century merchants' customary law had been highly localized.[99] Thus, there were substantial barriers to overcome before inter-city, inter-regional, and international trade could develop. Merchants spoke different languages and had different cultural backgrounds. Beyond that, geographic distances often prevented direct communication, let alone the building of strong inter-personal bonds that would facilitate trust. Numerous middlemen were required to bring about an exchange, including buyer's agents, seller's agents, and shipping agents. All of this "gave rise to hostility towards foreign customs and they ultimately led to mercantile confrontations."[100]

During this period, "the basic concepts and institutions of modern Western mercantile law—*lex mercatoria* ('the Law Merchant')—were formed, and, even more important, it was then that mercantile law in the West first came to be viewed as an integrated, developing system, a *body* of law."[101] By the end of the eleventh century, the Law Merchant had developed to such a degree that it governed virtually every aspect of com-mercial transactions in all of Europe (and in some cases outside Europe). In fact, the commercial revolution of the eleventh through the fifteenth centuries that ultimately led to the Renaissance and industrial revolution could not have occurred without the rapid development of this system of privately adjudicated and enforced customary law.

> Rulers who sought by means of national law to rigidify this free commerce would inhibit the success of exchanges in the market place—to the loss of both the foreign and the local merchant community. The only law which could effectively enhance the activities of merchants under these conditions would be suppletive law, i.e., law which recognized the capacity of merchants to regulate their own affairs through their customs, their usages, and their practices.[102]

How could merchants from such far-ranging backgrounds produce law? What is the source of recognition? Fuller suggested that free trade and commerce itself is the source, because traders

> enter direct and voluntary relationships of exchange. As for equality it is only with the aid of something like a free market that it is possible to develop anything like an exact measure for the value of disparate goods. . . Finally economic traders frequently change roles, now selling now buying. The duties that arise out of their exchanges are therefore reversible, not only in theory but in practice.
>
> This analysis suggests the somewhat startling conclusion that it is only under capitalism that the notion of moral and legal duty can reach its full development.[103]

The reciprocity necessary for the recognition of commercial law arose due to the mutual gains generated by exchange.

The Law Merchant evolved into a universal legal system through a process of natural selection. As merchants began to transact business across political, cultural, and geographic boundaries, they transported trade practices to foreign markets. Those previously localized customs that were discovered to be common to many localities became part of the international Law Merchant. Where conflicts arose, practices that were the most efficient at facilitating commercial interaction supplanted those that were less efficient.[104] By the twelfth century, mercantile law had developed to a level where alien merchants had substantial protection in disputes with local merchants and "against the vagaries of local laws and customs."[105]

The laws that were adopted "reinforced rather than superseded the cycle of business practice. . . . Moreover, [these laws] generally avoided complex legal forms and mandatory controls over business which had not already been sanctioned either in custom or in commercial habit."[106] Complexities that might hinder communication and thereby inhibit trade were avoided. Agreement was the overriding force in regulating business conduct.[107]

Commercial law coordinated the self-interested actions of individuals, but it also coordinated the actions of people with limited knowledge and trust. Medieval commerce involved traders traveling to fairs and markets all over Europe, exchanging goods about which they knew little with unfamiliar people. From 1000 to 1200 (and especially from 1050 to 1150), the rights and obligations of merchants developed to handle this uncertainty. In their dealings with each other, merchant law "became substantially more objective and less arbitrary, more precise and less loose."[108]

Furthermore, as the norms of commercial law became more precisely specified, they were increasingly recorded. These written laws were not in the form of statutory codes (although many governments ultimately adopted privately created mercantile law in their commercial legislation), but took the form of written commercial instruments and contracts.[109] Fuller explained that "the term *contract law*. . .refers primarily not to the law *of* or *about* contracts, but to the 'law' a contract itself brings into existence. . . . If we permit ourselves to think of contract law as the 'law' that parties themselves bring into existence by their agreement, the transition from customary law to contract law becomes a very easy one indeed."[110]

When it is recognized that individuals had to *voluntarily* enter into a contract, it becomes clear why the Law Merchant had to be objective and impartial. Reciprocity in the sense of mutual benefits and costs is the very essence of trade. Each party enters into an exchange with expectations of obtaining something that is more valuable than what is given up. But the legal principle of reciprocity of rights, as it was developed during the late eleventh and early twelfth centuries and is still understood today, involves more than mutual exchange. It involves an element of fairness of exchange.[111] Thus, fraud, duress, or other abuses of the will or knowledge of either party in an exchange meant that the transaction would be invalidated in a mercantile court. Beyond such procedural issues, however, "even an exchange which is entered into willingly and knowingly must not impose on either side costs that are excessively disproportionate to the benefits to be obtained; nor may such exchange be unduly disadvantageous to third parties or to society generally."[112] Fairness was a required feature of the Law Merchant precisely because obligation to obey it arose voluntarily from recognition of mutual benefits. No one would *voluntarily* recognize a legal system that was not expected to treat him fairly.

Merchants "governed" without the coercive authority of a state by forming their own courts to adjudicate disputes. As Wooldridge explained, merchant

> court decisions were generally respected even by the losers; otherwise people would never have used them in the first place. . . . Merchants made their courts work simply by agreeing to abide by the results. The merchant who broke the understanding would not be sent to jail, to be sure, but neither would he long be a merchant, for the compliance exacted by his fellows, their power over his goods, proved if anything more effective than physical coercion.[113]

Merchant court decisions were backed by the threat of ostracism, a very effective boycott sanction. If a merchant court ruled that a London-based merchant had breached a contract with a merchant from Cologne at a trade fair in Milan, for example, the London merchant had strong incentives to pay the compensation the court judged appropriate. If he did not, other merchants would no longer trade with him. But this sanction, while a real threat, was not often required. "Good faith was the essence of the mercantile agreement," Trakman concluded. "Reciprocity and the threat of business sanctions compelled performance. The ordinary undertakings of merchants were binding because they were 'intended' to be binding, not because any law compelled such performance."[114]

Merchants established their own courts for several reasons. First, royal law differed from commercial law. For instance, the king's courts typically would not consider disputes arising from contracts made in another nation. Nor would royal courts honor any contractual agreement involving the payment of interest, considering any interest usurious. Common-law courts would not consider books of account as evidence, even though merchants held such records in high regard.

Second, merchant courts developed to resolve commercial disputes involving highly technical issues. Merchant court judges were chosen from the relevant merchant community; when technical issues were involved, the merchant courts used judges who were experts in that area of commerce.

Third, speed and informality were important in adjudicating commercial dispute.[115] Merchants had to complete their transactions in one market or fair and quickly move to the next; even if they did not move on, they frequently dealt with others who did. A dispute had to be settled quickly to minimize disruption of business affairs. Speed and informality could not have been equitably achieved without judges who were knowledgeable about commercial issues and concerns and whose judgments would be respected by the larger merchant community. Participatory adjudication, therefore, was a necessary characteristic of the Law Merchant. The adjudicative procedures, institutional devices, and substantive legal rules adopted by merchant courts all reflected the Law Merchant's concern for facilitating commercial interaction.

For the same reason, rules of evidence and procedures were kept simple and informal. Appeals were forbidden to avoid undue delay and disruption of commerce.[116] Lengthy testimony under oath was avoided; notarial attestation was usually not required as evidence of an agreement; debts were recognized as freely transferable through informal "written obligatory," a process developed by merchants themselves to simplify the transfer of debt; actions by agents in transactions were considered valid without formal authority; and ownership transfers were recognized without physical delivery.[117] All of these legal innovations were validated in merchant courts despite their illegality in many royal courts, but they promoted speed and informality in commerce and reduced transactions costs, so merchant courts accepted them.

By the early thirteenth century the Law Merchant was an integrated system of principles, concepts, rules, and procedures. Berman concluded that, "a great many if not most of the structural elements of the modern system of commercial law were formed in this period."[118] Consider, for example, the development of credit devices. By the twelfth century, barter trade had been virtually replaced by commercial middlemen who bought and sold using commercial contracts involving credit. The main forms of credit extended by sellers to buyers were promissory notes and bills of exchange. When such commercial instruments "became common in the West in the late eleventh and twelfth centuries, they not only acquired the character of independent obligations, like money itself, but they also acquired another characteristic of money, namely, negotiability."[119] The practice of negotiability of credit instruments was "invented" by Western merchants because of the need for an improved means of exchange as commerce developed and because the rise of the Law Merchant generated sufficient confidence in the commercial system so that a reservoir of commercial credit could be established.[120]

Credit instruments became the means of exchange that allowed trade to flourish and the commercial revolution to take place. The Roman commercial system had functioned because of the availability of money to facilitate trade; but with the fall of Rome, a currency that could be trusted to maintain its value disappeared, and so did commercial trade. With no sound source of money, merchants had to develop their own exchange medium.

Many kinds of credit instruments developed, and all became part of the Law Merchant. Credit was extended from sellers to buyers in the form of negotiable instruments, and buyers extended credit to sellers through the use of various contracts for future delivery of goods. Third parties (e.g., bankers) extended credit to buyers, and devices such as mortgages of movables were developed to protect these creditors against default. In this way, creditors retained a security interest in goods that required payment before they could be resold; and if payment was not forthcoming, the goods could be taken for resale in order to satisfy the debt.

Other aspects of the Law Merchant could be examined to emphasize the integration of a wide variety of principles, concepts, rules, and procedures into a system of law. The Law Merchant's

> development was quite rapid, not only in its formative period but thereafter, in the thirteenth, fourteenth, and fifteenth centuries. ... [T]he objectivity of mercantile law, the specificity of its norms, and the precision of its concepts increased over time; its universality and generality, its uniformity, increasingly prevailed over local differences; reciprocity of rights became increasingly important as contractual opportunities expanded; adjudication of commercial disputes became increasingly regularized; and the degree of integration of commercial law increased."[121]

Commercial law grew and developed, changing and adopting in response to new conditions in commerce.[122]

CONCLUSIONS

Hayek suggested that the rules that emerge from customary law will of necessity possess certain attributes that authoritarian "law invented or designed by a ruler may but need not possess, and are likely to possess only if they are modelled after the kind of rules which spring from the articulation of previously existing practices."[123] The attributes of customary legal systems include an emphasis on individual rights because recognition of legal duty requires voluntary cooperation of individuals through reciprocal arrangements. Such laws and their accompanying enforcement facilitate cooperative interaction by creating strong incentives to avoid violent forms of dispute resolution. Prosecutorial duties fall to the victim and his reciprocal protection association. Thus, the law provides for restitution to victims arrived at through clearly designed participatory adjudication procedures, in order to both provide incentives to pursue prosecution and to quell victims' desires for revenge. Strong incentives for both offenders and victims to submit to adjudication arise as a consequence of social ostracism or boycott sanctions, and legal change occurs through spontaneous evolution of customs and norms.[124] But nation-states have taken on a substantial role in the creation and enforcement of law. Why, given the apparent effectiveness of customary law systems? The answer has been suggested in the brief discussion of the rise of kingship in England. A more complete answer is provided in the following chapter.

ENDNOTES

1. See Bronislaw Malinowski, *Crime and Custom in Savage Society* (London: Routledge and Kegan Paul, 1926).
2. Lon L. Fuller, *The Morality of Law* (New Haven: Yale University Press, 1964), p. 30.
3. Ibid., pp. 150–151.
4. Harold J. Berman, *Law and Revolution: The Formation of Western Legal Tradition* (Cambridge, Mass.: Harvard University Press, 1983), p. 274.
5. F. A. Hayek, *Law, Legislation and Liberty*, vol. 1 (Chicago: University of Chicago Press, 1973), pp. 96–97.
6. Fuller, *The Morality of Law*, pp. 23–24.
7. Lon L. Fuller, *The Principles of Social Order* (Durham, N.C.: Duke University Press, 1981), p. 213.
8. James Buchanan, "Before Public Choice," in *Explorations in the Theory of Anarchy*, ed. Gordon Tullock (Blacksburg, Va.: Center for the Study of Public Choice, 1972), p. 37.
9. Harold Demsetz, "Toward a Theory of Property Rights," *American Economic Review* 57 (May 1967): 347–359.
10. Hayek, *Law, Legislation and Liberty*, p. 99.

11. See for example, E. Adamson Hoebel, *The Law of Primitive Man* (Cambridge, Mass.: Harvard University Press, 1954); R. F. Barton, "Procedure Among the Ifugao," in *Law and Warfare*, ed. Paul Bohannan (Garden City, N.Y.: The Natural History Press, 1967); Bruce L. Benson, "Enforcement of Private Property Rights in Primitive Societies: Law Without Government," *Journal of Libertarian Studies* 9 (Winter 1989): 1–26.

12. Walter Goldsmidt, "Ethics and the Structure of Society: An Ethnological Contribution to the Sociology of Knowledge," *American Anthropologist* 53 (October/December 1951): 506–524; David Friedman.

13. See Bruce L. Benson, "The Evolution of Law: Custom Versus Authority" (ms., Tallahassee, Fl.: Florida State University, 1990).

14. Bruce L. Benson, "The Spontaneous Evolution of Commercial Law," *Southern Economic Journal* 55 (January 1989): 644–661; Leon E. Trakman, *The Law Merchant: The Evolution of Commercial Law* (Littleton, Colo.: Fred B. Rothman and Co., 1983); Berman, *Law and Revolution.*

15. Joseph R. Peden, "Property Rights in Celtic Irish Law," *Journal of Libertarian Studies* 1 (1977): 81–95. "Private Creation and Enforcement of Law: A Historical Case," *Journal of Legal Studies* 8 (March 1979): 399–415. Also see Terry Anderson and P. J. Hill, "An American Experiment in Anarcho-Capitalism: The *Not* So Wild, Wild West," *Journal of Libertarian Studies* 3 (1979): 9–29, for examples from the eighteenth-century American West.

16. Recognition of duty to obey rules of conduct exist in any interactive group, but see Robert A. LeVine, "The Internalization of Political Values in Stateless Societies," *Human Organization* 19 (1960): 58.

17. See Fuller, *The Principles of Social Order*, p. 134.

18. Carl Menger, *Problems of Economics and Sociology*, trans. Francis J. Nook, ed. Louis Schneider (Urbana: University of Illinois Press, 1963), and Adam Smith, *An Inquiry into the Nature and Causes of the Wealth of Nations* (New York: Modern Library, 1937). As Hayek explained, however, while Smith's and Menger's insights regarding the evolution of social order "appear to firmly establish themselves [in several of the social sciences] another branch of knowledge of much greater influence, jurisprudence, is still almost wholly unaffected by it." See *Studies in Philosophy, Politics and Economics* (Chicago: University of Chicago Press, 1967), p. 101.

19. Quoted in Leopold Popisil, *Anthropology of Law: A Comparative Theory* (New York: Harper and Row, 1971), p. 65.

20. Ibid., p. 66.

21. Ibid., p. 67.

22. Ibid.

23. Ibid., pp. 68–69.

24. Ibid., pp. 69–70.

38   FROM VOLUNTARY TO AUTHORITARIAN LAW

25. See ibid., p. 69.
26. Ibid., p. 80.
27. Ibid.
28. Ibid., p. 36.
29. Ibid.
30. Ibid., p. 93.
31. Ibid., p. 65.
32. Ibid.
33. Ibid., p. 93. See also Benson, "Enforcement of Private Property Rights in Primitive Societies."
34. Ibid., p. 94.
35. Fuller, *The Morality of Law,* p. 159.
36. Popisil, *Anthropology of Law,* p. 107.
37. See for example, Karl N. Llewellyn and E. Adamson Hoebel, *The Cheyenne Way* (Norman: University of Oklahoma Press, 1961): 53.
38. Fuller, *The Principles of Social Order,* p. 243. See also Malinowski, *Crime and Custom in Savage Society*; Max Gluckman, *The Judicial Process Among the Barotse of Northern Rhodesia* (Manchester, England: Manchester University Press, 1955).
39. Popisil, *Anthropology of Law,* p. 111.
40. The villages actually had no political or legal function. One sublineage might occupy several villages, and one village might contain families from different sublineages. The legal function rested with the sublineage, not the village. Ibid., p. 120.
41. Ibid., p. 111.
42. Ibid., p. 205.
43. Ibid., p. 110.
44. See Benson, "Enforcement of Private Property Rights in Primitive Societies."
45. Hoebel, *The Law of Primitive Man,* p. 294.
46. Benson, "Enforcement of Private Property Rights in Primitive Societies."
47. Friedman, "Private Creation and Enforcement of Law"; Peden, "Property Rights in Celtic Irish Law"; Anderson and Hill, "An American Experiment in Anarcho-Capitalism"; John Umbeck, *A Theory of Property Rights With Application to the California Gold Rush* (Ames: Iowa State University Press, 1981).
48. Sir Frederick Pollock and Frederick W. Maitland, *The History of English Law,* vol. 1 (Washington, D.C.: Lawyers' Literary Club, 1959), pp. 10–27.
49. Sir James F. Stephen, *A History of the Criminal Law of England,* vol. 1 (1883; reprint, New York: Burt Franklin, 1963), p. 52.
50. Pollock and Maitland, *The History of English Law,* vol. 1, p. 27.
51. Stephen, *A History of the Criminal Law of England,* vol. 1, p. 53.

52. Pollock and Maitland, *The History of English Law,* vol. 1, p. 57.
53. Bruce Lyon, *A Constitutional and Legal History of Medieval England,* 2d ed. (New York: W. W. Norton, 1980), p. 83.
54. This corresponds to the Irish honor price system described by Peden, "Property Rights in Celtic Irish Law."
55. Lyon, *A Constitutional and Legal History of Medieval England,* p. 83. See also Peden, "Property Rights in Celtic Irish Law"; Friedman, "Private Creation and Enforcement of Law."
56. Lyon, *A Constitutional and Legal History of Medieval England,* p. 83.
57. Ibid., p. 59.
58. J. H. Baker, *An Introduction to English Legal History* (London: Butterworths, 1971), p. 10.
59. Peter Hunter Blair, *An Introduction to Anglo-Saxon England* (Cambridge, England: Cambridge University Press, 1956), p. 232.
60. Stephen, *A History of the Criminal Law of England,* p. 66.
61. Pollock and Maitland, *History of English Law,* p. 48.
62. Leonard P. Liggio, "The Transportation of Criminals: A Brief Political Economic History," in *Assessing the Criminal: Restitution, Retribution and the Legal Process,* ed. Randy E. Barnett and John Hagel III (Cambridge, Mass.: Ballinger Press, 1977), p. 274.
63. See also Friedman, "Private Creation and Enforcement of Law"; Blair, *An Introduction to Anglo-Saxon England,* p. 240.
64. Stephen, *A History of the Criminal Law of England,* p. 68.
65. Ibid., p. 67.
66. Lyon, *A Constitutional and Legal History of Medieval England,* p. 84.
67. Blair, *An Introduction to Anglo-Saxon England,* p. 235.
68. See for example, Peden, "Property Rights in Celtic Irish Law."
69. Stephen, *A History of the Criminal Law of England,* p. 62.
70. See Pollock and Maitland, *History of English Law,* vol. 2, p. 50; Stephen, *A History of the Criminal Law of England,* p. 58.
71. Pollock and Maitland, *History of English Law,* vol. 2, p. 451.
72. Stephen, *A History of the Criminal Law of England,* p. 62.
73. Pollock and Maitland, *History of English Law,* vol. 1, pp. 47–48.
74. Lyon, *A Constitutional and Legal History of Medieval England,* p. 84.
75. See ibid., pp. 84, 85.
76. Pollock and Maitland, *History of English Law,* vol. 2, p. 451.
77. Ibid., p. 449.
78. See E. Adamson Hoebel, "Law-Ways of the Comanche Indians," in *Law and Warfare,* ed. Paul Bohannan (Garden City, N.Y.: The Natural History Press, 1967).
79. Pollock and Maitland, *History of English Law,* vol. 1, p. 48.

80. Stephen, *A History of the Criminal Law of England*, p. 57.
81. Pollock and Maitland, *History of English Law*, vol. 1, pp. 40–41.
82. Blair, *An Introduction to Anglo-Saxon England*, p. 196.
83. Ibid., p. 198.
84. See for example, Lyon, *A Constitutional and Legal History of Medieval England*, pp. 39, 59; Blair, *An Introduction to Anglo-Saxon England*, p. 197).
85. Lyon, *A Constitutional and Legal History of Medieval England*, p. 40.
86. See ibid., pp. 74, 78, 86.
87. Blair, *An Introduction to Anglo-Saxon England*, p. 261.
88. Ibid., p. 87.
89. Ibid., p. 262.
90. Lyon, *A Constitutional and Legal History of Medieval England*, p. 32.
91. Ibid., p. 33.
92. Pollack and Maitland, *History of English Law*, vol. 1, p. 48.
93. Ibid., p. 49.
94. Ibid., vol. 2, pp. 453–454.
95. Lyon, *A Constitutional and Legal History of Medieval England*, p. 42.
96. For a different view, see Lyon, *A Constitutional and Legal History of Medieval England*, p. 85.
97. Pollock and Maitland, *History of English Law*, vol. 1, pp. 31–32.
98. It must be noted that Roman commercial law was also customary law. See Bruno Leoni, *Freedom and the Law* (Los Angeles: Nash Publishing, 1961), p. 83.
99. Trakman, *The Law Merchant*, pp. 7–8. Much of the remainder of this chapter appears in Benson, "Spontaneous Evolution."
100. Ibid., p. 11.
101. Berman, *Law and Revolution*, p. 333.
102. Trakman, *The Law Merchant*, p. 13.
103. Fuller, *The Morality of Law*, p. 24.
104. Trakman, *The Law Merchant*, p. 11.
105. Berman, *Law and Revolution*, p. 342. See also W. Mitchell, *Essay on the Early History of the Law Merchant* (New York: Burt Franklin, 1904), pp. 7–9.
106. Trakman, *The Law Merchant*, p. 18.
107. Ibid., p. 10.
108. Berman, *Law and Revolution*, p. 341.
109. Ibid.
110. Fuller, *The Principles of Social Order*, pp. 224–225.
111. Trakman, *The Law Merchant*, p. 12.
112. Berman, *Law and Revolution*, p. 343.
113. William C. Wooldridge, *Uncle Sam, the Monopoly Man* (New Rochelle, N.Y.: Arlington House, 1970), pp. 95–96.
114. Trakman, *The Law Merchant*, p. 10.

115.   Berman, *Law and Revolution*, p. 347. See also Mitchell, *Essay on the Early History of the Law Merchant*, p. 13.
116.   Trakman, *The Law Merchant*, p. 16.
117.   Ibid., p. 14.
118.   See Berman, *Law and Revolution*, pp. 349–350.
119.   Ibid., p. 350.
120.   Ibid., p. 351.
121.   Ibid., pp. 354–355.
122.   See ibid., p. 355; and Mitchell, *Essay on the Early History of the Law Merchant*, pp. 29–30.
123.   Hayek, *Law, Legislation and Liberty*, vol. 1, p. 85.
124.   See the Appendix to Chapter 12, as well as Anderson and Hill, "An American Experiment in Anarcho-Capitalism"; Benson, "The Evolution of Law"; Umbeck, *A Theory of Property Rights With Application to the California Gold Rush*; Jerold S. Auerback, *Justice Without Law* (New York: Oxford University Press, 1983); Bruce L. Benson, "The Lost Victim and Other Failures of the Public Law Experiment," *Harvard Journal of Law and Public Policy* 9 (Spring 1986): 399–427.

3

THE RISE OF AUTHORITARIAN LAW

When government becomes involved in the enterprise of law, both the rules of conduct and the institutions for enforcement are likely to change. The primary functions of governments are to act as a mechanism to take wealth from some and transfer it to others, and to discriminate among groups on the basis of their relative power in order to determine who gains and who loses. The theory of government implicit to this contention (explored in some detail in Chapter 4) assumes that the actors in the process are motivated by their own interests. This includes both those who demand transfers and those who grant them. Government officials attempt to enhance their own well-being with transfers to themselves and to others who are powerful enough to affect the decision-makers' well-being. I will "test" this theory of government using historical data. Before beginning the test, however, a few implications of the theory must be recognized.

Consider the basis of power for determining wealth transfers. In inter-governmental competition, power is a function of the ability to use force. That same source of power can be an important discriminatory criterion in determining internal wealth transfers as well, although a group's political power may also be a function of its economic power, the number of its members, and its ability to effectively organize and voice its demands in the political arena. These factors are important because intra-governmental competition often involves an exchange process. Political decision-makers discriminate between competing groups on the basis of what they can give to the politician. In early kingdoms, powerful individuals could exchange military support for special privileges, rights, and property from the king. As kings centralized the military function, however, military power became relatively less important in intra-governmental competition, and other forces became increasingly relevant.[1]

The self-interest motives of government decision-makers *must* be recognized in the context of a transfer theory of government. Kings demanded transfers for their own benefit when they had sufficient power to do so. Even when they entered an exchange, thereby transferring to others, the support gained generally enhanced their own wealth and power. In this light, the effort by those in government to reduce the power of other groups (and vice versa) becomes clear: those other groups may threaten sources of wealth for decision-makers.

Some wealth transfers are at least superficially obvious. Taxes are collected and the resulting government outlays indicate at least some of the benefactors of the transfer. The major benefactor of such transfers during the development of kingship was often the king himself. Indeed, an important purpose of internal transfers was to strengthen the king in warfare, the external function of government. Another fairly obvious transfer occurs when property of some kind is confiscated, and given to or used for the benefit of others.[2]

Some transfers are less obvious. In particular, property rights can be altered through authoritarian changes in law. The fact is that authoritarian rights modifications "have a dual nature: The recognition of granting a right to A means the exposure of B, and visa-versa; the resulting A-B rights conflict is ubiquitous. For A to have a right is for A's interests to count and B's not to count, *pro tanto*."[3] An important implication of a transfer theory of government is that there will be a "train of readjustments through time" as a consequence of a modification in property rights.[4] Some of these changes are predictable. For instance, a rights modification tends to increase the incentives of unorganized losing interests to enter the political arena, so we can expect political demands for rights modifications to grow over time.[5] There are other reasons to expect growth in political demands, as well. After a group is organized, for example, the additional costs of demanding more benefits are relatively low and the group may become interested in issues beyond its earliest concerns. As organized power increases, goals expand—whether that power is accumulated by a government seeking to expand its borders or an interest group demanding wealth transfers.

Because authoritarian law is intended to produce an involuntary transfer of wealth, it only needs the support of a politically powerful minority of the people affected. Laws are relatively more likely to change when they are a reflection of shifting and growing political demands than when they must be voluntarily adopted by all the affected parties. Evolution of authoritarian law, therefore, can be much less gradual than the evolution of customary law.

The time and resources of government decision-makers are limited, so increased political demands ultimately force delegation of responsibilities. There are at least three consequences of such delegation. First, competition between bureaucracies for rights to enforce certain laws and the accompanying budgets, power, and prestige becomes prevalent.[6] Second, as these bureaus increase in number or size, the ability of decision-makers to monitor their actions decreases. Third, as bureaucratic discretion increases and bureaus grow in size, they generally become active political interest groups, demanding more rights modifications enforced to generate wealth transfers to bureaucrats in the form of larger budgets and greater prestige and power.

Property rights provide incentives that condition behavior, so a change in rights is likely to change behavior. Because customary legal systems emphasize private property and individual rights, authoritarian rights transfers at least initially imply restrictions on private property and individual rights. When such rights are significantly altered, individuals will quit performing functions that were previously worthwhile. If the function is demanded by politically powerful groups, government will either try to force the previous behavior or directly produce the function.

Furthermore, when reciprocity does not provide the underpinnings of law, it will not provide the basis for law enforcement. Enforcement of authoritarian laws requires relatively more coercion, while customary legal institutions evolve to facilitate voluntary interaction. As the effective purpose of law changes, a different set of institutions is required to replace those that cannot effectively facilitate involuntary transfers. Similarly, government institutions cannot be as effectively employed to facilitate voluntary interaction as the institutions of customary law that have been replaced or altered.

Government institutions and laws have evolved to build upon or *replace* private institutions and customary law. This does not prove that laws and institutions are necessary for maintaining social order *or* for supporting a system that emphasizes individual freedom and private property. Authoritarian government laws and institutions are likely to do precisely the opposite, since their function is to facilitate involuntary transfers rather than voluntary interaction.

EARLY DEVELOPMENT OF AUTHORITARIAN LAW

The Anglo-Saxon Roots of English Royal Law.   Remember that Anglo-Saxon England gradually yielded to consolidation and centralization of power. As the king's military power increased and his church-supported divine rights were accepted, his role as a lawgiver was also gradually established. The king's earliest law enforcement function was to support an individual who was unable to induce some relatively powerful offender into the private hundred court. The king collected a portion of the offender's fine for the service, which developed into a payment to the king (*wite*) for *any* violation of the "king's peace." The "profits" from enforcing the king's peace accrued only to the king or those to whom he had granted an "unusual favour."[7] Law enforcement and its profits became something the king could exchange in the political arena.

Ealdormen were granted special status as royal representatives within shires; they received "one third of the fines from the profits of justice" and one-third of the revenues from tolls and other duties levied by the king.[8] In exchange, the ealdormen mustered and led men into combat, represented the king in shire courts, and executed royal commands. By the tenth century, a few powerful families provided all the ealdormen in England. Under Canute, the very small number of ealdormen, now called earls, had obtained a great deal of national political power. When single ealdormen began to represent the king in groups of shires, the office of sheriff was created in each shire.[9] In exchange for his services, a sheriff received grants of land from the king and the right to retain some of the profit from the royal estates he supervised. Furthermore, "by the reign of Edward the Confessor judicial profits had come to be lumped in with the farm of the royal manors and all these had to be collected by the sheriff"[10] in exchange for part of the profit.

The king's attending household developed substantial "opportunities both for personal advancement and for exercising influence on decisions of all kinds."[11] In origin, the Anglo-Saxon royal household was military, however, and this function continued to dominate until the Norman invasion, but other functions also began to develop.[12] In particular, as the king's land holdings and legal role increased and his finances became more complex, he began to delegate certain administrative, financial, and judicial functions.[13]

During the early Anglo-Saxon period, the *witan* or king's council probably consisted of local headmen or elders, and early royal law always included recognition of consent of the group of "wise men of the nation." Thus, the earliest "codes are in fact not so much the introductions of new principles as the declarations of the customs or common law of the race, dating from far beyond the existence of written record, preserved in the memories of the wise and kept for the most part in constant general experience."[14] Later, the king's household, the earls, and the church would be represented in the *witan*, and some authoritarian laws began to reflect the interests of these groups. More important, their interests were closely intertwined with the king's interests because of the grants and privileges they received. In this way, codes began to reflect the desires of the king. Little substantive change from customary law was made in the definition of offenses. The most significant changes were probably in the specifications of *wite* for kings and lords and the designation of increasing numbers of offenses as violating the king's peace.

Early Norman Rule. Because England's Norman rulers were almost always involved in military struggle, political power remained in the hands of those who had military power. A major recipient of transfers under Norman kingship was the king himself. William seized virtually all the lands of England, bringing a system of feudalism. In turn, he granted fiefs to Norman vassals (barons) and the church in exchange for various payments and services.

Although the Normans were in no position to simply overturn Anglo-Saxon customary law, some important institutional changes occurred immediately. Saxon kings had gradually been concentrating and consolidating power through reciprocal arrangements with earls, sheriffs, and the church. As Pollock and Maitland noted: "The chief result of the Norman Conquest in the history of law is to be found not so much in the subjection of race to race as in the establishment of an exceedingly strong kingship."[15]

The Norman kings used law and law enforcement to generate revenues needed to finance their military operations, to enhance their own wealth, and to buy the support of powerful groups.[16] In this regard, one of the earliest and most significant changes the Normans made in English law was replacing the old restitution-based system of *bot, wer,* and *wite* with a system of fines and confiscations along with corporal and capital punishment.[17] This change had significant implications for the institutions of law enforcement, because it substantially reduced citizens' incentives to maintain their reciprocal arrangements for protection, pursuit, prosecution, and insurance and to participate in the local court system (hundreds). Thus, Norman kings had to establish a law enforcement and judicial apparatus in order to collect their profits from justice.

The first permanent tribunal representing the king consisted of Henry I's financial administrators:

> Twice a year this group, taking the name of "the exchequer," sat round the chequered table, received the royal revenue, audited the sheriffs' accounts and did incidental justice. From time to time some of its members would be sent through the counties to hear the pleas of the crown, and litigants who were great men began to find it worth their while to bring their cases before this powerful tribunal.[18]

By 1135, the exchequer court had developed its own legal tradition; it imposed swift justice on royal debtors and assessed substantial fines on anyone who did not meet his financial obligation to the king.

Very early in the Norman period, the office of chancellor supervised the royal chapel, which served as the writing office, guarded the seal, produced all documents the king desired, and developed a law enforcement role for itself. A writ issued by the chancellor was a royal command purchased by a plaintiff in a civil dispute which ordered the accused to surrender certain lands, property, or money. When this command was ignored, litigation in a royal court followed; thus, the profits of justice were extended to the civil arena.

Barons, prelates of the church, and members of the royal household were obliged to attend court to consider matters of law, war, and justice. This *curia regis* reflected the opinions of the most powerful members of Anglo-Norman society and was a source of backing for the king in his relations with the pope and other foreign powers. In addition, "the *curia regis* was first of all a feudal court governed by Norman feudal custom and procedure."[19] Cases of high treason were considered by the royal court, as were civil disputes between the "great men" of the realm.[20] The *curia regis* had some independence, and occasionally the barons ruled against the king's wishes and the king might be forced to concede. Clearly there was a reciprocal arrangement between the king and his vassals; each required the other in order to advance their own ends.

The term *curia regis* also referred to the fairly permanent court or small council that assisted the king in the general routine of governing. Constantly in attendance to the king, this small group was the core of the larger council, but it often served as a court. It should be emphasized here that the exchequer was also part of the *curia regis,* so the barons of the exchequer who comprised its court should be viewed as the *curia regis* sitting to hear financial cases.

"The greatest contribution of the Normans," Lyon judged, "was in the close surveillance established by the central administration upon local organs of government."[21] The Anglo-Saxon shire became the Norman county, and sheriffs quickly became the most important local officials in the Norman system. Sheriffs' legal functions were numerous; they were the king's permanent judicial representatives, presiding over the county court, and were responsible for ensuring the attendance of members of these courts and those summoned to appear. They empaneled inquisitional juries for the king, enforced the royal courts' decisions, led the pursuit of law offenders, made arrests, and carried out the orders of royal writs.[22]

When the sheriffs got too greedy and siphoned off too much revenue, or tried to take it all through revolt, the king took away their power to consider the king's pleas and replaced them with residential justices, who were also soon replaced by itinerant justices traveling from county to county. But the struggle for power between local and central authorities was far from over.

A major reason for the need for local arms of the king's justice was that the hundreds and tithings became much less important than they had been during the Anglo-Saxon period. Apparently many of the hundreds ceased functioning altogether under William. As the business of justice increasingly became the accumulation of royal revenues, voluntary participation in the justice process naturally declined. In this light, the Normans also instituted a local arrangement called the frankpledge. With similar functions to an Anglo-Saxon tithing, the members of a frankpledge were expected to pursue and capture thieves and perform court duties. Based on requirements of feudal obligation rather than reciprocities, the frankpledge was ordered to ensure the appearance of members in court. If a frankpledge failed, the group could be fined; similarly, if a frankpledge did not assist in pursuit the group was subject to a fine. There is evidence that entire communities were so fined.[23]

Early Norman Law. Beginning with Henry I, authoritarian legislation became increasingly important.[24] During Henry's reign, an attempt was made to translate and state the codes of the Saxon king, Edward. Three other law books were added to the translations to produce the *Liber Quadripartitus*. "These law books have...one main theme. ... An offense, probably some violent offense, has been committed. Who then is to get money, and how much money, out of the offender."[25] Revenues from law enforcement were obviously the most important consideration in royal law. By this time, fines had become very complex. "The claims of the lords, the claims of the church, the claims of the king are adding to the number of various fines and mulcts that can be exacted, and are often at variance with each other...the old law...is falling to pieces under the pressure of those new elements which feudalism has brought with it."[26] Most offenses under the early Normans were still defined by Anglo-Saxon custom, but those offenses that were considered to be violations of the king's peace were significantly expanded: "In the growth of this list we may be certain that although the king's concern for law and order was a cause, another interest was need of money; to increase his income the king only needed to use his prerogative and throw his jurisdiction over another offense."[27]

In order to expand the profits to be made from justice, the Norman kings and their justices began to permit appeal to a royal court. The appellor could accuse the wrongdoer of violating the king's peace along with committing the actual offense, and the accused could not deny breaking the king's peace. "By the creation of this fiction, practically any offense could be interpreted as breach of the king's peace and so brought before the royal court."[28] Significantly, this also tended to undermine the recognition of the obligation to behave in accordance with customary laws, since appeal implied that royal law was superior to customary law.

The Norman kings also brought the concept of felony to England, by making it a feudal crime for a vassal to betray or commit treachery against a feudal lord. Feudal felonies were punishable by death, and all the felon's land and property were forfeited to the lord. Soon felony began to develop a broader meaning: "Again royal greed seems to be the best explanation for the expansion of the concept of felony. Any crime called a felony meant that if the appellee was found guilty his possessions escheated to the king. The more crimes called felonies, the greater the income, and so the list of felonies continued to grow throughout the twelfth century."[29]

As the discretion of the kings and their courts increased so did the arbitrariness of punishment:

> The outlaw forfeits all, life and limb, lands and goods. ... The king may take life and choose the kind of death, or he may be content with a limb; he can insist on banishment or abjuration of his realm or a forfeiture of chattels. The

man who has committed one of the bad crimes which have been causes of outlawry is not regarded as having a right to just punishment. Under the new Norman kings, who are not very straightly bound by tradition. . .the kings could favour now one and now another punishment.[30]

Law enforcement differed in many ways under the Norman kings from what had existed in Anglo-Saxon England, but it does not follow that it was more "just." When justice becomes discretionary it becomes arbitrary.

THE EVOLUTION OF ROYAL LAW INSTITUTIONS

Many foundations of the modern English system of law were laid during the reign of Henry II, a man who was "hungry for political power, both abroad and at home."[31] He developed the system of public administration in England begun under his predecessors by greatly increasing the functions and powers of permanent, professional, central governmental departments.[32] Legal innovations frequently credited to him include a permanent court of professional judges, frequent regularized missions of itinerant judges, inquisitional juries, and use of the "original writ" as a regular part of the machinery of justice.[33]

Henry II's Institutions of Law Enforcement.   When Henry II came to power, he consolidated and expanded his revenue-collecting system, making the delegated judicial function of the *curia regis* much more pronounced and definitive.[34] The king's court moved quickly to take on many of the functions that had historically fallen to county and hundred courts.[35] The judicial functions of the exchequer also evolved rapidly, and the barons of the exchequer began considering cases that had nothing to do with disputes regarding royal finances, except that they generated royal revenues. The upper exchequer became a royal court that considered the same kinds of pleas as the small council of the *curia regis*.[36] Yet, it was now considered as a separate court, "the first of the great common law courts to split off from the royal court,"[37] and by 1165, the ministers of the exchequer were referred to as justices.

By 1168, circuit tax collectors and itinerant justices had become another "great subdivision" of the royal court. The itinerant justices conducted royal inquests regarding financial issues and issues of justice, and they transmitted royal commands to counties and hundreds. The justices also amerced frankpledge groups that failed to or refused to fulfill their policing duties, fined communities that did not form all men into frankpledge groups, and amerced both communities and hundreds that failed to pursue criminals or to report all crimes through inquest juries. Such amercements were increasingly important, implying that the positive reciprocal incentives of the populace to participate in law enforcement were extremely weak.

The growing scope of royal justice created a backlog of cases for the king and his council, so in 1178 Henry established a permanent *curia regis* court to hear all suits except those that required his attention. This court met throughout the year and almost always at Westminster, becoming the first centralized king's court. The treasurer always sat on the ten- or twelve-man court, indicating the vital role of justice in revenue collection. Noblemen were sometimes absent, reflecting Henry's competition with them and efforts to reduce their power. Canon law had developed more rapidly than royal law as a system of administered authoritarian law, so two or three bishops lent their expertise to the court.[38] These men helped convert English law into a system that would ultimately rival canon law, gradually reducing a need for a separate canon system and incorporating various elements of it into royal law. Pollock and Maitland have suggested that "Henry's greatest, his most lasting triumph in the legal field was this, that he made the prelates of the church *his* justices."[39] But, Lyon suggested that

> the system of royal jurisdiction developed by the Angevins must take a place second to the procedural innovations. Herein lie the originality of the common law system and the reason why the royal courts so quickly snuffed out rival competition. The success of this procedure stemmed from two royal instruments —the writ and the jury.[40]

Through their chancellors, kings had been issuing writs for some time at the request of a complainant, directing an adversary to appear before a court. Under Henry II, precedents regarding different types of writs were established and legal forms were developed. By developing new writs, Henry and his bureaucrats inaugurated new civil trial procedures *and* almost continually established pleas that could be tried only in the royal courts.[41] All the various writs were "exposed for sale; perhaps some of them may already be had for a fixed price, for others a bargain must be struck. As yet the king is no mere vendor, he is a manufacturer and can make goods to order."[42]

The juries that Henry II used were

> intimately connected with royal power. Not only do the king and his officers make the freest use of [the jury] in the form of "an inquest *ex officio*" for the

purpose of obtaining any information that they want about royal rights, local customs or other matters in which the king has an interest, but, as a part of legal procedure, civil and criminal, the jury spreads outward from the king's own court.[43]

The jury's primary functions were to inform the king's justices on various matters and make accusations. Sheriffs made the appropriate arrests and established jails to contain those accused by the juries. Trial was not "by jury" however: it was by ordeal.

The development of the accusational juries and the growth of the king's court were not independent events. The use of itinerant judges in an attempt to centralize judicial power led to the development of the local juries. Henry was also searching for revenues, and an important source was that component of the justice system that was concerned with violations of the king's peace. It should be noted that "the king got his judicial profit whether the accused was found guilty or innocent."[44] If guilty, hanging or mutilation and exile, plus forfeitures of all goods were typical punishments; if the accused was found innocent, the plaintiff was heavily amerced for false accusation. Of course, this further reduced the incentives of crime victims and frankpledge groups to report crimes. Royal courts, sheriffs, and inquisitional juries were necessary innovations if the king was to collect his profits.

Henry and his judges defined an ever-growing number of actions as violating the king's peace.[45] These offenses came to be known as "crimes," and the contrast between criminal and civil causes developed, with criminal causes referring to offenses that generated revenues for the king or the sheriffs rather than payment to the victim. There were clearly strong incentives for freemen to have an offense considered as civil, and "the dilemma 'criminal or civil' is offered to every plea."[46]

Magna Carta. The king's drive for revenues and power caused considerable discontent, particularly during John's reign. In 1215, powerful barons renounced their homage to the king and revolted, demanding a document that would specify the laws and customs that would govern them.

On June 19, 1215, John put his seal on the Magna Carta, which is widely perceived as a significant foundation of Anglo-American constitutional government. "According to the great justice Sir Edward Coke and others, Magna Carta had saved England from the rule of tyrants, had consecrated basic civil and political rights, and had germinated English Constitutional government."[47] The thirteenth-century barons were depicted as men seeking to secure the rights of all men, not just the nobles. In fact, the charter reflected an effort by barons and other powerful groups (e.g., the English Church) to regain their power and privilege that kings subsequent to Henry I had been eroding. The revenue-taking of the kings in many forms, was now considered illegal, and Magna Carta re-established the barons' feudal right to confiscate felons' land. In addition, "no free man shall be taken or imprisoned or disseised or outlawed or exiled or in any wise destroyed, save by the lawful judgement of his peers or the law of the land."[48] This passage is widely interpreted as a guarantee of trial by jury for all Englishmen, as a prohibition of arbitrary imprisonment, and as a grant of equal justice for all (due process). In fact, it was intended to force King John to guarantee trial for barons before their peers under existing feudal procedure, and it established the "germ" of due process for the feudal aristocracy.

From this very early period of government expansion in law and law enforcement, legal "reform" was carried out in the context of the government institutional system of the time. This should not be surprising. Those institutions were developed to transfer wealth to powerful groups; the barons would likely retain them, anticipating their own benefit.

Three powerful groups combined in competition with King John to force him to affirm Magna Carta. In addition to the barons and the prelates of the English church, the merchants were eager to translate their growing economic power into political power. Magna Carta guaranteed freedom of travel, for instance (a privilege merchants had had for some time), merchants were freed from "evil and excessive tolls," and the boroughs were guaranteed the liberties and privileges already granted.[49] None of these really represented significant changes, but most of Magna Carta was backward-looking rather than forward-looking, re-establishing rights and privileges that barons had once enjoyed.

Parliament.   John died in October of 1216, leaving nine-year-old Henry III as heir to the throne. The government was dominated by powerful barons and prelates for several years, and by the time Henry III and then Edward I took control of the throne, the king's biggest problem was money. The economic and political power in England had shifted considerably; wealth was no longer exclusively linked to feudal rights and political power was no longer totally dominated by military power. Control of military forces by the barons remained vital; but the king and the barons increasingly sought support from the knights of the counties and the merchants and their boroughs, whose wealth was increasing. In return, the knights and merchants were given recognition in political decisions. The thirteenth century witnessed a continuous struggle for control of government institutions, especially for control of government taxing and spending, so the barons and the king found themselves competing with each other for the support of the new sources of wealth. The parliamentary institution developed out of this struggle.

The word *parliamentum* first appeared in the records of the King's Bench in 1236 to describe meetings of the *curia regis*. By the end of Edward's reign, the term could mean more: "from political and economic necessity the king was beginning to augment his great and small councils with men who represented the lesser aristocracy and freemen of the counties and the burgesses of the boroughs."[50] These additions to the king's council would become permanent in the fourteenth century and the resulting assemblies would be called parliament. But it is during the thirteenth century that we see the impetus for and beginnings of parliament.

Both Henry III and Edward I had to seek approval of the great council for most substantive law-making and for extraordinary taxes. In fact, thirteenth-century kings typically had to negotiate directly with the group being taxed. In 1254, Henry, at war and desperate for funds, assembled the great council, with two knights representing each county and clergy from each diocese. This was the first assembly of knights in conjunction with the great council. In 1258, during a baronial insurrection, both Henry and the barons summoned representatives of the county knights to assemblies in an effort to gain their support. The barons sent out the first call, then Henry sent his summons, "seemingly. . .attempting to sabotage [the barons'] meeting with one of his own."[51]

The barons defeated Henry in 1264, and their leader called an assembly consisting of the barons and four knights elected from each county. In 1265, he called another parliament, "apparently hop[ing] to gain a wider base of support from the county gentry and borough middle class."[52] He assembled five earls, eighteen barons, two knights representing each county, two burgesses from each of the boroughs, and two canons from each cathedral chapter, bringing together for the first time all of the elements that would ultimately make up the parliaments to come—earls, barons, and prelates of the church who would form the House of Lords, and knights and burgesses who would constitute the House of Commons. Once the king regained power, however, Henry and Edward continued to simply call upon those whose support they felt was required for a particular action.

Some seventy "parliaments" would be called between 1258 and 1300, with only nine including representatives of the county knights and the borough burgesses.[53] One, assembled by Edward in 1295, is often cited as the "model parliament." It was not a model by intentional design. Edward had a tremendous need for money, and he assembled representatives from all the powerful groups in the kingdom to secure consent for a large, broad-based tax. It was the largest medieval parliament ever assembled, containing all the elements found in later parliaments. But Edward called twenty more parliaments during his reign and only three had this form.[54] The model parliament did reinforce a precedent in the minds of the various groups it represented: kings could not arbitrarily collect taxes from powerful political groups without their consent.

In 1297 a war-beleaguered and desperate Edward forced a few barons to approve a tax on all barons, knights, and burgesses. He then seized wool assembled for export, promised to pay for it later, assessed a tax on the clergy with no negotiation, and left for the French war. As soon as he departed, the powerful groups of England rose up and refused to send any money until Magna Carta was expanded and confirmed. In November, Edward conceded in his Confirmation of the Charters, which guaranteed that the king would not levy extraordinary or direct taxes without the consent of the affected powerful groups in England. In the fourteenth century, "bargaining and concessions for supply became the theme of parliamentary history. By securing control of the royal purse strings, the community [made up of those with political power] of the realm discovered that it could limit the king."[55]

Edward's parliaments were embryonic in more than form. Summoning a parliament implied that the large and small councils were ready to do justice as a court, and summoning the knights and burgesses meant that the king was going to request taxes. Various groups could present petitions to the king, but the negotiation and exchange element of taxing was clearly relevant. In addition, the parliament might approve—or demand—a statute declared by the king. But the king was still the recognized source of legislation. Politics, legislation, and taxation would become the focus of parliament only after the barons took control of the small council from Edward III, and joined with the knights and burgesses to convert parliament's role.

The Common Law.   By the thirteenth century, the king and his councils were clearly in the business of law-making, but the busiest law makers during Henry III's reign were judges.[56] Henry gave his judges free rein in devising new rules and writs, and professionalized the judiciary. The term "common law" was not yet in wide usage among practitioners of royal law, but the idea of an evolutionary judge-made law based on precedent and custom seems to have been recognized. Edward I did not appreciate the way judge-made law grew, so he and his parliament began, through statutes, "to rigidify many points of law which judges and lawyers, however clever, cannot circumvent or modify."[57] The growth of the common law was substantially slowed, and judge-made law would lose ground relative to statute law from Edward's reign onward.

Courts. By the middle of the thirteenth century, the king's high courts were moving toward the institutional structure that would last into the late nineteenth century. The Court of the King's Bench, the Court of Common Pleas, and the Court of the Exchequer became identifiable entities with identifiable jurisdictions. Itinerant justices were commissioned to administer all types of royal justice on their judicial eyres to the counties, but their major duty continued to be amercing counties, hundreds, and tithings for failure to perform their assigned policing and governmental functions. Complaints were widespread, and Henry reduced the frequency of the itinerant visits, replacing them with judicial commissions whose only business was justice. These commissions substantially reduced the need for itinerant justices, as assize commissions considered increasing numbers of civil cases and as the gaol and oyer and terminers commissions took on larger criminal caseloads. Initially, local residents (knights and barons) had a substantial part of the judicial business of the commissions, but gradually these commissions were transferred to the central justices, so that common law was increasingly administered locally by royal justices from the central courts.

Lawyers. There were well-formulated reasons why the "evolution of the class [of legal advisors] has been slow, for it has been withstood by certain ancient principles."[58] Individuals not skilled in the art of pleading were less likely to be able to conceal their guilt. Furthermore, one litigant might be unable to hire a skilled spokesman while another could. Thus, rather than give one litigant an unfair advantage, custom developed whereby professional councillors and pleaders were not allowed. By the early thirteenth century, however, pleaders had begun to appear. The earliest records of a pleader identify John de Planez as pleading on behalf of Henry II, and Richard had a permanent contingency of pleaders. As with other legal developments under the English kings, the legal profession was developed to give additional advantage to the king.

By 1268, Henry III had a number of men under permanent retainer to act for him in his cases. The king gained an advantage in his own suits and was able to sell the same privilege to others. Edward I had a large number of "servants or sergeants at law" under retainer and a large number of "apprentices" who were their pupils. By 1292, these legal practitioners had clearly "acquired some exclusive right to audience."[59] More importantly, in that year Edward ordered his justices to provide for a sufficient number of attorneys and apprentices in each county so the king and the powerful might be well served.[60]

London began to license two distinct groups of legal professionals—attorneys and pleaders—in 1280, but the king's justices took control of the licensing function in 1292 and severely limited entry into both branches of the profession: "apparently a monopoly was secured for those who had been thus appointed."[61] The legal profession had begun to take shape. Attorneys and counters had become licensed court appointees and quickly evolved into an organized professional group. Common law was becoming case law; those who wished to learn the profession joined guilds or fraternities that eventually developed into the Inns of Court, the English law schools.

These professional lawyers had an immediate effect. Legal procedure became much more complex than it had previously been, and as Lyon noted, "It is hardly necessary to say that [lawyers] prolonged justice almost endlessly."[62] In addition, lawyers, rather than ecclesiastical clerics, became the primary candidates for royal judges. The resulting insulation from Roman law "permitted the common law system to become a confusing puzzle of undefined principles. It became cumbersome and ill equipped to keep pace with the new demands made upon it by political, economic, and social change."[63]

Jury Trials.   Most civil cases were jury trials by the reign of Edward I. These juries, which consisted of men of the community who presumably had witnessed or had knowledge of the facts, were empaneled by the sheriff to hear the pleading and render a verdict.[64] Trial by ordeal effectively ended for criminal cases in 1215, and "neither the law nor the lawyer knew what to do about the indicted men overflowing the inadequate jails."[65] Writs had developed for obtaining jury trials in a few criminal cases, but not for most criminal trials. For instance, an accused could obtain a writ to have a jury determine whether the accuser had made charges because of malice or to determine whether an inquisitional jury had acted maliciously.

These juries were called petty juries to distinguish them from the grand or inquisitional juries. This set the stage for criminal jury trials. The prevailing opinion of the day was that trial by jury meant a guilty verdict, so there was considerable resistance to acceptance of a jury trial. The justices began to search for ways to force defendants to accept a jury trial. Some defendants were locked in prison for a year and a day with little food and water, but still many refused the trial. In 1275, the first statute of Westminster declared that those accused of a felony who refused to accept a jury inquest would be "put in strong and hard imprisonment." Accused felons were loaded with heavy chains and stones, placed in the worst part of the prison, given a little water one day and a little bread the next, until they agreed to trial by jury or died. Many chose to die. If found guilty in a trial, the accused would be executed and forfeit all property to the crown. Death under "hard and severe pressure" meant that he was not convicted and his property went to his family.

The composition of the petty jury gradually began to change toward the end of the thirteenth century. Rather than the same men setting as an inquisitional and petty jury, the grand jury was augmented by men randomly chosen from neighboring communities. Occasionally, such juries would even reach not-guilty verdicts. The witness-bearing character still dominated, however, and throughout the thirteenth century petty juries were groups sworn to tell what they knew about a case. The presentment jury and petty jury would not be completely separated until the mid-fourteenth century, and it would be another five hundred years before juries could be characterized as impartial.[66]

Summation.   By the end of the reign of Edward I, the basic institutions of government law had been established, and in many instances older custom had been altered or replaced by authoritarian rules to facilitate the transfer of wealth to relatively powerful groups. "Public interest" justifications for a government-dominated legal system and institutions *must* be viewed as *ex post* rationalization rather than as *ex ante* explanations of their development. Rather than continuing an analysis of the entire evolutionary process between the thirteenth and the twentieth centuries, let us focus on inter-jurisdictional competition between common law and merchant courts, and on some of the consequences of the replacement of the restitution-based legal system by criminal law.

INTERJURISDICTIONAL COMPETITION AND
THE ABSORPTION OF THE LAW MERCHANT

The absorption of the Law Merchant into royal law began around the twelfth century, as most governments in Europe began systematically collecting and codifying the customary rules of the Law Merchant.[67] England was no exception with its codification of the *Carta Mercatoria* in the fourteenth century. Nonetheless, the merchants continued to enforce their own law through their own courts, and they had to be induced to take their disputes before royal courts.

Transferring the Cost of Enforcement. One reason why the Law Merchant was absorbed into common law appears to be that governments demonstrated a willingness to enforce merchant law.[68] When merchants judged and enforced their law, they had to bear the full cost themselves; if the royal authority was willing to enforce merchants' own law *and* bear part of the enforcement cost, then the merchants would benefit. The shifting of enforcement cost onto the government is consistent with the increasing political power and political activity of merchants. Indeed, the overall trend in economic regulation of the period was primarily motivated by merchant demands for monopoly rights.[69]

Undermining the Recognition of Duty to Obey the Law Merchant. During the fourteenth century, kings began to produce laws that made merchant courts relatively less attractive. In England, for example, the Statute of the Staple of 1353 codified custom by declaring that "merchant strangers" were to be given protection in the fourteen major trading centers for "staple" products—mainly wool, leather, and lead. The statute actually *dictated* that disputes involving these foreign merchants would be settled under mercantile law, but appeals could be taken to the chancellor and the king's council. By giving merchants access to royal appeal, the *appearance* of royal backing of the Law Merchant was created, and a role for the royal courts in enforcing commercial law was established. More importantly, the Law Merchant was made to appear to be the less decisive law. Through a gradual process of absorption by creating more attractive governmental enforcement arrangements and by undermining the recognition of the Law Merchant, common law institutions became more acceptable to the merchant community.

The Statute of Staples also began a process of concentrating foreign trade flows to make them easier for the state to control. Most foreign trade was compelled to pass through a few important towns and special courts were created in these "staple" towns to administer the Law Merchant.[70] These courts consisted of the town's mayor, two constables, and two merchants. Appeal could occur from these staple courts. Fairs and markets still held their own merchant courts.

Competition Between Courts.   During the fifteenth century, common law courts began to attract more and more commercial cases. Merchant courts remained available for commercial disputes until the early 1600s. But royal courts gradually took more cases away from the merchant courts because it was in the financial self-interests of judges who were paid in large part out of litigation fees.[71] Merchants remained free to choose between their own courts and the common law courts through the sixteenth century, so the fact that merchants chose the royal courts in increasing numbers implies that those courts must have been successfully applying the Law Merchant. There was always the threat of competition from private merchant courts, and if the royal courts wanted the merchants' business they had to enforce law to the merchants' satisfaction.

The competitive relationship between royal and merchant courts was altered substantially in 1606. In reviewing a case previously judged under private arbitration, Lord Edward Coke pronounced "that though one may be bound to stand to the arbitrament yet he may countermand the arbitrator...as a man cannot by his own act make such an authority power or warrant not countermandable which by law and its own proper nature is countermandable."[72] In other words, the decisions of merchant courts could be reversed by the common law courts because an arbitrator's purpose was to find a suitable compromise, while a judge's purpose was to rule on the merits of the case. In essence, Coke asserted that the Law Merchant was not a separate, identifiable system of law, but "part of the law of this realm."[73] This was interpreted to mean that merchants were bound to submit to the jurisdiction of the common law courts and subject to those courts' procedures. In effect, Coke's ruling withdrew the guarantee in the Statute of Staples. As a result, "merchant courts at fairs, guilds and market towns were abolished, or alternatively, they were integrated into the common law system."[74]

The Subjugated Law Merchant.   The Law Merchant changed during the sixteenth and seventeenth centuries, becoming less universal and more localized as it began to reflect the policies, interest, and procedures of the state. Still, the Law Merchant survived for a good reason. Custom still prevailed in international trade, and England was a great trading nation. English judges had to compete with other national courts for the attention of international merchants' disputes. To attract cases involving international trade, they had to recognize commercial custom. There was some fragmentation in the form of the Law Merchant across Europe, but there was little difference in its substance. Trade between these geographically contiguous countries had become vital, and they recognized that there was substantial benefit associated with "free trade unimpeded by needless legal restraint."[75] The Law Merchant remained vital in international commercial law, however, and eventually reemerged as a significant influence on common law, particularly in the United States.

THE EMERGENCE OF CRIMINAL LAW

Victims' resistance to the development of criminal law, along with the resulting loss of restitution and its accompanying incentives, meant that English citizens had to be "forced into compliance by a slowly evolving carrot and stick policy."[76] For example, royal law imposed coercive rules declaring that the victim was a criminal if he obtained restitution before he brought the offender before a king's justice where the king could get his profits.[77] This was not a strong enough inducement, so royal law created the crime of "theftbote," making it a misdemeanor for a victim to accept the return of stolen property or to make other arrangements with a felon in exchange for an agreement not to prosecute. In delineating the earliest development of misdemeanor offenses, Pollock and Maitland only discussed "crimes" of this type. They suggested:

> A very large part of the [king's] justices' work will indeed consist of putting in mercy men and communities guilty of neglect of police duties. This, if we have regard to actual results, is the main business of the eyre...the justices collect in all a very large sum from hundreds, boroughs, townships and tithings which have misconducted themselves by not presenting, or not arresting criminals...probably no single "community" in the county will escape without amercement.[78]

More laws were added. For instance, civil remedies to a criminal offense could not be achieved until after criminal prosecution was complete; the owner of stolen goods could not get his goods back until after he had given evidence in a criminal prosecution; and a fine was imposed on advertisers or printers who advertised a reward for the return of stolen property, no questions asked. Coercive efforts to induce victims and communities to pursue and prosecute criminals were not successful, however, and government institutions have gradually taken over production of these services.

Justices of the Peace. An early development in the evolution of public policing and prosecution was the explicit creation of justices of the peace in 1326. At that time, JPs were simply "assigned to keep the peace," but in 1360 they were empowered "to take and arrest all those they may find by indictment or suspicion and put them in prison."[79] Most JPs were local landholders appointed by royal commission for each county; and as with much of the local apparatus of justice, these men were expected to perform their functions without monetary compensation.[80] Through over thirty statutes issued from the late fourteenth to the middle of the sixteenth century, three basic functions in the criminal process were assigned to JPs: 1) the taking of presentment or indictment, 2) the conduct of jury trial, and 3) the power of summary conviction for lesser offenses.[81]

Victims or their support group continued to be responsible for pursuing criminals and prosecuting most cases. But after a 1555 statute, JPs were obliged to take active investigative roles in felony cases; to organize cases for prosecution, including examination documents; to assist the assize judge in coordinating the prosecution at trial; to bind over for appearance all relevant witnesses, including the accusers and the accused; and to act as a back-up prosecutor when a private citizen was not available.[82] A public element had been introduced into the prosecution.[83]

International military involvement served as a major impetus for the development of public prosecution and police during the eighteenth and nineteenth centuries (as well as prisons and other public institutions of criminal justice). The economy—and particularly the London economy, because it was strongly influenced by government demand for war materials (or lack of demand, as employment often declined immediately after a war)[84] —could not quickly absorb the large influx of veterans following a war. Furthermore, according to many observers, the soldiers were "unaccustomed to ordinary labor and were unwilling to take it up again when they came home."[85] Instead,

the conclusions of wars in the eighteenth century brought "a great harvest of crime," as was said in 1819. . . . The peace brought back to England large numbers of disreputable men who had spent several years being further brutalized by service in the armed forces, without any provision being made for their reentry into the work force. The same complaint was voiced after every war.[86]

The failure of the existing crime control apparatus was in part a function of the kinds of crime the returning veterans generally committed. They had had considerable on-the-job training in *organized violence.* "It is hardly to be wondered at that some might employ these same skills at home if it seemed necessary. It was the power of such men in gangs...that frightened so many commentators."[87] Large-scale gang crime was a new phenomenon, and it was this type of crime that proved to be the most difficult for the criminal justice system to handle.

Victim participation in criminal justice was getting expensive at the same time that gang crime was developing. When a victim filed a complaint before a JP, for instance, he might have to pay for subpoenas and warrants if his witnesses and the suspect were not present. Other fees were incurred for the recognizances in which he and witnesses were bound over for trial, for the clerk of the peace or of the assize for drawing up the indictment, for the officer of the court who swore the witnesses, for the doorkeeper of the courtroom, for the crier, and for the bailiff who took the prosecutor from the court to the grand jury room.[88] Beyond these fees, the level of the cost of attending court was uncertain, because the length of the wait for an appearance before a grand jury and the timing of the trial were not known. A victim often had to bear costs of food and lodging for both himself and his witnesses. The declining incentives for victim participation in crime control in the face of fluctuating urban and growing gang crime made public policing and prosecution inevitable.

As early as 1729, the central government began to support local law enforcement in Middlesex, where the seat of government and the residences of most government officials and parliamentarians were located. The self-interest motives of these government officials in shifting the cost of law enforcement onto taxpayers certainly comes into question. They were the first to benefit from such expenditures, while the rest of the citizenry was forced (under statute) to provide their own policing and prosecutorial services. In 1729, the government chose to financially support one Middlesex JP to provide criminal investigative and prosecutorial services; he became known as the "court JP." Similar arrangements developed in London soon thereafter.[89]

Sir Thomas deVeil was the first court JP from 1729 until 1746. Little record remains of his tenure, but it was clear that he was active in pretrial examination and as a committal officer. DeVeil was succeeded by Henry Fielding, who along with his successor (his brother John), appears to have had a dramatic effect on law enforcement in the London area.

Fielding's investigations had contrasting tendencies. On the one hand, he was trying to cast a wider net by following up on leads and by encouraging greater evidence for trial at the old Bailey. This side of the job anticipated what became the Criminal Investigation Division of Scotland Yard. On the other hand, Fielding was also sifting and discharging cases that would not stand up, if sent on for trial, and in this respect he was the forerunner of the judicialized pretrial committal officer of the nineteenth century.[90]

Many forces set in motion by the original development of the justice of the peace were accelerated during Fielding's tenure, and several interrelated institutional developments followed. All of these separate developments were intertwined, feeding on and aiding one another.

Confessions and "Crown Witnesses": The Beginnings of Rules of Evidence. The "crown witness" program arose as a result of JP's growing discretion regarding the decision to prosecute after his pretrial investigation. One gang member was admitted as a crown witness and excused from prosecution in exchange for testimony against his fellow gang members. This became the primary strategy for combating gang crime. What may seem to be a rather innocuous innovation (particularly in light of the use of the same type of programs in criminal prosecution today) appears to have been a major force leading to the development of rules of evidence for criminal trials.

Criminal court judges recognized a problem with the crown witness program almost immediately. In an 1837 precedent-setting ruling, it was noted that "the danger is that when a man is fixed, and knows that his own guilt is detected, he purchases impunity by falsely accusing others."[91] A criminal had incentives to commit perjury, which clearly affected the reliability of his testimony. As a result, "the crown witness system led to one of the earliest manifestations of what came to be the laws of criminal evidence, the corroboration rule."[92] In trials before 1735, Langbein noted, "evidentiary rules that later came to distinguish Anglo-American trial procedure were scarcely to be observed. By [the mid-1700s]...the tone of the criminal trial began to change in subtle ways that, in retrospect, appear to us to foreshadow the rise of adversary procedure and the law of evidence."[93] The beginnings of the corroboration rule was one of these changes. By 1751, a mandatory corroboration rule was in place as a directed verdict standard, and judges dismissed cases without hearing the defense if the prosecution was solely founded on uncorroborated crown witness testimony.[94] The precedent for the rule was *Rex v. Atwood & Robbins* (1788), which made such evidence admissible "under such directions and observations from the Court as the circumstances of the case may require, to say whether they think it sufficiently credible to guide their decision in the case."[95] Here we see the beginnings of what has developed into the often detailed instructions to the jury by judges regarding the rules of evidence.

A standard practice under the crown witness program was to set up a competition between suspected criminal gang members. The one who offered the most evidence against the largest number of potential criminals would win the competition and receive exemption from prosecution; the losers generally had to admit guilt. The courts became concerned over the use of such confessions and in 1783 ruled that they would give "no credit" to a confession "forced from the mind by the flattery of hope, or by the torture of fear."[96] This case provided the precedent for the confession rule, which

> presaged the future of the Anglo-American law of evidence. It was an "exclusionary rule." Like most of the rest of the remarkable structure that would be erected in the name of the law of evidence over the next decades, the confession rule worked by excluding from the trial jury concededly probative information for fear that the jury lacked the ability to evaluate the reliability of the information properly. However accustomed we have since become to this way of handling criminal adjudication we must remain aware that it was a recent invention . . . and one whose origins have yet to be explained.[97]

The explanation lies in forces set in motion hundreds of years earlier and is reflected in the transformation from a system of privately enforced customary tort law to publicly produced criminal law. Each change initiated by government created problems that required additional change. When law is deliberately designed, whether well-intended or not, there will always be manifestations that the designers did not anticipate. When some of those manifestations prove to be undesirable, new rules are designed, which will also have unanticipated consequences.

Criminal Trials.   By the mid-sixteenth century, familiarity with the crime was no longer required to be a jury member.[98] Langbein suggested that "this transformation of the active medieval juries into the passive courtroom triers is among the greatest mysteries of English legal history, still no better understood than [a century ago]."[99] But it really is no great mystery when we realize that the recognition of duty to perform law enforcement functions was originally built on restitution and reciprocity. Widespread criminalization under the Norman kings ultimately undermined even the kings' jury system.

Even as trial by jury developed, such trials were not at all like what we see today: "well into the eighteenth century when the old Bailey [London's criminal court] sat, it tried between twelve and twenty felony cases per day, and provincial assizes operated with similar dispatch. . . . How could the Old Bailey of the 1730s process a dozen and more cases to full jury trial in one day, whereas in modern times the average jury trial requires several days of court time?"[100]

In 1730 London, it was common to empanel two twelve-man juries to try all the roughly 150 felony cases in a session of Old Bailey (royal assizes typically empaneled a single jury that heard all cases). The juries' sittings were staggered so that one could hear evidence on a series of cases while the other was out deliberating on other cases. Many cases lasted only a few minutes, with little evidence presented, and little dispute. Most jurors were experienced, having served before, so judicial instruction of the jury was perfunctory.[101]

Judges had a great deal of control over the juries and the trial in general. A judge often acted as an examiner, questioning the accused and the witnesses and commenting at will on the merits of a case. Jurors questioned the accused and witnesses and made observations about facts, the character of witnesses, and so on. There was also a good deal of communication between the judge and the jurors. A judge could terminate a case prior to a verdict and remit the accused to jail if he believed that the jury was leaning toward an improper verdict or if it was clear that relevant evidence was not being provided. Judges could also direct "the jury to find a special verdict."[102] The jury might not follow the judge's directions, but in issuing such a statement the judge opened up new options. For instance, "it was open to the judge to reject a proffered verdict, probe its basis, argue with the jury, give further instruction and require redeliberation."[103] There are records of juries deliberating further and altering their verdicts as well as of juries persisting in their original finding. This judicial power did not imply that juries were forced to find as the judge wanted, but they had a second chance if the judge disagreed with them.

Evidence was likely to be accurate in seventeenth- and eighteenth-century criminal trials since it was not unusual for a trial to take place within a week of the crime when witnesses' recollections were relatively fresh. Also, the accused will virtually always be the most efficient possible witness at a criminal trial. Even when he has a solid defense, the accused has usually been close to the events in question, close enough to get himself prosecuted.[104]

The accused had no option but to speak in his own defense, because there were no defense lawyers to speak for him,[105] which brings us to the major explanation for the pace of criminal trials before the mid-eighteenth century.

The accused was forbidden counsel. . . . The victim or other complaining witness, sometimes aided by constable and by the justice of the peace, performed the role we now assign to the public prosecutor, gathering evidence and presenting at the trial. As a result, jury trial was not yet protracted by the motions, maneuvers and speeches of counsel that afflict the modern trial.[106]

The entry of lawyers into criminal trials would be a major factor in altering virtually all of the characteristics that facilitated the rapid disposition of criminal cases.

Criminal Lawyers. Lawyers where employed by the government as prosecutors in a long series of "State Trials" involving political crimes like treason, and also in some important criminal cases. By the mid-1730s, victims had begun to employ private prosecution attorneys. Prosecution counsel were not used in great numbers, and they did not significantly change the character of criminal trials, but there was a significant consequence to their participation.[107] Judges began to allow defense counsel if prosecution counsel was employed, and defense counsel had a tremendous impact on the criminal trial.

The primary defense counsel role was in cross-examination,[108] and a number of structural changes in criminal trials are directly traceable to that process. First, access to the accused was sharply limited. Second, the counsel had to know what the case for the prosecution was in order to defend his client. Consequently, "In place of the rambling altercation that had persisted into the practice of the early eighteenth century, the criminal trial underwent that articulation into prosecution and defense 'cases' that so characterizes adversary procedure."[109] Third, the demarcation of prosecution and defense cases meant that the burden of "proof could be recognized and defense motions for directed verdict at the conclusion of the prosecution case could come into play."[110] Fourth, the possibility of remaining silent to avoid self-incrimination became an option and ultimately a privilege. The idea that a defense was not necessary unless the prosecution had fully demonstrated guilt was forming.[111] Finally, excluding evidence became a significant issue: "the *necessary consequence* of [allowing defense counsel] was that objections to the admissibility of evidence were much more frequently taken, [and] the attention of the judges were directed to the subject of evidence."[112]

The two judicial changes of rules of evidence and defense counsel quickly began to feed on one another. Defense counsel called on the existing rules of evidence and questioned the admissibility of evidence not covered in the first rules. At the insistence of defense counsel, judges' attention became increasingly focused on issues of evidence; and the rules of evidence began to evolve into the complex result we rely on today. "These adaptations were meant as patches, applied for the purpose of repairing the inherited system. . . . No one could have foreseen that adversary procedure harbored an inner dynamic toward complexity so relentless that it would ultimately render criminal jury trial unworkable as a routine dispositive procedure."[113] Alternatives to the jury trial became necessary.

Plea Bargaining.   Beginning in 1586, a gradual increase in guilty pleas appears in the assize records. Many of those pleas involved altered indictments to allow for less severe punishment than would have been required under the original charges.[114] Cockburn has proposed two reasons for what may have been informal plea bargain arrangements. First, the government was trying to avoid loss of forfeitures as a consequence of acquittals, so JPs and judges preferred to obtain a conviction on lesser charges. Second, "the assize system, with its fixed schedule and inability to guarantee the attendance of trial jurors and local magistrates, was peculiarly incapable of absorbing increases in judicial business. When such increases occurred suddenly, as they apparently did on at least three occasions in Elizabeth's reign, traditional trial procedures came under intolerable pressure."[115] On the other hand, in London before the end of the eighteenth century, "so rapid was trial procedure that the court was under no pressure to induce jury waivers. We cannot find a trace of plea bargaining in the Old Bailey in these years."[116] In all likelihood, the same cyclical forces that put pressure on all the other aspects of the criminal justice process led to some plea bargaining, but it is also likely that the summary character of criminal trials meant that plea bargaining generally was not necessary. The question becomes, why has *widespread* use of plea bargaining developed rather than some other solution to the problem of crowded court dockets?

In Anglo-Saxon law, the victim prosecutor was free to pursue and prosecute, *but* he was also free not to. Even after criminal law mandated that individuals prosecute, some simply chose to ignore such authoritarian law. As public officials, particularly JPs, began to do pre-trial preparation of prosecution, the discretion to pursue prosecution appears to have passed to them. Under the crown witness competition, for instance, JPs could exempt guilty criminals from prosecution in exchange for testimony. It was a relatively small step to exempt a criminal from prosecution for some crime in exchange for a guilty plea to another crime.[117]

Another factor in the natural selection of plea bargaining was the long tradition of the guilty plea. Indeed, under Anglo-Saxon law, the fine paid was less if an offender admitted his guilt than if he tried to conceal it. Given prosecutorial discretion, however, "the guilty plea had an intrinsic convenience that pointed the Anglo-American system towards a nontrial procedure once jury trial had undergone the transformation that stripped it of its former efficiency."[118]

Another factor leading to plea bargaining was the insistence on trial by jury rather than by judge. Recall that juries initially were resisted as they were used to expand the power of the kings, but distrust of judges also was substantial. *In the context of the criminal law as it developed to assist the kings,* mistrust for one of the kings' institutions, juries, was clearly not as great as mistrust for another, royal judges. Juries became widely viewed as the only potential safeguard against the further manipulation of law enforcement for the political or financial benefit of the kings.

One other factor helps explain the ease with which plea bargaining was adopted. Thomas Green suggested: "One might conjecture that so long as the Crown had a monopoly on punishment, that punishment would be very severe."[119] Indeed, "as the emphasis shifted from restitution to the victim. . .to punishment for alleged crimes committed 'against the state,' the punishment exacted by the state became more and more severe."[120] Facts in capital cases that involved restitution in pre-Norman times, such as unplanned homicide and nonviolent thefts, were frequently manipulated by inquisitional juries to prevent capital punishment, thus blunting royal criminal law.[121] Jury mitigation continued and became particularly important during the seventeenth century political trials.[122] Jury mitigation reflects a longstanding precedent for reducing the severity of punishment in certain cases. Plea bargaining was another way to mitigate punishment.

There was considerable conflict over what punishment should be. Many judges and juries showed reluctance to impose severe physical punishments; others advocated such punishment. Lon Fuller pointed to the fact that restitution had two important consequences that promoted social harmony and maintained social order: 1) it tended to restore the victim and eliminate his desire for violent revenge, and 2) it benefited the offender in that he bought back the "peace" and his place in society.[123] Indeed, the creation of criminal law appears to have generated greater social *disorder* precisely because victims were no longer "restored" to their original level of satisfaction and therefore became more likely to demand severe physical punishment.

Punishment by Imprisonment. Prisons, or gaols, were used on a small scale as early as the tenth century to detain individuals accused of an offense but awaiting trial. But the Anglo-Saxons did not consider prison to be an appropriate punishment. It would force the offender to be idle, making it difficult for him to pay his restitution, and it would be costly to the community. By Henry II's time, detention prisons were becoming quite common as trials increasingly had to wait for the arrival of an itinerant judge. Henry III used prisons to prepare an offender to pay a fine. Indeed, imprisonment as a form of *punishment* arose chiefly in conjunction with the refusal to pay an amercement. Prisons were also used to force those accused of crimes to plead. Such individuals were put in prison and piled with chains and stones until they either agreed to plead or died.

Jails were not publicly financed. Sheriffs or others who obtained the right to run a jail, frequently by paying a fee to the crown, earned their income by levying fees on prisoners and selling them special accommodations.[124] As the use of prisons expanded, in many cases the king's justices no longer needed to threaten imprisonment to generate revenues. In these cases, of course, the profits from justice arose by keeping someone in prison.

"Houses of correction" were first established under Elizabeth to punish and reform able-bodied poor who refused to work.[125] A "widespread concern for the habits and behavior of the poor" is often cited as the reason for the poor laws regarding vagrancy and the establishment of facilities to "reform" the idle poor by confining them and forcing them to work at hard labor.[126] But Chambliss reported that "there is little question but that these statutes were designed for one express purpose: to force laborers (whether personally free or unfree) to accept employment at a low wage in order to insure the landowner an adequate supply of labor at a price he could afford to pay."[127] Such laws clearly reflected the transfer function of government.

The evolution of imprisonment is closely intertwined with the rise and decline of transportation. A 1597 Elizabethan act established the transportation option, and transportation of some criminals to various British colonies soon followed. Pardons could now be granted subject to the acceptance of transportation, and merchants transported healthy criminals to sell them into indentured servitude. After 1670, however, the system began to run into a number of problems. The colonies protested as the number of convicted felons sent to them increased.[128] The transportation system was easily interrupted during periods of war, and jails were so small that interruptions in the system caused significant overcrowding.

A postwar crisis in crime arose in 1713, 1714, and 1715, at the same time that a change in the character of government occurred. The new government was anxious to gain support of powerful political elements, many of which were concerned about crime. Faced with a rising number of criminals, the new regime was "strong enough, both politically and *financially*, to ensure that any new powers they were granted could be put into effect. One result was the Transportation Act of 1718."[129] England had undergone a significant "financial revolution" during the previous twenty years that had substantially expanded the government's revenue sources and its ability to tap them. Thus, the new government was willing to commit funds to crime control in order to meet the demands of powerful political interests. In fact, the eighteenth century witnessed a gradual increase in government financing of many aspects of criminal law, as it declined as a revenue source relative to other forms of revenue and as crime problems grew. Finally, the 1718 Transportation Act committed the treasury to pay for transporting criminals to the American colonies.

The transportation of criminals reached its peak in the 1750s and 1760s, and faith in its deterrent effect began to wane in the face of a series of wars and crime crises. Houses of correction had been used to "reform" vagrants and some criminals by subjecting them to hard labor, and influential voices advocated that such arrangements be used more extensively for criminals. On top of the growing political pressure, the American Revolution suddenly completely closed the American colonies to transportation. Parliament approved confinement at hard labor for prisoners liable to transportation in 1776. The London merchant community was a major supporter of the bill because convicts were to be used to dredge sand and gravel from the Thames to improve navigation on the river. The prisoners were to be housed on ships in the river, called hulks.

The hulks program was hardly imprisonment in a pure form; it had undoubtedly grown out of the experience of transportation of which it was conceived as a temporary substitute. . . . Nevertheless it was a form of incarceration with hard labor, and many of the practices established to punish and manage the convicts on board the ships anticipated fundamental aspects of the penitentiary as it was to be conceived in both theory and practice within a few years.[130]

Prisoners wore uniforms, for example, whipping was allowed for misbehavior, and inmates could earn early release for good behavior.

Prisons were soon seen as institutions that did more to corrupt men than to reform them, and demands were made for prison reform. The Penitentiary Act of 1779 was passed, supposedly because conditions in hulks had become "hideous" and the mortality rate was quite high. Perhaps a more important factor, however, was the security problem; battles between prisoners and their keepers had erupted, and several men had escaped.[131] But the act did not eliminate or change conditions on the hulks, which remained the only significant alternative to transportation. The legislation dictated that prisons be constructed wherein prisoners could be held in solitary confinement, thus reducing the interaction between prisoners and reducing the chance of organized riots. Prisoners were to be subject to hard labor, discipline, and religious instruction. But the prisons were not built.

Soldiers returning from the American war brought another crime crisis, putting tremendous pressure on the existing system of punishment. The hulks and houses of correction were expensive to operate, and costs were rising. The hulks could not absorb the "skyrocketing" convictions of the period and penitentiaries were not being built.[132] Finally, in 1786, political pressure forced the government to act. Despite heavy costs, the cabinet chose to transport prisoners to Botany Bay in New South Wales, Australia,[133] and transportation again became the most important punishment alternative.

But government had demonstrated a willingness to bear large costs to punish criminals and to use prisons as punishment. What was required was "larger economic resources and more concentrated and activist political power and . . . [even] greater participation of the state in the administration of justice."[134] By the early 1800s, imprisonment was the major form of punishment for felons, and parliamentary actions in 1823, 1865, and 1877 effectively transformed England's system of punishment into a public prison system financed by tax revenues.

Public Police. Pursuit of criminals and protection from them remained a duty of all private citizens, perhaps with the assistance (or the coercive urging) of semi-official sheriffs and JPs, at least until the nineteenth century. But as crime and income increased, private citizens began hiring specialists. Beginning in about 1500, private individuals or organizations paid watchmen, and private "thief-takers" (bounty hunters) pursued and captured offenders and recovered property in order to obtain rewards offered by individuals and private groups.[135]

The reliance on private policing changed modestly in 1737 when George II began paying some London and Middlesex watchmen with tax monies. In addition, Henry Fielding's system required people to seek out and apprehend suspects, assist in the retaking of goods, patrol, and infiltrate gangs. In the early 1750s, he began organizing a force of quasi-professional constables who came to be known as the "Bow Street Runners."[136] Because Fielding was a magistrate of the court, this group had some "public" status, and their income came from rewards for criminal apprehensions. By 1792, seven other magistrate offices in the London area had organized similar operations, and in 1805 the Bow Street organization formed a horse patrol for areas on the outskirts of London. William Wooldridge observed: "Fielding continuously agitated for governmental financial assistance so his platoon could be regularly salaried... [but] Englishmen opposed on principle the idea of public police during Fielding's lifetime. They feared the relation between police and what is known now as the police state."[137]

In 1822, Robert Peel was appointed Home Secretary. Peel believed that "you cannot have good policing when responsibility is divided,"[138] and that the only way to consolidate responsibility was through government. But it took Peel some time to actually set up a public police department. Even after Parliament gave Peel the authority and financing to form a London metropolitan police department in 1829, there was substantial opposition from the populace. Englishmen knew that the French public police, established in 1667, had always provided the king with detailed information about citizens and that, even after the Revolution, police had opened mail, controlled the press, and made arrests and imprisonments without trial.[139] Napoleon ultimately grew to fear the power of his minister of police, but the system remained intact through much of the nineteenth century. In an effort to alleviate the fears of the English, Peel's police officers wore identifiable uniforms so they could not secretly spy on citizens. But citizens remained concerned, and they were apparently justified. Between 1829 and 1831, for example, 3,000 of the 8,000 public police officers hired were fired for "unfitness, incompetence, or drunkenness."[140] The officers were referred to as "Peel's bloody gang" or "blue devils."[141]

Once the institution of public police was in place, it was gradually transformed. A plain-clothes detective unit was established after ten years, and by 1863 the visible truncheon had been added to the policeman's attire. Public police were in other cities and boroughs by 1835 and were established in the counties between 1839 and 1856. Substantial opposition prevented the full-scale development of public police for some time, but support gradually increased in the face of cyclical upsurges in crime. And once powerful individuals and groups began to see that they could shift the cost of their own protection to taxpayers, special interest support for public police began to grow.[142] Public police were not nearly as effective as their supporters had hoped, however, so private citizens still relied on private police and protection.[143]

Public Prosecution. Englishmen also resisted public prosecution because "a private prosecutorial system was necessary to check the power of the Crown. If not so limited, the power of criminal prosecution could be used for politically oppressive purposes."[144] Gradually, central government officials expanded their power in prosecution of "political" crimes, and by the late nineteenth century a "limited system of governmental prosecution" was in place.[145] The Public Prosecutions Office was formed, which began playing a small role in criminal prosecution. But even today only a small portion of criminal cases are actually prosecuted by that office; most of its work is reviewing the charges that the director approves prior to prosecution.

Considerable power in prosecutorial management had accrued to JPs during and after the Fielding era, but they apparently preferred not to personally perform the trial prosecution function. That role remained largely in victims' hands, and JPs tended to delegate their evolving trial prosecutorial or testimonial duties to constables. Of course, private victims received no restitution, and they bore substantial costs in fees, time, and trouble. It was not surprising when many citizens became willing to yield the prosecution role to someone else. Fear of public prosecution was primarily directed at the central government, so a localized bureaucracy was the natural government organization to take on such duties. Thus, "police departments *instituted* the policies of receiving the complaints of crime victims, investigating the charges, and if prosecution was believed appropriate, bringing the charges against the offender and managing the prosecution within their own office."[146] Police officers were soon conducting prosecutions in court, including presenting charges, examining witnesses, addressing the magistrate, and arguing with the defense counsel.[147]

Public prosecution in England required a legal fiction, however. Under common law, prosecution is still private: "English common law maintains that police officers are not distinct from the general body of citizens. . . therefore, when a police officer initiates a criminal proceeding he is legally acting not by virtue of his office but as a private citizen interested in the maintenance of law and order."[148] Theoretically, then, the vestiges of Anglo-Saxon law's reliance on private prosecution remains.[149]

CONCLUSIONS

The common law system we have inherited was largely shaped, not by some desire to organize society in the "public interest," but by the self-interested goals of kings, their bureaucrats, and powerful groups in England. One response to this might be: "So what? We now live in a representative democracy; there is no longer a powerful king, so our representatives can now shape the legal system to benefit the public at large." There are two problems with this argument.

1) Imposed Order vs. Spontaneous Order.   Under customary law, "the spontaneous order arises from each element balancing all the various factors operating on it and by adjusting all its various actions to each other, a balance which will be destroyed if some of the actions are determined by another agency on the basis of different knowledge and in the service of different ends."[150] The common law system that our representative democracy inherited was already flawed by a long history of "direct commands" that were intended to be "in the service of different ends." Furthermore, legislated rules determined on the basis of incomplete knowledge continue to alter the natural evolution of law and order. We have examined only a small part of the transition from customary to authoritarian law, and the most dramatic changes may have occurred in the twentieth century. Berman contended, for instance, that basic customary postulates are being undermined as Western societies have turned toward collectivism in the law, with an emphasis on state or public property, limitations on contractual freedom, and so on.[151] Entirely new areas of government law have come into being during this century, such as labor-management relations, securities regulation, public housing, and social security. So pervasive are the processes of government rule creation that Lon Fuller was led to conclude:

Now the tendency is to convert every form of social order into an exercise of the authority of the state. . . . Legislation, adjudication, and administrative direction, instead of being perceived as distinctive interactional processes, are all seen as unidirectional exercises of state power. Contract is perceived, not as a source of "law" or social ordering in itself, but of something that derives its whole significance from the fact that the courts of the state stand ready to enforce it. Custom is passed over in virtually complete silence. . .and is viewed by legal scholars as becoming worthy of attention only when it is recognized by the courts and thus has been converted into "law."[152]

This may seem surprising in light of historical events leading to the establishment of an independent nation in the United States. But when the Western countries rejected the power of the monarchy, they did not reject the idea that government was the supreme source of law, and therefore, of social order.

2) Facilitating Interaction vs. Facilitating Transfers.   The fact that government law has taken over as much as it has is not a reflection of the superior efficiency of representative government in making or enforcing law that facilitates interaction. It is, rather, a reflection of government's general purpose of transferring wealth to those with political power. Government power to coerce is needed to accomplish transfers. Under customary law, individuals had reciprocal incentives to recognize their rules of obligation and to participate in enforcement of such rules. The adversarial nature of authoritarian law that pits group against group in the taking/transfer process promotes disorder rather than order. Indeed, under government law, individuals have incentives *not* to participate in a cooperative effort to maintain order.

The expressed aim of government officials in a representative democracy may not be the accumulation and centralization of power, but that is a necessary consequence of the process as it has evolved within the institutions developed by medieval kings. Whether the government producing law is a totalitarian king or a representative democracy, power is centralized and coercion is used to impose rules beneficial to some upon the rest of the population. Government is still a wealth transfer mechanism.

ENDNOTES

1.   Military power is still a major consideration in many places (e.g., the Philippines, Nicaragua, El Salvador, Lebanon), and military-like terrorism is an important political factor.

2. Transfer payments can alter incentives of the recipients in ways which create wealth for third parties. See for example, Gary M. Anderson, "Welfare Programs in the Rent-Seeking Society," *Southern Economic Journal* 54 (October 1987): 377–386.
3. W. Samuels and N. Mercuro, "Property Rights, Equity and Public Utility Regulation; in *New Dimensions in Public Utility Pricing,* ed. H. Trebing (East Lansing: Michigan State University Press, 1976), p. 50.
4. Eric G. Furubotn, "Comment," in *New Dimensions in Public Utility Pricing,* p. 108.
5. Bruce L. Benson, "Rent Seeking from a Property Rights Perspective," *Southern Economic Journal* 51 (October 1984): 393–394.
6. Roger L. Faith, "Rent-Seeking Aspect of Bureaucratic Competition," in *Toward a Theory of the Rent-Seeking Society,* ed. James M. Buchanan, Robert D. Tollison, and Gordon Tullock (College Station: Texas A & M University, 1980), p. 33.
7. Sir Frederick Pollack and Frederick W. Maitland, *History of English Law,* vol. 2 (Washington, D.C.: Lawyers' Literary Club, 1959), p. 453.
8. Bruce Lyon, *A Constitutional and Legal History of Medieval England,* 2nd ed. (New York: W. W. Norton and Co., 1980), pp. 62–63.
9. Ibid., p. 63. Sheriffs actually evolved from royal *reeves* who were the kings' representatives in hundreds and royal manors.
10. Ibid., p. 65.
11. William Stubbs, *The Constitutional History of England* (Chicago: University of Chicago Press, 1979), p. 42.
12. Peter Hunter Blair, *An Introduction to Anglo-Saxon England* (London: Butterworths, 1971), p. 211.
13. Lyon, *A Constitutional and Legal History of Medieval England,* p. 52.
14. Blair, *An Introduction to Anglo-Saxon England,* p. 208.
15. Pollock and Maitland, *History of English Law,* vol. 1, p. 94.
16. Lyon, *A Constitutional and Legal History of Medieval England,* p. 163.
17. Pollock and Maitland, *History of English Law,* vol. 1, p. 53.
18. Ibid., pp. 109–110.
19. Lyon, *A Constitutional and Legal History of Medieval England,* p. 145.
20. Ibid., p. 146.
21. Ibid., p. 148.
22. In exchange for services, sheriffs received land, but they "derived their largest income from what they extorted from the people. . . . This was a perquisite of the office and was taken for granted; it was why so many men were willing to pay dearly for the office." See ibid., p. 170.
23. Ibid., p. 196.
24. Pollock and Maitland, *History of English Law,* vol. 1, p. 111.
25. Ibid., p. 106.

26. Ibid., pp. 106–107.
27. Lyon, *A Constitutional and Legal History of Medieval England*, p. 189.
28. Ibid., p. 190.
29. Ibid.
30. Pollock and Maitland, *History of English Law*, vol. 2, pp. 461–462.
31. Harold J. Berman, *Law and Revolution: The Formation of the Western Legal Tradition* (Cambridge, Mass.: Harvard University Press, 1983), p. 439.
32. Ibid., p. 443.
33. Pollock and Maitland, *History of English Law*, vol. 1, p. 138.
34. Ibid., p. 153.
35. Ibid.
36. Lyon, *A Constitutional and Legal History of Medieval England*, p. 282.
37. Ibid.
38. Pollock and Maitland, *History of English Law*, vol. 1, p. 154.
39. Ibid., p. 132. Emphasis added.
40. Lyon, *A Constitutional and Legal History of Medieval England*, p. 288.
41. Ibid.
42. Pollock and Maitland, *History of English Law*, vol. 1, p. 151.
43. Ibid., p. 141.
44. Lyon, *A Constitutional and Legal History of Medieval England*, p. 295.
45. Pollock and Maitland, *History of English Law*, vol. 1, p. 455. See also Richard E. Laster, "Criminal Restitution: A Survey of Its Past History and an Analysis of Its Present Usefulness," *University of Richmond Law Review* 5 (Fall 1970): p. 75.
46. Pollock and Maitland, *History of English Law*, vol. 2, p. 165.
47. Lyon, *A Constitutional and Legal History of Medieval England*, pp. 310–311.
48. Pollock and Maitland, *History of English Law*, vol. 1, pp. 171–172.
49. Lyon, *A Constitutional Legal History of Medieval England*, p. 316.
50. Ibid., p. 413.
51. Ibid., p. 417.
52. Ibid.
53. Ibid., p. 418.
54. Ibid., p. 420.
55. Ibid., p. 421.
56. Ibid., p. 433.
57. Ibid., p. 436.
58. Pollock and Maitland, *History of English Law*, vol. 1, p. 211.
59. Ibid., p. 216.
60. Ibid.
61. Ibid.
62. Lyon, *A Constitutional and Legal History of Medieval England*, p. 447. Unlike civil case litigants, criminal defendants were not permitted legal representation, so criminal procedure was much less complex.

63. Ibid., p. 438.
64. The judgment itself was not final, however. A defendant could obtain another trial by alleging error, or he could purchase a writ in order to sue the jury for bringing a false verdict.
65. Lyon, *A Constitutional and Legal History of Medieval England*, p. 450.
66. Ibid., p. 452.
67. Berman, *Law and Revolution*, p. 341.
68. Ibid., p. 343.
69. Robert B. Ekeland and Robert D. Tollison, "Economic Regulation in Mercantile England: Hecksher Revisited," *Economic Inquiry* 18 (October 1980): 565–572.
70. W. Mitchell, *Essay on the Early History of the Law Merchant* (New York: Burt Franklin, 1904), p. 72.
71. Baker, *An Introduction to English Legal History*, p. 31. See also William M. Landes and Richard A. Posner, "Adjudication as a Private Good," *Journal of Legal Studies* 8 (March 1979): 258.
72. Quoted in Steven Lazarus, et al., *Resolving Business Disputes: The Potential for Commercial Arbitration* (New York: American Management Association, 1965), p. 18.
73. Quoted in Leon E. Trakman, *The Law Merchant: The Evolution of Commercial Law* (Littleton, Colo.: Fred B. Rothman and Co., 1983), p. 26.
74. Ibid., p. 26.
75. Ibid., p. 25.
76. Laster, "Criminal Restitution," p. 76.
77. See ibid. for discussion of and citations to the following legal changes.
78. Pollock and Maitland, *History of English Law*, vol. 2, pp. 521–522.
79. Quoted from Sir James F. Stephen, *A History of the Criminal Law of England* (New York: Burt Franklin, 1883), p. 190.
80. John H. Langbein, *Prosecuting Crime in the Renaissance: England, Germany and France* (Cambridge, Mass.: Harvard University Press, 1974), p. 5.
81. Ibid., p. 66.
82. See John H. Langbein, "The Origins of Public Prosecution at Common Law," *American Journal of Legal History* 17 (1973): 334; J. H. Gleason, *The Justice of the Peace in England 1558–1640* (Oxford: Clarendon Press, 1969), p. 2.
83. Langbein, *Prosecuting Crime in the Renaissance*, pp. 34–35.
84. J. M. Beattie, *Crime and the Courts in England, 1660–1800* (Oxford: Clarendon Press, 1986), p. 228.
85. Ibid., p. 229.

86. Ibid., p. 226.
87. Ibid., p. 227.
88. Ibid., p. 41.
89. John H. Langbein, "Shaping the Eighteenth-Century Criminal Trial: A View from the Ryder Sources," *University of Chicago Law Review* 50 (Winter 1983): 76.
90. Ibid., p. 63.
91. Quoted in ibid., p. 97, from *Regina* v. *Farler*, 8C and pp. 106, 108, 173 Eng. Rev. 418, 419 (Worcester Assizes 1837).
92. Ibid., p. 96.
93. Ibid.
94. Ibid., p. 98.
95. Quoted in ibid., p. 102, from 1 Leach at 465–466, 168 Eng. Rep. at 334–335 (1788).
96. Quoted in ibid., p. 103, from *Rex* v. *Warickshall* 1 Leach 263, 168 Eng. Rep. at 235 (1783).
97. Ibid., p. 104.
98. J. S. Cockburn, *Calendar of Assize Records: Home Circuit Indictments, Elizabeth I and James I* (London: Her Majesty's Stationary Office, 1985), p. 57.
99. Langbein, "The Origins of Public Prosecution at Common Law," p. 314. See also Thomas A. Green, *Verdict According to Conscience: Perspectives on the English Criminal Trial Jury, 1200–1800* (Chicago: University of Chicago Press, 1985), p. 105.
100. John H. Langbein, "The Criminal Trial Before the Lawyers," *University of Chicago Law Review* 45 (Winter 1978): p. 274.
101. Ibid., pp. 276, 277; Beattie, *Crime and Courts in England, 1660–1800*, p. 376.
102. Langbein, "The Criminal Trial Before the Lawyers," p. 345.
103. Ibid., p. 291.
104. Ibid., p. 284.
105. It should be noted, however, that there was a substantial level of acquittals during the seventeenth century. See ibid., p. 267; Beattie, *Crime and the Courts in England, 1660–1800*, p. 418.
106. John H. Langbein, "Understanding the Short History of Plea Bargaining," *Law and Society Review* 13 (Winter 1979): 263–264.
107. Beattie, *Crimes and the Courts in England, 1660–1800*, p. 354.
108. Ibid., p. 361.
109. Langbein, "Shaping the Eighteenth-Century Criminal Trial," p. 131.
110. Ibid.
111. Beattie, *Crime and the Courts in England, 1660–1800*, p. 375.
112. W. Best, quoted in Langbein, "Shaping the Eighteenth-Century Criminal Trial," p. 131.

113. Ibid., p. 134.
114. Cockburn, *Calendar of Assize Records,* p. 65.
115. Ibid., p. 69.
116. Langbein, "The Criminal Trial Before the Lawyers," p. 278.
117. Langbein, "Understanding the Short History of Plea Bargaining," p. 267.
118. Ibid., p. 268.
119. Green, *Verdict According to Conscience,* p. 367.
120. Murray N. Rothbard, "Punishment and Proportionality," in *Assessing the Criminal: Restitution, Retribution and the Legal Process,* ed. Randy E. Barnett and John Hagel III (Cambridge, Mass.: Ballinger Press, 1977), p. 262.
121. Green, *Verdict According to Conscience.*
122. Ibid., p. xviii.
123. Lon Fuller, "The Law's Precarious Hold on Life," *Georgia Law Review* 3 (1969): 539.
124. Beattie, *Crime and the Courts in England, 1660–1800,* p. 290; Stephen, *A History of the Criminal Law of England,* p. 484.
125. Beattie, *Crimes and the Courts in England, 1660–1800,* p. 492.
126. Ibid., p. 497.
127. William Chambliss, "A Sociological Analysis of the Law of Vagrancy," *Social Problems* 12 (Summer 1964): 69.
128. Beattie, *Crime and the Courts in England, 1660–1800,* p. 479.
129. Ibid., p. 503. Emphasis added.
130. Ibid., p. 567.
131. Ibid., p. 573.
132. Ibid., p. 593.
133. Ibid., p. 599.
134. Ibid., p. 617.
135. Truett A. Ricks, Bill G. Tillett and Clifford W. Van Meter, *Principles of Security* (Cincinnati: Criminal Justice Studies, Anderson Publishing Company, 1981), pp. 2–3; Beattie, *Crime and Courts in England, 1660–1800,* p. 192.
136. Langbein, "Shaping the Eighteenth-Century Criminal Trial," p. 67.
137. William C. Wooldridge, *Uncle Sam, the Monopoly Man* (New Rochelle, N.Y.: Arlington House, 1970), pp. 119–120.
138. Quoted in Richard S. Post and Arthur A. Kingsbury, *Security Administration* (Springfield, Ill.: Charles C. Thomas, 1970), p. 13.
139. Frank Morn, *The Eye that Never Sleeps* (Bloomington: Indiana University Press, 1982), p. 10.
140. Ricks, et al., *Principles of Security,* p. 6.
141. Ibid., p. 6.
142. Beattie, *Crime and Courts in England, 1660–1800,* p. 67.

143. Ricks, et al., *Principles of Security,* p. 8. See Benson, "The Evolution of Law: Custom Versus Authority" (ms, Tallahassee, Fl.: Florida State University, 1990).
144. Juan Cardenas, "The Crime Victim in the Prosecutional Process," *Harvard Journal of Law and Public Policy* 9 (Spring 1986): 361.
145. Ibid., p. 362. The Prosecution of Offenses Act of 1879 established the Office of Director of Public Prosecutions with a very "circumscribed list" of functions. The office's power in the area of criminal prosecution has since expanded, however.
146. Ibid., p. 363. Emphasis added.
147. A majority of the criminal prosecutions in England are still conducted by police. If a case is especially complex, a solicitor or barrister may be hired; and there is a growing trend in urbanized areas of England for police departments to retain permanent prosecuting solicitors.
148. Cardenas, "The Crime Victim," p. 365.
149. Roughly three percent of defendants are still privately prosecuted. Ibid.
150. F. A. Hayek, *Law, Legislation and Liberty,* vol. 1 (Chicago: University of Chicago Press), p. 51.
151. Berman, *Law and Revolution,* pp. 36–37.
152. Lon L. Fuller, *The Principles of Social Order* (Durham, N.C.: Duke University Press, 1981), pp. 156–157.

PART II

A PUBLIC CHOICE
APPROACH TO
AUTHORITARIAN LAW

4

LAW AND JUSTICE AS A POLITICAL MARKET

Many of the public institutions of our modern enterprise of law were developed to facilitate monarchs' efforts to centralize and consolidate their power. These institutions operate today in a representative democracy. Nonetheless, government actions still reflect responses to the demands of politically active pressure groups. This claim is not new. Indeed, the political nature of and interest group influence on the justice system have been recognized by many.[1] James Eisenstein reported:

> One point should be unmistakably clear: the legal process is an integral part of the political process. It not only displays the major characteristics of the political system in recruitment, operation, and impact, but appears to play a particularly crucial role in shaping patterns of who gets what. Because it is intimately bound up in the legitimate use of coercive force in society, it lies at the heart of politics.[2]

Because the legal system allocates costs and benefits of the political system, parties in interest have strong incentives to try to influence the inputs to and outcomes of the legal system.

Political pressure groups play a significant role in determining legal policy emanating from the legislative process. In fact, as Rhodes pointed out, "as far as crime policy and legislation are concerned, public opinion and attitudes are generally irrelevant. The same is not true, however, of specifically interested criminal justice publics, particularly in the politics of legislation."[3] What gets defined as criminal behavior by statute, for instance, is the result of a political process. One must understand this political process in order to understand crime.[4]

Interest group pressure influences more than the legislative definition of criminal activities and sanctions. All areas of law are subject to interest group manipulation through the legislative process. Furthermore, once laws are passed, the administration of justice is also influenced by interest groups. After all, the mere legislative passage of rules does not provide any guidance or incentive for enforcement. Attempts will be made to influence the courts, the police, the prosecutors, and the rest of the administrative system to assure that the laws each group desires are enforced.

Special interest views of government have been around for a long time, but it has only been recently that attempts were made to develop any formal rigorous theory of special interest government.[5] George Stigler's work was probably one of the most influential contributions, although he drew his thoughts from many previous examinations of the political process.[6] Stigler described government regulation as a supply-and-demand process, with interest groups on the demand side and legislative representatives and their political parties on the supply side. Several theorists have expanded on this perception by examining the demand or supply sides of the exchange. One question of interest is what is being demanded by interest groups and supplied by the government.

THE ASSIGNMENT AND ENFORCEMENT OF PROPERTY RIGHTS

Those who adopt the interest group theory of government assume that the object of interest group demand is a transfer of wealth.[7] This view might be somewhat misleading if it is interpreted to imply that individuals become involved in interest group activities only if they can gain or avoid losing monetary or physical wealth. Many who are active in the political arena gain little or no personal monetary wealth from their efforts. Rather, they gain considerable satisfaction by influencing the outcome of the political process so that it more closely meets their view of what the "public interest" should be. Of course, if "wealth" is more broadly defined to mean well-being or satisfaction, there is little cause for confusion. Nonetheless, let us define the objects of interest group demand and the functions of government law as: 1) the assignment of property rights and 2) enforcement of each property rights assignment.[8] Property rights specify the "norms of behavior" that persons must observe while interacting with one another.[9]

In doing so, they "convey the right to benefit or harm oneself or others."[10] In other words, property rights dictate the distribution of wealth and changes in property rights transfer wealth. In addition, the concept of property rights encompasses all law, even criminal statutes, which define or attenuate various "human rights" as well as rights over material property. Governments govern by creating and enforcing rights and by modifying and changing rights as wealth transfers are instituted.[11]

INTEREST GROUP DEMANDS

Stigler contended that interest groups demand favorable treatment from their political representatives. This political market distributes favors to those with the highest effective demand. A small interest group with a large per capita stake tends to dominate a larger group with more diffused interests because of the relationship between group size and the cost of obtaining favorable political treatment. Two costs are involved. The first is the cost of information. Voting for legislative representatives is infrequent and usually concerned with a package of issues, so individuals must incur costs to become informed about particular issues and politicians. This investment is not worthwhile unless the expected gains in rights, or the potential loss of rights due to the demands of other interest groups, are relatively large.[12]

There are also costs of organizing. Individuals must first recognize their interest (obtain information) and then organize to express that interest to politicians and bureaucrats. The expression of interests includes mobilizing votes and money as well as informing government officials of the group's desires and political strengths (lobbying). These organizing costs tend to rise faster than group size.[13]

Posner added to Stigler's interest group theory with a more detailed discussion of the costs of organization in the context of the theory of cartels and the free rider problem.[14] There are two major costs of cartelization: 1) arriving at an agreement and 2) enforcing an agreement. Potential members of an interest group view the cost of organizing to seek beneficial rights assignments as an investment. Individuals are likely to make this investment if they do not have a more attractive alternative investment. Thus, the expected net per capital gain from participation in interest group activities will be compared to other investments by individuals.

Once a potential interest group has reached an agreement on objectives and strategies, each member has the incentive to avoid paying his full share, either monetarily or in terms of time. Such organizations tend to break down because of the free rider problem.[15] The free rider problem explains the observation that small groups may be effective in obtaining regulatory benefits while large groups may not be effective. It is easier to organize an effective interest group and disperse the costs if the interest group is small. If a potential benefactor refuses to participate in the cooperative effort, the effort will generally collapse: "Thus all will tend to participate, knowing that any defection is likely to be followed promptly by the defection of the remaining members of the group, leaving the original defector worse off than if he had cooperated."[16]

The cost of arriving at an agreement tends to be less when the potential interest group has homogeneity of interests, so groups with a very narrow focus are often successful. But groups can be effective even if they have heterogeneous interests. Stigler pointed out that some members of a group may have incentives to take the initiative in forming a coalition or in seeking benefits, despite the lack of support by other benefactors when there is significant asymmetry among the members.[17] Laws and criminal enforcement policies can take a variety of forms and can affect potential members of the interest group differently. Some individuals, therefore, will have strong incentives to press the group's interests to reflect their views. Stigler argued that even though small groups can generally organize easier than large groups, with asymmetry a large group of individuals may be effectively represented by a few individuals with strong interests.

Pressing this point even further, James Q. Wilson classified the demand for regulation into three categories. First, with "interest-group politics" both costs and benefits are narrowly concentrated so groups on both sides of an issue organize and compete. Second, "client politics" applies when benefits of a policy are concentrated but costs are widely dispersed, so only one group makes demands on the political system. Finally, "entrepreneurial politics" describes a situation in which benefits of a policy are dispersed but a "skilled entrepreneur" serves as a "vicarious representative of groups not directly part of the legislative process."[18]

While such a breakdown is useful for a more complete understanding of the political process, the term "interest group" will be used here to refer to all organizations that apply political pressure in an effort to generate a governmental change in property rights. This does not mean that all interest group members or their representatives are motivated solely by selfish interests. In fact, while potential self-interest motives can often be identified for groups seeking changes in law, many firmly believe that the changes they demand are in the "public interest." As Wilson noted, "a complete theory of regulation politics—indeed, a complete theory of politics generally—requires that attention be paid to beliefs as well as interests."[19] Of course, the "public interest" is a normative concept. It is what each individual believes it to be, and his perception is often affected by his own self-interests. Nevertheless, using "interest group" to describe all political pressure groups should not imply any negative judgments about the members of such groups.

How do interest groups make their demands effective? Posner listed three bases for interest groups' political strength: 1) favorable treatment can be rewarded by the members' votes; 2) monetary payments (i.e., campaign contributions) can be made to obtain favorable rights assignments; and 3) rights are "awarded to groups that are able to make credible threats to retaliate with violence (or disorder, or work stoppage, or grumbling) if society does not give them favorable treatment."[20] Interest groups with sufficient monetary backing may also effectively obtain their desired ends through litigation. For example, interest groups that turn to the judicial process often believe they do not have enough political power to obtain the rights assignment they desire from a legislature or bureaucracy. Initiated changes through the courts may yield the desired rights directly, or they may indirectly force legislative action.[21]

Other factors should also be noted. First, Peltzman observed that more than one interest group can obtain benefits from a particular policy, and interest group coalitions may arise.[22] Second, Hirshleifer pointed out that the enforcement bureaucrats themselves constitute an interest group that benefits when laws are passed that must be enforced, and those bureaucrats may demand changes.[23] Government employees' unions are also likely to play a considerable role in the policy-making process. Regulatory bureaucracies appear to have an advantage over other interest groups in terms of organizing and lobbying costs because they can often appropriate a portion of their budget to cover some of the costs.[24] They also have ready access to elected officials who pass laws and set budgets, so lobbying costs appear to be relatively low. Public employees' unions are also at a relative advantage because of their ability to disrupt services that only they can legally provide. Finally, an interest group may be forced to organize and demand retention of the status quo in order to avoid losses due to potential changes that benefit another interest group.[25] Thus, the number of interest groups seeking rights can change over time, and the politically dominant interest groups can change.

GOVERNMENT RESPONSES TO INTEREST GROUP DEMANDS

Interest groups may target their efforts at several levels of the legal system, including the legislature, the enforcement bureaucracy, and the judicial bureaucracy. In theory, these governmental organizations might be expected to respond to interest group demands in different ways. Peltzman assumed that the utility-maximizing behavior of politicians could be predicted by viewing them as majority maximizers.[26] He concluded:

1. The legislature will tend to favor the most politically powerful interest groups.
2. More than one organization may be favored at the expense of others.
3. When there are differences between members of an interest group, the benefits (or costs) to members that result from a particular rights assignment will differ among members.
4. The favored interest group will not be favored to the extent that it could be; a legislature never acts as a perfect broker for a single interest group.

Because legislators wish to meet the marginal conditions of the political exchange, Stigler and his followers argue that this transfer process should efficiently accomplish what it is designed to do. Posner concluded:

> A corollary of the economic theory of regulation is that the regulatory process can be expected to operate with reasonable efficiency to achieve its ends. The ends are the product of a struggle between interest groups, but . . . it would be contrary to the usual assumptions of economics to argue that wasteful or inappropriate means would be chosen to achieve those ends.[27]

So, the interest group theory of government implies that legislators attempt to efficiently allocate political favors. The political efficiency desired by legislators is not equivalent to economic efficiency. The theory implies that the legislature attempts to efficiently meet desires that are in the interests of small powerful groups rather than the public at large.

Considerable evidence in support of the predicted legislative efforts for political efficiency has been found in the case of economic legislation.[28] Legislators have established many organizational and institutional arrangements in an attempt to achieve this political efficiency. For example, a legislature could make all decisions itself, as a committee of the whole. But legislative bodies have high decision-making costs that rise sharply as the number of decisions increases. Bargaining among a large number of individuals involves high transactions costs, which rise sharply as the number of bargainers increases.[29] Therefore, a legislature cannot respond efficiently by increasing its size. Legislatures delegate primary decision-making powers to their committees; and political efficiency is improved. The number of bargainers involved in making each decision is reduced, and legislators are allowed to specialize. A small number of legislators become relatively well versed in a few areas, and they are able to better determine the relative strengths of interest groups and group demands. The committee system facilitates the logrolling process that is vital for efficiently supplying interest group desires.

Enforcement (and often rule-making) powers are delegated to bureaucratic agencies for the same reason that legislatures delegate decision-making powers to committees, because of the high transactions costs of decision-making in a large group. Of course, when enforcement and rule-making powers are delegated to agencies, the bureaucrats' incentives must be examined to see if they prefer to regulate efficiently. These authorities can be seen as firms producing a service—the enforcement of legislatively determined property rights assignments. Niskanen's model of the exchange of bureaucratic services for a budget has been modified to fit the supply of property rights in the context of the special interest theory of government.[30] The model predicts that bureaucrats generally have incentives to over-enforce and to produce any level of enforcement inefficiently. Legislators, in turn, should attempt to force bureaucrats to produce in a politically efficient manner by using various control devices.

The term "over-enforcement" is not intended to imply that the law enforcement bureaucracies are arresting too many criminals and punishing them too severely. It means that whatever rights assignments are supported by powerful political interests will be over-enforced. For example, if powerful interest groups obtain more rights for the accused or for prisoners, those rights will be enforced more diligently than the legislature would prefer. This could mean fewer arrests and less severe punishment than is politically optimal from the legislature's point of view. Bureaucratic agencies also will try to inefficiently enforce rights by spending a larger budget per unit of enforcement than is necessary, if they can appropriate part of the budgets allocated by the legislature for their own benefit. A bureaucratic manager might use a portion of his discretionary budget, for example, to improve his office environment or enlarge his staff.

Constraints do exist to force relatively efficient behavior among bureaucrats. Assume that legislators have only two functions: 1) choosing the appropriate rights assignments and 2) controlling enforcement bureaucracies. Legislators' time and staff must be allocated between these two functions while attempting to maintain political support. In this case, a typical legislator's majority is a function of the amount of time he spends assessing demand conditions to determine rights assignments, the property rights assignments he selects, and the net benefits to favored interest groups (net of the losses to others) that result from the enforcement of the rights. The net benefits are a function of the level of enforcement that the legislature allows.

A legislator's choices are not quite this simple, but the implication is that a lawmaker's vote-maximizing efforts are subject to constraints. Actual budget allocations approach politically optimal allocations as more of a legislator's time is directed to controlling bureaucrats. Time available for assessing relative interest group demands decreases, however, as a legislator spends more time scrutinizing bureaucratic performance. Therefore, legislators face a trade-off, and some bureaucratic inefficiency and over-enforcement is anticipated. As one former state legislator remembered:

> When, as a young man, I went to the state legislature as a freshman member, I was utterly confounded by the amount of time devoted to sorting out special-interest legislation. . . .
>
> In any stable of interest groups an individual legislator must please, there are two types of horses: those whom he must not actively antagonize and who can be induced to support or at least be neutral about his candidacy and those who actively help his election either by delivering voters or by delivering money that can be used to deliver voters.
>
> In the service of the second group, the average legislator uses up all of his personal credit, political credit and most of his creative energy *and time*. . . .
> It is not possible to initiate programs; the most we can expect is for legislators to react to programs.[31]

Clearly, monitoring the performance of bureaucrats is not high on the typical legislator's list when it comes to allocation of his time and effort. Nonetheless, there should also be evidence of legislative efforts to control law enforcers.

One important legislative control device is the maintenance of alternative sources of enforcement. When the legislature has different enforcement authorities to choose from, then bureaucrats are forced to compete for the enforcement budget. In effect, each agency faces relatively elastic demand. In this case, the bureaucrats' budget requests and enforcement levels are closer to the legislators' optimal budget and enforcement.

One other implication of this theoretical model of property rights enforcement must be stressed. Because bureaucratic salaries or perquisites are directly related to output level and budget size, it follows that bureaucrats often find it rewarding to shift their own demand. This leads to two important implications. First, bureaucrats may be willing to use some of their own resources or their discretionary budget to influence the legislature. That is, law enforcement bureaucrats constitute interest groups that demand laws. Second, bureaucrats have incentives to inform lawmakers of the strength and wishes of other interest groups, so they serve as an important source of information for the legislature.

Of course, because legislatures often delegate rule-making power to bureaucrats, interest groups directly pressure bureaucracies for favorable rights. The enforcement budget still comes from the legislature, however, so bureaucrats must inform the legislature of changes that occur in the workload as a consequence of meeting interest group demands. Thus, interest group pressure on bureaucrats is relatively ineffective unless bureaucrats can persuade the legislature to expand the enforcement budget as a consequence of such pressure.

The Niskanen type of bureaucratic model only considers the incentives of the bureau manager to be important and ignores the incentives of the rank-and-file civil servants. Furthermore, bureau managers may come from very different circumstances and have very different goals. In this light, James Q. Wilson chose to categorize regulators into three distinguishable but often overlapping groups: 1) careerists "who identify their careers and rewards with the agency" so that "the maintenance of the agency and their position within it is of paramount importance"; 2) politicians who "see themselves as having a future in elective or appointive office outside the agency" so the enhancement of their image outside the agency provides their primary motivation; and 3) professionals whose rewards depend "on their display of professionally approved behavior and technical competence" to "organized members of similar occupations" in and outside the agency.[32]

These considerations can provide insights for understanding bureacratic performance, but they do not change the primary predictions of Niskanen's model. Wilson's careerists, for instance, are assumed to be most concerned with avoiding scandal, which is likely to be the only threat to their position and their agency. If a careerist is in a position of power, however, he does not wish to be accused of doing nothing, so he will "proliferate rules to cover all possible contingencies." Wilson observed that "critics of regulatory agencies notice this proliferation of rules and suppose that it is the result of the 'imperialistic' or expansionist instincts of bureaucratic organizations [à la Niskanen]. Though there are such examples, I am struck more by the defensive, threat-avoiding, scandal-minimizing instincts of these agencies."[33] So, the same outcome arises but for a different reason. If an agency has both Niskanen bureaucrats and Wilson careerists, their incentives will complement each other, leading to too many rules that require a larger bureaucracy and more resources. Furthermore, Niskanen bureaucrats will strive to avoid scandals. Wilson "politicians" are like Niskanen bureaucrats in that they will tend to be "energetic advocates of regulation."

Adding Wilson's "professionals" makes a modest contribution to the predictive power of Niskanen's theory. Professionals in the criminal justice area, for example, may include lawyers in prosecutors' offices and police officers. Many attorneys in prosecutors' offices are young and ambitious, and, Wilson contended, they seek the "maximum display of legal acumen. The lawyers' opportunities to prove their legal talent in the courtroom or in other negotiations substantially enhances their market value" for both prospective private sector employers and other public sector employers.[34] These lawyers, therefore, have incentives to "prosecute vigorously," but they also tend to prosecute certain kinds of crimes and avoid others. Wilson argued that professionals in law enforcement favor 1) simple cases that can be investigated and prosecuted in a reasonably brief time in order to maximize the number of convictions and 2) cases that are designed to meet the demands of some relatively vocal individual or group.[35] If an agency is dominated by such professionals, laws will be vigorously enforced if they are easily enforced or if some interest group demands that they be enforced.

COURTS IN THE POLITICAL SYSTEM

Courts made up of long-term appointee judges can be characterized as a bureaucracy.[36] The constraints and incentives may be different for these judges than for the police and other law enforcement agencies, but the same general model can be applied. Judges who are elected for short terms and are frequently up for re-election may face incentives similar to those of elected representatives. As West Virginia Supreme Court Justice Richard Neely observed: "The lower the level of the judge and the shorter his or her term of office, the more intense his or her political involvement tends to become."[37] Courts may be very attractive avenues through which to pursue interest group goals. They are much less expensive to use and more accessible than legislatures, so litigants increasingly use courts to initiate legal change. Such cases "cause courts to become a terrifying political force to a host of vested interests."[38]

Because the advantages that courts can generate for an interest group can be lost if the judge in power does not favor that group's position, interest groups actively pursue favorable judicial appointments. As Judge Neely explained, "Any concept of merit selection—that is, selection based exclusively on objective standards rather than politics—is chimerical. . . . In the final analysis, interest groups are not looking for brilliant lawyers, they are looking for lawyers who will decide cases in their favor."[39] Courts not only fit into the special interest/bureaucratic view of the legal system, but they are also an integral part of that system.

Most judges are appointed for long tenures, so their incentives are not unlike those of other civil servants. Neely contended that "there are four personal advantages a. . . [judgeship] can offer: income (including all fringe benefits); power; prestige; and leisure. A fifth may be intrinsically interesting or worthwhile work, but I would subsume this under the category of power."[40] This characterization sounds much like the Niskanen bureaucratic model, except for the importance of leisure (something easily added to Niskanen's model as one of the perquisites of office). As Neely explained, a lawyer's reputation and income depend on winning cases, but a judge's salary is paid "regardless of whether he is good, mediocre, or abjectly incompetent."[41] Like civil service bureaucrats, a judge's income is not based on the quality of his work, and his incentives to efficiently provide quality justice are relatively weak.

THE COMMONS PROBLEM

Legislatures, courts, and police are like any other public property; when ownership rights are not assigned to a good or resource and prices are not charged to ration its use, the resource is overused and inefficiently allocated. Publicly owned property is available on a first-come, first-served basis, with no user charge to discourage those whose desires for using the property generate relatively less welfare than those of others who might come later. Typical examples of the "tragedy of the commons" include the near extinction of the buffalo and the whale, the destruction of the eastern forests during the 1800s, and the crowding of, littering on, and deterioration of public parks, beaches, roadsides, and waterways. The same type of tragedy applies to legislatures, police, and courts.

Legislation.   Laws and bureaucratic enforcement policies are frequently shaped to reflect the demands of special interest groups, and there is a high cost associated with organizing most groups. Thus, one might conclude that the potential benefits must be very large if the group is able to organize and voice its demands. The commons problem arises once a group has been organized and the largest cost of applying political pressure has been overcome. The marginal cost of demanding more laws is extremely low relative to those initial organizational costs. Thus, organized groups are likely to demand many more laws that generate far fewer benefits than would have been sufficient to induce them to organize. Auerbach observed that laws "have proliferated so rapidly as to suggest (even to lawyers) that American society is choking from legal pollution,"[42] which is to be expected when the public sector provides a service for which a rationing price is not levied. This is exemplified in the area of criminal law by the "over-criminalization" of so-called "victimless" crimes. As David Friedman put it:

> People who want to control other people's lives are rarely eager to pay for the privilege. . . . And those on the receiving end—whether of laws against drugs, laws against pornography, or laws against sex—get a lot more pain out of the oppression than their oppressors get pleasure. . . . So compulsory puritanism— "crime without victims"—should be much rarer if [those demanding the laws have to pay the full cost of the laws].[43]

Laws against marijuana use, pornography, and prostitution may be on the books because the laws could be obtained at virtually a zero price, while the costs of the laws (including enforcement) are shifted to others.

Police.   Blumberg argued that approximately 80 percent of police resources are used up in "social-worker, caretaker, baby-sitter, errand-boy" activities.[44] Many of these activities clearly generate benefits for individuals, but because the individuals do not bear the full cost, they tend to overuse them. It is doubtful that people would be as quick to call the police to quiet noisy neighbors or get cats out of trees if they were responsible for the full cost of the resources that taxpayers incur. More significantly, there can be substantial negative externalities from using police services in that manner, because police are then unavailable for what may be far more valuable uses.

The seriousness of the commons problem with police services is evident in the direct links that individuals and businesses have between alarm systems and the police. Most studies of such systems find a false alarm rate of well over 95 percent.[45] In Beverly Hills, California, for example, a survey of 1,147 alarm calls to which police responded found that 99.4 percent were not warranted.[46] These false alarms have been attributed to several factors, including problems with equipment and subscriber error.[47] But the analysis here suggests another reason. Those using alarm systems do not pay the cost of each police response so they have no incentive to minimize those costs; therefore, they have no incentive to minimize the number of false alarms. If the users were liable for such costs, subscribers would make far fewer "errors" and the alarm companies would see that their equipment failed less frequently. But the real cost of these false alarms goes well beyond the outlays for police labor and equipment used in responding to the calls. The opportunity cost of those resources is the alternative, more valuable uses to which the resources could be put—to respond to real emergencies, to deter crime, to produce other goods and services (that is, reduce the size of the tax-supported police system).

These examples suggest that the public sector law enforcement system must be large relative to what an optimal system providing similar services would be. Special interest groups will demand laws (and their enforcement) for which the social costs exceed the social benefits. The government responds by allocating resources to enforce those laws. In addition, due to the commons problem arising with enforcement resources—the fact that some government-provided resources are diverted from uses for which they might be more highly valued—additional resources will have to be provided to try to meet demands of the interest groups (including, presumably, demands for crime prevention and protection).

Courts.   Among many others, Chief Justice Burger has complained that the courts are overcrowded and that there is an excess demand for the courts' services.[48] In response to such observations, Mabry, et al. noted that when a queue of people waiting to consume the good is observed, that good is under priced.[49] It is because courts are supposedly available free of charge that court delays arise.[50]

> [S]ince demand for free court services exceeds supply, rationing must occur, and it is accomplished by standing in line. Unfortunately, the people who can afford to stand in line the longest are not necessarily the people who have the most urgent need to litigate. . . .
>
> Since a place in line cannot be sold or exchanged, all litigants must pay essentially the same price for use—a price that bears no relationship to the urgency of individual needs or the importance to the public. . . .

In the civil courts customers come in competitive pairs. . .where the alternatives available to at least one of the pair are significantly less attractive than the product that can be obtained free from a court. Often the attractive products that the court delivers free are delay itself or a forum that provides the stronger litigant with an opportunity to wear out or outgun the opposition. . .the nature of the adversary system leads then to the irrational and needless consumption of private resources. Whenever opposing sides can match expenditures, enormous amounts of money are spent that secure no improvement at all in the basic product. When one side cannot match his opponent's expenditure, the financial power of the stronger side will usually determine the result.[51]

The waste and inefficiency associated with common access is considerable, but its consequences for justice are also significant.

One example of the commons problem with the courts is the rapid growth of malpractice suits. As the size of awards has increased, so have the incentives to bring suit. The resulting increase in litigation has generated the external costs of higher legal fees, higher insurance rates (and higher fees by physicians and others susceptible to malpractice suits), and court crowding. The plaintiffs in such cases clearly bear only a portion of the costs.

Litigants not only do not pay the full cost of the court's services, but they often do not pay the full cost of the privately held resources that are consumed in the process of litigation.[52] A plaintiff in a civil suit may pay his own lawyer's fees, but he does not always pay the defendant's legal fees, even if the defendant wins. Furthermore, the time associated with such a case can be more costly than direct legal fees, and a defendant who may be in the wrong can drag a case on for a long time, forcing higher legal fees and other costs to the plaintiff. Mabry, et al. concluded that the legal system encourages trials involving weak cases for plaintiffs and discourages trials where the plaintiff's case is strong but his anticipated gains or the resources available for pursuing the case are small. Similarly, suits against defendants are encouraged where the plaintiff wants to force an out-of-court settlement. Such cases clearly do not promote justice.

Rationing court services according to willingness to wait creates incentives to misuse the judicial system. "Since parties who are in the wrong do not want to pay money or be enjoined to do something, disputes are concocted so that the court will get bogged down and delayed in extracting payment. . . . There are endless examples of nondisputes that are in major courts."[53] Such considerations led Mabry, et al. to advocate a "loser-pays rule" for court proceedings, in effect, to alleviate the commons problem.[54] Neely apparently agreed, but he also noted that many groups have considerable vested interest in maintaining an inefficient court system:

The way today's lawyers, business-people, and political community do business is predicated on a court system that allows anyone who alleges a dispute to go to court. Anyone who suggests the alternative—that those who abuse the process be punished—threatens to turn the world of lawyers and their clients upside down. But the status quo of free access has much more going for it than just [these] self-interest[s]. ... What in fact the whole concept of penalizing frivolous litigation does is threaten the existing distribution of wealth.[55]

Thus, reform in the pricing of court services is unlikely.

The same problem applies to criminal cases. A loser-pays system should discourage criminals from dragging court cases out and discourage prosecutors and police from bringing cases where evidence is clearly insufficient to warrant prosecution. It is not particularly surprising that the present criminal justice system suffers from the same commons problem that the civil system faces. In most states and in the federal system, the criminal court and the civil court are actually the same institution. The excess demands on the civil court system due to non-price allocation must spill over and affect the criminal system because they compete for the same resources.

Government Failure. Those who advocate government production are quick to point out the externalities associated with markets but, as Tullock pointed out, the externalities generated by the government process are often ignored.[56] The argument presented here is that public production of law and order produces negative externalities. Police are inefficiently used to produce services that do not warrant the costs, too many laws are passed, and too many court cases are brought. The private-public issue is not simply one of detailing the potential inefficiency of private law and order and opting for public provision.

When the commons problem of public law enforcement services is combined with bureaucratic tendencies to over-produce and inefficiently produce the resulting output, it becomes obvious that the public production of law and order is not an efficient substitute for market production. Bureaucratic over-enforcement precludes political efficiency which, if it were achieved, would not translate into economic (or allocative) efficiency because of the commons problem. Beyond that, it *must* be remembered that government institutions of law have a different purpose than the institutions of customary law. Customary law and its institutions facilitate voluntary interaction; government law and its institutions facilitate involuntary transfers.

ENDNOTES

1. See for example, Robert McCormick and Robert Tollison, *Politicians, Legislation, and the Economy, An Inquiry into the Interest Group Theory*

of Government (Boston: Martinus Nijhoff Publishing, 1981); Bruce Benson, "Land Use Regulation: A Supply and Demand Analysis of Changing Property Rights," *Journal of Libertarian Studies* 5 (Fall 1981): 435–451; Ralph Nader, "Introduction," in *With Justice for Some: An Indictment of the Law by Young Advocates*, ed. Bruce Wasserstein and Mark Green (Boston: Beacon Press, 1970), p. ix; Charles Reasons and Jack Kuykendall, eds., *Race, Crime, and Justice* (Pacific Palisades, Calif.: Goodyear Publishing, 1972), pp. 1–2; Melvin Sikes, *The Administration of Injustice* (New York: Harper and Row, 1975), p. 119; Richard Quinney, *Crime and Justice in Society* (Boston: Little, Brown and Company, 1969); James Eisenstein, *Politics and the Legal Process* (New York: Harper and Row, 1973), pp. 9–10.

2.   Eisenstein, *Politics and the Legal Process,* p. 351.

3.   Robert Rhodes, *The Insoluble Problems of Crime* (New York: John Wiley and Sons, 1977), p. 13.

4.   William Chambliss, "The State, the Law, and the Definition of Behavior as Criminal or Delinquent" in *Handbook of Criminology,* ed. Daniel Glaser (Chicago: Rand McNally, 1974), p. 39.

5.   Richard Posner, "Theories of Economic Regulation," *Bell Journal of Economics and Management Science* 5 (Autumn 1974): 335–358.

6.   George Stigler, "The Theory of Economic Regulation," *Bell Journal of Economics and Management Science* 2 (Spring 1971): 3–21.

7.   See for example, Sam Peltzman, "Toward a More General Theory of Regulation," *Journal of Law and Economics* 19 (August 1976): 211–240.

8.   Bruce Benson, "Regulation: The Demand and Supply of Property Rights," *Appalachian Business Review* 8 (1981): 22–28. See also Benson, "Rent Seeking from a Property Rights Perspective," *Southern Economic Journal* 51 (October 1984): 388–400.

9.   Eric Furubotn and Svetazor Pejovich, "Introduction: The New Property Literature" in *The Economics of Property Rights,* ed. E. Furubotn and S. Pejovich (Cambridge, Mass.: Ballinger Publishing, 1974), p. 3.

10.   Harold Demsetz, "Toward a Theory of Property Rights," *American Economic Review* 57 (May 1967): 348.

11.   Benson, "Rent Seeking from a Property Rights Perspective."

12.   Stigler, "The Theory of Economic Regulation."

13.   Ibid.

14.   Posner, "Theories of Economic Regulation."

15.   Ibid., pp. 344–345.

16.   Ibid., p. 345.

17.   Stigler, "Free Riders and Collective Action: An Appendix to Theories of Economic Regulation," *Bell Journal of Economics and Management Science* 5 (Autumn 1974): 359–365.

18.   James Q. Wilson, *The Politics of Regulation* (New York: Basic Books, Inc., 1980), p. 370.

19. Ibid., p. 372.
20. Posner, "Theories of Economic Regulation," p. 347.
21. For example, see Benson, "The Economic Theory of Regulation as an Explanation of Policies Towards Bank Mergers and Holding Company Acquisitions," *Antitrust Bulletin* 28 (Winter 1983): 839–862.
22. Peltzman, "Toward a More General Theory of Regulation."
23. Jack Hirshleifer, "Comment," *Journal of Law and Economics* 19 (August 1976): 241–244.
24. Benson, "The Economic Theory of Regulation."
25. Benson, "Rent Seeking from a Property Rights Perspective."
26. Peltzman, "Toward a More General Theory of Regulation." See also Bruce L. Benson and M. L. Greenhut, "Interest Groups, Bureaucrats and Antitrust: An Explanation of the Antitrust Paradox," in *Antitrust and Regulation,* ed. Ronald E. Grieson (Lexington, Mass.: Lexington Books, 1986), pp. 53–90.
27. Posner, "Theories of Economic Regulation," p. 350.
28. See for example, Benson, "The Economic Theory of Regulation."
29. James Buchanan and Gordon Tullock, *The Calculus of Consent* (Ann Arbor: University of Michigan Press, 1962), Chapter 7.
30. William Niskanen, *Bureaucracy and Representative Governments* (Chicago: Aldine-Atherton, 1971); Niskanen, "Bureaucrats and Politicians," *Journal of Law and Economics* 18 (December 1975): 617–643; Niskanen "The Peculiar Economics of Bureaucracy," *American Economic Review* 58 (May 1968): 293–305; Benson and Greenhut, "Interest Groups, Bureaucrats and Antitrust."
31. Richard Neely, *Why Courts Don't Work* (New York: McGraw-Hill, 1982), pp. 67–80. Emphasis added.
32. Wilson, *The Politics of Regulation,* p. 374.
33. Ibid., pp. 377–378.
34. Ibid., p. 380.
35. Ibid.
36. See Abraham Blumberg, *Criminal Justice* (Chicago: Quadrangle Books, 1970).
37. Neely, *Why Courts Don't Work,* p. 27.
38. Ibid., p. 26.
39. Ibid., pp. 37–38.
40. Ibid., p. 44.
41. Ibid., p. 46.
42. Jerold S. Auerbach, *Justice Without Law* (New York: Oxford University Press), p. 9.
43. David Friedman, *The Machinery of Freedom* (New York: Harper and Row, Publishers, 1973), p. 174.
44. Blumberg, *Criminal Justice,* p. 185.
45. James S. Kakalik and Sorrel Wildhorn, *Private Police in the United States: Findings and Recommendations* (Santa Monica, Calif.: The Rand Corporation, 1971), p. 29.

46. Ibid.
47. Ibid.
48. "Burger Sees High Court Case Load Doubling by 1978 if 'Appalling Mass of Litigation' Persists," *New York Times,* January 7, 1974, p. 16.
49. Rodney H. Mabry, Holly H. Ulbrich, Hugh H. Macauley, Jr., and Michael T. Maloney, *An Economic Investigation of State and Local Judicial Services* (Washington, D.C.: National Institute of Law Enforcement and Criminal Justice, Law Enforcement Assistance Administration, Department of Justice, 1977), p. 111.
50. Neely, *Why Courts Don't Work,* p. 164.
51. Ibid., pp. 164–165.
52. Mabry et al., *Economic Investigation of Judicial Services,* p. 111; Neely, *Why Courts Don't Work,* pp. 172–173.
53. Ibid., pp. 166–168.
54. Ibid., p. 112.
55. Neely, *Why Courts Don't Work,* p. 184.
56. Gordon Tullock, *Private Wants, Public Means: An Economic Analysis of the Desirable Scope of Government* (New York: Basic Books, 1970), p. 78.

5

THE DEMAND SIDE OF THE POLITICAL MARKET

The proposition that the formation and application of law is largely designed to meet interest group demands has been made numerous times, particularly with regard to criminal law. Richard Quinney, for example, stated that "criminal definitions describe behaviors that conflict with the interests of the segments of society that have the power to shape public policy," and "since interests cannot be effectively protected by merely formulating criminal law, enforcement and administration of the law are required. The interests of the powerful, therefore, operate in applying criminal definitions."[1] Similarly, William Chambliss and Robert Seidman observed:

> Deviancy is not a moral issue, it is a political question. No act, nor any set of acts, can be defined as inherently 'beyond the pale' of community tolerance. Rather, there are in effect an infinite number and variety of acts occurring in any society which may or may not be defined and treated as criminal. Which acts are so designated depends on the interest of the persons with sufficient political power and influence to manage to have their views prevail. Once it has been established that certain acts are to be designated as deviant, then how the laws are implemented will likewise reflect the political power of the various affected groups.[2]

Judge Neely's view is not quite so all-encompassing, as he pointed out that Anglo-American common law has always made a distinction between customary law crimes (such as murder, robbery, and rape) and positive-law crimes, which "have become crimes exclusively because some group lost a political battle."[3] Developments in criminal law are just as political today as they were when the breaking of basic customary law was declared a crime against the king so he could collect revenues. Today the objectives of criminalization are somewhat less clear because of multiple demands of special interest groups, but "criminal law is in every regard political."[4]

INTEREST GROUPS AND THE PASSAGE OF CRIMINAL LEGISLATION

Chambliss and Seidman argued that "every detailed study of the emergence of legal norms has consistently shown the immense importance of interest-group activity, not the public interest, as the critical variable in determining the content of legislation."[5] Historical studies of legislation tend to agree with the conclusion. When Chambliss examined the origins of vagrancy laws in England, he concluded that vagrancy laws were created and later altered to protect the interests of such specific groups as landowners and merchants.[6] Hall's study of the growth of modern theft laws and Platt's examination of the rise of the juvenile court in the United States reached similar conclusions.[7] Joseph Gusfield's examination of the Volstead Act concluded that temperance advocates represented the interests of a relatively small segment of the population.[8]

Recent Changes in Criminal Statutes.   More recent research on statutory changes in criminal law indicates that the determinants of such laws remain political. Perhaps the most significant investigation is the empirical study of changes in the California Penal Code by Berk, Brackman, and Lesser.[9] The researchers found that during the early 1950s, the making of criminal law in California could be characterized as an "agreed bill" process that involved only a few major criminal justice lobbies, generally the California Peace Officers Association (made up of district attorneys, sheriffs, and police chiefs), the American Civil Liberties Union, and the State Bar of California. Legislators did not initiate or shape criminal law policy; they simply reacted to the demands of the lobbies.[10]

The agreed-bill process is one wherein lobbyists and a few members of relevant legislative committees negotiate directly in making significant decisions.[11] The important part of the legislative process takes place behind closed doors, and most open legislative debate is simply rhetoric for public consumption. This domination by lobbyists in setting legislative agendas is not unique to criminal law issues or to California. Judge Neely, a former West Virginia legislator, wrote that because of tremendous demands on legislators' time and resources,

> the most we can expect for legislators is to react to programs. . . paid lobbyists on all sides bang out the compromises and refine legislation long before a legislator is required to take a position on it. The development of comprehensive, politically acceptable legislative packages requires scores of man-years of work, and no single legislator or even group of legislators has resources like that at their disposal. . . .
>
> When my court proposes changes to the legislature, we have a completed, polished bill already drafted and ready for introduction by members of each house. The same is true of every other organized interest group that is aggressively seeking positive legislative action.[12]

During the 1960s, criminal law in California began to involve a wider range of groups than were active in the 1950s, but the process did not change.[13] The most active groups continued to be the ACLU (and its oft-times ally, the Friends Committee on Legislation), the CPOA, and the Bar Association; but small vocal groups of citizens also appeared to initiate attempts to alter the Penal Code. Often they allied themselves with the law enforcement interests or the ACLU. Several established interest groups whose original purpose was not directed at criminal justice also supported an established criminal justice lobby. For example, the ACLU often enjoyed support from the state NAACP, the Mexican-American Political Association, the Northern and Southern California Council of Churches, the Association of California Consumers, and the Federation of the Poor.[14]

Berk, Brackman, and Lesser went beyond other studies of interest groups' impact on changes in criminal justice to provide statistical support for the contention that this influence is extremely important. They looked at the strength of the law enforcement lobby (LEL), primarily the CPOA, and the civil liberties lobby (CLL), primarily the ACLU and FCL, recognizing that these principal groups often worked with others. "Effective influence" was identified in a number of ways. Using newsletters and journals published by the interest groups and information from journalists, politicians, and criminal justice professionals, the three researchers made independent evaluations of how effective lobbyists were in shaping the Penal Code. Their statistical analysis used both zero-order correlations and multivariate analysis. They found that year by year, the LEL achieved significant changes leading to increasing criminalization, more severe penalties, and more resources and powers for police. The LEL also had a significant negative impact on rights for defendants, judicial discretion, and, to a lesser degree, the rights and resources going to corrections officials. The CLL's efforts were positively correlated with substantial gains in defendants' and corrections officials' rights and in judicial discretion; it had a negative impact on criminalization, penalty severity, and police powers. The two groups were not in direct and constant opposition in all instances, however, and their agendas and impacts were somewhat different. The LEL apparently emphasized criminalization and penalties, while the CLL was more interested in limiting police powers and expanding judicial discretion.[15]

The multivariate analysis reinforced the zero-order correlation results, showing that both lobbies were effective, but in different areas. The civil libertarians may have been more effective when the two groups were in direct conflict, because the CPOA's "core concerns" involved procedure, an area in which the CPOA was relatively ineffective.[16]

The Berk-Brackman-Lesser study also found that "public opinion" played no identifiable role in Penal Code revision. Moreover, legislators did not develop and seek support for their own criminal justice agendas; they simply responded to the interest groups that were concerned with such legislation. They concluded that criminal law was unquestionably enacted for the benefit of interest groups rather than for the public good.

Nonetheless, no one interest group got everything it demanded. As the interest group theory predicts, there was clear evidence of legislative efforts to balance the costs and benefits when conflicts arose. Furthermore, "the horse-trading endemic to the legislative process produced criminal law that at least diluted and often distorted original intent. . . . [W]hat might have begun as incipient law soon became a hybrid whose content reflected what was politically acceptable."[17]

These findings are not unusual. For instance, when Pamela Roby examined the 1965 revision of New York State's prostitution statutes, she found that different interest groups contended with each other during the revision process.[18] The civil libertarians and welfare groups appeared to be the winners over business and police interests, since prostitution was reduced from a criminal offense to a "violation," and patronizing a prostitute was declared to be a violation. Subsequent to passage of the new statute, however, Roby found that police and business interests were able to get enforcement policies adopted in which prostitutes' patrons were rarely arrested. Roby's study emphasized two important points: first, bureaucrats (i.e., police) themselves may be an important interest group, and second, interest groups can apply pressure at the bureaucratic as well as the legislative level.

LAW ENFORCEMENT BUREAUCRATS AS
POLITICAL INTEREST GROUPS

Police are traditionally very active in the political arena, acting as lobbyists and frequently employing tactics common to labor unions, such as strikes, demonstrations, and protests. Police strikes are often illegal, but "blue flu" has a long history and is increasingly giving way to outright strikes. Thus, "it should come as no surprise. . .to learn that police have a profound impact on the content of law-as-applied. They have both the opportunity and motivation to make countless decisions that have a direct bearing on who gets what from the legal process."[19]

Enforcement personnel are in a unique position to create social disorder, so they often have a great deal of political power relative to their numbers (for voting) and financial resources. The managers of enforcement bureaucracies also are in a unique position. Daniel Glaser observed: "the leaders of a law enforcement bureaucracy have special advantages for promulgating their views because of their ready access to the heads of the executive and legislative branches of government, their ability to issue official reports and call news conferences, and their consequent control over public information on the effectiveness of the law and need for it."[20]

Howard Becker's study reinforces the claim that law enforcement bureaucracies may apply pressure for changes in criminal statutes.[21] Because of pressure from the Narcotics Bureau of the Treasury Department, for example, the Marijuana Tax Act was passed in 1937. The bill encountered considerable resistance from users of hempseed oil and from the birdseed industry, who argued that hempseed was a vital ingredient in many birdseed mixtures. These interest groups managed to stall passage of the bill until it was amended to exempt hempseeds from control. The legislature tried to efficiently balance the demands of conflicting interests, following the theoretical prediction that it never acts as a perfect broker for a single interest when conflicts exist.

Judges also wield political influence in the legislative arena. As Judge Neely noted:

> Every state court system has some centralized administrative authority, even if it is only the state's highest court itself. In the federal system the Department of Justice has an entire bureau devoted to administering the federal judiciary. . . . It is through either the Justice Department or the state courts' administrative offices that the courts sponsor legislation as an organized, collective intelligence. In addition, of course, local judicial associations may concoct bills and urge their adoption, but these are usually concerned with improving pay, perquisites, working conditions, or systems of judge selection—basically private interest bills.[22]

Government law enforcement employees use their positions and influence to lobby for laws they can enforce, as well as for issues regarding pay and perquisites. But their goals can go well beyond these private interest objectives. Judges may lobby for "public interest" court reforms that they expect to improve the efficiency of the judicial process, and police may similarly apply political pressure in support of their perception of the public interest. All these bills have impacts on the size, power, level of work, and prestige of the bureaucracy, so self-interest motives may at least influence the "public interest" arguments presented by bureaucrats.

The Legal Service Corporation. There are times when the political activities of public law enforcement officials may even violate the law by using public funds or publicly purchased labor, time, and resources. One well-documented case of such abuse involves the Legal Services Corporation (LSC), an "independent private corporation" set up by Congress and funded by federal tax dollars.[23] It is a bureau in all aspects except its name. The LSC's statutory function is to "provide equal access to the system of justice...to those who would be otherwise unable to afford adequate legal counsel." In setting up this quasi-bureaucracy, however, Congress specifically outlawed political activity. In addition, Congress mandated that no LSC funds may be used

> to support or conduct training programs for the purpose of advocating particular public policies or encouraging political activities, labor or antilabor activities, boycotts, picketing, strikes, and demonstrations, as distinguished from the dissemination of information about such policies or activities except that this provision shall not be construed to prohibit the training of attorneys or paralegal personnel necessary to prepare them to provide adequate legal assistance to eligible clients.

And finally, no LSC funds may be used

> to initiate the formation, or act as an organizer, of any association, federation, or similar entity, except that this paragraph shall not be construed to prohibit the provision of legal services to eligible clients.[24]

These passages from the Legal Service Corporation Act of 1974 are instructive for two reasons. First, there is the implication that Congress felt compelled to include such explicit prohibitions of political activity because they had strong reasons to expect LSC officials would engage in them. Second, LSC management and employees have obviously undertaken extensive political activity in direct violation of the act. Bennett and DiLorenzo found that "under the ruse of providing access for the poor to the justice system, taxpayers are being forced to finance social and economic policy changes that many of them would oppose. In short, those who are connected with the LSC are pursuing their own interests with taxpayers' money."[25] For instance, LCS provided a $61,655 grant to the Proposition 9 Task Force, an organization whose purpose was to defeat California's Proposition 9. The funds went through the Western Center on Law and Poverty, Inc., an LSC Los Angeles affiliate that also had four registered legislative lobbyists and administrative advocates in Sacramento. Thirty other local legal service programs supplied staff for voter registration and media relations. The grant was illegal, as were the activities of the participants.[26]

When President Reagan was elected, a "survival task force" was established within the LSC to "develop a campaign that would nullify the effects of any changes in LSC operations that the Reagan administration might attempt to implement." The task force director was particularly concerned that the new administration would try to place "control on social activism of legal services staff who are engaged in aggressive advocacy."[27] The task force strategy was composed of three elements.

First, the Coalition for Legal Services was formed, with active participation by LSC officials, as an outside lobby on behalf of the LSC. Many of those actively involved in this lobbying organization had direct links to the LSC as grant recipients, and LSC grant funds found their way into the Coalition.[28] This was not the only LSC-supported lobby effort on its own behalf, however. Joseph Lipofsky of Legal Services of Eastern Missouri received an LSC grant; his letter accompanying the application stated that the Coalition for Sensible and Humane Solutions' purpose was:

1. To publish a handbook for the "People's Lobbyists."
2. To. . .continue training of community activists in both substantive issue and the process of community education and action, legislative and administrative advocacy as well as their relationship to litigation.
3. To research and to publish a "People's Alternative" to budget cuts and tax issues on a state and local level.
4. To develop an ongoing bimonthly communication on a statewide basis to focus on budget and tax questions and ways to impact them.[29]

This LSC-funded lobbying organization was formed as a direct result of Reagan's 1981 budget message.

Second, the LSC survival task force organized a network of "grass roots" lobbying campaigns directed at congressmen. Every LSC regional office and local affiliate designated "survival coordinators," and each state had a coordinator. The network had four objectives: 1) to produce a flood of letters to congressmen advocating re-authorization of LSC; 2) to stimulate newspaper editorials supporting the LSC; 3) to pressure local bar associations to pass resolutions supporting the LSC; and 4) to set up meetings with congressmen to lobby for re-authorization.[30] When the General Accounting Office ruled that such activities were illegal, the president of the LSC agreed to make "changes," but "rather than ceasing political activity, LSC officials decided that alternative organizational structures had to be developed to carry out activities that Congress had expressly prohibited and activities that were likely to be prohibited in the future."[31]

Third, the LSC began to set up "mirror corporations" to "launder funds so that congressional restrictions on political advocacy and representation could be subverted."[32]

In 1982, when President Reagan appointed new LSC board members and officers, many files in the corporation's Washington office were destroyed, apparently in an effort to prevent the new appointees from obtaining evidence of illegality. A major media campaign was also organized to discredit the new members of the board. The smear campaign appears to have worked. Congress continues to fund the LSC with larger budgets, and "despite abundant evidence of blatant wrongdoing, virtually nothing has been done to correct LSC's abuses of its mandate."[33]

Political activism is common among government employees, be they firefighters, school teachers, welfare workers, or military officers. The preceding examples make it clear that employees involved in our justice system, from police, to judges, to legal aid lawyers, are just as politically active. Political pressure may be mounted for obvious self-interest motives (higher salaries or job security) or for what civil servants see as the "public interest." Whatever the reason, the end result is that the political character of law and order is enhanced.

INTEREST GROUP PRESSURE ON LAW ENFORCEMENT BUREAUCRACIES

Interest groups often go beyond influencing legislation and attempt to influence the enforcement of laws. In the courts, for example, "groups which judges support support judges."[34] Jack Peltason contended that groups attempting to instigate wider roles for federal judges are typically those that consider their chances to be small when it comes to influencing selection of legislators and administrators who will represent their interests.[35] He listed several examples of this kind of interest group including Federalists, slave owners, industrialists, trade unions, racial minorities, and civil libertarians.

Peltason's view of the court's role in the interest group form of government is consistent with the position taken by Landes and Posner, and supported empirically by Crain and Tollison.[36] These researchers argued that benefits gained through legislative actions are easily taken away if the beneficiary group is unable to maintain its position of strength. But it is more difficult for opposition groups to change rights assignments made by the courts, even if opposition groups become politically superior. Thus, as Peltason contended, groups that are not confident in their ability to obtain or maintain legislative support may attempt to gain their ends through the courts. Of course, one should not carry this argument too far. Court assignments of rights are not necessarily guaranteed. As Peltason noted:

> No Governmental agency necessarily has final word in any interest conflict. In this case of legislation or administrative agencies this is clearly recognized. . . . Yet a court decision is no more conclusive of interest conflict than a decision of other agencies. The constitution, or anything else, is what judges say it is only when the judges represent the dominant interest within the community.[37]

In the context of an interest group form of government, even the court's rulings are not permanent.

One of the most obvious channels of influence by interest groups is in the recruitment of judges. Eisenstein found that bureaucrats, lawyers, bar associations, and various other organized interest groups actively seek to influence judicial appointments at *all* levels of government.[38] The recent special interest circus involving the attempted appointment of Judge Bork to the Supreme Court was unusual only in the degree to which the activities of special interest groups attracted so much press attention.

There are good reasons for interest groups to try to influence judicial appointments. Some judges do not face reelection or reappointment, for instance, so typical political tools of influence are relatively ineffective. Thus, deciding who holds the office is a *relatively* more important avenue of political influence for judges than for legislators. Appointees may not wish to offend those who contributed to their past success. In fact, judgeships are often "political rewards" for individuals who have demonstrated support for the desires of powerful interest groups. Those judges who do face reelection or reappointment or who aspire to higher appointment recognize that they will need the support of powerful groups, so they also tend to maintain the interests of their political sponsors. "In fact," Blumberg observed, "the *easy* decision is the one that is politically inspired."[39]

The frequency of the involvement of organized interest groups in litigation is well documented. Several studies have focused on celebrated Supreme Court decisions and found interest group support from the outset.[40] Others have documented comprehensive patterns of group involvement by examining *amicus curiae* briefs in the Supreme Court.[41] Interest groups plan their use of litigation just as meticulously as their legislative lobbying efforts. The factors affecting success include the makeup of the court bureaucracy, the status (or power) of the group, and the skill of the group's presentation.[42] Interest groups: 1) find a person willing to break a law in order to set up a test case and challenge the constitutionality or applicability of a law; 2) arrange for a plaintiff and a defendant to have a friendly suit in which the group's lawyers prepare the arguments for both sides; 3) have a member act as a plaintiff to enjoin administrative officials from enforcing a statute; 4) file class action suits; 5) help a non-member who is already involved in litigation that touches on the group's interests; and 6) file an *amicus curiae* brief.[43] In each instance, the group must have sufficient financial resources to retain skilled lawyers. As Murphy and Pritchett noted, a favorable judicial decision can produce considerable benefits, but litigation is an expensive and time-consuming process. Thus, an interest group with sufficient resources to retain a permanent legal staff with relevant expertise has a definite advantage over another litigant with limited financial resources.[44]

Interest group activity through the courts can have numerous goals. The group's purpose may be to use judges as a source of legislation—to create new property rights or change existing rights structures. For example, in 1967 the NAACP's Legal Defense and Education Fund initiated class actions to block all executions in Florida and California, and subsequently secured delays in virtually all executions in the nation pending the resolution of various constitutional issues. The LDF successfully secured a "*de facto* moratorium" on all executions for several years.[45] The LDF's efforts have been supported by several church groups, the National Council on Crime and Delinquency, the American Civil Liberties Union, and the American Correctional Association and the Ethical Culture Society. The American League to Abolish Capital Punishment has taken an active role.[46] Interest groups may have very commendable goals, but it is important to remember that most Americans support the death penalty.[47] This is clearly a case of interest group rule rather than majority rule.

Interest groups may use the courts to alter the nature or severity of law enforcement. For example,

> the fight over enforcement [of environmental laws] is viewed by the offending industries as a legitimate battle for survival. The real fight is a political battle over income shares. How long shall polluters have to clean up their processes? Who pays the cost of pollution control? As long as enforcement is slack the income share of polluters and their employees rises because existing plants can still be used.[48]

In an effort to thwart enforcement, the interested party may challenge procedural issues through courts, thereby delaying or limiting the implementation of the offensive laws. Or an attempt could be made to limit the ability of the enforcement authority by limiting the resources available. It is often easier "to scuttle enforcement appropriation" than to "scuttle" the passage of a statute.[49]

Efforts to influence law enforcement clearly reach beyond the courts. In his examination of eight communities, Wilson found that police law enforcement activities are governed by the dominant values of the local "political culture."[50] Eisenstein, Nimmer, and others have reached similar conclusions.[51] Melvin Sikes calls the police "pawns of politics and power."[52] And Bruce Smith found that

> Political manipulation and law enforcement seem always to have been closely associated in the United States. . . . The political influences are so numerous and so varied that their effect is kaleidoscopic. Sometimes they are so diametrically opposed that they tend to offset each other. Usually, however, either some one political interest is able to dominate or conflicting partisan interests are reconciled.[53]

Gordon Tullock found two problems with governmental definition and enforcement of property rights. First, government is used as an instrument for changing people's property rights, which means that government can also be used to transfer benefits to those with sufficient power to influence those changes.[54] Second, the government production of law and order creates external costs.

INEFFICIENCIES WITH AUTHORITARIAN JUSTICE

Because the costs of forming an interest group can be high, strong incentives (high per capita gains) are probably required to induce individuals to overcome them. The benefits accruing to a particular group from passage of a law that provided the initial incentive to organize are probably very large, but the *additional* cost of demanding further statutory changes may be very small. In other words, the "price" paid for additional laws is effectively zero, and laws are supplied to active interest groups because they press their demands. Furthermore, the laws that are supplied need not generate sufficient benefits to even cover the cost of their enforcement, since those demanding laws do not have to pay for enforcement.

Under this institutional arrangement, enforcement requirements arising from the quantity of laws demanded and instituted through legislation should exceed the limited supply of enforcement resources. The legislature and the courts can pass laws at fairly low cost, of course, so the commons problem is really reflected in the allocation of enforcement resources. Laws that generate relatively low value when enforced will compete for the attention of law enforcers with laws that can generate relatively greater value. Allocation of enforcement resources according to willingness to pay would mean that the laws producing the greatest value would typically be enforced. Still, interest groups have a great deal of input into the rationing of law enforcement. In addition, "first come first served" is an important rationing mechanism, so police may find themselves responding to a call regarding a prostitute, a gambling operation, or a marijuana user, while a murder, assault, rape, or robbery is in progress. Furthermore, given non-price means of allocating prison space, relatively early release of potentially violent criminals in order to accommodate incoming marijuana users or other criminals without victims becomes a distinct possibility.[55] There is an increasing trend to criminalize more and more activities. For example, Cole reported that an important

> factor in the crisis of criminal justice is the "law explosion"—the increasingly complex and demanding pressures placed on law and legal institutions to resolve conflict in...society. ... [Included] has been the tendency to utilize the criminal law to perform a number of functions for society outside the traditional concerns for the protection of persons and property.[56]

These functions are typically associated with so-called victimless crimes or with the provision of "community services," but they appear to be taking up larger portions of the resources of the criminal justice system, leaving relatively few resources available for control of violent and property crimes.

Decriminalization of victimless crimes and "the consequent reduction of pressure on police, courts, and correctional services would have a massive impact on the criminal justice system."[57] In fact, one reason for the failure of police to apprehend most criminals, as well as for criminal court delays and prison overcrowding, is that an estimated 30 to 50 percent of the criminal justice system's resources are employed against people who have not harmed persons or property.[58] Large amounts of resources are devoted to the apprehension, prosecution, and punishment of prostitutes, drug users, gamblers, pornography salesmen, and others who have no identifiable victims. Clearly, a reduction in the criminalization of such crimes would free up resources that could be redirected at the control of violent and property crimes. For instance, in 1971, the Los Angeles district attorney began filing all marijuana possession cases as misdemeanors rather than as felonies. As a direct result, approximately 10,000 fewer felony cases were filed during 1971–1972 than during the previous year, cutting the system's felony caseload by 25 percent.[59] If decriminalization has this effect, then increasing criminalization should have the opposite effect; more "crimes" to enforce means relatively fewer resources devoted to protecting against or solving violent and property crimes.

Interest Groups and the Commons Problem for the Courts.   Advocates of court reform have typically pressed for a larger and "better" version of the existing system. "Most active members of institutionalized 'law reform' groups," Judge Neely concluded, "particularly the bar association, are lawyers who have devoted their lives to mastering the current system. This fact alone encourages all improvement to be predicated on making a bigger and better model of the current system."[60] But why are their demands not fully met, given public sector responsiveness to organized pressure groups? The answer is that there are even more powerful interest groups that benefit from the inefficiencies in the court system, and that, therefore, resist changes. Neely pointed out that

> every effort at court improvement has from the perspective of some political interest group negative components. . . . While the political establishment in most places is genuinely against murder, armed robbery, and dope peddling. . . that same establishment is less enthusiastic about prosecuting consumer fraud, antitrust violations, or political corruption, because they are often involved in these activities themselves. . . . Efforts to increase staff for prosecution of violent crime. . . becomes impaled on the well justified fear that the same prosecutorial staff that can do a number on the longhaired denizens of the underworld can also do a number on all our well-manicured country-club friends who engage in an occasional payoff, rigged election, or a little consumer fraud.[61]

Because court and prosecution resources are common pool resources, they can be used for a wide variety of enforcement functions. Political demands and the self-interest motives of judges and prosecution bureaucrats are some of the factors that will determine how the new resources will be rationed. A tremendous amount of additional resources would be required to eliminate all excess demand (rationing by waiting would still apply, of course, although queues might be shorter), so the solution may threaten some whose "crimes" currently go unnoticed.

Economists often suggest that the solution for a commons problem is allocation by willingness to pay—that is, price allocation. This would reduce litigation by discouraging the frivolous, low-valued use of the justice system. But several justice groups would vehemently resist such a change. For example, "lawyers are reluctant to accept any rules that discourage litigation, since litigation is their bread and butter. While the tragedy of the common may have a disastrous effect on litigants, it is a bonanza for tens of thousands of new lawyers who graduate from law schools each year."[62] Actually, not all litigants view the consequences of the allocation system as disastrous. There are special interest groups who benefit substantially because they can use the judicial system with its current rationing mechanism. Neely cited some of the "endless" number of examples of such "frivolous disputes" or "non-disputes."[63] For instance, in most landlord and tenant disputes the only issue is back rent, and the court will ultimately decide that the landlord is right and the tenant is wrong.[64] The tenant can refuse to pay and threaten to go to court, however, forcing the landlord to bear court costs, which may be greater than the benefit of gaining the back rent. So the landlord simply gives up. If the loser of such cases had to pay the court costs of the winners, fewer cases would be threatened or brought.

In the insurance industry, if a company wants to reduce its settlement when a house and its contents have been destroyed by fire, then the company can demand proof of the fair market value of the house's contents, forcing litigation for full recovery.[65] In order to avoid the court costs, the policyholder may be forced to settle for less than he is legally owed. One of the most significant court costs arises directly from the commons problem, as rationing by waiting leads to court delay. Sufficient delay substantially reduces the value of the ultimate award and benefits some groups.

The longer a loser can delay a decision in a civil case, the longer he can use the money he will have to pay. Given that judgments do not include the full cost of litigation, many litigants who expect to lose have incentives to litigate. This can be a substantial benefit for insurance companies, but it can also be significant for other political interests. For example, slightly over one-fifth of the civil cases concluded in New York City in the 1979–1980 fiscal year were brought against the city government.[66] Neely reported: "New York City cannot afford an efficient court system because it would be bankrupt beyond bail-out if all the suits go to trial in one or two years."[67] When faced with several years in delay, a plaintiff may also have strong incentives to settle out of court for much less than he might otherwise receive. This benefits insurance companies, New York City, and many others who face large liabilities. Delay may also benefit guilty criminals, because prosecutors have incentives to settle and reach an agreeable plea bargain. The longer the court delays, the stronger is a criminal's bargaining position.

Political pressure to maintain the common pool character of the courts and, more generally, the entire justice system comes from many sources, ranging from business interests to governments to those involved in the legal process to those outside the law. In fact, there are many "special interests that actively seek mediocre, if not downright incompetent, court performance."[68] Any change in the current system makes the transfer of wealth from some group to another more (or perhaps less) efficient, and someone's interests suffer. The public sector justice system will continue to be inefficient because it will continue to be part of the political battleground over the allocation of property rights and wealth.

Inefficient Political Compromises.   Conflicting political pressures often force the implementation of laws or law enforcement procedures that are relatively inefficient in achieving a particular end. Perhaps the most visible set of inefficient enforcement procedures are those resulting from the exclusionary rules. The Supreme Court's rulings on acceptable evidence reflected its efforts to protect civil rights and individual liberties from abuse by law enforcement bureaucracies. But the only tool available to the courts was their power to exclude evidence, which, as Neely observed, is like "trying to do brain surgery with a meat ax."[69]

Citizens, judges, police, and prosecutors all decry the set of complicated procedural rules and the frequent release of obviously guilty criminals. The National Advisory Commission on Criminal Justice Standards and Goals, for example, found that one major factor contributing to increases in serious crime is that courts have applied more stringent standards for admitting evidence without adequately justifying the changes, and often without providing sufficient guidelines for obtaining admissible evidence.[70] Similarly, David Jones reported that lower court judges and prosecutors generally complain that the extension of exclusionary rules has shackled their ability to bring the guilty to justice.[71]

A significant consequence of exclusionary rules is that the intended goal of protecting civil liberties has not been effectively achieved, particularly where the rights of the *innocent* are concerned. For instance, if the police enter a person's home, destroy or damage his property, and find nothing incriminating, exclusionary rules do not protect him. His only recourse is to file a damage suit with its accompanying costs to recover.[72] Furthermore, such damage suits are frequently not successful, as many states require proof of vicious intent or prior knowledge of innocence before damages will be paid. Thus, "there is little effective remedy against the police available to those who are not guilty," and "for every search that produces contraband there are untold scores that do not."[73] The exclusionary rule protects criminals, not innocent victims.

Exclusionary rules have also led to a fairly costly method of protecting the rights of the guilty. For example,

> Twenty years of court decisions on search and seizure, the warrant requirement for certain types of arrests, and police interrogation have spawned an entirely artificial system of procedural rules that even lawyers find difficult to master. When a five-judge state supreme court after three months' deliberation splits three to two on whether a particular search was within the narrow exceptions to the warrant requirement, how can the average police officer be expected to decide the issue correctly in the approximately fifteen seconds allotted to him out on the street?[74]

These complexities have resulted in additional demands on the court and prosecutory system and a considerable expenditure in additional police "training" so that officers can understand the complex procedural rules for obtaining acceptable evidence.

It should be noted that, given its goals, the court system had little option but to establish an exclusionary rule. Rules of evidence are under the court's control, but more efficient means of achieving the desired end are not. The court does not actually require release of felons whose rights have been violated; it simply has dictated that release will be the solution until another means of protecting civil rights is established.[75] But Congress and state legislatures have not taken up the problem because, as Neely explained, the logical remedy would require a civil fine on the offending officers or their government departments.[76] Nevertheless, such remedies are much more likely to achieve the protection of civil rights, especially of the innocent.

"Every serious student of the exclusionary rule," Neely observed, ". . .agrees that the exclusionary rule is a limited deterrent to the most persistent forms of police bullying."[77] The exclusionary rule provides no direct sanction against police, and the only personal cost to a police officer for improperly obtaining evidence is indirect. Should an officer consistently violate the rights of criminals so that convictions cannot be obtained, then he *might* expect a lower salary or loss of his job. Even these sanctions are extremely tenuous when an officer is protected by his union and when firing a civil servant is virtually impossible. At some point, the officer *may* be passed over for promotion, but such possibilities are so uncertain that they provide little perceived threat.

If sufficiently direct sanctions were applied, then police "bullying" would be significantly reduced *without* any exclusionary rule. There would be more direct incentives to perform properly if police departments and governments were liable for damages any time police violate a citizen's rights. Neely argued that damage awards of no more than five hundred dollars plus attorney fees and any property damage would affect local budgets enough to cause policy-makers to deter police abuse.[78] The assumption here is that budgetary pressure would translate into pressure on police officers to "clean up their act." A more direct course would be to make officers themselves liable for such damages by requiring monetary payment to their victims. In either case, Neely contended that if a state legislature was to enact a comprehensive compensation system for all citizens with reasonable damages for *all* unconstitutional police intrusion and simultaneously prohibit the exclusionary rule in the state's courts, the Supreme Court would be forced to reconsider its exclusionary rules.[79]

No state legislature is likely to seriously consider such a law. The political power of police organizations would be mobilized so quickly that any legislator supporting the bill would be in considerable trouble. Local governments would also strongly oppose the legislation because, at least initially, it would be very costly. From the point of view of local government officials, an exclusionary rule is inexpensive. It does not cost tax dollars to release guilty felons. From the point of view of legislators and executives at the local, state, and federal levels, an exclusionary rule has other political advantages as well. Citizen or interest group outrage over the government's failure to successfully convict and imprison criminals to a large extent is directed at the courts and "their" rules of evidence. This is one factor that has led to the recent demand for stricter penalties: "These grass-roots groups are expressing their anger and frustration at judges who hand down lenient sentences, at parole boards who free violent offenders to commit mayhem, at prosecutors who plea bargain serious offenses down to minor charges, and at laws that allow the guilty to go free on legal quirks or small police errors."[80] Their "frustration" is not with legislators or executives, but with judge-made laws, even though the laws are in force because legislators have chosen not to overturn them. And the frustration is not with police, who benefit when such outrage is directed elsewhere. In fact, the police have frequently justified larger budgets to cover the cost of additional training and other needs that arise from the complex procedures associated with the courts' rules of evidence.

While the exclusionary rule is an inefficient and ineffective means of protecting civil rights, it is not likely to be changed because it is a politically attractive "solution." It demonstrates an effort to protect individual rights, but more importantly it does so without the large negative impact on police and politicians that more efficient procedures would have. Many other inefficiencies arising from political compromise could be cited, but few are as obvious or notorious as the exclusionary rules.

ENDNOTES

1. Richard Quinney, *The Social Reality of Crime* (Boston: Little, Brown, 1970), pp. 15–18; Quinney, *Critique of Legal Order* (Boston: Little, Brown, 1974), p. 16; William Chambliss, "Toward a Political Economy of Crime," *Theory and Society* 2 (Summer 1975): 152; Peter Manning, "Deviance and Dogma," *British Journal of Criminology* 15 (January 1975): 14; Francis Allen, *The Crimes of Politics: Political Dimensions of Crime* (Cambridge, Mass.: Harvard University Press, 1974), p. 21; Stuart Hill, *Crime, Power and Morality: The Criminal Law Process in the United States* (Scranton, Pa.: Chandler Publishing, 1971); Austin Turk, "Conflict and Criminality," *American Sociological Review* 31 (June 1966): 346; George Cole, *Politics and the Administration of Justice* (Beverly Hills: Sage, 1973); Richard Berk, Harold Brackman, and Selma Lesser, *A Measure of Justice: An Empirical Study of Changes in the California Penal Code, 1955–1971* (New York: Academic Press, 1977); Jack Peltason, *Federal Courts in the Political Process* (New York: Random House, 1955); James Eisenstein, *Politics and the Legal Process* (New York: Harper and Row, 1973); Raymond Nimmer, *The Nature of System Change: Reform Impact in the Criminal Court* (Chicago: American Bar Foundation, 1978); Walter Murphy and C. Herman Pritchett, *Courts, Judges, and Politics* (New York: Random House, 1961), Chapter 8.

2. William Chambliss and Robert Seidman, *Law, Order, and Power* (Reading, Mass.: Addison-Wesley Publishing, 1971), p. 67.

3. Richard Neely, *Why Courts Don't Work* (New York: McGraw-Hill Book Co., 1982), p. 29.
4. Ibid., p. 162.
5. Chambliss and Seidman, *Law, Order, and Power*, p. 73.
6. William Chambliss, "A Sociological Analysis of the Law of Vagrancy," *Social Problems* 12 (Summer 1964): 69.
7. Jerome Hall, *Theft, Law and Society*, 2nd ed. (Indianapolis: Bobbs-Merrill, 1952); Anthony Platt, *The Child Savers* (Chicago: University of Chicago Press, 1969).
8. Joseph Gusfield, *Symbolic Crusade* (Urbana: University of Illinois Press, 1963).
9. Berk, et al., *A Measure of Justice.*
10. Ibid., pp. 85–86.
11. Ibid., p. 11. See also John Heinz, Robert Gettleman, and Morris Seeskin, "Legislative Politics and the Criminal Law," *Northwestern University Law Review* 64 (July 1969): 277–356.
12. Neely, *Why Courts Don't Work*, p. 80.
13. Berk, et al., *A Measure of Justice*, p. 86.
14. Ibid., p. 62.
15. Ibid., pp. 201–203.
16. Ibid., p. 200.
17. Ibid., p. 276.
18. Pamela Roby, "Politics and Criminal Law: Revision of the New York State Penal Law on Prostitution," *Social Problems* 17 (Summer 1969): 83–109.
19. Eisenstein, *Politics and the Legal Process*, pp. 95–97. For similar findings, see Carl Heustis, "Police Unions," *Journal of Criminal Law, Criminology and Police Science* 48 (November 1958): 643; Alan Bent, *The Politics of Law Enforcement: Conflict and Power in Urban Communities* (Lexington, Mass.: Lexington Books, 1974), p. 77.
20. Daniel Glaser, *Crime in Our Changing Society* (New York: Holt, Rinehart and Winston, 1978), p. 22.
21. Howard Becker, *Outsiders: Studies in Sociological Deviance* (New York: The Free Press, 1963), pp. 121–146. For similar findings, see Donald Dickson, "Bureaucracy and Morality: An Organizational Perspective on a Moral Crusade," *Social Problems* 16 (Fall 1968): 142–156; Joseph Oteri and Harvey Silvergate, "In the Marketplace of Free Ideas: A Look at the Passage of the Marihuana Tax Act," in *Marihuana: Myths and Realities*, ed. J. L. Simmons (North Hollywood: Brandon House, 1967), pp. 136–162. See also Alfred Lindesmith, *The Addict and the Law* (New York: Vintage Press, 1965); and Hill, *Crime, Power, and Morality*, p. 98.
22. Neely, *Why Courts Don't Work*, p. 81.

23. James T. Bennett and Thomas J. DeLorenzo, "Poverty, Politics, and Jurisprudence: Illegalities at the Legal Services Corporation," *Cato Policy Analysis* 49 (February 26, 1985): 1–29. The discussion that follows draws heavily from this paper.
24. Legal Services Corporation Act (1974), Section 1007 (a)(5), (b)(6), (b)(7).
25. Bennett and DiLorenzo, "Poverty, Politics, and Jurisprudence," p. 5.
26. Ibid., pp. 7, 8.
27. Ibid., p. 8.
28. Ibid., p. 10.
29. Quoted in ibid., p. 10.
30. Ibid., p. 12.
31. Ibid., p. 14.
32. Ibid., p. 16.
33. Ibid., p. 22.
34. Peltason, *Federal Courts in the Political Process*, p. 11.
35. Ibid., p. 11. See also Murphy and Pritchett, *Courts, Judges, and Politics*, p. 274.
36. William Landes and Richard Posner, "The Independent Judiciary in an Interest-Group Perspective," *Journal of Law and Economics* 18 (1975): 875–901; Mark Crain and Robert Tollison, "Constitutional Change in an Interest Group Perspective," *Journal of Legal Studies* 8 (January 1979): 165–175.
37. Peltason, *Federal Courts in the Political Process*, p. 55.
38. Eisenstein, *Politics and the Legal Process*, pp. 66–67. See also John Schmidhauser and Larry Berg, *The Supreme Court and Congress: Conflict and Interaction, 1945–1968* (New York: Free Press, 1972), pp. 81–99; Peltason, *Federal Courts in the Political Process*, Chapter 4; Abraham Blumberg, *Criminal Justice* (Chicago: Quadrangle Books, 1970).
39. Blumberg, *Criminal Justice*, p. 127.
40. See for example, Clement Vose, *Caucasians Only: The Supreme Court, the NAACP and the Restrictive Covenant Cases* (Berkeley: University of California Press, 1959); David Manwarning, *Render Unto Caesar* (Chicago: University of Chicago Press, 1962).
41. See for example, Samuel Kirslov, "The *Amicus Curiae* Brief," *Yale Law Journal* 72 (1963): 694–721; Fowler Harper and Edwin Etherington, "Lobbyists Before the Court," *University of Pennsylvania Law Review* 101 (1953): 1172–1177.
42. Murphy and Pritchett, *Courts, Judges, and Politics*, p. 275.
43. Ibid., pp. 276–278.
44. Ibid., p. 280.
45. Hugo Bedau, *The Courts, the Constitution and Capital Punishment* (Lexington, Mass.: Lexington Books, 1977), p. 76. See also Michael

Meltsner, *Cruel and Unusual: The Supreme Court and Capital Punishment* (New York: Random House, 1973).

46. See also Hugo Bedau, "The 1964 Death Penalty Referendum in Oregon: Some Notes from a Participant-Observer," *Crime and Delinquency* 26 (October 1980): 528–536.

47. H. Erskine, "The Polls: Capital Punishment," *Public Opinion Quarterly* 34 (1970): 290–301; "Public Opinion About Capital Punishment," *Gallup Opinion Index* (1978), pp. 20–25; Research and Forecasts, Inc., *America Afraid: How Fear of Crime Changes the Way We Live, Based on the Widely Publicized Figgie Report* (New York: New America Library, 1983).

48. Neely, *Why Courts Don't Work*, p. 29.

49. Ibid.

50. James Q. Wilson, *Varieties of Police Behavior* (Cambridge, Mass.: Harvard University Press, 1968).

51. Eisenstein, *Politics and the Legal Process*; Nimmer, *The Nature of System Change.*

52. Melvin Sikes, *The Administration of Injustice* (New York: Harper and Row, 1975), p. 119.

53. Bruce Smith, *Police in the United States,* 2nd rev. ed. (New York: Harper and Row, Publishers, 1960), p. 4.

54. Gordon Tullock, *Private Wants, Public Means: An Economic Analysis of the Desirable Scope of Government* (New York: Basic Books, 1970), p. 146.

55. Bruce L. Benson and Laurin Wollan, "Prison Crowding and Judicial Incentives," *Madison Paper Series* 3 (February 1989): 1–22.

56. Cole, *Politics and the Administration of Justice,* pp. 23–24.

57. Abraham Goldstein and Joseph Goldstein, *Crime, Law, and Society* (New York: The Free Press, 1971), p. 293.

58. Robert W. Poole, Jr., *Cutting Back City Hall* (New York: Universe Books, 1978), p. 53.

59. Ibid., p. 53.

60. Neely, *Why Courts Don't Work,* p. 61.

61. Ibid., p. 20.

62. Ibid., p. 183.

63. Ibid., pp. 168–170.

64. Ibid., p. 169.

65. Ibid., p. 108.

66. Ibid., p. 16.

67. Ibid., p. 17.

68. Ibid., p. 241.

69. Ibid., p. 137.

70. National Advisory Commission on Criminal Justice Standards and Goals, *Report on Police,* 1973, p. 206. Also see Fred Graham, *The Self-Inflicted Wound* (New York: Macmillan, 1970).

71. David Jones, *Crime Without Punishment* (Lexington, Mass.: Lexington Books, 1979), p. 83.
72. Neely, *Why Courts Don't Work*, pp. 144–145.
73. Barnett, "Public Decisions and Private Rights," p. 54.
74. Neely, *Why Courts Don't Work*, p. 142.
75. Ibid., pp. 139–140.
76. Ibid., p. 140.
77. Ibid., p. 141.
78. Ibid., p. 148.
79. Ibid., p. 162.
80. Michael Satchell, "Victims Have Rights Too," *Parade*, March 17, 1985, p. 15.

6

THE SUPPLY SIDE OF THE POLITICAL MARKET

Two conclusions of the theory of bureaucracy have now been supported for criminal justice bureaucracies. First, police bureaucrats and judges attempt to expand the size and power of their agencies. Second, criminal justice bureaucrats act as interest groups. Considerable support also exists for the conclusion that a strong incentive of bureaucrats is to increase the size (i.e., level of rights enforcement) of the bureaucracy. This chapter will provide a few examples of such incentives and, perhaps more significantly, examine the consequences of such incentives on the effectiveness of the resources allocated to public sector provision of law and order. But first, how effective have bureaucrats been in expanding their budgets?

GROWTH IN THE CRIMINAL JUSTICE SYSTEM

During the 1960s public sector law enforcement personnel per capita increased by 27 percent while expenditures per capita for public law and order increased by 70 percent. During the same period the purchasing power of the dollar declined by only 21 percent. Between 1960 and 1969, the number of law enforcement personnel employed by all levels of government grew by 42 percent, while the population only increased by 12 percent.[1] These trends have continued, as evident in the growth in employment (Table 6.1), payroll (Table 6.2), and total expenditures (Table 6.3) for the various components of the public criminal justice system.

Table 6.1 Full Time Equivalent Employees in Federal, State and Local Criminal Justice Systems, 1970–1979.[a]

Year	Total Employment	Police	Services and Judicial	Legal Public Prosecution	Defense	Corrections	Other
1970	774,551	489,367	95,524	38,171	3,063	148,044	582
1971	861,766	528,594	107,129	39,725	3,510	179,961	2,857
1972	898,305	547,555	111,686	43,789	4,155	185,793	5,326
1973	945,305	575,142	115,490	47,304	5,178	196,279	5,916
1974	1,011,205	607,913	125,129	52,215	6,119	213,197	6,628
1975	1,050,503	625,045	131,988	55,364	6,357	224,520	7,229
1976	1,079,892	628,347	137,451	59,306	7,255	239,293	8,240
1977	1,131,780	645,015	150,546	63,902	8,104	255,008	9,206
1978	1,157,288	655,720	149,336	69,234	8,268	265,503	9,041
1979	1,177,263	653,579	155,707	73,189	9,081	276,549	9,158
% change 1970–79	52.0%	33.6%	63.0%	91.7%	196.5%	86.8%	1463.5%

a. SOURCE: *Sourcebook of Criminal Justice Statistics* (Washington, D.C.: U.S. Department of Justice, Bureau of Justice Statistics, Various Years.)

Table 6.2 Payroll for the Month of October ($ thousand) for Federal, State, and Local Employees of the Criminal Justice System, 1970–1979.[a][b]

Year	Total Payroll	Police	Services and Judicial	Legal Public Prosecution	Defense	Corrections	Other
1970	604,203	388,015	76,686	34,420	2,715	106,655	712
1971	714,873	445,289	88,698	37,922	3,439	136,810	2,715
1972	804,241	501,277	97,634	43,925	4,367	152,299	5,235
1973	912,176	570,871	107,916	50,978	5,728	170,405	6,278
1974	1,043,104	645,612	124,817	59,585	7,201	198,462	7,427
1975	1,158,872	708,888	141,122	67,695	8,213	224,635	8,319
1976	1,277,120	772,867	154,466	77,140	9,821	252,890	9,935
1977	1,426,801	846,197	178,918	89,734	12,219	287,924	11,859
1978	1,540,955	908,221	190,541	101,288	12,529	314,864	11,679
1979	1,681,947	973,276	211,109	114,623	15,247	355,247	12,446
% change 1970–79	178.4%	150.8%	175.3%	233.0%	461.6%	233.1%	1648.0%

a. SOURCE: *Sourcebook of Criminal Justice Statistics* (Washington, D.C.: U.S. Department of Justice, Bureau of Justice Statistics, Various Years.)
b. Perhaps it should be stressed that these figures are for *one month's* payroll, rather than for total annual payroll—that month being October in each case.

Table 6.3 Criminal Justice Expenditures of Federal, State, and Local Governments by Type of Activity ($ thousands), 1970–1979.[a]

Year	Total Expenditures	Police	Services and Judicial	Legal Public Prosecution	Defense	Corrections	Other
1970	8,571,252	5,079,808	1,190,416	441,764	102,291	1,706,291	50,498
1971	10,517,083	6,164,918	1,355,282	491,326	128,547	2,291,073	82,937
1972	11,731,802	6,903,304	1,490,649	580,381	167,630	2,422,330	167,508
1973	13,006,721	7,624,178	1,579,457	663,810	206,705	2,740,208	192,363
1974	14,842,053	8,511,676	1,798,153	770,762	244,593	3,240,396	276,473
1975	17,248,860	9,786,162	2,067,664	933,126	280,270	3,843,313	338,325
1976	19,681,409	11,028,244	2,428,472	1,047,925	331,102	4,385,512	460,150
1977	21,573,756	11,864,875	2,638,251	1,225,344	403,754	4,934,067	507,465
1978	24,131,955	13,120,193	3,067,221	1,459,859	523,735	5,522,711	438,276
1979	25,871,357	13,811,815	3,388,874	1,648,084	597,262	5,986,464	439,058
% change 1970–79	201.8%	171.9%	184.7%	273.1%	483.9%	250.1%	769.5%

a. SOURCE: *Sourcebook of Criminal Justice Statistics* (Washington, D.C.: U.S. Department of Justice, Bureau of Justice Statistics, Various Years.)

During the 1970s, employment in the criminal justice sector grew at about five times the percentage change in total population, and in real terms, expenditures on publicly produced criminal justice services almost doubled (in nominal terms they more than tripled). But has this growth alleviated problems inherent in the public sector criminal justice?

CONSEQUENCES OF BUREAUCRATIC INCENTIVES AND NON-PRICE RATIONING

We have seen how public sector criminal justice resources are often inefficiently used because of the common pool problem which arises when resources are not privately owned. The allocation of these resources are not determined by prices (willingness to pay), so there are no incentives for demanders to conserve on resource use or for suppliers to make certain that resources are employed in their highest valued use. But allocation by willingness to pay does much more than prevent commons problems. Prices provide suppliers of goods and services with clear signals of what consumers want, and relative prices are an important source of information that markets use to represent the relative value of alternative uses of resources. Willingness to pay a high price to a supplier typically means that the producer is doing a very good job of providing for consumers. If that high price generates high profits, then the producer is able to employ more resources and produce more of the desired commodity.

Non-price Measures of Performance.   Because legislators do not enjoy a clear information source like prices when determining how to allocate publicly employed resources, they are forced to consider less reliable measures of performance. Typically, this means using some statistical representation of the "quality" of work being done by a bureau, since market prices do not place a direct value on that work. For instance, the function of police in the minds of most citizens is to "fight crime." But how can we tell if they are doing a good job in order to justify a particular budget? They must demonstrate their effectiveness like any other bureau. What statistic is readily available to demonstrate that police are fighting crime? The number of arrests is a natural measure, and other legal sector bureaucrats rely on similar statistics.

The important question is, what incentives does reliance on statistical measures of effectiveness provide? When the price that consumers are willing to pay measures effectiveness, producers have strong incentives to provide the quality of goods or services that consumers desire. If a private security firm is hired to protect a home or business, then that firm will have incentives to prevent crime through watching and wariness. Private individuals who join neighborhood watch groups do so largely to set up patrols that deter criminals and thus prevent crimes. But public police must produce arrest statistics and have no strong incentives to watch or patrol. Public police have incentives to wait until a crime is committed in order to make an arrest. Prosecutors have similar incentives to bargain for convictions on lesser charges, perhaps with concurrent sentences, in order to generate conviction statistics. All such incentives arise because these bureaucracies are not market institutions.

Once again, public sector bureaucrats are not by nature bad people, but like most people, they respond to incentives. Judge Neely noted: "The point is not that human failings play a central part in the breakdown of the courts but rather that courts as an institution tend to breed many of the observed failings."[2] Life tenure or long elected terms for judges, he observed, encourages "arrogance and indolence," while occupations such as working as a salesperson tends to mask them.[3] Salespersons compete in markets for the expenditures of consumers, while judges supply a service within an institutional setting that requires potential consumers to compete for their attention.

Bureaucratic Discretion.   Public law enforcement bureaucrats also have tremendous discretion in the allocation of bureau resources. As Bent noted:

> With upwards of 30,000 federal, state, and local statutes to uphold, the average policeman is faced with a monumental task of applying these laws evenly and performing his duties in a set standard of behavior. Theoretically the multiplicity of laws may be construed as a traditional administrative device to define conditions of illegal or disorderly behavior that the policeman may encounter, thereby precluding any discretionary responsibility on the part of the individual police officer. In actuality, however, the overload of statutes has made impractical the mechanical application of law by police. Instead, this overload invites the influence of prejudices of individual police officers. . . resulting in the law being administered unevenly and selectively.[4]

With such discretion, police can choose which laws to enforce strictly and which not to enforce at all. In fact, this discretion is an important ingredient for meeting the demands of powerful special interests; police can not only choose which laws to enforce, but which laws to enforce *for whom.*

A person's chances of police protection correspond closely to his position in the "geography of political power."[5] Much more attention is paid to the robbery of an important political figure than to the murder of an out-of-work, uneducated member of a racial minority.

Commons problems in the courts generate similar discretion for prosecutors and judges. To a large extent, court time is rationed by waiting time, but prosecutors can also decide which cases to prosecute and which to plea bargain and judges can decide which cases deserve consideration and which do not. "The point is frequently made as a tribute to our society that ours is a government of laws and not of men," Judge Neely observed. "Yet the decision regarding...the disposition of each case [is] entirely within the discretion of the prosecuting attorney in the first instance and the judge later on."[6]

Monitoring could sharply curtail this bureaucratic discretion, but monitoring incentives are very weak. An individual voter or taxpayer recognizes that he has relatively little to gain from monitoring, because he bears all the cost of such an effort but must share the benefit with many others. Furthermore, each individual has relatively weak incentives to cooperate with others in a joint monitoring effort, because if the group is successful the individual can share in the benefits without bearing any of the costs.

Bureaucratic Inefficiency. Producers in private markets provide commodities in hopes of making a profit. Because profit is the difference between revenues and costs, private profit-seekers have strong incentives to minimize the costs of producing the quantity *and* quality of the commodity that consumers demand. Public sector producers, however, typically cannot claim any profits that they generate. If revenues (the bureau's budget from tax dollars) exceed operating costs, then the excess revenues are simply returned to the general treasury. Thus, bureau managers' incentives to monitor production and prevent excess costs may be *considerably* weaker than those of private entrepreneurs. Bureau managers may gain personal satisfaction from the power they wield and the prestige their position enjoys. Larger bureaus imply greater power and prestige, of course, and relative bureau size is typically measured by relative budgets. A true budget maximizer may actually have incentives *not* to minimize costs—that is, to produce inefficiently—in order to spend a larger budget.

We now turn to an examination of the performance of various justice sector bureaucracies. The main emphasis will be on whether or not bureaucrats respond to the incentives they face. Consider first the public police.

Police. After an extensive study of police performance, Lawrence Sherman, director of the Police Foundation, concluded: "Instead of *watching to prevent crime,* motorized police patrol [is] a process of merely *waiting to respond* to crime."[7] Sherman noted that the budget process rewards those who successfully dispose of cases after crimes are committed more than those who quietly prevent crimes. Police policy-makers are "preoccupied" with the questions of how many police are needed and how big the police budget should be. Of course, the answers to these questions depend on what police must do, so police lobby for more budget and personnel in order to reduce response time and catch more criminals.[8] Efficiency considerations would dictate that the additional cost of such resources be justified by improved performance of at least equal value. Is this a valid assumption?

A 1976 study by the Police Foundation and the National Institute of Law Enforcement and Criminal Justice found that cutting response time by seconds or even minutes makes little difference in whether or not a criminal is apprehended.[9] The study measured the impact of police response time on the chances of intercepting a crime in progress and making an arrest. The difference in the probability was nil when comparing arrivals of between two minutes and twenty minutes. The main reason is that citizens take such a long time to report a crime that the criminal is gone long before the police arrive. The average victim of a crime where the victim and criminal confront each other delayed calling the police for fifty minutes. Sherman concluded that these studies suggest three options in terms of the allocation of resources to police work: 1) maintain current levels of police and response time while trying to educate citizens to call police more quickly; 2) reduce the number of police drastically since the current response time is unnecessarily rapid; or 3) re-allocate existing police so they are employed in systematic watching efforts rather than in waiting to respond.[10] In other words, *police manpower is being inefficiently allocated.* Studies of police on duty have found that about half of an officer's time is spent simply waiting for something to happen. Police officials claim that this time is spent in preventative patrolling, but systematic observation has discovered that such time is largely occupied with conversations with other officers, personal errands, and sitting in parked cars on side streets. Few police officers aggressively "watch" when there are no calls to answer.[11] Sherman lamented: "In general, as the level of crime prevention watching has declined, the level of crime has risen, and so has public dissatisfaction with public police."[12]

Inefficient use of police goes beyond the inappropriate emphasis on response time. For instance, police officials contend that patrol cars should have two officers because they can more efficiently deal with criminal incidents and are less likely to be resisted or harmed. A year-long Police Foundation study of one- versus two-man patrol cars in San Diego, however, contradicts these claims. The report found "clearly and unequivocally it is more efficient, safer, and at least as effective for the police to staff patrol cars with one officer."[13] The overall performance of the 22 two-man car sample and the 22 one-man car sample was about the same in terms of calls for service and officer-initiated activity. The primary differences were that two-man cars wrote several more traffic tickets, one-man cars received far *fewer* citizen complaints, and one-man cars were far more cost effective. The total annual cost of two-man units was 83 percent greater than for one-man units. One-man units called for back-up more frequently, but not nearly enough to make up for the cost differential. Furthermore, there were fewer cases of resisting arrest and assaults on officers in one-man units than in two-man units.

Do police departments use appropriate cars? Many cities still use large cars for police patrol even though there is an estimated 33 percent per year savings in operating costs when compact cars are used. But police officials argue that compact cars simply are not adequate for police work. John Christy, executive director of *Motor Trend* magazine, designed seven separate evaluations for the Los Angeles Sheriff's Department in 1977, including slow- and high-speed performance, ease of maintenance, radio suitability, fuel economy, and human factor checks. The vehicle that performed best overall was a compact, followed by two intermediate-sized cars. The tests were designed to assure that the highest scoring vehicle would be "not only the best-suited but also the most cost-effective" according to L.A. Sheriff Department Captain W. F. Kennedy.[14]

Abraham Blumberg reported in 1970 that there is a

bureaucratic fetish...to ferret out...those cases which can be most easily processed. Often this becomes the major consideration in expending limited resources and personnel. As a result, we have spent much of our limited resources...[to arrest] addicts, alcoholics, prostitutes, homosexuals, gamblers, and other petty offenders, simply because they are readily available and produce the desired statistical data that indicate "production."[15]

Blumberg's findings reinforce the contention that statistical indicators of performance are a major bargaining chip in bureaucratic efforts to obtain more resources. These indicators are expanded when violators of "victimless crime" statutes are arrested rather than participants in violent crimes. Thus, the over-criminalization result of interest group pressures in the context of the commons problem is exacerbated by the enforcement incentives of police. And, of course, over-criminalization is a major factor in providing police with sufficient discretion to allocate resources in the fashion indicated by Blumberg.

Arrest statistics may be the primary statistical indicator of police performance, but it is not the only important statistic used in bargaining for larger police budgets. Milakovich and Weis noted that police have a "vested interest" in keeping crime rates relatively high. If crime rates drop too much, then support for more police and larger budgets declines; and "like all bureaucracies, criminal justice agencies can hardly be expected to implement policies that would diminish their importance."[16] Thus, additional funding need not lead to a substantial decrease in reported crime rates, since high crime rates are clearly an important element in arguments for expanded criminal justice budgets. This reinforces the incentives police face because arrest statistics are viewed as an indicator of performance. In order to keep crime rates up *and* make growing numbers of arrests, for example, police have strong incentives to seek criminalization of increasing numbers of activities.

The Commons Problem and Police Manpower. There is a commons problem arising directly from the allocation of police services, and naturally police administrations cite the consequences of non-price rationing and excess demand as justifications for larger bureaus. Police typically ration patrol responses on a first-call-first-served basis, so some calls receive no response until it is much too late to do anything about the crime. Investigative services also must be rationed, and the discretionary powers that result have led to many crimes (e.g., burglary and other property crimes) receiving relatively little attention. And relatively large amounts of police resources are allocated to the pursuit of arrests for "easier" crimes to solve (e.g., prostitution and drug use).

Is increasing the size of the police bureaucracy likely to solve these problems? Consider the impact of increasing the size of the police department in New York City between 1940 and 1965. Over that twenty-five-year period, the number of police in the city was increased from 16,000 to 24,000, but the *total number of hours worked by the entire force actually declined.*[17] The 50 percent increase in personnel was more than offset by shorter hours, longer vacations, more holidays, more paid sick leave, and longer lunch periods. The taxpayers of New York received no benefits from the large increase in police manpower. If this is true elsewhere (and with increasing unionization of police, it appears to be), then expanding the police bureaucracy does not appear to solve the problems in public police service arising from non-price rationing. This is not surprising. Commons problems are rarely solved by additional resources. In fact, such additions typically lead to increases in effective demand, as many who would have chosen not to use the service because of congestion decide to seek services. This will become clearer after examining common pool problems with the courts.

Prosecutors' Discretion and Plea Bargaining.   In his detailed examination of plea bargaining, David Jones found that prosecutors' incentives are tied to maximizing the number of *criminals convicted*.[18] Such behavior is certainly predictable when prosecutors are considered in light of Wilson's characterization of "professionals" in the bureaucracy.[19] The dominant goal for such professionals is to demonstrate their legal talent in order to enhance their future market value. Therefore, they "prosecute vigorously" *but* selectively. According to Wilson, such professionals should favor simple cases that can be investigated and prosecuted in a short time so that they can maximize their number of convictions.[20] Interestingly, the criminals that are easiest to prosecute are frequently not the criminals that are easiest to apprehend. Victimless offenses divert police resources because they generate easy arrests, but prosecutors routinely dismiss such cases.[21] Judges and juries take most victimless crime less seriously than murders and robberies. In addition, police efforts to enforce drug possession laws lead them to violate constitutional prohibitions against unreasonable search and seizures,[22] making convictions difficult to obtain because of the exclusionary rule. So police have incentives to arrest people who prosecutors are not likely to prosecute. Other than some relatively minor deterrent effect that police harassment might have, police resources devoted to such arrests are largely wasted; they are not going to have much impact at all on criminal behavior or the level of criminal activity.

Eisenstein found that because the conviction rate is the main concern of most prosecutors, it is more important "not to lose than to win."[23] As a result, many prosecutors dismiss a case or plea bargain, giving them a large number of convictions at a low cost in terms of their time and effort. Criminals are generally convicted on fewer or lesser counts and receive lighter punishment, of course, but guaranteed conviction statistics more than make up for that. Furthermore, due to widespread plea bargaining, the process has become easier since "cases are processed in a routine bureaucratic manner."[24]

A plea bargain is an exchange, and it might be expected to improve the efficiency of the criminal justice system. Indeed, plea bargaining appears to relieve some of the pressure on the prosecutorial and judicial systems arising from non-price allocation and the resulting court delay and waiting time rationing process. This is, in fact, the typical justification for the widespread use of plea bargaining. But there is a significant difference between the goals of those participating in a market exchange and those participating in plea bargaining. The criminal who agrees to a plea bargain gains since his punishment (or perhaps legal expenses) must be less than he expects it to be if his case goes to trial. Prosecutors gain since their conviction statistics increase and their workload decreases. Judges benefit as pressure on the court docket is relieved.

Notice that there is no advantage for crime victims in these exchanges. After all, the only potential benefit accruing to victims under the current system might be the satisfaction of revenge, knowing that the perpetrator is being punished for his crime, or that he will be prevented from committing another crime for a significant period of time. Plea bargaining generally leads to shorter and concurrent sentences. The victim often feels violated by the justice system as well as by the criminal because of plea bargained forgiveness of crimes. These exchanges make bureaucrats and criminals better off, but it is not clear that they enhance justice.

How much do prosecutors bargain away in their plea bargaining? It probably depends on the jurisdiction, but a New York study found that most people arrested as felons are *not* prosecuted and convicted as felons. The odds that a person arrested for a felony would be sentenced to prison were one in 108.[25] This startling figure represents more than just plea bargaining, however. Over 84 percent of New York felony arrests in 1979 (88,095 out of 104,413) were simply dismissed.[26] Prosecutors pointed to a lack of staff and to police failure to secure items of evidence or lists of witnesses. And many cases are routinely dismissed because convictions are difficult to obtain. In addition, a 1971 study of the New York City bail system discovered that almost one-third of the city's criminal defendants simply disappeared.[27] Some were ultimately recaptured but many were not. Even more significantly, 29 percent of those who disappeared were *not* out on bail; they disappeared while in the custody of the city's Correction Department. In 1979, of the more than 15 percent of the felony arrests (16,318) that led to indictments, 56 percent resulted in guilty pleas to lesser felonies, 16 percent ended with misdemeanor guilty pleas, 12 percent were dismissed after indictment, 3 percent resulted in some "other" disposition, and 13 percent went to trial. Significantly, the largest number of sentences that did not involve a prison term arose due to prosecutors' willingness to permit felons to plead guilty to lesser charges.[28]

It is not clear that the efficiency gains in reduced common pool problems through plea bargaining are significant. The large caseload and backlog are the most widely cited justifications for the "need" for plea bargaining. However, Jones found that guilty plea rates are not a function of caseloads. In fact, he contended that prosecutors and judges have apparently established an "artificial quota" on the proportion of felony cases pending that can be taken to trial during any time period. The quota varies across jurisdictions, but it is generally less than 10 percent. Furthermore, these quotas have remained at virtually constant percentages for perhaps as long as 70 years.[29]

Plea bargaining is also rationalized on the grounds that rising crime rates necessitate the practice, but the historical data cast significant doubt on that argument. Even though crime rates increased steadily for the last thirty years of Jones' study, guilty plea rates remained almost constant for more than 70 years.[30] Of course, prosecution and judicial bureaucrats have every incentive to claim that plea bargaining at its current (and historic) level is necessary because of the higher crime rates and caseloads that tax the bureaucracies' limited resources. In this way, they can apply pressure for increased budgets and add leverage to their other demands. As H. H. A. Cooper observed, plea bargaining is "less an independent ill than a symptom. More properly it is part of a collection of symptoms of a general sickness. It is but one manifestation, albeit a significant one, of a system which is not operating properly."[31]

The conclusions that Jones and other analysts reached may be too strong. Clearly, plea bargaining is a function of the court backlog, as judges and prosecutors claim—just not in the way that they claim it is. Because those who bring cases do not pay prices that cover the full marginal cost of trying those cases, the commons problem arises and court congestion results. Price is an allocating mechanism and when price is not used other discriminatory rationing mechanisms take over.

It is the congestion problem resulting from non-price rationing that gives prosecutors and judges the discretionary power to selectively ration trials and plea bargains. This does not deny the conclusions reached by Jones and others: it simply requires that they be reinterpreted. The evidence indicates that although plea bargaining occurs because of the case backlog, increasing resources allocated to prosecutors and the public courts to reduce the backlog are not likely to affect the portion of cases settled through plea bargaining. The congestion problem will not go away, at least not without a tremendous influx of resources, given the relatively low price of litigation (relative to costs). Besides, the bureaucratic incentives for expansion mean that the existence of delays and plea bargaining provide "justifications" for larger budgets and bureaus. Adding more personnel has never changed the ratio of plea bargaining cases to tried cases, as Jones demonstrated, and it is not likely to do so in the future.

Judicial Discretion and the Rationing of Court Time. Pretrial delay does not arise exclusively because of increasing crime and caseloads, and research on both federal and state courts has failed to uncover a link between criminal case loads and the pace of litigation.[32] Church, et al. found very little connection between processing time and either the number of felony filings per judge or the number of pending felonies per judge. They concluded that both speed and backlog are largely determined by "established expectations, practice, and informal rules of behavior of judges and attorneys."[33] In other words, like plea bargaining, pre-trial delay is a rationing device that is largely controlled at the discretion of the bureaucrats in the criminal justice system. Indeed, "all proposals for reforms predicated on the supposition that expanding personnel, streamlining procedures, or increasing the number of courts will cure the courts' problems are naive and doomed to failure."[34] Under the current system, which is dominated by rationing by waiting, many individuals opt out because the time costs are too high. One implication of rationing by waiting is that "the people who can afford to stand in line the longest are not necessarily the people who have the most urgent need to litigate."[35] In fact, those with the lowest value of time are most likely to wait. Shortening the wait by increasing judicial resources will bring some people back into the court system who would have opted out, and the wait will quickly return to what it was before the resources were added.

For example, Judge Neely described a four-county rural circuit in West Virginia that was served by a single judge prior to 1976. Roughly 1600 cases were filed during his last year in office. After he retired, the legislature added a second judge to the circuit. By 1979, case filings had risen to 2400 even though there had been no significant change in the area's population or economy. Neely concluded: "It was merely the prospect that cases would be heard quickly and disposed of conveniently (since there were more sittings each year in each county) that encouraged the greater number of filings. Since human conflict is almost limitless, I infer from my experience that given the current system, which encourages litigation, the volume of work will always press against the capacity of any existing judicial machinery to get work done."[36] When prices are not used to equate quantity demanded and supplied, excess demand arises. All markets eventually clear, however, because alternative rationing systems arise. In the case of rationing by waiting, the time cost of waiting means that potential litigants opt for settlement without trial. The supply of additional court time will not lead to satisfaction of all excess demand unless the expansion in the court system is so substantial that quantity demanded equals quantity supplied at a zero price. In the absence of a tremendous influx of resources, court delay is likely to remain roughly as it is, reflecting the willingness of a large number of people to wait roughly the amount of time they now wait in order to litigate. "Even if every judge in the system worked fourteen hours a day, six days a week, and the budget for supporting services were doubled, the courts still would not perform significantly better than they do now."[37]

There is little doubt that the levels of both plea bargaining and court delay are at least in part functions of the incentives arising in bureaucratic institutions of the criminal justice system. These rationing mechanisms benefit bureaucrats by providing arguments for expanding bureaucratic budgets and resources and, in the case of plea bargaining, provide a means of generating conviction statistics without the danger of losses when cases go to trial. Criminal justice resources *must* be rationed, of course, because they are not allocated by a pricing mechanism and willingness to pay. Without such rationing mechanisms, congestion and delay would be even greater. Therefore, they often appear to be desirable. But as we will see in Chapters 9 through 13, other techniques could be chosen.

Judges and prosecutors have other incentives that are similar to some faced by police. Police may prefer that crime rates not decline too much, for instance, for fear of losing support and budget. Similarly, judges and prosecutors may fear substantial drops in delay. In Cook County, Illinois, during the 1970s, for example, the criminal court system was expanded and the prosecutor's office began to indict people for burglary and auto theft, crimes that had previously been plea bargained.[38] Court congestion was maintained but the make-up of the caseload changed significantly. One implication of this example is that prosecutors have considerable discretion over the allocation of court time and the disposition of cases due to the tremendous excess demand for law enforcement.

Judges often determine which cases will be heard and which will be dismissed. They quickly indicate what type of cases will attract their attention, and those are the cases that lawyers pursue.[39] The primary criterion for allowing a case to come to trial, according to one observer, is that judges "ration justice by turning their backs to comparatively weaker claims and defenses that require additional judicial time to resolve fairly. By dismissing these 'weaker' claims and defenses, the overworked judge disposes of such time-consuming matters and moves on to the stronger (i.e., easier) cases, where the claims or defenses are more obvious and compelling."[40] In this way, judges can consider more cases, of course, and have more free time. This may have the ring of efficiency, but it should be noted that one argument presented as a justification for public provision of courts is that private courts will not produce sufficient precedents because they have a "public good" character.[41] If judges choose to consider the easy cases as their incentives dictate—that is, the obvious cases given *existing* law and precedent—while dismissing those cases that are going to be difficult or time-consuming, then it is likely that the public courts underproduce precedents whether private courts do or do not. The difficult cases are the ones that are likely to require precedent-setting decisions.

If judges have the same incentives as prosecutors and police, then the motivation for choosing the easy cases and avoiding the difficult, time-consuming ones *might* be to increase some statistical measure of performance. But it is not at all clear that this is the only, or even the primary, reason for such behavior. In this instance, the judicial bureaucracy may appear to differ from police and prosecutors. But remember that police rely on more than just arrest statistics to justify their budgets; high crime rates are also an indication of greater *need* for police services. In the case of judges, the tremendous excess demand for their services may be a more powerful argument for an expanded budget than a statistical measure of output. Under these circumstances, indication of some "adequate" level of output given expectations based on historical performance may be desired, but production beyond that level could imply less need for additional resources. Therefore, "since judges can blame the court system's failure on others—on society's lack of consensus or society's parsimony in funding supporting services—there is no gnawing sense of shirked responsibility on the part of the judiciary. This is a convenient attitude; a gnawing sense of inadequacy would suggest a great deal of very hard work."[42]

Do judges actually respond to the incentives they face and use their discretionary control of court time to work less? There is at least some evidence that they do. According to Judge Neely, when the fee system in West Virginia for county justices of the peace was eliminated and replaced by salaries, the number of hearings per day handled by each judge dropped dramatically, the quality of court paperwork deteriorated, and minor court dockets got crowded.[43] When justices of the peace were paid by the case, they had incentives to dispose of cases quickly to make way for more cases. The justices of the peace also made fewer mistakes in the accompanying paperwork, presumably to avoid spending additional time on the case.

Bureaucratic Discretion and the Rationing of Prisons.   The over-criminalization aspect of the commons problem for legislation manifests itself in many ways. Excess demands for police services and courts have been emphasized, but there is also tremendous excess demand for prison space. Thus, a major constraint on sentencing is the shortage of space in correctional facilities.[44] The commons problem with prisons means that limited space must be rationed, so judicial discretion extends to sentencing. As a consequence, "the amount of variation in sentencing that exists and that is not related to the apparent facts of the case or the nature of the defendant is substantial."[45] One 1977 study found that the average sentence for robbery in Baltimore was 56.5 months while a 25.1-month sentence was the average in Chicago.[46] Whether or not these differences can be explained in terms of differences in prison crowding is not clear, but that is not the point. The commons problem means that rationing of prisons is required, and one rationing mechanism is judicial discretion in sentencing.

Another obvious means of rationing prison space is plea bargaining, which generates smaller penalties than guilty criminals can expect if they choose to go to trial. Potential demands on the prison system are also reduced when prosecutors choose to dismiss cases rather than bring charges.

Other rationing devices also play major roles in allocating limited prison space. Parole boards, for instance, have considerable discretion in determining how much of a sentence is actually served, whether the sentence comes from plea bargaining or a trial judge. Waiting time is important in many jurisdictions, as criminals sentenced to state prisons sit in county jails queuing up for limited prison space. All these rationing mechanisms are apparently inadequate. As of 1983, 41 states and the District of Columbia were either under federal court order to alleviate problems of or in litigation as a consequence of inhuman treatment of prisoners, arising to a very large extent from prison crowding.[47]

Some might argue that plea bargaining and judicial sentencing discretion are necessary because rationing of prisons must occur, but there are other options. Under the current system, a crowded prison may include several "criminals" convicted of victimless crimes, forcing judges or prosecutors to plea bargain or limit the sentence of more serious criminals. Or perhaps a relatively insecure city or county jail is forced to hold someone convicted of violent crimes because a marijuana user has been assigned space in the relatively secure state prison. In this light, perhaps non-violent or non-repeat offenders could be fined or put in supervised work projects while violent or repeat offenders are put in prison. Or restitution could be made an alternative to prison. The point is that when there is excess demand there must be *some* means of rationing. The potential number of rationing mechanisms is typically quite large. In the case of rationing public sector law enforcement resources, the rationing techniques we observe reflect the demands of interest groups and the incentives of public bureaucrats. But they are not necessarily the only or the most efficient options available.

The Political Requirements of Bureaucratic Discretion.   Judicial (as well as prosecutorial and police) discretion is an inevitable and necessary component of a government dominated by interest group politics. Judges must be free to discriminate among potential cases for consideration by congested courts in order to favor those pressure groups that have supported the judge. An interest group competes to have judges appointed who hold positions that will favor that group's positions. Then, because of judicial discretion, it follows that "much of law really reflects the political judgments and emotional passions of judges."[48]

It should be clear by now that poor performance by the courts and police results from complex political causes and not simply from the observed symptoms of those causes, an apparent shortage of staff and funding.[49] The political nature of the justice system manifests itself in many ways. For example, both academic researchers and the press frequently complain about bureaucratic efforts to protect the inner workings of the system from outside scrutiny. This, too, has as its source the political character of the process of law and order.

BUREAUCRATIC SECRECY

Perhaps the most important conclusion of the theoretical analysis of interest group government and bureaucratic performance is that government policies represent the private interest of politically active pressure groups rather than the public interest. This implies that politicians and bureaucrats do not want their policies and procedures to be easily understood by the general public.[50] A number of studies of criminal justice bureaucracies have found bureaucratic secrecy to be commonplace. Alan Bent found "the police have long practiced bureaucratic secrecy to the exacerbation of relations with the community. . . . True to the bureaucratic practice of maintaining barriers between itself and the public, police officials have resisted investigations of their internal affairs and attempts to impose controls over their activities."[51] Similarly, Eisenstein reported that secrecy and resentment toward outside interference generally prevail in the operation of courts where most actual work occurs in private.[52] Much of what the public sees is little more than a ceremony culminating private negotiations.

Such secrecy does have some "legitimate" purposes *within the institutional setting* of this political market. In order to successfully accomplish the law enforcement function as mandated by the political process, some actions must be taken that will not meet with the approval of all citizens.[53] For example, a prosecutor recognizes that a legitimately honest witness will not handle himself well on the stand, thus risking acquittal of a guilty criminal. Therefore, the prosecutor decides to plea bargain, which many citizens might find unsatisfactory. If the reason was made public, however, the criminal might refuse to bargain. In this case, the prosecutor's secrecy is a necessary part of his job, in the same way that a lawyer in a civil case would be justified if he settled out of court rather than risked a loss because of his client's poor demeanor. Similarly, police must protect the identity of undercover agents and informants in order to make legitimate arrests.

But bureaucratic secrecy does much more than serve "legitimate" actions. It also makes it difficult for non-interest group members to discover what bureaucrats are doing and "who is getting what" from the government. Furthermore, bureaucratic secrecy is an obvious attempt to limit the effectiveness of legislative monitoring and control of bureau production. This is expected in light of the prediction that enforcement bureaus typically desire a higher level of enforcement than is politically optimal.

One reason for bureaucratic secrecy is the police incentive to "solve" crimes that can most easily be processed.[54] In fact, "law enforcement agencies have applied the principle of 'benign neglect' to certain types of crime ranging from teenage extortion of money from younger children, to bicycle and other property theft, and even breaking and entering."[55] Many police departments tend to ignore property crimes as they concentrate their resources on easier cases or on more highly visible crimes that the media and interest groups are likely to demand be solved. Clearly, however, this is an aspect of the criminal justice system's operation that bureaucrats would prefer to keep quiet, particularly if the laws they choose to enforce relatively vigorously can be traced to political pressure that was originally applied by the same bureaucrats acting as interest groups.

IMPROVING BUREAUCRATIC PERFORMANCE

The theoretical presentation of bureaucratic production suggests one way to improve bureaucratic performance: competition for law enforcement bureaus. Legislators have liberally used this control device in an effort to force politically efficient production on the system. For example, Frederick Kaiser reported that in 1980 more than 110 federal agencies competed in overlapping police, investigation, and law enforcement jurisdictions.[56] In addition, of course, virtually every political jurisdiction has its own police and court bureaucracies. With the large number of competing bureaucracies, we might predict that the system should be operating reasonably efficiently. But three points must be made.

First, even if law enforcement agencies produce efficiently, they produce output that meets the desires of special interests rather than the public interest. The purpose of government is generally the coercive transfer of property rights, so discontent by the unorganized general population that loses in the transfer process can be expected.

Second, creating more bureaucratic agencies has an effect on the political demand and supply process. The number or size of public sector bureaucratic interest groups also is increased. Thus, demand for more criminalization will be stronger, and non-government interest groups will have relatively less power. This brings us to another problem with expanding public sector law enforcement. Bureaucrats become so powerful as interest groups that many laws appear to be designed primarily to increase their power and size rather than to protect the potential victims of crime. Government activity in law enforcement, therefore, decreasingly serves the private sector, including private sector interest groups. Consequently, such interest groups will be unhappy and will continue to apply pressure.

Third, even if the output produced by law enforcement agencies was efficiently produced in the sense of minimizing the cost of production, the actual output produced will be inefficiently chosen because of the commons problem. People who do not pay a user fee obtain police and court services that generate personal benefits of lesser value than potential services would generate for other users who wait or forgo the services because of congestion.

When these three points are added to the undeniable fact of bureaucratic inefficiency, one cannot help but be sympathetic to Smith's conclusion:

"From such as these, the observer turns away in disgust and very likely with the conviction that no police system can remotely approach its objectives."[57]

CRIME VICTIMS AND AUTHORITARIAN LAW

So far, a major component of the crime picture has been almost completely ignored: the victims. Why? Simply because they have been almost completely ignored by the politicized criminal justice system. "In contemporary America," McDonald reports, "the victim's well-being and fair treatment are not the concern of the criminal justice system or any other institution. The victim has to fend for himself every step of the way."[58] This is in stark contrast with the legal system's historical concern for obtaining restitution for victims. And because of the incentives arising with restitution, victims willingly pursued and prosecuted offenders. But the politicization of crime has led to an ever-diminishing role of and concern for victims. Let us consider the effects that removing victims from consideration has had on both victims and law enforcement.

Bureaucratic Treatment of Victims.   Consider first how the incentives that bureaucrats face (and apparently respond to) affect victimization. The police, who have incentives to wait and respond rather than watch to prevent, in effect *create* victims. When arrest statistics are important, then crime victims must be created. Furthermore, "the criminal justice system's interest in the victim is only as a means to an end not as an end in himself. The victim is a piece of evidence. The police want to know 'just the facts.' "[59]

Similarly, the relative ease of making arrests in cases of victimless crimes tends to divert police resources away from controlling crimes that have victims. Because crimes with victims receive relatively less attention than they would with less criminalization, fewer of these crimes are solved and deterred and there are more victims. Little wonder that citizens are increasingly dissatisfied with the public crime control process and are increasingly turning to the private sector for crime prevention. But the victim is at a disadvantage there as well. In their interest group role, police have consistently raised strong opposition to many private efforts at crime prevention. Thus, a victim who takes a self-protection initiative faces significant risks of violating the law. And, of course, "when a victim's self-protective measures do lead him to violate the law, it is no defense to say that police protection was inadequate."[60]

Conviction statistics are of primary concern to prosecutors, so the role that victims play in prosecution is generally conceived in terms of their function as witnesses.[61] If the victim is likely to appear unconvincing or unsympathetic, if he has "done something stupid" and appears to deserve what he got, or if he has a criminal record, the prosecutor will dismiss the case or plea bargain in order to generate a conviction or avoid a loss. There is one perverse implication of this tendency. Lower-income individuals are victims of a disproportionate number of crimes but are also more likely to have criminal records themselves and to make less articulate witnesses. "Thus, it is more likely that these cases are given away by prosecutors than those of higher income victims."[62] Ironically, of course, one *rhetorical* justification for public prosecution is to ensure that poor victims receive the same justice as rich victims would be able to purchase if private prosecution still existed. Instead, the opposite has occurred. Under private prosecution, rich and poor victims acted as prosecutors themselves and were generally on a relatively equal footing.

The characteristics and aspirations of the lawyers in the prosecutor's office also affect victims. Recall that many lawyers use the public prosecutor's office as a stepping stone to higher political office or to private law firms, so turnover among assistant prosecutors is very high and a prosecutor's office is usually staffed with young relatively inexperienced lawyers. This "means that the prosecutors must use an assembly line organization for their work. . . . [D]ifferent prosecutors are stationed along the various stages of the process and handle all the cases that reach the processing stage. . . . [T]his means that the victim, who may have already explained his case to several different police officers now has to retell it to each new prosecutor."[63]

The victims' cost of cooperating with prosecutors can be staggering. In *addition* to the initial loss to the criminal, victims face the costs of transportation, babysitting, and parking. More importantly, they can lose wages and they endure seemingly endless delays and continuances. There are also considerable emotional and psychological costs of having to confront an assailant, for example, or enduring a defense attorney's questions.

Why would a victim choose to bear such additional costs *beyond* the original loss due to the crime? In the case of property crimes, perhaps they hope to recover some of what they lost. In the case of personal crimes, the hope may be that the criminal will be put in prison so that he cannot attack someone else. But the portion of reported crimes that are ultimately cleared by arrest is only about 20 percent and is declining (see Table 6.4). More significantly, only a small portion of arrests result in convictions.

Table 6.4   Percentage of Offenses Known Cleared by Arrest.

Year	Total Crime*	Violent Crimes**	Murder and Non-Negligible Manslaughter	Forcible Rape	Robbery	Aggravated Assault
1980	19.2	43.6	72.3	48.8	23.8	58.7
1975	21.0	44.7	78.3	51.3	27.0	63.5
1970	21.0	47.6	86.5	56.4	29.1	64.9
1965	24.6		90.5	64.0	37.6	72.9
1960	26.1		92.3	72.5	38.5	75.8
1955			92.7	78.6	42.8	77.4
1950			93.8	80.3	43.5	76.6

SOURCE: U.S. Department of Justice, *Uniform Crime Reports,* Federal Bureau of Investigation, for various years.
*The values for the Aggregated Crime Index were not reported for 1950 and 1955.
**The Aggregated Violent Crime Index was not reported for 1950, 1955, 1960, and 1965.

In Alameda County, California, for example, 98,218 felonies were *reported* to the police during 1973.[64] The police arrested 13,695 adults and 6,798 juveniles that year, but 2,377 of the 13,695 adults were released because of insufficient evidence, and misdemeanor complaints were filed against 1,315 of them. Of the 10,043 felony complaints filed, the district attorney's office found that only 4,946 had sufficient evidence to warrant pursuing. The municipal court dismissed or processed as misdemeanants 2,714 of the 4,946; 2,232 were sent to superior court for felony trials, and 1,656 of those were convicted of felonies. That means that 1.7 percent of all reported felonies and perhaps 0.8 percent of all actual felonies (because at least half are not reported) ultimately led to felony convictions. And this ignores the fact that many of those felony convictions may have been achieved through plea bargaining so that the punishment was for a lesser crime than was committed.

But the story does not end here. Only 329 of the 1,656 convicted felons actually went to prison, a few went to state mental institutions or youth authority facilities, and 1,172 were given local jail sentences. Of those 1,172, about half went to jail for less than a year and were given probation, 62 got straight jail terms, 3 paid fines, and roughly half received *only* probation. These kinds of figures are not atypical. A 1977 study found that less than 30 percent of the felony arrests in Washington, D.C., resulted in *any* kind of conviction.[65]

At the federal level the lengths of sentences have been increasing, but actual time served has been decreasing (see Figure 6.1). A 1973 study of

Figure 6.1   Average sentence for, and average time served by, first releases from federal institution, 1965–1975

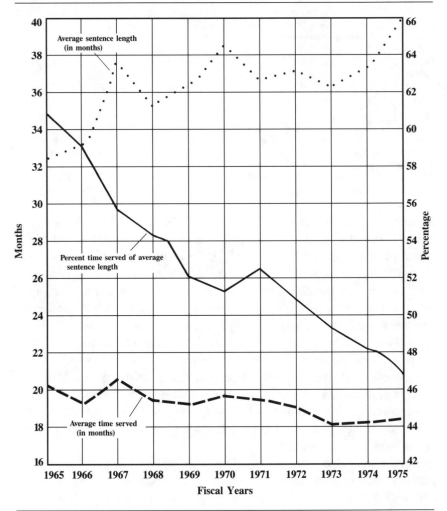

SOURCE: U.S. Department of Justice, *Sourcebook of Criminal Justice Statistics,* Bureau of Justice Statistics, 1976.

property crime estimated that the probability that an adult burglar will be sent to prison for a single offense is .0024; the risk for a juvenile was .0015. Furthermore, if an adult was actually sent to prison, he or she spent an average of only 26.8 months; juveniles were institutionalized for an average of about nine months.[66] Any hope that cooperating with police and prosecutors will protect the victim or others from the same criminal is a false one. Over 70 percent of the offenders released from prison are re-arrested for committing another crime.[67] The *major* reason for victim cooperation appears to be the potential satisfaction of knowing that the criminal who violated the victim's person or property is being punished. As Wilson explained, there are few offsetting benefits for the cost of cooperating in prosecution except a desire for revenge, since stolen property is often not recovered, money loss is not restored, and there is generally no compensation for injury.[68]

Suppose victim cooperation is successful and a criminal is arrested and convicted. Here, too, the criminal justice system shows little regard for the victim. The victim's views on sentencing are not represented to the judge, even though "defense counsel will be allowed to appeal to the judge, to beg for mercy, to try to sway the judges' emotions, and to recount in pathetic details his client's tragic childhood." Yet, recent political demands to have victim representation at sentencing have been met with the argument that it would be "improper, because the victim would play on the emotions of the judge."[69]

It should be clear that the typical crime victim has little to gain from participating in the criminal justice system. "If anything, the victim is exploited by criminal justice officials and defense attorneys to serve their personal and organizational self-interest."[70] But victims have not simply ignored such abuse. Many have simply chosen not to participate in the prosecution process, and others have begun to organize politically and apply pressures for changes in the criminal justice system.

Victims Opting Out.   It is estimated that about one-half the FBI Index crimes are not reported to police.[71] The *Figgie Report* estimated that 60 percent of personal larceny cases where there is no contact between the thief and his victim go unreported and that less than half of all assaults, less than 60 percent of all household burglaries, less than 30 percent of household larcenies, and only a little more than half of all robberies and rapes are reported.[72] Non-reporting is a natural reaction to the high cost of victim involvement with the criminal justice system, a reaction that has been common since the inception of criminal law. The avoidance of additional costs that exceed the personal satisfaction of seeing the criminal punished is not the only reason for not reporting crimes. The U.S. Department of

Justice report on crime victimization in 1979 found that in approximately 10 percent of unreported crimes victims believed that the police did "not want to be bothered."[73] This belief is probably justified given that many crime reports receive little or no attention by police departments facing common pool problems. Fear of reprisal is another factor, but this also reflects victims' perceptions that the criminal justice system is failing.[74]

The role of the victim in the publicly provided crime control process and his subsequent treatment within that process provide significant disincentives for him to report crimes or cooperate in the prosecution of criminals. Many victims respond to those incentives by opting out, which clearly reduces the effectiveness of the public sector in achieving criminal justice. After all, "to the extent that there is less victim involvement than there would be if other sorts of remedies were available—such as restitution—then fewer crimes will be reported, fewer criminals will be successfully prosecuted, and more rights violating conduct will result."[75]

Political Actions by Organized Victims.   The second response by victims has been to organize. A number of victim-oriented pressure groups have been formed over the last few years, such as Parents of Murdered Children (POMC) and Mothers Against Drunk Drivers (MADD). These groups "are expressing their anger and frustration at judges who hand down lenient sentences, at parole boards who free violent offenders to commit new mayhem, at prosecutors who plea bargain serious offenses down to minor charges, and at laws that allow the guilty to go free on legal quirks or small police errors."[76] They demand tougher sentencing laws, victim compensation, the right of victims to testify prior to sentencing about the effect of crime on their lives, and numerous other reforms. For instance, the Stephanie Roper committee (named after a Maryland College student who was raped, beaten, shot, set afire, and partially dismembered by two men who were sentenced to life in prison but who would be eligible for parole after less than 12 years), with some 11,500 members and 92,000 signatures on petitions, persuaded the Maryland legislature to require a minimum of 20 years in prison before parole can be considered in a capital crime, to eliminate drugs and alcohol as mitigating circumstances in violent acts, and to mandate that a written victim-impact statement be provided to judges before sentencing.[77] They have also lobbied for judges to be given the option of imposing life sentences with no parole and for in-person testimony by victims prior to sentencing, as well as notification of victims and their families before a criminal is paroled.

Society's League Against Molestation (S.L.A.M.) was organized in California following the sexual torture and murder of a two-year-old child by a pedophile with a 20-year history of violent sexual abuse. S.L.A.M.'S initial efforts in Sacramento were ineffective, but they returned the next year with 500 people and 60,000 signatures on a petition.[78] A number of new laws were the result, including mandatory prison terms for repeat molesters or violent first offenders, elimination of the hospital treatment program that freed the murderer whose crime led to the group's formation, and access by organizations to criminal records of anyone seeking a job that brings them into close contact with children. In 1989, S.L.A.M. had 75 chapters in 43 states, which lobby for legislative change, actively monitor court cases, and provide counseling for victims and information for parents. California established a victim-assistance program in 1965 and by 1986 thirty-seven states and the District of Columbia had followed suit (most since 1979).[79] The National Organization for Victim Assistance now coordinates the lobbying efforts of about 25 groups in Washington, D.C.[80]

It is important to remember that this reform legislation often reflects a compromise between potential conflicting interests and is often designed to achieve the self-interest goals of a group that does not obviously benefit from the statute. Consider public compensation for crime victims, an integral part of several states' victim relief programs. The American Bar Association has actively pursued such a program, even at the federal level. Why? Most federal bills, as proposed, include a payment of the victim's lawyer by the compensation board whether the victim's claim is successful or not.[81] Similarly, several state victim compensation programs mandate a 15 percent legal fee from a victim's award, which produced enough revenues to support about 1,000 full-time lawyers in 1975.[82]

Lawyers are not the only non-victim advocates of victim compensation. The International Association of Chiefs of Police have supported such legislation since 1966. In attempting to produce the political compromise necessary to pass federal compensation legislation, such bills have been joined with proposals for federal payments to policemen and firemen killed in the line of duty.[83] Of course, police may support victim compensation out of concern for victims or out of recognition that victims would then have greater incentives to cooperate in generating arrests and convictions, but the linkage of the two pieces of legislation together suggests strong self-interest motives as well.

Other bureaucrats have also consistently advocated victim compensation programs. The Department of Justice would administer the federal compensation commission and the program funds, which "would account for the LEAA study, which pushed for adoption of the program, claiming that the cost would be trivial."[84] The LEAA study estimated annual compensation of about $25 million, allowing roughly $1,000 payment to perhaps 2 percent of the victims of reported crime with injury at that time. Roger Meiners suspected that the federal government would be forced to cover the true costs of the program, because congressmen would find it difficult to vote for reduced benefits to innocent crime victims.[85] Therefore, by underestimating costs, the bureaucracy might achieve its ends and then be able to maintain its new position and power.

Victim compensation is like so many other programs that characterize the criminal justice system. It appears to be a desirable program, but "in reality, victim compensation threatens to emerge as another tentacle of leviathan, encompassing far more in territory and dollars than ever envisioned."[86] It is just another example of a policy chosen because it benefits bureaucrats, lawyers, and other political interests and expands the role of existing institutions. It is becoming apparent that the political approach to the problems of victim alienation is no better than simply opting out.

There is one more important response that victims and potential victims are making to the political criminal justice process. The private sector offers numerous alternatives to the use of public police and courts for crime prevention and protection of property rights. These are not considerations that are likely to get much attention in the political arena, but are being increasingly adopted by private citizens.

ENDNOTES

1. James S. Kakalik and Sorrel Wildhorn, *Private Police in the United States: Findings and Recommendations* (Santa Monica, Calif.: The Rand Corporation, 1971), pp. 1, 12.
2. Richard Neely, *Why Courts Don't Work* (New York: McGraw-Hill, 1982), p. 34.
3. Ibid., p. 35.
4. Alan Bent, *The Politics of Law Enforcement: Conflict and Power in Urban Communities* (Lexington, Mass.: Lexington Books, 1974), pp. 3–6.
5. Neely, *Why Courts Don't Work*, p. 131.
6. Ibid., p. 91.
7. Lawrence W. Sherman, "Patrol Strategies for Police," in *Crime and Public Policy*, James Q. Wilson, ed. (San Francisco: Institute for Contemporary Studies Press, 1983), p. 149.

8. Ibid., p. 156.
9. Tony Pate, et al., *Police Response Time, Its Determinants and Effects* (Washington, D.C.: Police Foundation, 1976).
10. Sherman, "Patrol Strategies for Police," p. 153.
11. Ibid., p. 151.
12. Ibid., p. 149.
13. John E. Boydstun, Michael E. Sherry, and Nicholas P. Moelter, *Patrol Staffing in San Diego: One- or Two-Officer Units* (Washington, D.C.: Police Foundation, 1977).
14. Robert W. Poole, Jr., *Cutting Back City Hall* (New York: Universe Books, 1978), pp. 46–47.
15. Abraham Blumberg, *Criminal Justice* (Chicago: Quadrangle Books, 1970), pp. 184–185.
16. Michael Milakovich and Kurt Weis, "Politics and Measures of Success in the War on Crime," *Crime and Delinquency* 21 (January 1975): 10.
17. E. S. Savas, "Municipal Monopolies Versus Competition in Delivering Urban Services," in *Improving the Quality of Urban Management*, ed. Willis D. Hawley and David Rogers, vol. 8 of *Urban Affairs Annual Review* (Beverly Hills, Calif.: Sage Publications, 1974), p. 475.
18. David Jones, *Crime Without Punishment* (Lexington, Mass.: Lexington Books, 1979), p. 201.
19. James Q. Wilson, *The Politics of Regulation* (New York: Basic Books, Inc., 1980), p. 374.
20. William Chambliss also found that criminal justice is a selective process in which the types of cases that most easily yield convictions are most likely to arise. See Chambliss, *Crime and the Legal Process* (New York: McGraw-Hill, 1960), p. 84. Also see James Eisenstein, *Politics and the Legal Process* (New York: Harper and Row, 1973); Abraham Blumberg, "The Practice of Law as a Confidence Game," *Law and Society Review* 1 (1967): 15–39; Brian Grosman, *The Prosecutor: An Inquiry into the Exercise of Discretion* (Toronto: University of Toronto Press, 1969).
21. Randy Barnett pointed this out in his review of an earlier draft of this book.
22. Randy E. Barnett, "Public Decisions and Private Rights," *Criminal Justice Ethics* 3 (Summer/Fall 1984): 54.
23. Eisenstein, *Politics and the Legal Process*, pp. 104–105. Also see John Kaplan, "The Prosecutorial Discretion: A Comment," *Northwestern Law Review* 6 (1965): 180.
24. Eisenstein, *Politics and the Legal Process*, p. 112.
25. Neely, *Why Courts Don't Work*, p. 16.
26. Ibid.
27. William M. Landis, "Legality and Reality: Some Evidence of Criminal Procedure," *Journal of Legal Studies* (June 1974): 289.

28. Neely, *Why Courts Don't Work*, p. 16.
29. Jones, *Crime Without Punishment*, pp. 81, 191, 193–197.
30. Ibid., p. 81.
31. H. H. A. Cooper, "Plea Bargaining: A Comparative Analysis," *International Law and Policy* 5 (1972): 427, 446.
32. See for example, Thomas Church, Jr., et al., *Justice Delayed: The Pace of Litigation in Urban Trial Courts* (Williamsburg, Va.: National Center for State Courts, 1978); W. M. Rhoades, "The Economics of Criminal Courts: A Theoretical and Empirical Investigation," *Journal of Legal Studies* 5 (1976): 319–320; W. J. Campbell, "Delays in Criminal Cases: Before the Conference of Metropolitan Chief Judges of the Federal Judicial Center," *Federal Rules Decisions* 55 (1973): 230; R. W. Gillespie, *Judicial Productivity and Court Delay: An Exploratory Analysis of the Federal Courts* (Washington, D.C.: Government Printing Office, 1973); J. O. Williams and R. J. Richardson, *Delay in Superior Courts of North Carolina and an Assessment of Its Causes* (Raleigh, N.C.: Administrative Office of the Courts, 1973).
33. Church, et al., *Justice Delayed: The Pace of Litigation in Urban Trial Courts*, pp. 28, 54.
34. Neely, *Why Courts Don't Work*, p. 7.
35. Ibid., p. 105.
36. Ibid., p. 58.
37. Ibid.
38. Randy Barnett provided this example in his review of an early draft of this book. Barnett suggested that "the average case load of a felony court judge now is boring compared to ten years ago."
39. Neely, *Why Courts Don't Work*, p. 25.
40. Carl Person, "Justice Inc.," *Juris Doctor* 8 (March 1978), p. 32.
41. See for example, William M. Landes and Richard Posner, "Adjudication as a Private Good," *Journal of Legal Studies* 8 (March 1979): 238; Rodney H. Mabry, Holly H. Ulbrich, Hugh H. Macauley, Jr., and Michael T. Maloney, *An Economic Investigation of State and Local Judiciary Services* (Washington, D.C.: National Institute of Law Enforcement and Criminal Justice, Law Enforcement Assistance Administration, Department of Justice, 1977), p. 82.
42. Neely, *Why Courts Don't Work*, p. 44.
43. Ibid., p. 198.
44. James Q. Wilson, "Thinking Practically About Crime," in *Assessing the Criminal: Restitution, Retribution, and the Legal Process*, ed. Randy E. Barnett and John Hagel III (Cambridge, Mass.: Ballinger Press, 1977), p. xxi.
45. Ibid., p. xxi.
46. James Eisenstein and Herbert Jacob, *Felony Justice* (Boston: Little, Brown and Co., 1977), p. 281.

47. Charles H. Logan and Sharla P. Rausch, "Punishment and Profit: Emergences of Private Enterprise Prisons," *Justice Quarterly* 2 (September 1985): 304.
48. Neely, *Why Courts Don't Work*, p. 10.
49. Ibid., p. 32.
50. Bruce L. Benson, "The Economic Theory of Regulation as an Explanation of Policies Towards Bank Mergers and Holding Company Acquisitions," *Antitrust Bulletin* 28 (Winter 1983): 839–862.
51. Bent, *The Politics of Law Enforcement*, pp. 6–11.
52. Eisenstein, *Politics and the Legal Process*, p. 120.
53. This point was raised by Randy Barnett in his review of an early draft of this book. He noted that "[t]he main group that is deliberately excluded from access to the inner workings of the courts are academics seeking to 'study' the system—who then go on to write about the hidden workings of the system."
54. Blumberg, *Criminal Justice*, p. 184.
55. Research and Forecasts, Inc., *America Afraid: How Fear of Crime Changes the Way We Live, Based on the Widely Publicized Figgie Report* (New York: New America Library, 1983), p. 16.
56. Frederick Kaiser, "Federal Law Enforcement: Structure and Reorganization," *Criminal Justice Review* 5 (Fall 1980): 101–118.
57. Bruce Smith, *Police Systems in the United States*, 2nd ed. (New York: Harper and Row, 1960), pp. 2–3.
58. William F. McDonald, "The Role of the Victim in America," in *Assessing the Criminal: Restitution and the Legal Process*, ed. Randy. E. Barnett and John Hagel III (Cambridge, Mass.: Ballinger Publishing Co., 1977), p. 298.
59. Ibid., pp. 299–300.
60. Ibid., p. 298.
61. Ibid., p. 302.
62. Ibid., p. 300.
63. Ibid., p. 301.
64. These statistics are reported in Poole, *Cutting Back City Hall*, pp. 51–52.
65. Brian Forst, Judith Lucianvic, and Sarah J. Cox, *What Happens After Arrest?* (Washington, D.C.: Institute of Law and Social Research, 1977).
66. G. Krohm, "The Pecuniary Incentives of Property Crime," in *The Economics of Crime and Punishment*, ed. S. Rottenberg (Washington, D.C.: American Enterprise Institute, 1973), p. 33.
67. J. L. Barkas, *Protecting Yourself Against Crime*, Public Affairs Pamphlet No. 564 (New York: Public Affairs Committee, 1978), p. 20.
68. Wilson, "Thinking Practically About Crime," p. xv.
69. McDonald, "The Role of the Victim in America," pp. 301–302.
70. Ibid., p. 307.
71. Wilson, "Thinking Practically About Crime," p. xv.

72. Research and Forecasts, *America Afraid*, p. 105.
73. Ibid.
74. Wilson, "Thinking Practically About Crime," pp. xv–xvi.
75. Randy E. Barnett, "Pursuing Justice in a Free Society, Part One: Power vs. Liberty," *Criminal Justice Ethics* 4 (Summer/Fall 1985): 50–72.
76. Michael Satchell, "Victims Have Rights Too," *Parade*, March 17, 1985, p. 15.
77. Ibid.
78. Ibid., p. 16.
79. Juan Cardenas, "The Crime Victim in the Prosecutorial Process," *Harvard Journal of Law & Public Policy* 9 (Spring 1986): p. 357.
80. Satchell, "Victims Have Rights Too," p. 17.
81. Roger E. Meiners, "Public Compensation of the Victims of Crime: How Much Would It Cost?" in *Assessing the Criminal: Restitution, Retribution, and the Legal Process*, ed. Randy E. Barnett and John Hagel III (Cambridge, Mass.: Ballinger Publishing Co., 1977), p. 314.
82. Ibid.
83. Ibid., pp. 314–315.
84. Ibid., pp. 315–316.
85. Ibid., p. 316.
86. Ibid., pp. 328–329.

7

CORRUPTION OF LAW ENFORCEMENT OFFICIALS

"Chicago Cop Goes Undercover to Crack a Police Dope Ring," "This Judge Is the Defendant," "A Federal Judge Goes on Trial in Nevada on Bribery Charges," "More Miami Cops Are Arrested," "A Prosecutor on Trial," "Jailed U.S. Judge Resists Resigning."[1] This sample of headlines from news magazine and newspaper articles only touches the surface of the corruption problem among law enforcement officials. Political corruption has been a fact of life since government got into the business of law enforcement. Corruption is actually just a black market for the property rights over which politicians and bureaucrats have allocative power.[2] Rather than assigning rights according to political power, rights are sold to the highest bidder. If bureaucrats are not monitored closely, then self-interest motives may really take over and corruption is likely. To get some idea of the level of corruption in law enforcement, we must examine the opportunities for corruption and the institutionalized incentives to carry out corrupt acts that face public sector law enforcement officials.

OPPORTUNITIES FOR CORRUPTION

Corruption is a direct consequence of discretionary authority by government officials. When common pool congestion arises, public law enforcement bureaucrats have tremendous discretion in allocating limited bureau resources among competing demands. For example, overcriminalization enhances the possibility for corruption, as police are in a position to choose which laws to enforce and which to ignore. This power invites corruption. Commons problems also generate considerable discretion for judges and prosecutors. Court time is to a large extent rationed by waiting time, but prosecutors can also ration court time by deciding which cases to prosecute, which to plea bargain, and which to drop; judges similarly decide which cases deserve consideration and which do not. The discretionary power to allocate many rights because of the commons problem of overcriminalization combines with bureaucratic secrecy to enhance opportunities for corruption.

For example, where government has modified a rights structure to prevent a competitive market and has, consequently, created *incentives* for an illegal market to arise, the potential illegal transaction can often be easily detected.[3] As a result, successful underground markets require illegal transactions to have the appearance of legality or have agreements with officials that the law will not be enforced. Perhaps the property is durable and immobile (e.g., land subject to zoning), or the property is subject to close scrutiny by government officials (e.g., liquor license requirements). Under such circumstances, an illegal property rights modification must be accomplished through the actions of a government official. As a consequence, land use and building regulations appear to generate considerable opportunities for political corruption.[4] Corruption need not go as far as outright changes in statutes or regulations. Public officials may simply ignore violations or make it easy for individuals to find their way through the red tape quickly. In 1972, the Knapp Commission to Investigate Alleged Police Corruption in New York City discovered that the second largest source of police corruption was

> legitimate business seeking to ease its way through the maze of City ordinances and regulations. Major offenders are construction contractors and subcontractors, liquor licensees, and managers of businesses like trucking firms and parking lots, which are likely to park large numbers of vehicles illegally. If the police were completely honest, it is likely that members of these groups would seek to corrupt them, since most seem to feel that paying off the police is easier and cheaper than obeying the laws or paying fines and answering summonses when they do violate the laws.[5]

There is a closely related opportunity for corruption that has clear and direct applications to criminal law enforcement. In instances where illegal activities could be prevented or severely limited through relatively inexpensive enforcement efforts (e.g., gambling, prostitution), public officials have a valuable set of property rights that may be sold. They can allow certain individuals or groups to operate illegally while preventing other potential participants from entering the market. That is, they can sell monopoly rights to a private sector underground market and then enforce that rights allocation.

Schelling argued that organized crime is really monopolized crime, and both Rubin and Anderson contended that criminal firms possess market power because there are economies of scale in buying corruption from police and other governmental officials.[6] Demsetz, however, explained that economies of scale are not sufficient for such monopoly pricing.[7] Exploiting a monopoly position requires entry restrictions, typically arising from governmental policy. In the case of underground markets, all entry is illegal; but if enforcement is easy, corrupt public officials can sell the right to produce to selected illegal firms. In this instance, an underground market for governmentally controlled property rights may be required for a private sector underground market to operate. Not surprisingly, the Knapp Commission discovered that "organized crime is the single biggest source of police corruption" in New York City.[8] Similarly, Charles Ashman reported that "organized crime cannot function without organized justice."[9]

The potential for government corruption arises for precisely the same reason that underground private markets can exist. Legal rights modifications prevent a competitive allocation of resources, creating opportunities for markets that are designed to avoid the laws. Under many circumstances, these illegal markets must involve corrupt law enforcement officials in order to exist, particularly when the market requires rights over which public officials have allocative discretion. But corruption requires more than opportunities; it requires a desire to take advantage of them.

INCENTIVES FOR CORRUPTION

Decisions are made on the basis of information and incentives, and public officials react to incentives just as private individuals do. Thus, relatively strong incentives to become corrupt are likely to result in relatively more corruption. The relevant incentives are those that Becker delineated in his economic theory of crime: the size of expected payoffs relative to a public official's alternatives, the likelihood of being detected and punished, and the severity of the potential punishment.[10]

The Payoffs to Corruption. The attractiveness to a public official of the expected payoff from corruption depends on a number of factors. The potential returns to corruption will be weighed against returns to other activities that may have to be foregone if the official chooses to participate in an illegal market. Of course, law enforcement officials cannot capture profits when they abstain from corruption and concentrate on enhancing efficiency in the production of law enforcement services. They may be able to move to a better-paying public sector job, but few public officials receive large salaries. Officials may also gain satisfaction from the prestige and power they acquire, but "some experts note that judicial virtue has been tested more than usual of late by failure of salaries to keep pace with the earnings of private attorneys."[11] Furthermore, many public officials are severely constrained as to how and how much they can legally obtain beyond their public salaries. Thus, assuming that public sector employment was chosen because it was an official's best alternative, any reasonably large expected payoff from corrupt activity may be tempting.

The magnitude of the potential payoff from corruption is determined by several factors. The expected value of the rights that the official is able to allocate is a prime determinant. Thus, *the greater the market distortion created by the laws being enforced*, the greater the potential payoff to officials doing the enforcing. Strict building codes or rigorous and geographically expansive zoning laws, for instance, generate the potential for large payoffs.[12] In addition, when a market is entirely outlawed (e.g., drugs and prostitution), the potential payments to public officials for protecting a black market's monopoly are enormous. The Knapp Commission found evidence of payoffs to a plainclothes police officer from gambling interests in New York to range from $400 to $1,500 *per month*.[13] But this is small-time compared to narcotics-related payoffs, which run into the hundreds of thousands of dollars. In 1982, for example, ten Chicago police officers were convicted of taking $250,000 in protection money from narcotics dealers.[14] In 1986, a federal prosecutor was charged with receiving payments of $210,000 and a boat in exchange for tipping off a drug smuggler to the evidence-gathering activities of U.S. Drug Enforcement Administration officers.[15] Similarly, if an official has allocative power over a number of different rights, the payoff could be large even though no single right has tremendous value. The Knapp Commission found that "while individual payments to uniformed men were small, mostly under $20, they were often so numerous as to add substantially to a patrolman's income."[16]

When the discretionary power to allocate rights in a common pool is concentrated in the hands of a few officials, the corruption payoff to those individuals can be extremely large. Judges, for example, have near-monopoly control over the dispensation of cases that come before them. One of the four judges found guilty as of January 20, 1986, as a consequence of "Operation Greylord" (a federal undercover operation to detect corruption in the Cook County court system) was convicted of, among other things, accepting bribes totaling $400,000 in cash and eight automobiles.[17] A New Jersey judge was convicted in 1982 of taking $22,000 to release one convict from prison and put another on probation.[18] Investigating officers have similar monopoly powers. If an investigator puts together a case against a particular criminal, then he is in position to extort money or accept a bribe from that criminal. The Knapp Commission found that investigating detectives' "shakedowns of individual targets of opportunity" frequently "come to several thousand dollars."[19]

If the power to influence a rights assignment is widely dispersed and difficult to coordinate, however, the payoff to any one official is likely to be relatively small. Organized crime may have to bribe several police officers, for instance, to assure the relatively unmolested operation of their underground markets in drugs and prostitution, but this means that the payoff to any one police officer will be relatively small and less acceptable. Similarly, if a buyer of illegally allocated rights has several alternative sources (competitive corruption, if you will), then the return to any one corrupt seller is likely to be small. A pimp, for example, may be indifferent as to whether his prostitutes work in one or another of several geographically contiguous political jurisdictions.

An obvious determinant of the payoff to corruption is the private buyer's willingness to pay for an illegal governmental rights allocation. Naturally, buyers in the underground market for governmentally controlled property rights react to the same kind of incentives that participants in any illegal activity do. Is the potential return relatively large or small? Is the action likely to be detected? How severe might the punishment be if the activity is detected? Given the evidence of police and judicial corruption, a substantial number of private sector individuals find the potential returns from illegal dealings with officials to be high enough to be worth the risk.[20]

The Probability of Detection.   If there is a high probability that an illegal rights allocation will be detected and that a corrupt official will be identified and prosecuted, then an official is less likely to become corrupt. There are several ways to monitor law enforcement activities. Individual citizens in general and taxpayers and voters in particular might make efforts to monitor individual officials. But this is far from a major threat because of rational ignorance and the free-rider problem. A citizen's *share* of the benefits derived by eliminating one corrupt official is so small relative to his costs that he has virtually no economic incentive to act as a monitor. Monitoring costs are quite high and simply learning enough about the inner workings of a single bureaucracy to be able to identify a corrupt official can take a tremendous investment in time and effort.

Furthermore, a citizen has little incentive to join in a collective effort to monitor government, because he can share whatever benefits such a collective action may generate without bearing any of the costs. There are several fairly active government watch organizations, of course, and they may pose some threat to potentially corrupt officials, but it is likely that these efforts will be relatively unsuccessful because they simply will not be able to attract sufficient resources to be effective.

The common pool characteristics of law enforcement cast a slightly different light on the typical explanation of free-rider incentives. There are incentives to overuse common pool resources, but there are also strong incentives to underinvest in maintaining the common pool. Those who harvest whales have few incentives to replenish the stock so that others will be free to harvest those new animals. In much the same way, individuals have little incentive to invest in maintaining the integrity of public officials so that others will be free to share the benefits of the investment. In fact, the probability of any direct benefit of such an investment will be very small. What is frequently characterized as a free-rider problem, then, may be a common pool underinvestment problem.

The news media is another potential source of monitoring. News does have some public good (or, more accurately, externality) characteristics, so there is a potential free-rider problem. But because consumers of news pay indirectly through advertising, the undersupply of news services is not likely to be a significant problem. Nonetheless, there are reasons to expect that the news media will not be a major threat to most corrupt officials. Few members of the media devote much time to trying to *detect* corruption of criminal justice officials. Corruption exposed by others is certainly reported, but there are relatively few instances in which news personnel have actively sought out illegal activity. This is partly because newspapers and other media require daily output, and most reporters must concentrate on news that can be obtained easily and quickly. Detecting corrupt officials and proving their guilt are generally difficult and time consuming, and such efforts are likely to take place only when the potential payoff is substantial. A reporter might be willing to spend considerable time trying to demonstrate that an important public official is corrupt because the potential payoffs are large (e.g., front page headlines, recognition by peers and citizens, and greater income opportunities), but he is unlikely to invest much time and effort in detecting corruption by a police patrol officer.

Peers can be a source of monitoring. Most governmental institutions have established self-monitoring systems and have actually discouraged (and in some cases even prevented) monitoring from external sources. Police departments have their internal affairs divisions, for example, and court systems have judicial review boards. But such monitoring is not likely to be very effective. No matter what the goal of a government official might be, he has strong incentives *not* to expose corruption or inefficiencies within his governmental unit. Suppose that a police official derives his satisfaction by working for what he believes is the "public interest" and is convinced that what his bureau is doing is vital. If he reveals that his colleagues are corrupt, the unit's effectiveness may be jeopardized. This public-spirited individual may try to suppress corruption internally, but it seems likely that he would prefer not to know about the corruption at all.

The Knapp Commission attributed police officers' extreme reluctance to bring evidence against or to effectively investigate fellow officers to "intense group loyalty." This in turn supposedly manifested itself in a "public spirited" concern for the effectiveness and morale of the department which produced suspicion and hostility directed at any outside interference with the department. This mixture of hostility and pride created the most serious roadblock to a rational attack on police corruption: a stubborn refusal at all levels of the department to acknowledge that a serious problem exists.[21]

Police are not the only bureaucrats with strong tendencies to protect their own. Most states have judicial review boards that involve judges monitoring other judges. "Some critics complain, however, that judges cannot be counted upon to act against their own colleagues...the idea of firmly rooting out judicial corruption remains an especially sensitive one...[with] worries about the manifest danger of losing public respect."[22] It is interesting to note the similarity between the justification for not revealing police corruption and the justification for not revealing judicial corruption.

It must be emphasized that the kind of incentives and behavior discovered by the Knapp Commission (and many other investigative commissions) can easily be attributed to self-interested motives rather than public-spiritedness. For the public official for whom power and prestige are major sources of satisfaction, for example, corruption within his organization may lead to reductions in budget, discretionary power, and prestige. Finally, an official who may be corrupt or who wishes to keep the corruption option open obviously does not want to attract attention to the corruption potential of his position. This explanation is particularly compelling in the Knapp Commission case because "police corruption was found to be an extensive, department-wide phenomenon, indulged in to some degree by a sizable majority of those on the force."[23]

It is not surprising, therefore, to find that in the few instances in which an official has reported corruption he has generally been ostracized by colleagues and superiors, denied promotions, and ultimately forced to resign. When honest officials face such potential costs, it is evident that corrupt officials probably have little to fear from their peers.[24] Thus, "with extremely rare exceptions, even those who themselves engage in no corrupt activities are involved in corruption in the sense that they take no steps to prevent what they know or suspect to be going on about them."[25]

Another source of potential detection comes from other governmental units. One function of elected representatives is to monitor bureaucracies to see that they are doing what his constituents want them to do. This monitoring could conceivably be very effective (assuming that the representatives themselves are not corrupt) if there are relatively few officials to monitor and relatively few rights over which those officials have allocative powers. But as more time and resources are spent in monitoring, less are available for determining the nature and strength of constituencies' demands, meeting those demands through legislative enactment, and taking advantage of outside income sources and benefits associated with legislative service.[26] So, even if there were relatively few officials and rights modifications to be monitored, it would not necessarily follow that legislative oversight would substantially reduce corruption.

A legislature may choose to delegate the monitoring function to some other governmental unit. Results of the Federal Bureau of Investigation's corruption detection efforts, for example, have been evident. Similar efforts by state and local criminal justice agencies are also possible. Operation Greylord, for instance, produced initial expectations of indictments of 30 court officials, including ten circuit judges, on charges of fixing cases, bribery, extortion, mail fraud, and racketeering in the Cook County court system.[27] But this was the culmination of a three-and-one-half year undercover investigation. Law enforcement officers are expected to enforce a wide range of laws with limited budgets. Expensive police efforts appear to involve a few, possibly spectacular arrests (e.g., Operation Greylord), perhaps in the hopes that the visibility of these actions will lead potentially corrupt officials to overestimate the risk of detection (but also because they often follow a highly publicized scandal that results in a temporary political commitment to provision of investigative resources). This may have the desired impact over the short term, but it may not work for long. Thus, resources devoted to corruption detection should not pose a great threat to the overwhelming majority of corrupt officials.

In many cases, the officials' incentives for monitoring their counterparts in separate government bureaus are quite weak. Prosecutors' offices, for instance, might appear to be in a good position to investigate police corruption, but "in the case of the district attorneys, there is the additional problem that they work so closely with policemen that the public tends to look upon them—and indeed they seem to look upon themselves—as allies of the police."[28] The Knapp Commission found citizens had a general mistrust of the district attorneys primarily because of those close ties. One implication of this distrust, of course, is that many prosecutors were also involved in the corruption.[29]

This brings up a relevant point. When a government official has the responsibility of preventing corruption by other officials, he also has a potentially valuable right to sell: the right to be corrupt. He faces the same kinds of incentives as officials who are supposed to prevent private sector underground activities. Thus, it should not be surprising that public officials pay off police officers in order to practice corruption.[30]

Another reason for corrupt officials to be relatively unconcerned with potential detection is that investigations are costly. Operation Greylord required over three years of undercover work, and the cost ran into the millions of dollars.[31] New York State had a staff of 45 monitoring judges in 1983 at a cost of $1.5 million a year,[32] but most states, counties and cities cannot commit such resources to the monitoring of public officials. They rely on existing law enforcement bureaucrats to monitor themselves and each other, at least until a major scandal erupts. But common pool problems provide those bureaucrats with a ready excuse for not actively searching out corruption. In a situation where bureaucrats face excess demand and have substantial discretion to choose how to allocate their resources, they can frequently justify ignoring corruption, particularly if it is not brought to the public's attention. Whether the public is better served by use of those scarce resources in pursuit of corruption or in the provision of other services does not appear to be a question that is raised.[33]

There have been numerous instances where a major corruption scandal has been exposed and a special commission or task force has been appointed to investigate the problem. But there are problems with the "scandal reaction" approach to corruption control. Any alternative regime that does not address the fundamental institutional issues—the information and incentives generated—is unlikely to be successful over the long run. First, those who are corrupt can appeal to a concentrated constituency for campaign funds. Second, and more important, without changes in the fundamental institutions the replacements for those who are convicted, forced to resign, or defeated in an election are likely to degenerate into corruption themselves.[34]

In New York City, the Knapp Commission reported that their "findings were hardly new. As long ago as 1844, when the State legislature created the New York police department as the first in the country, historians record an immediate problem with extortion and other corrupt activities engaged in by police."[35] The city has since been hit periodically by major corruption scandals followed by special investigations, revelation of large-scale corruption, official expressions of outrage, and finally "reforms"; but in each case "the basic pattern of corrupt behavior was never substantially affected and after the heat was off, it was largely back to business as usual."[36] A major investigation of police corruption seems to take place about every 20 years in the city.[37]

New York is certainly not unique in this regard. A major investigation of police corruption took place in Chicago between 1970 and 1976,[38] but the corruption did not end. Over twenty Chicago officers were at some stage of investigation (arraignment, indictment, or conviction) for drug-related charges in July of 1982.[39] Charles Ashman has concluded that "scandalous corruption seems to be contagious among judges in certain states."[40] Corruption does not end when the "rascals" have been thrown out. They are probably no more "rotten" by nature than any other typical resident of the same city or state. The institutional setting creates the opportunity and incentives for corruption, and discretion occurs because of the excess demands on common pool resources (e.g., over-criminalization). As Ashman noted, "the argument that there are just as many crooked television repairmen or auto mechanics and the like doesn't hold up. No repairman or mechanic or anyone but a judge has unlimited control over the freedom and property of each member of his community."[41]

The Severity of Punishment.   One other potential source of disincentives for corruption is the severity of the punishment that arises when that corruption is detected. The impact of punishment is difficult to assess, however, since severity is a subjective concept. An official who obtains satisfaction from a prestigious position may view the embarrassment of public exposure for corruption and the loss of a job as severe punishment; another with attractive outside alternatives might view exposure as an inconvenience. The same can be said of punishment as a deterrent to private sector illegal activity, so at least some inferences can be drawn from a comparison of the types of punishment that corrupt officials face relative to punishment given criminals in the private sector.

If it is correct that officials who detect corruption in their own organizations are likely to suppress information and downplay its significance, then any internally generated punishment is likely to be relatively mild. Mild punishment should make the corruption appear to be relatively less significant to those outside the organization (e.g., legislators and private sector government-watch groups), thus minimizing the attention that exposure might attract. Judicial disciplinary boards hear more than 3,500 complaints of misconduct each year, many on such charges as favoritism, abusive language, and other forms of overt misbehavior.[42] While some complaints are unfounded, coming from persons disgruntled over losing a case, many are valid. Through the 1970s, however, review boards dismissed virtually every complaint, taking some action against only about a dozen judges per year.[43] The number of cases found for complaintants increased during the early 1980s, but even so, of the 152 judges found quilty in 1981, only 16 were forcibly removed from office and 11 were suspended. Another 55 were officially reprimanded, but 70 simply resigned while under investigation and received no official punishment. Of 89 grievances filed against federal judges, 11 resulted in unspecified "corrective action" and one ended with a judge's retirement.[44]

Retirement or resignation are the routes frequently taken when a corrupt official is identified.[45] A May 14, 1970, letter from the Law Department of the City of New York to the mayor recommending formation of the independent investigative committee (the Knapp Commission) pointed out, for instance, that

> under present law a city employee is required to give 30 days' notice before his retirement becomes effective. The Police Department has found that in many instances this time period does not permit a proper investigation and disposition of charges of corruption against members of the police force, particularly if criminal charges are under investigation. Other city departments have encountered similar problems with regard to allegedly dishonest employees seeking to retire and obtain their pension benefits.[46]

Punishment of a corrupt official could be relatively severe when the conviction is as a consequence of detection by another organization or a private government-watch group. One might even expect such punishment to be relatively severe if the strategy is to make examples of the officials who are caught in order to deter other potential corruption. But this is not an appropriate deduction. Although there is little statistical evidence, public officials (particularly high-ranking officials) seem to receive relatively short prison terms and to be paroled relatively quickly. During the four and one half years following the Serpico incident (beginning in 1968 and ending in the middle of 1972), for instance, the five district attorneys' offices in New York City initiated 136 police corruption cases involving 218 officers, including 158 patrolmen, 39 detectives, 9 sergeants, 11 lieutenants, and 1 assistant chief inspector. Sixty-three of the defendants pleaded guilty, and 28 were convicted after trial; 46 were acquitted or dismissed and 81 were still awaiting trial when the Knapp report was issued. Eighty of the 91 officers found guilty had been sentenced at the time of the Knapp report: 49 were either *freed or given suspended sentences* and 31 received jail terms, 14 of which were for less than a year. The

> Bronx County District Attorney. . .testified before the Commission that light sentences were common in cases involving police officers. . . . It is clear that the risks of severe punishment for corrupt behavior are slight. A dishonest policeman knows that even if he is caught and convicted, he will probably receive a court reprimand or, at most, a fairly short jail sentence. Considering the vast sums to be made in some plainclothes squads or in narcotics enforcement the gains from corruption seem to far outweigh the risks.[47]

Interestingly, from 1970 through 1973 there was also a 90 percent turnover in the rank of captain and above, apparently due to retirement, but almost every criminal charge was brought against those holding the rank of lieutenant or below. The obvious implication is that punishment for police corruption is likely to be relatively light and is likely to decline as the official's rank increases.

CONSEQUENCES OF CRIMINALIZATION

If historical trends toward more criminalization and increased growth of public enforcement bureaus continue, then one can predict increased corruption among law enforcement officials. At first glance, such a prediction may appear trivial: Growth of law enforcement bureaucracies means more government employees, so that if some portion of public officials is corrupt, corruption should increase. But this prediction goes beyond such an obvious relationship. Based on our explorations of the opportunities for and the incentives to commit corruption, we can anticipate that the number of law enforcement officials involved in corruption should rise *at an increasing rate*. The relationship between public sector growth and the opportunities for corruption is obvious. Greater criminalization means that more property rights are controlled by government officials, so there are greater possibilities for the illegal sale of such rights. Incentives for participation in private sector underground markets increase, so officials have additional opportunities to accept bribes in return for altering rights structures or for allowing some individuals or groups to operate in a private illegal market without fear of punishment. Clearly, if the incentives to commit corrupt acts do not change with growth in public sector law enforcement, we could still predict increasing corruption simply because of the expanded number of opportunities for corruption. But such growth also leads to stronger and stronger incentives to become corrupt.

Consider the impact of an expanding governmental role for the potential payoff to corruption. Governmental growth means that private sector or market activities are increasingly constrained as property rights allocations gravitate toward public officials. The more severe the legal constraints on private markets and private behavior in general, the more valuable become the rights controlled by public officials. Correspondingly, the payment that is likely to accrue to a corrupt official increases. Furthermore, as the power to make ever greater numbers of rights allocations is placed in the hands of public officials, the potential returns to corruption expand even if no single right has tremendous value. Because increasing criminalization leads to greater potential payoffs to corruption, the incentives to be corrupt become stronger as government grows.

The growth in the size of enforcement bureaus has two implications for corruption. First, an increase in the number of government employees with some rights allocation powers means that monitoring for corruption becomes increasingly ineffective. Monitoring efforts must be spread over more and larger agencies, so detection of a corrupt public official becomes less likely and each official's incentive to avoid corruption is reduced. If resources devoted to monitoring are expanded *proportionately* to governmental growth, corruption incentives need not increase, but this possibility is doubtful. I have found no legislation that delegated power to enforce a new law and *simultaneously* provided resources to monitor for possible corruption. There appears to have been some recent general increase in resources committed to corruption control, but this commitment falls far short of being proportional to the tremendous growth in government. The incentives for private citizens to become involved with government-watch organizations should also increase, so private sector monitoring efforts may expand as government grows. The free-rider or common pool underinvestment problem, however, is still likely to stand in the way of effective monitoring.

The second implication of the growth of public enforcement agencies is that the risk of detection to individuals paying bribes falls concurrent with a reduction of risk to those receiving bribes. Thus, individuals become more willing to enter into underground transactions with public officials, and more opportunities for corruption become available. Furthermore, the reduced risk to bribe-payers is likely to make them willing to pay even larger bribes to corrupt officials. The payoff to corruption increases, and corruption becomes more attractive.

Many government officials would probably counter this argument by pointing out the stepped-up efforts and the success of law enforcement authorities in detecting corruption during recent years. The U.S. Department of Justice's public-integrity section has been pursuing charges of corruption since 1976, the FBI's Abscam and Operation Greylord were very successful, and even state governments have become active in detecting corruption. The official conclusion typically sounds like this: "Most experts believe there is less crookedness in law enforcement today than in the past," or "all in all, misbehavior on the bench stands a better chance today of being corrected than ever before."[48]

There have been numerous corruption scandals in recent years, but is the surge of judicial and police corruption cases evidence of the success of increased policing of corruption as officials claim or is it evidence of increased corruption itself? Certainly, if corruption increases with government growth, then the likelihood increases of some official making a mistake that brings him into the public eye and necessitates an official inquiry. Operation Greylord was not initiated by the FBI out of the blue. Widespread suspicion of cases being fixed in the Chicago court system sent the state's attorney's office to the FBI for help.[49] One judge who cooperated with the investigation indicated how blatant the corruption had become when he characterized many of those charged as "political hacks about as smart as a bag of rocks."[50] The point is that as corruption increases, the likelihood of scandal and politically motivated responses also increases. Governments at all levels will put additional resources into corruption detection as a consequence. But committing additional resources does not guarantee that they will be used effectively.

CONCLUSIONS

How widespread is corruption among law enforcement officials? If the arguments proposed here are true, then it is impossible to estimate since most corruption is never reported. Smith, however, believed that his examination of U.S. police systems revealed "the prevailing influence of corruption."[51]

Of course, from some perspectives, corruption may not be all that bad. As Becker and Stigler point out, the desirability of the suppression of corruption

> depends on whether laws are passed in the "social" interest or to reward special interest groups. . . . For example, bribes that reduced the effectiveness of many housing codes, of the laws of Nazi Germany against the Jews, or of the laws restricting oil imports, would improve, not harm social welfare (although not as defined by the legislature).[52]

We may be better off, for example, if bribes persuade police to ignore many of the victimless actions that have been criminalized so that police resources can be used to prevent violent and property crimes. And victimless crimes (prostitution, gambling, narcotics) are the areas that seem to dominate police corruption. But it is not clear that corruption is this selective. And perhaps we should be concerned with the moral foundation of a society that requires corrupt public officials to achieve desirable ends.

ENDNOTES

1. *Time*, July 26, 1982, p. 17; *Newsweek*, February 7, 1983, p. 59; *Time*, April 7, 1984, p. 64; *Newsweek*, February 10, 1986, p. 68; *New York Times*, January 16, 1986, p. 1.
2. This chapter draws heavily from Bruce L. Benson, "A Note on Corruption of Public Officials: The Black Market for Property Rights," *Journal of Libertarian Studies* 5 (Summer 1981): 305–311; Benson and John Baden, "The Political Economy of Government Corruption: The Logic of Underground Government," *Journal of Legal Studies* 14 (June 1985): 391–410. See also Benson, "Corruption in Law Enforcement: One Consequence of the 'Tragedy of the Commons' Arising with Public Allocation Processes," *International Review of Law and Economics* 8 (June 1988): 73–84; Benson,

174 A PUBLIC CHOICE APPROACH TO AUTHORITARIAN LAW

"An Institutional Explanation for Corruption of Criminal Justice Officials,"
Cato Journal 8 (Spring/Summer 1988): 139–163.

3. Benson, "A Note on Corruption of Public Officials."

4. John Gardiner and Theodore Lyman, Decisions for Sale: Corruption and
Reform in Land-Use and Building Regulation (New York: Praeger, 1978).

5. Whitman Knapp, Chairman, The Knapp Commission Report on Police
Corruption (New York: George Braziller, 1972), p. 68.

6. Thomas Shelling, "What Is the Business of Organized Crime?" American
Scholar 40 (Autumn 1971): 643–652; Paul Rubin, "The Economic Theory
of the Criminal Firm," in The Economics of Crime and Punishment, ed.
S. Rottenberg (Washington, D.C.: American Enterprise Institute, 1979);
Annelise Anderson, The Business of Organized Crime (Stanford: Hoover
Institute Press, 1979).

7. Harold Demsetz, "Why Regulate Utilities?" Journal of Law and Economics
11 (April 1968): 55–65.

8. Knapp, The Knapp Commission Report on Police Corruption, p. 68.

9. Charles R. Ashman, The Finest Judges Money Can Buy (Los Angeles: Nash
Publishing, 1973), p. 11.

10. Gary S. Becker, "Crime and Punishment: An Economic Analysis," Journal
of Political Economy 78 (March/April 1968): 526–536. See the Appendix
to Chapter 10 for a detailed discussion.

11. Richard Lacayo, "Passing Judgement on the Judges: A Spate of Legal Trouble
for the Judiciary," Time, January 20, 1986, p. 66.

12. Gardiner and Lyman, Decisions for Sale.

13. Knapp, The Knapp Commission Report on Police Corruption, p. 75.

14. Kurt Anderson, "A True Prince of the City: In Chicago, a Cop Goes Undercover to Crack a Police Dope Ring," Time, July 26, 1982, p. 17.

15. Aric Press and Mark Starr, "The Friends of David T.: A Prosecutor on
Trial," Newsweek, February 10, 1986, p. 68.

16. Knapp, The Knapp Commission Report on Police Corruption, pp. 2–3.

17. Lacayo, "Passing Judgement on the Judges," p. 66.

18. Ted Gest, "Crackdown on Judges Who Go Astray," U.S. News and World
Report, February 28, 1983, p. 42.

19. Knapp, The Knapp Commission Report on Police Corruption, p. 2.

20. For example, see Lawrence W. Sherman, ed., Police Corruption: A
Sociological Perspective (Garden City, N.Y.: Anchor Books, 1974); Sherman,
Controlling Police Corruption (Washington, D.C.: National Institute of Law
Enforcement and Criminal Justice, Law Enforcement Assistance Administra-
tion, 1978).

21. Knapp, The Knapp Commission Report on Police Corruption, pp. 6–7.

22. Lacayo, "Passing Judgement on the Judges," p. 66.

23. Knapp, The Knapp Commission Report on Police Corruption, p. 61.

24. An honest official may even become a target for revenge. See ibid., p. 197.
25. Ibid., p. 3.
26. Bruce L. Benson, "Why Are Congressional Committees Dominated by High-Demand Legislators?" *Southern Economic Journal* 48 (July 1981): 68–77; Benson, "High Demand Legislative Committees and Bureaucratic Output," *Public Finance Quarterly* 11 (July 1983): 259–281; Isaac Ehrlich and Richard Posner, "An Economic Analysis of Legal Rule-Making," *Journal of Legal Studies* 3 (January 1974): 257–286; W. Mark Crain, "Cost and Output in the Legislative Firm," *Journal of Legal Studies* 8 (June 1979): 607–621.
27. Mark Starr and Michael Reese, "Stinging the Chicago Courts," *Newsweek*, August 22, 1983, p. 21.
28. Knapp, *The Knapp Commission Report on Police Corruption*, p. 14.
29. Ibid., p. 5.
30. Sherman, *Controlling Police Corruption*, p. 6.
31. Starr and Reese, "Stinging the Chicago Courts," p. 21.
32. Gest, "Crackdown on Judges Who Go Astray," p. 42.
33. Knapp, *The Knapp Commission Report on Police Corruption*, p. 257.
34. See Smith, *Police Systems in the United States*, pp. 5–6.
35. Knapp, *The Knapp Commission Report on Police Corruption*, p. 61.
36. Ibid., p. 61.
37. In 1984, 1912, 1932, 1950, and 1972. See ibid., pp. 61–64.
38. See Beigel and Beigel, *Beneath the Badge*.
39. Anderson, "A True Prince of the City," p. 17.
40. Ashman, *The Finest Judges Money Can Buy*, p. 6.
41. Ibid., p. 173.
42. Gest, "Crackdown on Judges Who Go Astray," p. 42.
43. Ibid.
44. Ibid.
45. See for example, Ashman, *The Finest Judges Money Can Buy*, p. 202.
46. Knapp, *The Knapp Commission Report on Police Corruption*, p. 266.
47. Ibid., pp. 252–253.
48. See "Corruption Is Still a Fact of Life," *U.S. News and World Report*, November 1, 1982, p. 46; Gest, "Crackdown on Judges Who Go Astray," p. 42.
49. Starr and Reese, "Stinging the Chicago Courts," p. 21.
50. Ibid.
51. Smith, *Police Systems in the United States*, p. 13.
52. Gary S. Becker and George J. Stigler, "Law Enforcement Malfeasance and Compensation of Enforcers," *Journal of Legal Studies* 3 (January 1974): 6.

PART III

REEMERGENCE OF PRIVATE ALTERNATIVES

8

CONTRACTING OUT FOR LAW AND JUSTICE

While the cost of local government services has been rising, many local government decision-makers are facing considerable resistance to tax increases.[1] Costs are rising faster in the public sector than in any other major sector of the economy (except construction),[2] and local public officials are being forced to explore options that might allow them to more efficiently supply the goods and services various interest groups have demanded and have come to expect. One option that has received widespread attention is contracting out to private firms.

The interest in contracting out for the delivery of various goods and services has been heightened by several well-publicized studies whose authors imply that private profit-seeking firms can deliver the same or superior quality goods and services at a substantial cost savings over (or perhaps we should say under) public sector production.[3] Documented cost savings reach as high as 50 percent for fire services in Scottsdale, Arizona, for example.[4] The national average savings from private garbage collection in cities with over 50,000 people is 40 percent. Orange County, California, has saved 33 percent on data processing, and there are savings of from 10 to 20 percent in such services as tree trimming, pavement striping, and park maintenance.[5] Virtually everything that local governments do is being contracted out by some city somewhere, including fire services, paramedics and ambulance services, road construction and maintenance, water, parks, recreation services, garbage pick-up, tax assessment, police, and jails. By

1980, "the question of whether or not a local government should contract on its services is. . . being replaced by another: How much contracting should be encouraged?"[6]

Most of the contracting out by local governments has been for "professional and housekeeping services" like those provided by architectural, engineering, and legal firms, as well as for street construction, street and building maintenance and repairs, garbage collection, and waste disposal.[7] Contracting with private police has not been accepted as quickly.[8] But the idea of contracting for police services is beginning to catch on. A few small communities have contracted for full police services, and many more have opted for partial contracting for specialized security services such as park patrols, public housing project guards, and patrols.

A similar story can be told in the area of corrections. Record increases in the prisoner population and budgets have forced local, state, and federal administrators to consider contracting with private firms.[9] The nation's prison population increased by one-third between 1978 and 1982, and state and federal prison populations increased by approximately 74 percent from 1979 to 1986.[10] According to recent court rulings, 60 to 80 percent of the nation's jails and prisons are "overcrowded."[11] As prison costs rise, taxpayer dissatisfaction with the correctional system is mounting.[12] They see prisons as ineffective and costly, with high rates of recidivism and repeat offenders, and the critics are calling for reform and innovation. But as Peter Greenwood concluded in his study of the correctional system, "when you're looking for innovators you don't look to government; you look to business."[13]

THE CURRENT LEVEL AND SCOPE OF CONTRACTING OUT

Government units are beginning to recognize the potential benefits of partial privatization of the enterprise of law. Consider the following information on the level of contracting.

Police Services. In 1972, a survey found no city that contracted directly with a private firm for all police services, and less than one percent of cities surveyed dealt with private firms for subservice functions like crime labs.[14] Today, many local governments contract with private firms for certain traditional police functions. For example, Wackenhut, Inc., has provided patrols for parks and recreation areas to St. Petersburg, Florida, during hours of peak vandalism. Beginning in 1970, a four-man, twenty-four-hour

Wackenhut patrol provided security for a public housing project in Lexington, Kentucky. Wackenhut received a "merit of safety" award from Lexington in recognition of the fact that no crimes were reported in the area after the private patrols were instituted.[15] The firm also provides complete police services to the Tampa Airport and predeparture security at several other airports. Wackenhut provides the entire police force for the Energy Research and Development Administration's 1,600-square-mile Nevada nuclear test site.[16] The firm has a similar arrangement with the Kennedy Space Center in Florida, where it also provides fire and rescue services.

Many other firms are also getting into the police business. Houston, Texas, hired a private firm to guard its city hall.[17] IBI Security Services, Inc., which has worked for several New York City area neighborhood associations since the early 1970s, contracted with the Suffolk school district in New York for school patrol services. Maricopa County, Arizona, contracted with the Mesa Merchant Police for security services for the county's administration, superior court, mechanical engineering, and highway department buildings, as well as the general hospital.[18]

Police investigative services have also been contracted to private firms. In the mid-1960s, Florida Governor Claude Kirk was not satisfied with the performance of the public criminal justice system in his "war on organized crime" program, so he commissioned Wackenhut to fight the "war."[19] The $500,000 contract lasted about a year and led to over 80 criminal indictments; many of those arrested were local politicians and government employees. In 1973, Multi-State, Inc., began "renting" skilled narcotics agents to small-town police forces in Ohio and West Virginia.[20] Established by a former Columbus, Ohio, police chief, the firm employed thirteen former police officers with narcotics experience as "undercover" agents. In their first few months of operation, Multi-State was responsible for over 150 arrests and the seizure of about $200,000 in drugs.

One of the longest-standing contract police arrangements is in San Francisco. The northern section of the city has 62 "private police beats" which are "owned" by private "patrol specialists."[21] All of the police officers have completed academy training and have full rights to carry firearms and make arrests, but they received no public support. They are paid by the businesses, homeowners, and landlords on their "beat." Each patrolman purchases a beat from its previous owner and negotiates contracts with each property owner who wishes to purchase his services. The level of attention a customer requires determines the fee. In describing this system, Robert Poole pointed out that "the San Francisco system thus provides vast diversity of police services, tailored to the needs of the individual customers who pay for what they want."[22] In 1979, these private police would watch a vacationer's house, rotate house lights, and take in papers and mail for $10 to $20 per month; a large apartment house could have as many as six nightly inspections for $450 per month. Small retailers paid as little as $35 per month.

Perhaps the most intriguing development in recent years is communities contracting for complete police services. In 1975, Oro Valley, Arizona, contracted for police services with Rural/Metro Fire Department, Inc.[23] Guardsmark, Inc., began providing full police services to Buffalo Creek, West Virginia, in 1976.[24] Wackenhut had contracts with three separate Florida jurisdictions in 1980.[25] Reminderville, Ohio, contracted with Corporate Security, Inc., for police services in 1981.[26] Contracting for police services is becoming increasingly attractive as communities have begun to recognize its benefits in terms of cost savings and enhanced service quality.

Corrections. Perhaps the most widely used and fastest growing aspect of contracting out in law enforcement is in corrections. The Federal Bureau of Prisons has contracted out all 300 or so of its halfway-house operations since 1979, and several states are contracting some or all of their halfway-house programs.[27] In 1985, 32 states had nonsecure, community-based facilities (e.g., halfway houses, group homes, community treatment centers) under contract.[28] In that same year, approximately 34,080 juvenile offenders were held in nearly 1,996 privately run facilities nationwide. So far, most correction contracting has been for juvenile facilities and adult support services, and several for-profit firms are involved in these markets (although most of these facilities are operated by private, non-profit organizations). But almost every aspect of corrections, including food services, counseling, industrial program, maintenance, security, education, and vocational training, is under contract with private firms on a piecemeal basis.[29] More significant, however, is the move to privately owned and operated high-security institutions. The first arrangement of this kind was with RCA, which in 1975 established a high-security intensive treatment unit for 20 juveniles at Weaversville, Pennsylvania; by 1983, there were 73 private juvenile facilities with security systems (guards and/or security hardware).[30] Behavioral Systems Southwest, the first company to operate a major adult detention facility, currently runs minimum security facilities for 600 to 700 illegal aliens for the Immigration and Naturalization Service in San Diego and Pasadena, California, as well as in Arizona.[31] The company also had a contract for a facility in Aurora, Colorado, but the contract ended in 1987 when Wackenhut got a contract to build a new facility there. Behavioral

Systems Southwest also has small contracts with the U.S. Marshalls and the Federal Bureau of Prisons.

In 1985, the Federal Bureau of Prisons awarded a contract to Palo Duro Private Detention Services for a 575-bed, minimum security prison for illegal aliens. Corrections Corporation of America, Inc., formed in 1983, had two facilities operating by August 1984, and 13 facilities in five states with 3,215 beds by mid-1988.[32] Their first two contracts were for a 35-bed juvenile facility in Memphis and a 350-bed minimum security jail in Houston for the Immigration and Naturalization Service (INS). In 1985, the company received a second INS contract for a Laredo, Texas, facility with a daily population of 175.[33] It now incarcerates alien criminals for the Federal Bureau of Prisons, operates a 250-bed medium security facility for Hamilton County, Tennessee, and the Bay County jail in Panama City, Florida, and manages the Santa Fe Detention Facility. On July 1, 1988, CCA received a contract from the state of New Mexico to design, finance, construct, and operate a prison that will hold all of the state's female felons, becoming the first private minimum-through-maximum security state prison in recent history. Similarly, Southwest Detention Facilities has owned and operated county jails in Texas and Wyoming since September 1985. A private prison was opened in Marian County, Kentucky, on January 6, 1986, by U.S. Corrections Corporation as a minimum security institution for inmates nearing parole.[34] In 1987, private companies held roughly 1,200 adults for state and local governments alone (and many more were held for the federal government), and twelve states had privately run juvenile facilities.[35]

The government has prevented even more rapid privatization of prisons. Buchingham Security wanted to construct a 716-bed "interstate" jail in Lewisburg, Pennsylvania, for protective-custody prisoners from several government jurisdictions.[36] Negotiations were underway with seventeen states, and by April 1984 the company had letters of intent for more prisoners than they had planned space for. The project would have cost an estimated $20 million and was widely supported by the community, but it was abandoned following defeat of enabling legislation in the Pennsylvania legislature. Similarly, when Corrections Corporation of America proposed to take over the entire Tennessee prison system, state lawmakers turned down the offer despite substantial cost savings.

Despite these setbacks, Philip Fixler, Jr., contends

private prison construction *and* operation is the next logical step in an orderly evolution. Private firms have proven their capabilities by first providing housekeeping and support services such as prisoner transportation and medical care, then progressing to halfway houses and detention centers, and now accepting the responsibility for operating high-security facilities.[37]

Judicial Services. I could find no examples of complete contracting out in the area of judicial services. Instead, more complete privatization (e.g., arbitration, mediation, private courts) is becoming widespread. There is, however, contracting for what might be called judicial support services. In February, 1980, for example, a Pomona, California, law firm was awarded a contract to provide the municipal court with public defender services.[38] The contract covered hundreds of cases each year in which the public defender's office could not represent a defendant, primarily because of conflict of interest. Prior to the contract, these cases had been handled by court-appointed attorneys who were paid by the hour and had no incentives to efficiently conserve on the time allocated to the cases. The winner of the competitive bidding process for a 1978 pilot study, however, agreed to payment based on case volume. During the first eight months of operation, the firm's average cost per case was $205, compared to the $800 average cost under the previous system.[39]

Actually, private defense lawyers perform public defender functions quite regularly, but on a less formal basis than a contractual arrangement. A standard practice, for example, is for private defense lawyers to represent defendants where a conflict exists between multiple offenders. Arrangements are typically made on a case-by-case basis with different firms, apparently providing a way for young lawyers to gain experience.[40]

THE BENEFITS OF CONTRACTING OUT

Why should there be any difference between the quality and costs of services provided by private firms and public bureaus? The Institute for Local Self Government has dismissed contracting out for full police services as infeasible, because "there are no secret methods, known only to the private sector, of running an entire police department."[41] But the *incentives* facing public bureaucrats are very different from those facing private producers. As Robert Poole observed, "What this statement blithely ignores is the role of incentives in affecting the choices decision makers end up making."[42] It is not a difference in knowledge or even in desires that generates the cost differentials.

> In a market system dominated by private enterprise, the chief guarantor of product quality, the chief incentive to efficient operations, and the chief force

operating to hold prices reasonably close to production costs are competition coupled with the profit motive. One of the main objections to the way in which government bureaucracies operate lies in their tendency to disregard and place their own convenience over the needs and wishes of their clientele, which is attributed in turn to absence of any counterpart to the profit motive.[43]

The incentives facing bureaucrats generally lead bureau managers to strive for expanded budgets and power, with relatively little concern for efficiency. Some argue that private firms have similar incentives. They, too, want to expand and prosper, so they seek economic power. But there is a very important difference here. Private firms' desires for expanding power are limited by two factors: 1) they must produce something consumers are willing to buy at a price that consumers are *willing* to pay, and 2) they must compete for the attention of consumers in a market with other firms offering similar goods or services. Private firms must *persuade* consumers to buy their product, while government can *coerce* taxpayers into buying something they do not want. When coercive power and a bureaucrat's incentives are added to the rigidities of most civil servant employment systems, the inefficiencies of government production are not too surprising. The question becomes: Can the incentives and competitive pressures of the market system be harnessed through contracting out so bureaucratic inefficiencies can be avoided? Yes, they can be, and the benefits are likely to be significant.

In 1980, Reminderville, Ohio, and the surrounding Twinsburg Township contracted with a private security firm. The arrangement was made following an attempt by the Summit County Sheriff's Department to charge the community $180,000 per year for an emergency response service and an occasional patrol. For $90,000 a year, Corporate Security provided twice as many patrol cars and a six-minute emergency response (the sheriff department offered a 45-minute response time). The firm agreed to select trained, state-certified candidates for the police positions so the village could choose among the candidates. Corporate Security then paid the seven officers' salaries, provided and maintained two patrol cars, maintained the department's electrical, communications, and radar equipment, and carried the auto and liability insurance for the force.[44] The arrangement has been challenged by the Ohio Police Chiefs Association, but they have not been able to find anything in Ohio law to prevent it. The community has been satisfied with their private police force, and no complaints or charges have been registered.

A similar but even more completely private sector police force was established in Oro Valley, Arizona, in 1975. In Reminderville, the village officials hired, fired, disciplined, and organized the police force, but Rural/Metro Fire Department, Inc. (which provides fire protection for approximately 20 percent of Arizona's population), took responsibility for full operations management of Oro Valley's police force. Rural/Metro kept all the records required by the state and decided what equipment and how many officers were needed, what salaries to pay, and when to use non-police personnel (e.g., to write parking tickets and direct traffic)—all for $35,000 per year. As a consequence of policies established by Rural/Metro's police chief (e.g., twice-a-day checks of homes whose residents were away), burglary rates in the 3.5-square-mile town dropped from 14 to 0.7 per month and remained at that level.[45]

The Oro Valley-Rural/Metro arrangement was challenged by the Arizona Law Enforcement Officers Advisory Council, which argued that under Arizona law an employee of a private firm could not be a police officer. Rural/Metro could not bear the high court fees required to fight the challenge, so in 1977 the arrangement was terminated. In 1982, the Oro Valley police budget was $241,000, "a typical police operation with typical costs."[46]

Cost savings arise because private profit-seeking firms in competition for government contracts have strong incentives to monitor costs and avoid unnecessarily expensive means of production. For example, a Corrections Corporation of America's vice-president pointed out: "We can...get better prices from contractors. Contractors always charge the government more money."[47] Corporate Security's Reminderville police operation purchased a used Kustom HR-12 radar for $350 instead of a new one for $2,600.[48] They also used one-man patrol cars (unlike many public police forces), which studies have shown are more cost effective than two-man cars.

Perhaps the major source of savings from contracting out is labor costs. Even in corrections, 70 percent of the total costs over the useful life of a prison is in staffing.[49] Corrections Corporation of America reported that because they are not restricted by civil service rules, they can pay less in wages than government agencies by hiring nonunion labor. But labor savings go beyond avoiding public employee unions. "We can build prisons for almost nothing by designing them so they need a smaller staff," reported D. A. Wolfberg of Metro Support Services in Miami.[50] Travis Snelling, vice-president of Corrections Corporation of America, explained on CBS's *60 Minutes*:

> The major expense in corrections is personnel, and the area of personnel is a function of good corrections practice and also the design of the building in

which you're working. As an example, for a post—and that's corrections vernacular—where you have to have someone doing a function 24 hours a day at a given point in your institution, that's going to take you five-point something people per post. If you can eliminate one post by your architectural design, just one, that'll save you well over $100,000 in a given marketplace, as far as labor cost is concerned. So, if you have a large facility, and you can eliminate one or two or three posts you can start to see those type of savings start to accrue.[51]

One reason for more cost-effective government service production by private firms under contract is their flexibility. Fitch argued that one reason for the dissatisfaction with local government provision of crime control (and many other services) is that government units are not able to quickly respond to changing demands. This inability is at least partly due to "the political and organizational inflexibility of many local governments."[52] St. Petersburg, Florida, officials responded to rising vandalism in their parks and recreational facilities by contracting with a private firm rather than adding more city police, both because it was cost-effective and because it would be easier to end a private contract when the need diminished than it would be to reduce the number of public police.[53]

This flexibility has been an especially important consideration in contracting out for corrections. In 1975, for example, the Pennsylvania attorney general informed corrections officials that they could not keep hard-core juvenile delinquents in state prisons. The state's public institutional system was unable to respond quickly to this dilemma, so "they turned for help to RCA, which was then contracting with the state to provide educational programs for delinquents. RCA set up Weaversville [where Pennsylvania's worst delinquents are still kept under RCA's supervision] in a state owned building in just 10 days and was rewarded with a contract to run it."[54] Corrections Corporation of America received their contract for the Houston Immigration and Naturalization Service facility because they could build in seven months what the government would spend two or three years and millions of dollars planning.[55] When the Federal Bureau of Prisons contracted for its new medium security facility in 1985, a Bureau spokesman noted:

Rather than build our own institution for something that might be a temporary phenomenon, we decided not to take the risk. Besides it takes two or three years for us to site and build a place. This is an immediate need, which the private sector has offered to fill. If at some point we don't need the place anymore, we can terminate the contract.[56]

It is much more difficult to "terminate the contract" with a public employees' union and close a publicly owned facility.

The relative flexibility of private firms is also reflected in a greater likelihood of innovation. The profit motive reinforced by the threat of competition for contracts leads private firms to seek cost savings and quality improving innovations. As Lou Witzman, president of Arizona's Rural/Metro Fire Department, Inc., noted: "We have the greatest incentive in the world to innovate, to pioneer, to analyze every little step. Sheer survival."[57] When firms must compete every year or two to renew their contracts, they must look for ways to keep the cost (and, therefore, the price) of their services lower than that of their potential competitors, but they must still make a profit. Thus, they have tremendous incentives to look for cost-cutting innovations. In addition, if a firm offers better services than potential competitors at similar costs, then the firm will be in a strong position for contract renewal and for obtaining new contracts elsewhere.

Consider the Associated Marine Institute's facility for "serious" juvenile offenders in Florida. The Institute has implemented what is considered a "unique" program involving a four-phase process of increasing the privileges of offenders based on good behavior.[58] The juveniles start out working in a wilderness camp and gradually earn their way to a city job through a step-by-step program. Other innovations are also being made. The vice-president of Corrections Corporation of America reported to 60 Minutes that "we bring hot meals to the people versus bringing people to the classic large dining facility, which has always been a corrections problem. And so, we're operating. . .15 to 20% under what the national norm is per day, per inmate, and I'll guarantee you our food quality and nutritional levels are equal to or better than anywhere in the country."[59]

Potential cost savings through contracting out also arise because economies of scale differ for various governmentally provided services. There is no reason to expect that the optimum-size city in terms of minimizing average production cost is the same for, say, water, sewer, and police services. And there is no reason to expect that all police "subservices" are provided at minimum per-unit costs for the same size city. Even if they are, it is doubtful that most cities are of the efficient size for producing them. As Robert Poole pointed out: "Whatever the size of the city or county, it's not likely to be the optimum (most efficient) size for producing more than one or two of its public services—if that."[60]

The implication is that cities can reduce costs by purchasing services from suppliers that produce at the efficient scale of operation. Some services are likely to require relatively large-scale operations in order to achieve the cost-minimizing level of production. In those cases a single firm may contract with several customers—both private and public.[61] Several cities contract for maintenance of communications equipment, for example, because they do not have enough maintenance work to keep full-time employees busy and they cannot afford to employ a specialist.[62] Similarly, several small communities in Ohio and West Virginia contracted for professional narcotics agents from Multi-State, Inc., because their small departments could not afford to staff their own narcotics division with people of comparable skills and experience.

Other services may be more efficiently produced at scales that are smaller than what single production organizations need to serve an entire city. One example is the use of private towing services to remove illegally parked cars. These services appear to be done best when performed by a number of small units; besides, it "takes at least a certain amount of police attention away from more important duties, the more so because police forces seem to be incapable of handling towing functions efficiently."[63] Contracting out does not necessarily have to involve big firms.

There are many reasons to expect lower costs as a result of contracting out, and a substantial amount of evidence indicates that the expectations are met. Tom Beasley, president of Corrections Corporation of America, noted on *60 Minutes* that his firm's minimum security facility for illegal aliens cost $23.84 a day per inmate, including debt service and profit and operation; the same kind of facility operated by the federal government costs around $34 per day.[64] But there is some concern about the quality level of government services purchased from the private sector:

> Many local officials express the view that the quality of basic services will suffer if basic protective and other crucial services are provided privately. If the objective of a private firm is to maximize profit in the short run, the public, they believe, may not receive adequate service.
> [On the other hand]. . .elected officials have, as their basic objective, the public good, and can thus assure that public services are in fact being provided efficiently by public agencies.[65]

Mark Cunniff, director of the National Association of Criminal Justice Planners, expects private firms that provide prisons to cut back on costs by cutting back on services, making the prison situation worse than it already is.[66] Similarly, Sandy Rabinowitz of the American Civil Liberties Union sees the concept of privately provided prisons as "really frightening." The already inadequate food and medical treatment in publicly operated prisons, she believes, would only get worse because of profit incentives. There are at least two major flaws in these arguments. First, very few firms are short-run profit-maximizers. This seems to be particularly true of private firms that sell police services to government units or that provide private prisons. Many of these firms have been in business for a long time and intend to be in business for a lot longer. As Morley Safer noted on *60 Minutes*, "they are not fly-by-night outfits."[67] They have reputations to maintain so that they can continue to attract new customers. Perhaps more importantly, they are likely to have to compete for new customers and for the renewal of existing contracts. A survey of 89 municipal governments regarding contracting out found that the most frequently applied criteria used for awarding large contracts was *documented past performance*.[68]

The second flaw in the arguments against contracting out is the implicit assertion that the objective of public officials is to serve the "public good," which ensures that public production will generate quality services. But consider that in 1983, 41 states and the District of Columbia were either under court order to remedy prison conditions or were involved in litigation regarding prison conditions.[69] If a government unit demands a certain standard from a private firm, it will get it or the contract can be voided. But in public bureaucracies, civil service rules and union contracts virtually prevent the firing of one inefficient worker, let alone an entire production organization.

Compare the histories of two correctional institutions. RCA has been running the Weaversville, Pennsylvania, juvenile facility since 1975. Weaversville is small, with an average of twenty inmates at a time. It resembles a college dormitory, and "unlike many juvenile institutions, it is clean, quiet, and relaxed."[70] Thirty staff members include psychologists, caseworkers, and teachers, some of whom are specialists in remedial education. There are daily group therapy sessions and regular family visits for counseling sessions.

> "Weaversville is better staffed, organized, and equipped than any program of its size I know," said James Finckenauer, a Rutgers University professor of criminal justice who has studied delinquency programs nationwide. He thinks the fact that the facility is privately run helps: "In a lot of public institutions, you find that the staff has the attitude that it is just there to do a job and then leave at the end of the day. At Weaversville you've got people who see their job as more expansive."[71]

Contrast Weaversville with the Florida School for Boys at Okeechobee. The school was taken over from the state in 1982 by the Jack and Ruth

Eckerd Foundation, a nonprofit enterprise that had been running "wilderness experience" programs for troubled children for several years. The Foundation hoped to do a better job than the state and tried to make improvements in the facility. Neglected buildings were painted and patched, food was improved, broken toilets and screens were repaired, and dilapidated equipment was replaced. The Foundation contributed $280,000 for salaries in 1984 to attract better staff and purchased shoes for inmates and computer terminals for the education program.[72] But even though the facility was clearly improved relative to what it had been under state control, the American Civil Liberties Union and a coalition of other groups filed suit against the state of Florida because of "cruel and abusive conditions of confinement" at Okeechobee.[73] Allegations included overcrowding, unsanitary conditions, inadequate food and clothing for inmates, poor security resulting in sexual assaults on and beating of inmates, and inadequate medical care and psychological counseling.

The Eckerd Foundation was not named in the suit, "nor do most of the school's critics blame the Foundation for the alleged conditions there. Critics say that Eckerd has inherited the fruits of the state's antiquated and harsh policies toward delinquents—policies that make it difficult for anyone to run a decent facility."[74] Florida was funding Eckerd at less than half the money for each inmate that Pennsylvania was giving RCA for the Weaversville facility. On top of that, the state used Okeechobee as a "dumping ground," sending first-time offenders, hard-core delinquents, and a "large and increasing number" of retarded and severely disturbed offenders there.[75] State Senator Don Childers concluded: "I don't think there's anything Eckerd can do that will have a meaningful effect if they don't control the budget and they don't control who gets sent to them."[76] Quality services clearly must be paid for, even when profit is not the motivating force for producing the services.

This brings up another advantage of contracting out. The contracting firm shares part of the liability risk that could arise in a damage suit—clearly a benefit for taxpayers. A representative of Corrections Corporation of America told *60 Minutes* that "there is no way that...any government entity can ever completely duck their responsibility so far as liability for any actions that we take, whether it was through contracting or operating the facilities yourself. But if you are sued, our attorneys will defend you in that suit. If any damages are awarded, those damages will be borne by Corrections Corporation of America and, thereby, we will reduce the liability exposure of your state."[77] This benefits anyone harmed by a firm under contract as well, since many government entities and their employees are protected from liability for certain action.

The primary advantages gained from contracting out are virtually all (except perhaps economies of scale) generated because of the incentives that face private firms. Competition is the automatic safeguard of the market process that forces self-interested individuals to efficiently use the resources they control. There is little doubt that such competition can exist. As Savas noted, "Under the right conditions, potential contractors will compete vigorously for this [government contract] business."[78] When the municipal court in Pomona, California, requested bids for public defender services, seven firms responded.[79] In the area of contract prisons, there are already "a number of energetic competitors."[80] Fisk, et al. worried that reasonable levels of competition might not exist in the contracting process because "few, if any, private firms exist to provide [certain services]...in most places,"[81] but if the market is attractive (profitable), many firms will try to enter. These need not be previously existing firms who are already producing the same service. RCA is certainly not known for producing correctional services nor is Wackenhut, but both are actively pursuing contracts in that area. Control Data Corporation, a conglomerate that deals mainly in computers, has also bid for corrections contracts and obtained controlling interest in City Venture, which sells vocational-training programs to prisons.[82]

How do companies enter the corrections market when they have no previous experience or expertise? It is easy since, as Poole observed, "privatization is nothing more than the application of businesslike ideas to the process of dispensing justice—ideas like specialization, division of labor, and payment for services rendered."[83] Corrections Corporation of America was founded by Thomas Beasley and backed by the Massey Burch Investment Group, which also started Hospital Corporation of America. Beasley had no prison management experience, so he hired several former corrections officials, including a former commissioner of corrections from Arkansas and Virginia, and a retired chairman of the U.S. Parole Commission. Corrections Corporation is run "with large purchase orders and centralized accounting and management, and by hiring experienced professionals from public agencies to run the day-to-day affairs of the institutions."[84] The company has been one of the most active and aggressive bidders for contracts and now runs several facilities.

If production of services for sale to the government is profitable and competition is encouraged, the private sector will respond. Problems arise only if competition is eliminated. Unfortunately, there are characteristics of government that threaten competition and, therefore, the success of contracting out.

THE SHORTCOMINGS OF CONTRACTING OUT

Krajick has warned: "Efficient as these profit-making concerns may be, the institutions they run are bound to reflect to some extent the aims, the limitations, and perhaps the abuses of the government systems of which they become a part."[85] Perhaps governments will do a poor job of contracting just as they do with most other tasks they undertake. For one thing, the bureaucratic attitudes and incentives that influence government production will also affect the contracting process.

Consider the belief that "one efficient firm and a knowledgeable government official can reach an agreement to provide services at a cost no higher than it would be if ten suppliers were bidding."[86] This attitude could quickly destroy the effectiveness of the contracting process. The threat of competition forces the private firm to produce efficiently; furthermore, if an official is so "knowledgeable" why is he or she unable to keep a public bureau producing efficiently? When a single private firm is given a contract with no fear of future competition it begins acting like a monopolist, not an efficient competitor. Also, according to Fitch, "the continuous use of one or a few firms lends itself to the creation of friendly relationships which may make difficult the exercise of appropriate controls."[87]

Bureaucratic behavior by contracting agencies can destroy competition in bidding even when the bureau claims to seek competition. This occurs because government agencies have imposed a large number and variety of regulations, standards, and other requirements on the contracting process itself and on post-contract production.[88] The result is predictable:

> The high cost of obtaining government contracts, the limitations on salaries and other costs frequently imposed by government regulation, and the problems raised by zealous auditors make government contracting for the typical small firm, and for many large firms, a chancy business. The risks impel many firms to limit the amount of government business they seek, and some now go after government contracts only because of ancillary advantages (such as access to information not otherwise available).[89]

The federal government, in contracting out for prisons, for example, specifies standards for all aspects of prison life and stations observers in private institutions.[90]

The rationale for the regulations is supposedly to prevent dishonest private firms from providing poor services. Of course, a sufficiently competitive contracting process would do precisely that, as potential competitors monitor those providing services in hopes of spotting inefficiencies or abuses that will allow them to offer a superior contract. But even with all the regulations, many critics remain "afraid that contract prisons will generate the same kinds of scandals as contract nursing homes, which despite numerous inspectors and standards have still frequently become substandard facilities."[91] Such concerns are clearly warranted. As Fitch noted, many of the regulations "have the effect of putting a greater strain on honest firms than on dishonest firms, which can often find some way of beating the regulation, if only by buying cooperation of government contracting officers."[92]

This brings us to another potential barrier to competition in the contracting out process—corruption. Poole observed that "instances of corruption have occurred, in cases where the selection process was not an openly competitive situation."[93] But the threat of corruption goes beyond that. Corruption may *prevent* the selection process from being "an openly competitive situation." In fact, "contracts are one of the most common and lucrative sources of corruption in government."[94]

Political corruption becomes possible when government officials control the allocation of valuable property rights. The right to act as exclusive supplier of some government service without fear of competition can be extremely valuable, particularly if a public official is willing to turn away when a producer cuts quality to increase profits. Note that in such cases critics may be absolutely correct in arguing that private firms reduce costs by cutting quality. But this is not because of the market forces of competition. Rather, the uncorruptible market regulator called competition has been terminated and replaced by the regulation of a corrupt public official. Incentives for private contractors to engage in bribery, kickbacks, and payoffs obviously exist, and corruption is inevitable if public officials in charge of the contracting process are sufficiently self-interested.

Of course, firms do not have to resort to illegal means in order to "purchase" contracts and other advantages from government. Government decisions reflect the demands of politically active and powerful interest groups, and it is not surprising to find that "private contractors doing business with government are. . .one of the principal sources of campaign funds."[95] In fact,

In the political community, contractors are expected to make political contributions in order to be eligible for contracts. Contributions may take the form of outright bribes and graft but. . .the more popular form is the campaign contribution—outright grants, subscriptions to fund-raising dinners, and so on.

Such potlatch may be expected to take its toll by raising the costs of contract services and loosening the assiduousness of inspection, though the more cautious political operators will insist that work be at least passable, and only the more venal will tolerate [extreme reductions in quality].[96]

Corrections officials have expressed some concern that companies will now try to influence state and local politics in their drive to secure contracts.[97] A Texas law was passed in September 1983, for example, that authorized counties to contract for private jails. This "private interest bill" passed because of the political pressure brought to bear "by former lawmen interested in getting into the business" through their influence with the Texas Sheriffs' Association.[98]

In fact, one of the major reasons for the political interest in contracting out has been the political influence of firms who want to get into the contract business.[99] This political pressure has certainly had an impact. Several respondents to the Florestano-Gordon survey, for example, admitted that one "criterion" that had been important in awarding large contracts had been "political considerations."[100] In addition, "giant firms such as a Lockheed— and smaller firms whose output is crucial to certain government programs —have received special assistance to keep them in business."[101]

The implications of this discussion are much more far-reaching than simply the potential for granting contracts to relatively inefficient producers or overlooking quality cutting. For instance, some of the major criticisms of the government production of law and order are not alleviated by contracting out. One problem—bureaucratic inefficiency—may be partly overcome if corruption and the bureaucratic tendencies for over-regulation do not eventually destroy the potential for such benefits. But the other problems remain. Private firms under contract to the government will produce what interest groups want, not what individual taxpayers want. And contracting creates *new* interest groups—the contracting firms and their employees—that will demand greater output of whatever good or service they sell to the government (not unlike bureaucrats). As Levenson noted, contracting out "can make for an invisible and often a shadow work force which could result in the dependency of more people upon the government."[102] The two biggest federal departments—Health and Human Services and Defense—supported four workers under contract in 1979 for every one federal employee.[103] Contracting in law enforcement is much less significant, but it does emphasize the dangers of assuming that contracting for services will necessarily reduce the size of the resource pool controlled by government, particularly the number of persons dependent on public funds.[104] Furthermore, because consumers who directly benefit from the services do not pay a unit price, the excess demand will lead to crowding or congestion and alternative allocation techniques will have to be established. The misallocation of resources due to interest group demands and nonprice rationing could be far more significant than misallocation due to bureaucratic production inefficiencies. Thus, the major shortcoming of contracting out is that it can only overcome a few of the problems that arise from government failure: "in reality, the factors which militate against efficient production in the public sector also militate against getting highest-quality results from contracts."[105] Of course, gains in production efficiency are better than no gains at all.

ENDNOTES

1. Patricia S. Florestano and Stephen B. Gordon, "Public vs. Private: Small Government Contracting with the Private Sector," *Public Administration Review* 40 (January/February 1980): 29.

2. Lyle C. Fitch, "Increasing the Role of the Private Sector in Providing Public Services," in *Improving the Quality of Urban Management*, ed. Willis D. Hawley and David Rogers, vol. 8 of *Urban Affairs Annual Review* (Beverly Hills, Calif.: Sage Publishing, 1974), p. 502.

3. Donald Fisk, Herbert Kiesling, and Thomas Muller, *Private Provision of Public Services: An Overview* (Washington, D.C.: Urban Institute, 1978), p. 2; Florestano and Gordon, "Public vs. Private," p. 29; Robert W. Poole, Jr., *Cutting Back City Hall* (New York: Universe Books, 1978), p. 27.

4. Poole, *Cutting Back City Hall*, p. 27.

5. Ibid.

6. Rosaline Levenson, "Public Use of Private Service Contracts in Local Government: A Plea for Caution," in *Public-Private Collaboration in the Delivery of Local Public Services: Proceedings of a Conference* (Davis: University of California, April 1980), p. 18.

7. Florestano and Gordon, "Public vs. Private," p. 34.

8. Robert Poole, Jr., "Why Not Contract Policing?" *Reason* 14 (September/ October 1983): 10.

9. Kevin Krajick, "Punishment for Profit," *Across the Board* 21 (March 1984): 20–21.

10. Robert W. Poole, Jr., "Rehabilitating the Correctional System," *Fiscal Watchdog* 81 (July 1983): 4; President's Commission on Privatization, *Privatization: Toward More Effective Government* (Washington, D.C.: President's Commission on Privatization, March 1988), p. 146.

11. Poole, ibid., p. 3.
12. On prison costs, see E. W. Zedlewski, "The Economics of Disincarceration," *NIS Reports* (May 1984): 4–8; U.S. Department of Justice, *Report to the Nation on Crime and Justice: The Data* (Washington, D.C.: Bureau of Justice Statistics, 1983), p. 93; B. Cory and S. Gettings, *Time to Build? The Realities of Prison Construction* (New York: Edna McConnell Clark Foundation, 1984), p. 17; Charles H. Logan and Sharla P. Rausch, "Punishment and Profit: The Emergence of Private Enterprise Prisons," *Justice Quarterly* 2 (September 1985); p. 304; Poole, "Rehabilitating the Correctional System," p. 3; G. Funke, *Who's Buried in Grant's Tomb?—Economics and Corrections for the Eighties and Beyond* (Alexandria, Va.: Institute for Economic Policy Studies, 1983), p. 3.
13. Quoted in Poole, "Rehabilitating the Correctional System," p. 3.
14. Fisk, et al., *Private Provision of Public Services*, p. 33.
15. Ibid.
16. Poole, *Cutting Back City Hall*, pp. 41–42.
17. Ibid., p. 40.
18. Fisk, et al. *Private Provision of Public Services*, pp. 33–34.
19. Ibid., p. 34.
20. "Rent-a-Narc," *Newsweek*, August 27, 1973. p. 25.
21. Christine Dorffi, "San Francisco's Hired Guns," *Reason* 10 (August 1979).
22. Poole, *Cutting Back City Hall*, p. 39.
23. Theodore Gage, "Cops Inc.," *Reason* 14 (November 1982): 25.
24. Poole, *Cutting Back City Hall*, p. 42.
25. Ibid., p. 43.
26. Gage, "Cops, Inc.," p. 24.
27. Poole, "Rehabilitating the Correctional System," p. 1.
28. Joan Mullen, Kent Chabotar, and Deborah Carrow, *The Privatization of Corrections*, Abt Associates report to the National Institute of Justice (Washington, D.C.: U.S. Department of Justice, February 1985), pp. 56–68.
29. Logan and Rausch, "Punishment and Profit," p. 307.
30. Ibid., p. 307. Also see Charles H. Logan, *Private Prisons: Cons and Pros: A Report to the National Institute of Justice* (Washington, D.C.: National Institute of Justice, 1989).
31. Philip E. Fixler, Jr., "Can Privatization Solve the Prison Crisis?" *Fiscal Watchdog* 90 (April 1984): 2.
32. "Operating Private Prisons," *Venture* (August 1983): 18; Corrections Corporations of America press release, July 26, 1988.
33. Logan and Rausch, "Punishment and Profit," p. 307.
34. Peter Binzen, "Free Enterprise: Private Concerns Begin Delivering Public Services," *Philadelphia Inquirer*, August 12, 1984, p. 10-C.
35. Judith C. Hackett, et al., "Contracting for the Operation of Prisons and Jails," *Research in Brief: National Institute of Justice*, June 1987, p. 2.

36. Logan and Rausch, "Punishment and Profit," p. 307.
37. Fixler, "Can Privatization Solve the Prison Crisis?" p. 4.
38. Poole, "Can Justice Be Privatized?" p. 1.
39. Ibid., pp. 1–2.
40. This information was provided by Randy Barnett in his review of an earlier draft of this book.
41. Quoted in Poole, "Why Not Contract Policing?" p. 11.
42. Ibid., p. 11.
43. Fitch, "Increasing the Role of the Private Sector," p. 509.
44. Gage, "Cops, Inc.," p. 23.
45. Ibid., p. 26.
46. Ibid.
47. Krajick, "Punishment for Profit," p. 24.
48. Poole, "Why Not Contract Policing?" p. 11.
49. "Privatization Spreads to Prisons," *Energy News-Record*, April 5, 1984, p. 10.
50. Ibid.
51. "Crime Pays," *60 Minutes*, vol. 14, no. 11, transcript of a broadcast over the CBS Television Network, Sunday, November 25, 1984, 7:00–8:00 p.m., EST, p. 10.
52. Fitch, "Increasing the Role of the Private Sector," p. 502.
53. Fisk, et al., *Private Provision of Public Services*, p. 36.
54. Krajick, "Punishment for Profit," pp. 22–23.
55. Ibid., p. 24.
56. Ibid., p. 23.
57. Quoted in Poole, *Cutting Back City Hall*, p. 28.
58. Poole, "Rehabilitating the Correctional System," p. 3.
59. "Crime Pays," p. 10.
60. Poole, *Cutting Back City Hall*, p. 28.
61. This source of cost savings is not a result of incentives, but rather of technological production relationships. Thus, a community may be able to reduce its costs of, say, police services by contracting with another government unit. See for example, Poole, "Why Not Contract Policing?" p. 10.
62. Fisk, et al., *Private Provision of Public Services*, p. 35.
63. Fitch, "Increasing the Role of the Private Sector," p. 510.
64. "Crime Pays," p. 10.
65. Fisk, et al., *Private Provision of Public Services*, p. 2.
66. Krajick, "Punishment for Profit," p. 27.
67. "Crime Pays," p. 8.
68. Florestano and Gordon, "Public vs. Private," p. 32.
69. Logan and Rausch, "Punishment and Profit," p. 304.
70. Krajick, "Punishment for Profit," p. 25.
71. Ibid.

72. Ibid., p. 27.
73. Ibid., p. 25.
74. Ibid.
75. Ibid., p. 26.
76. Quoted in ibid.
77. "Crime Pays," pp. 9–10.
78. E. S. Savas, "Municipal Monopolies Versus Competition in Delivering Urban Services," in *Improving the Quality of Urban Management*, ed. Willis D. Hawley and David Rogers, vol. 8 of *Urban Affairs Annual Review* (Beverly Hills, Calif.: Sage Publishing, 1974), p. 489.
79. Poole, "Can Justice Be Privatized?"
80. Krajick, "Punishment for Profit," p. 24.
81. Fisk, et al., *Private Provision of Public Services*, p. 8.
82. Krajick, "Punishment for Profit," p. 24.
83. Poole, "Can Justice Be Privatized?" p. 3.
84. Krajick, "Punishment for Profit," p. 23.
85. Ibid., p. 24.
86. Fisk, et al., *Private Provision of Public Services*, p. 5.
87. Fitch, "Increasing the Role of the Private Sector in Providing Public Services," p. 512.
88. Ibid., p. 517.
89. Ibid., p. 518.
90. Kevin Krajick, "Private, For-Profit Prisons Take Hold in Some States," *Christian Science Monitor*, April 11, 1984, p. 27.
91. Ibid.
92. Fitch, "Increasing the Role of the Private Sector," p. 517.
93. Poole, *Cutting Back City Hall*, p. 29.
94. Fitch, "Increasing the Role of the Private Sector," p. 517.
95. Ibid., p. 516.
96. Ibid., p. 513.
97. Krajick, "Punishment for Profit," p. 27.
98. Ibid., p. 27.
99. Fisk, et al., *Private Provision of Public Services*, p. 2.
100. Florestano and Gordon, "Public vs. Private," p. 32.
101. Fitch, "Increasing the Role of the Private Sector," p. 518.
102. Levenson, "Public Use of Private Service Contracts in Local Government," p. 21.
103. Barbara Blumenthal, "Uncle Sam's Army of Invisible Employees," *National Journal*, May 5, 1979, pp. 730–733.
104. Levenson, "Public Use of Private Service Contracts in Local Government," p. 21.
105. Fitch, "Increasing the Role of the Private Sector," p. 504.

9

CURRENT TRENDS
IN PRIVATIZATION

There are now more private security personnel than public law enforcement personnel in the United States, and during the past fifteen to twenty years, the growth rate of the private securities industry has substantially outpaced that of public law enforcement.[1] As Lawrence Sherman observed, "Few developments are more indicative of public concern about crime—and declining faith in the ability of public institutions to cope with it—than the burgeoning growth in private policing. . . . Rather than approving funds for more police, the voters have turned to volunteer and paid private watchers. . . ."[2] But private responses to crime have gone well beyond voluntary participation and hiring guards. During the 1960s and 1970s, when crime rates were rising rapidly, households and firms adopted private means of protection "on an unprecedented scale,"[3] including the increased use of alarm systems, safes, automatic telephone dialers, window bars, and other protection devices. Private sector involvement in the enterprise of law is quite substantial.

PRIVATE CRIME PREVENTION AND DETECTION

Sherman classified crime control into three categories: 1) "watching," 2) "walling," and 3) "wariness."[4] "Watching" refers to observing people and places that criminals may attack and apprehending criminals in the act.

"Walling" describes actions designed to prevent criminal access to persons or property through locks, bars, fences, and other obstructions. "Wariness" characterizes adjustments in behavior to avoid crime, such as self-defense or firearms classes, staying home at night, and leaving lights on when away from home. All of these activities are on the rise.

The *Figgie Report on Fear of Crime* asked citizens what protective measures they take in their homes and when they go out. "The answers revealed an extremely cautious and security-minded America."[5] For instance, 56 percent of those responding to the survey said they kept their car doors locked most of the time while driving, and 70 percent did so more often than not. Sixty percent phoned at least sometimes to inform others that they had safely reached their destination when traveling, and 44 percent indicated that they often planned their travel routes to avoid potentially dangerous places. When going out at night, 25 percent of the sample frequently had a whistle, carried a weapon, or were accompanied by a dog. Fifty-four percent of the women made certain they had a companion for trips at night (only 15 percent of the males surveyed took such action). Seventy-eight percent of blacks dressed plainly to avoid attracting attention, while only 54 percent of the whites surveyed did so.[6]

Almost everyone interviewed for the *Figgie* survey locked their doors when leaving and made people identify themselves before opening doors. Fifty-two percent had added extra locks to their doors, 82 percent had someone watch their homes when they were away for a weekend, and 70 percent had newspaper and mail delivery stopped. Approximately one-fourth of the survey sample had automatic timers to switch lights on and off, and many had installed more sophisticated devices to turn the television or stereo on and off as well. Fifteen percent had burglar alarms and 8 percent barred windows. In addition, 36 percent of the survey had engraved their valuables in the hope of discouraging theft or aiding in the recovery of stolen items.[7]

"Quite often the gun is a household protective device," the report found. "Gun ownership *clearly* has the effect of substantially reducing formless fear" of crime.[8] Of the 1,043 respondents to the *Figgie Report*'s questionnaire, 542 indicated that they owned a gun to protect their homes. An estimated fifty million guns are in private hands in the U.S, and the Federal Bureau of Alcohol, Tobacco, and Firearms reported domestic production of 835,169 pistols and 1,702,062 revolvers in 1981, with another 305,576 guns imported that year.

And people are using their guns for protection. Private citizens legally shoot almost as many criminals as public police do, while in some places citizens legally kill up to two or three times as many violent criminals as do police. There were 126 justifiable homicides by private citizens in California during 1981, compared to 68 justifiable homicides by police. Residents of Houston, Texas, killed 25 criminal suspects in 1981 and 17 during the first ten months of 1982. Residents of Dallas killed 13 suspects in self-defense in 1981, while 15 criminals died at the hands of private citizens in New York that year. Houston police and prosecutors concluded that the city's rising crime rate (up 17.7 percent in the first half of 1982) was a key factor in the shootings by citizens, as "residents and small-business owners in Houston are turning to deadly force to protect themselves and their property."[9] Private citizens not only own guns for protection, but they are using them.

Corporate Executives.   The *Figgie Report* also examined the effects of rising crime on corporate policy and the lifestyle of *Fortune 1000* business executives. Seventy-five percent of the senior executives surveyed secured their homes with burglar and fire alarms, had guards and guard dogs, had unlisted phone numbers, or kept their addresses confidential.[10] In addition, 46 percent of the surveyed executives nationwide and 62 percent of those in large cities indicated that crime in their corporate neighborhoods had affected programming, planning, and security policies. Most corporate headquarters had a "vast array" of security procedures and devices: 88 percent had building security checks; 87 percent had fire alarms; 84 percent had automatic sprinkler systems; 66 percent had burglar alarms; 64 percent had flood-lighting; 50 percent had automatic light timers; 48 percent had closed circuit television; 38 percent had electronic card identification systems; 30 percent had photoelectric timers; and 24 percent had armed guards.[11] Four hundred of the 1,000 companies used at least six of these ten security systems, and unarmed guards, plainclothes security personnel, and coded door locks were common. Most of the surveyed corporations also had comprehensive security programs, including education programs for employees (73 percent), crisis management plans (63 percent), and employment of a security specialist (62 percent).

Corporate executives took numerous measures to protect themselves and their families. Fifty-three percent of those surveyed had burglar and fire alarms in their homes, for example. Thirty-five percent varied their daily route to work, and 19 percent alternated cars. The *Figgie Report* concluded: "It's obvious that the development of a corporate security program is a tremendously time-consuming, cumbersome, and expensive process that places a burden on the employee as well as the employer."[12]

Efforts to avoid crime are expensive. A 1970 study by Predicast, Inc., estimated that sales of crime deterrent equipment grew at an annual rate of 8.8 percent between 1958 and 1963, increasing to 11 percent between 1963 and 1968 (see Tables 9.1 and 9.2). Sales of monitoring and detection equipment grew by 7.1 percent per year over the 1958–1963 period and 10.4 percent per year from 1963 to 1968. These equipment sales accounted for considerably less than half the total expenditures on security during this period (41 percent in 1958 and 36 percent in 1968). The largest category of spending was for guard and investigative services.

Table 9.1   Sales of Private Security Equipment ($ Million).

Products	1958	1963	1968
Deterrent Equipment			
Fixed Security Equipment			
Safes and chests	15	14	21
Safe deposit boxes	9	12	15
Bank vaults and other bank equipment	21	33	54
Insulated filing cabinets	11	12	12
Other fixed security equipment	13	20	42
Total	69	91	144
Security Lighting Equipment			
High intensity lamps	8	15	31
Area floodlighting systems	12	27	45
Poles and accessory items	3	7	15
Total	23	49	91
Total Deterrent Equipment	92	140	235
Monitoring and Detection Equipment			
Central Station Alarm Services	55	80	110
Local and Proprietary Alarms	30	36	54
CCTV Devices	5	9	23
Detection, Surveillance, and Other	27	40	83
Total Monitoring and Detection	117	165	270
Fire-Control Equipment	83	118	245
Total Security Equipment	511	780	1,395

SOURCE: Predicast, Inc., "Special Study 56" (March 5, 1970).

Table 9.2   Market for Sales of Private Security Equipment.

Market	1958	1963	1968
Financial, Commercial and Retail	190	274	468
Industrial and Transportation	249	393	729
Consumer	10	15	23
Institutions and Others	62	98	175
Total	511	780	1,395

SOURCE: Predicast, Inc., "Special Study 56" (March 5, 1970).

The industry anticipated spending approximately $5.3 billion in intruder detection equipment sales alone during 1980–1985, with half of those purchases being made in North America.[13] There is a growing business in providing bullet-proof cars and vehicle security systems for those in positions of wealth or power who face high risks of assassination or kidnapping. In 1983, there were roughly a dozen U.S. firms specializing in armoring cars at prices ranging from $32,000 to $250,000, depending on the degree of safety required. Many other privately provided forms of protection equipment are available to those willing to pay.[14]

VOLUNTARY GROUP ACTION AGAINST CRIME

A recent Gallup poll indicated that organized volunteer crime prevention efforts were in place in the neighborhoods of 17 percent of the Americans surveyed.[15] Voluntary groups have sponsored and organized youth-oriented activities to keep young people off the streets, neighborhood improvement programs, organized property protection activities (e.g., Operation ID), escort services, and neighborhood and building patrols. Some groups have even bought the streets and fenced in their neighborhoods. Participatory organizations may not be the dominant institutions of the enterprise of law that they were in Anglo-Saxon England, but they are certainly important.

Programs for Youth. "Most of the activities reported as 'doing something about crime,' " Podolefsky and Dubow concluded in 1981, "involve attempts by groups of neighbors to improve the 'quality of life' in their neighborhood."[16] In particular, voluntary efforts are directed to keeping children from turning to criminal activities. In a random digit telephone survey of residents of San Francisco, Chicago, and Philadelphia, Podolefsky and

Dubow found that youth-oriented activities accounted for 19.9 percent of all crime control activities, the largest proportion of all group anti-crime activities. These activities included providing employment or recreation for youths (70 percent of all efforts in this activity group) as well as counseling and dealing with gang problems.[17] Many volunteers see youth programs designed to keep children busy, particularly sports programs, as major contributions to crime control, but many groups indicate that "recreation is not enough, there is a need to combine education, economics and recreation."[18] Thus, community groups also provide activities ranging from job counseling to employment opportunities. One community group even tried to set up a non-profit business to hire youths, using funds donated by local businessmen.

Neighborhood Improvement. Voluntary groups pursued programs to 1) improve the physical and social conditions of their neighborhoods or communities, 2) alter conditions seen as particularly conducive to crime, 3) reduce access to the community, 4) make changes that facilitate group watching efforts (e.g., pruning trees and shrubs or installing lighting), and 5) improve the overall economic conditions of the area. Improving or cleaning up the neighborhood was the third most frequently mentioned crime control activity in the Podolefsky-Dubow survey, accounting for 8 percent of the responses.[19] Neighborhood groups cleaned up streets, parks, alleys, business areas, and housing projects and fixed or destroyed abandoned buildings to make the area more hospitable. Groups have also tried to establish or improve neighborhood recreational facilities. One group responding to the Podolefsky-Dubow survey, for example, claimed responsibility for closing six blocks to traffic to allow for children's play.

Another, but relatively infrequent, group activity is the "sanctioning of wrongdoers" (e.g., drug addicts, pushers, drunks, prostitutes, and troublesome families) in an attempt to expel them from the community. After the murder of a seventeen-year-old youth, for example, a community group in South Philadelphia organized a demonstration to pressure drug dealers (who apparently were not connected with the murder) to leave the neighborhood. Between 500 and 900 residents marched to the residence of two dealers and shouted at them for 45 minutes to get them to leave. The dealers did not return.[20] It should be noted that such sanctioning activities are illegal according to authoritarian law. Such actions are not necessarily to be commended, but they should be noted in order to stress that private individuals, when faced with a choice between breaking a legislated law and taking what they perceive to be a protective action, may choose to break the authoritarian law. Illegal firearm ownership for protection is another example of such behavior.

The norms of the community may ultimately rule even when they conflict with statutory law. Such "vigilante" behavior is a part of our American tradition, and as Roger McGrath observed:

> The classic era of frontier vigilantism ended by 1900. . . . However, a tradition of "neo-vigilantism" lives on. Examples include. . .the self-protection patrol groups of the 1960s and 1970s operating in urban neighborhoods beset by crime or racial problems. The ideology of vigilantism, which stresses popular sovereignty, self-preservation, and the right of revolution, continues to attract Americans even though frontier rationales for vigilantism have disappeared.[21]

The vigilante tradition is still alive, but McGrath is incorrect in claiming that the "rationale" has disappeared. When it imposes laws, the government has a reciprocal duty to adequately enforce those laws. When government fails to adequately fulfill its duty, it has been the custom in both English and American society to re-establish the rule of customary law through revolution or vigilante justice.

Property Protection.   Community groups promote awareness and home security by holding meetings, arranging lectures, and distributing crime prevention literature.[22] Some groups go beyond simply providing information by organizing property engraving (e.g., Operation I.D.) programs that advocate marking valuables. Participants are also urged to display decals that announce to potential burglars that they have marked their property.[23] Participation in such programs is estimated to range from 10 to 25 percent in target areas, and 31 percent of those surveyed by Podolefsky and Dubow reported marking their property.[24]

Personal Protection.   Group personal protection activities include escort services and organized responses to signaling devices (e.g., whistles or freon horns), as well as educational programs. Escort services are typically designed for a particular purpose, such as escorting senior citizens when they cash pension, social security, or welfare checks, accompanying children home from day care centers, or escorting women students crossing a campus after dark.

The Podolefsky-Dubow survey found that 5 percent of the respondents carried signaling devices.[25] Many people participated in such programs as

WhistleSTOP, a community signal system. Participants carry a whistle that they can blow in emergencies or if they encounter trouble in the streets. Other WhistleSTOP members respond to a signal by first calling the police and then blowing their own whistles to signal others that a crime situation or emergency exists.

Surveillance Patrols.   In 1977, between 800 and 900 resident patrols operated in urban areas with over 250,000 people, and there were over 50,000 block watches nationwide.[26] An estimated 63 percent of the patrols were composed of volunteers, 18 percent hired guards, 7 percent paid residents, and the remaining 12 percent involved a combination of voluntary and hired watchers. Patrols can be found in neighborhoods at all income levels (an estimated 55 percent of all patrols are found in low income areas, 35 percent in middle income areas, and 10 percent in high income neighborhoods). Building patrols frequently operate in low crime areas for preventative purposes, and neighborhood patrols are often formed in areas experiencing serious crime problems. In 1980, roughly 10,000 of New York's 39,000 city blocks had functioning block associations to compensate for inadequate city services, and nearly all had some kind of security patrol.[27]

Building patrols typically operate in areas that receive little attention from public police. Such patrols are primarily intended to deter crime and keep undesirable strangers out of the building. These patrols often place guards at building entrances or gates, and they may also use closed circuit televisions and other electronic aids. One building patrol set up by the Woodlawn Organization for the TWO housing complex in a predominantly black neighborhood of Philadelphia adopted an especially interesting strategy. Most of the TWO patrol force were or had been members of the Blackstone Rangers gang. Staff members hired gang members "because they know the area and the gangsters. That has a pretty good effect on some people who might be involved in burglaries."[28] Residents of the housing complex reported few crime problems and said that the areas with TWO patrols were very safe.[29]

Neighborhood patrols primarily cover streets and public areas rather than buildings. Unlike building patrols, neighborhood patrols have frequent contact with public police and often may coordinate their efforts with police. If the patrols are responsible for large areas, they are not likely to be able to distinguish strangers from residents so they must focus on observing undesirable or suspicious behavior. Neighborhood patrols may operate on foot or in cars, and some observe crime-prone areas from fixed vantage points in buildings. They often employ radios to report observations to a base station or directly to the police.

A "typical" voluntary patrol might be the East Midwood Patrol in Brooklyn.[30] In 1980, the patrol had 120 volunteer members who performed all-night patrols 365 days per year. They taught security techniques to households and watched for prowlers and muggers. Expenses were covered by $10/year donations from houses in the 25-block patrol area; 85 percent of the households contributed in 1980.

Many neighborhood patrols supplement police services and are organized with the help of public police. Others have taken a more adversarial role, substituting for a perceived lack of public police presence.[31] For instance, the West Park Community Protection Agency was organized by a black resident of Philadelphia because "when Blacks began moving into the area police became lax."[32] The organizer performed stakeouts and patrols, checked in with businesses and signed in on police sign-in sheets. The police initially accused him of vigilantism, but they eventually recognized the benefits of cooperating with the West Park patrol group, and after a change in the organization's name, links with police were established. But this kind of cooperation does not always develop. The Black Panthers began as a small ghetto patrol organization but not to protect the neighborhood from criminals. "Blacks wanted protection from the. . . [police department] that was supposed to protect them," so the Panthers supplied "guards for the guards" by following the police cars that patrolled the area and monitoring arrests.[33] They carried legal weapons to discourage the idle harassment of blacks by police. The Black Panthers subsequently became involved in some controversial projects, and little cooperation between the group and police appears to have developed.

Private Streets.   One of the most complete cooperative privatization schemes in recent history is underway in St. Louis and University City, Missouri. As Oscar Newman noted,

> the decline of St. Louis, Missouri, has come to epitomize the impotence of federal, state, and local resources in coping with the consequences of large scale population change. Yet buried within those very areas of St. Louis which have been experiencing the most radical turnover of population are a series of streets where residents have adopted a program to stabilize their communities to deter crime, and to guarantee the necessities of a middle-class life-style. These residents have been able to create and maintain for themselves what their city was no longer able to provide: low crime rates, stable property values and a

sense of community. . . . The distinguishing characteristic of these *streets* is that they have been deeded back from the city to the residents and are now legally *owned and maintained by the residents themselves.*[34]

The continued existence of private streets in St. Louis, along with increased petitioning by residents for the conversion of their streets to private status, indicates that privatizing and closure provide increased security and stability. In 1970, for example, Westminster Place in St. Louis was dying economically. Middle income residents had seen property values plummet during the 1960s as "urban blight" set in. In addition, an estimated 6,000 cars per day used Westminster Place to avoid traffic lights on nearby major boulevards. Prostitutes found the neighborhood to be an attractive business area. But in 1970 the remaining residents petitioned the city to deed the streets to them: "Standing up to the urban blight, the crime, and the fear that causes residents to flee, the people of [Westminster Place and several other] neighborhoods. . .found an unconventional solution to a common problem—they bought their neighborhoods."[35]

The city complied with the requests for privatization in return for the residents' assumption of responsibility for street, sewer, and streetlight maintenance, garbage pickup, and any security services above normal fire and police response. The titles to the streets are vested in an incorporated street association to which all property owners must belong and pay dues. The street associations, most of which own one or two blocks, have the right to close the street to traffic, so the only cars on the street belong to residents and their visitors. "It is *their* street and that ownership gives the neighborhood a high degree of cohesiveness."[36] Indeed, a large study of St. Louis and University City private streets found that residents "needed assurance that neighboring homeowners shared both their values and financial capacity to maintain the standards of homeownership. . .concern for security of their investment was a critical factor which led urban oriented residents to the selection of a house on a private street."[37] The study found that such cooperative behavior has substantially reduced crime. A comparison of crime rates on private streets and adjacent public streets found significantly lower crime on private streets in virtually every category. The crime rate was 108 percent higher on an adjacent public street than on Ames Place, a private street. In general, private streets surrounded by socially dissimilar populations in high-crime areas have substantially lower levels of crime than their neighbors.[38] Newman concluded: "The ultimate effect of this symbolic definition of the street is that residents come to think of the street as their neighborhood.[39]

Privatization creates a bond that allows for reciprocal cooperation in crime prevention that is reminiscent of the Anglo-Saxon neighborhood tithing system. If a stranger enters the area he is likely to be noticed. As a consequence, privatization of streets appears to have the greatest effect in deterring crimes against persons and crimes of opportunity, such as assault, purse snatching, and auto-related theft.[40] Criminals apparently realize that private street residents are more likely to notice them as strangers, so crime rates are lower on middle-income private streets despite their proximity to poorer neighborhoods.

Such private street arrangements are becoming increasingly common, although few examples are documented to the same degree as the St. Louis arrangement. Many residential and commercial developments involve private streets and private security arrangements. The development I live in in Tallahassee, Florida, has private streets including rules for traffic flow and a neighborhood crime watch to supplement the county sheriff's provision of general police services. Other developments in the area have more substantial private security, with walls, private security guards, or gates requiring codes for entry. In California and Florida, entire developments have been walled and security guards are posted at the gates.[41] Large commercial developments generally have their own security force and traffic enforcement, and shopping centers typically have lanes for traffic flow in their expansive parking lots, with stop signs, fire lanes, and other traffic control rules. Private streets are not very unusual.

PRIVATE POLICE

During the 1960s, contract and security services expenditures and employment grew by 170 and 130 percent.[42] According to a Virginia law enforcement research firm, in a report prepared for the Department of Justice, private security services now involve substantially more employment and money than local, state, and federal law enforcement services combined.[43] Table 9.3 details the number of firms and employees in detective agencies and the protective services industry (SIC 7393). This is only a fraction of the total employment of private police and guards, however, since many firms and organizations have their own security forces. For instance, there were an estimated 142,000 private guards in California alone in 1984. "They seem to be visible on nearly every city block—wherever there are office buildings and industrial plants that stand as inviting targets of theft, arson or sabotage."[44] In 1982, $21.7 billion was paid to an estimated 1.1 million full-time security employees, 449,000 of them in individual enterprises,

Table 9.3   Number of Firms and Employees in SIC 7393: Detective
Agency and Protective Services, 1964–1981.

Year	Number of Firms	Number of Employees
1964	1988	62,170
1965	2146	71,427
1966	2418	85,057
1967	2558	96,614
1968	2981	118,451
1969	3145	133,238
1970	3389	151,637
1971	3570	163,700
1972	3822	182,665
1973	4182	202,561
1974	5295	249,663
1975	5533	253,125
1976	5841	248,050
1977	6312	268,684
1978	6204	287,380
1979	6502	310,333
1980	6752	337,617
1981	7126	331,294
% Changes		
1964–81	285.5%	432.9%
1970–79	91.9%	104.7%

SOURCE: County Business Patterns (Washington, D.C.: U.S. Department of Commerce, Bureau of the Census, various years.

and the rest involved with contractual services (guard units, investigation, alarm services, etc.).[45] Large numbers of new firms enter the market virtually every year, while the average size of firms has also grown. Each firm employed an average of 31.3 employees in 1964, which increased to 46.5 in 1981. Furthermore, security industry experts expect the growth rate in private security to accelerate even more as private firms take over more responsibility for crime control.

Private police perform many functions beyond patrolling or guarding residential buildings, neighborhoods, and corporate headquarters. They also provide security for airports, sports arenas, hospitals, colleges, state and municipal government buildings, banks, manufacturing plants, hotels, and retail stores. They provide armored-car services and central-station alarm systems. Private security employees range from minimum-wage contract guards or watchmen in retail establishments where skill requirements are minimal, to guard positions in corporate headquarters that required college educations and substantial additional training, to highly trained body-guards and security consultants. The industry has developed a high level of specialization over the last 25 years. In fact, "there is emerging a new security person, highly trained, more highly educated and better able to satisfy the growing intricacies of the security profession."[46]

The market for police is growing for several reasons. The rising crime rate of the 1960s contributed to the industry's growth, but that growth has continued during the 1970s and 1980s when crime rates have been somewhat more stable. Furthermore, as the Hallerest Systems report noted, the accelerating growth in private security employment has occurred at the same time that "growing numbers of Americans undertook self-help measures against crime, increasing the use of locks, lighting, guns, burglar alarms, [and] citizen patrols."[47] Technology has played an important role in the rapid expansion of private police services as new electronic equipment has made detection and deterrence more efficient. Training has also improved dramatically, making private police more attractive sources of security. Finally, the net effect of all private sector crime control efforts has been to reduce the demand for city police services relative to what it would be, so there has been a transfer of the policing function from the public to the private sector.[48]

PRIVATE COURTS

During the last several years, private courts have come into existence to resolve many disputes. The private sector has not yet moved into criminal adjudication to a great extent, but there are indications that such a move may be underway. Furthermore, one of the primary reasons for the rapid expansion of private courts in dispute resolution is the long pre-trial delays in the public court system. Because criminal cases can move ahead of civil cases on the court docket, civil litigations suffer the greatest delay, which gives greater incentive to move the cases out of public courts.

Mediation and arbitration are the primary techniques of nonjudicial dispute resolution.[49] Mediation involves impartial third parties who help the parties in dispute reach an agreement. Arbitration involves impartial persons who are given authority to determine the outcome of the dispute. Mediators generally work toward a compromise, but arbitrators reach decisions based on the merits of the case. Both non-judicial mediation and arbitration are used in commercial and consumer disputes, labor-management relations, neighborhoods and family strife, and even in environmental clashes. It has been suggested that "the manifold possible applications of various forms of dispute resolution are just beginning to be explored."[50] But such methods of dispute resolution have a much longer history than do government courts, and their "possible applications" are simply beginning to re-emerge.

Mediation.   Mediation has been an integral part of business practice for as long as trade has been significant. As Edmund Burke explained in 1791, "the world is governed by go-betweens. These go-betweens influence the person with whom they carry on the intercourse, by stating their own sense to each of them as the sense of the other; and thus they reciprocally master both sides."[51] When an agreement between two parties is reached with the aid of a go-between, then the agreement is reached through mediation. There is a mediation element in the negotiation of many and perhaps all contracts. "That there is a close connection between *mediation* and the ordering principle of contract certainly requires no demonstration. . . . One of the most common tasks of the mediator is to facilitate the negotiation of complicated contracts."[52] Therefore, because ever-increasing specialization and trade characterizes all modern societies and increasingly complex contractual agreements are needed to facilitate such trade, the use of mediation in this area has been growing continuously for centuries.

One of the most visible uses of mediation is in labor-management disputes. The consequence of this conflict resolution generates mutual gains, which are sought by two traders and achieved with the help of a mediator. Trade that requires a contract typically involves two parties attracted by potential reciprocal gains and repelled by lack of mutual familiarity and trust. The level of trust may be sufficient for two parties to negotiate their contract without a mediator, of course, but under these circumstances the two parties have joined to perform the "mediational function."[53] Potential conflict still exists, or the contract would not be necessary.

Mediation can resolve a dispute only when both parties *voluntarily* agree to the *suggested* solution. Thus, there must be potential for reciprocal gain if mediation is to be a viable option for solving a disagreement. Indeed, a primary "function that the mediator can perform . . . [is] that of reminding the parties that their negotiations constitute a cooperative enterprise and that one does not necessarily make a gain for himself simply because he denies the other fellow something he wants."[54]

One particular example of mediation is especially intriguing. It is typically argued that the existence of environmental externalities requires intervention by a coercive authority because private sector individuals will not be able to solve such problems (this argument parallels the argument for authoritarian provision of law and order in Chapter 11). But environmental disputes are increasingly being solved through private mediation. For instance, a proposed logging operation in South Carolina's Francis Marion National Forest threatened the nesting grounds of the rare Backman's warbler. As Denenberg and Denenberg reported: "The warbler dispute. . .was settled simply and amicably, because the antagonists, the National Wildlife Federation and the U.S. Forest Service, hit upon an ingenious way around their impasse."[55] Each side of the dispute chose a biologist to sit on a mediating panel, and they jointly chose a third. After six months of deliberation, the three scientists proposed that no logging would occur in the bottomland hardwoods environment the warblers preferred, and that cutting of upland pines would be allowed. Both sides accepted the recommendation.

A National Wildlife Federation attorney found the experience to be "unexpectedly agreeable" and concluded that a judge and jury clearly are not always needed to solve environmental disputes. "Increasingly, his belief is shared on both sides of the environmental battle lines, reflecting *disenchantment with the courtroom as the forum for making decisions* about the use of natural resources, protection of flora and fauna, preservation of clean air and water, disposal of toxic wastes, and a host of related issues. The antagonists have begun to turn to the services of an *expanding corps of environmental mediators.*"[56]

There are numerous examples of successful mediation of environmental disputes, including 1) an agreement on water levels between a lakeside community in Maine and the hydroelectric dam controlling the levels; 2) agreements needed to convert a large power plant in Massachusetts from burning (imported) oil to (domestic) coal; 3) the settlement of a dispute over the siting of a city landfill in Wisconsin; and 4) the establishment of a recreation trail along an abandoned rail spur in Missouri. These and other successes have led some observers to conclude that "litigation is just not efficient. There are incredible delays, high costs and even when someone is declared the winner he doesn't feel like a winner."[57] For example, public court rulings may be made on the basis of some narrow technical point that leaves the basic issue unresolved. Furthermore, the adversarial court system does not seek a compromise; it *forces* a solution and virtually guarantees future confrontations between the parties.

The private sector is capable of generating agreements even when no guiding law (like a contract) exists, so that adjudication (that is, the clarification of existing property rights) is all that is needed. Arbitration, for example, is used primarily to adjudicate disputes over existing contracts. Beyond that, mediation has other advantages. It may be used to focus discussion on the real dispute. For example, in a confrontation regarding the siting of a landfill for Eau Claire, Wisconsin, various groups had been quarrelling about the adequacy of the environmental impact statement for the proposed site. The quarrel appeared to focus on water pollution concerns, but the mediator identified the real concerns—how the site was to be operated, what hours it would be open, who could use it, what kinds of trucks would be traveling to it, and what would happen to the site when it was full. Once the true concerns were delineated, it took only three meetings to reach an agreement guaranteeing the neighbors that the site would be operated in an acceptable manner.[58]

Community Dispute Resolution Centers.   Since the 1960s, mediation has been used in about 100 programs to resolve "conflicts that courts may find too trivial or too elusive: domestic quarrels, squabbles between neighbors and similar animosities among ethnic groups."[59] Programs in Los Angeles, Philadelphia, Kansas City, Atlanta, San Francisco, Miami, Boston, Garden City, New York, and Cleveland have been designed to seek compromise solutions to disputes by using neighborhood volunteers to serve as mediators (and sometimes arbitrators). These programs recently have been going beyond domestic and neighborhood disputes to consider criminal incidents. In one example, a Los Angeles grocer filed a complaint against a black youth who had robbed his store. The store owner did not want to involve the police because he wanted to avoid alienating his black customers.[60]
    One of the earliest community dispute resolution projects was run by the American Arbitration Association in Philadelphia, which began hearing minor criminal cases in 1969. The success of this private court provided the impetus for moving minor criminal cases into neighborhood justice centers. Some of these arrangements were not actually voluntary private alternatives to the public courts; they required a substantial authoritarian role in their development, financing, and administration. If the programs fail when funding is withdrawn, as it has been over the past few years, some observers may conclude that the private sector is simply unable to provide neighborhood- or community-based conflict resolution services. We must recognize the potential for such failures at this point and realize

that in all likelihood, the failures reflect the characteristics of those particular community-based systems that have been imposed by public officials.

Potential Failure of "Community Conflict Resolution" Arrangements: Private Sector or Government Failure ? The concept of "alternative dispute resolution" became a focal point for legal reformers some time ago, but it was also picked up by the American Bar Association and by judges as a potential remedy for court congestion. Lawyers and judges began designing new mediation programs for low income and minority neighborhoods in an effort to move their disputes out of the public courts. These "minor" disputes were considered to be "inappropriate for adjudication" by government courts. Many of the new neighborhood justice centers were sponsored and financed by the Department of Justice "and securely located within the judicial system."[61] Virtually all cases were referred to the centers by judges or prosecutors, and few members of the "community" voluntarily have taken disputes there for resolution. In a 1980 report, the Justice Department recognized that several of its projects were basically extensions of the public court system.[62] In many cases, prosecutors and other officials in the criminal justice system have used "very persuasive" means to get people involved in "neighborhood dispute resolution" arrangements. A Department of Justice report found that "subtle forms of coercive pressure (like the threat of criminal prosecution if someone failed to appear) are important elements in the building of sizable caseloads."[63] These courts are accurately perceived as part of the public sector justice system. Mediators may be community volunteers, thus giving them certain private sector appearances, but the disputants are not volunteers and a program's failure should not be characterized as a failure of the private sector.

Does this mean that private mediation is not a viable alternative for dispute resolution? Definitely not. The role of mediation in contracting, in environmental disputes, and in some communities, continues to grow. Community dispute resolution centers in stable neighborhoods founded on voluntary recognition of reciprocities rather than government coercion may succeed. The failure of a government-sponsored program does not imply that other institutions truly designed for the benefits of potential disputants would fail.

Arbitration. It has been argued that the modern resurgence of commercial arbitration in the United States can be traced to the American Civil War.[64] The naval blockade of the South resulted in tremendous court congestion in England due to contract disputes over the purchase, delivery, and sale of cotton to British markets. Many ship owners were unwilling to run the blockade, vessels were sunk, and prices fluctuated unpredictably. Further complications arose due to British neutrality and contraband-of-war laws. Insurance was either unavailable or it carried new and extremely complex provisions developed because of the tremendous uncertainty. These provisions required reinterpretation with each new contingency.

Because of the difficulties and uncertainties associated with the blockade and the resulting backlog in the public court, the Liverpool Cotton Association agreed to insert arbitration clauses in their contracts to avoid government courts when disputes arose. "Arbitration proved so successful in adjusting differences without the expense, inconvenience, and hard feelings of suits that other Liverpool commercial associations took up the device, first the Corn Trade Association and then the General Brokers Association."[65]

The success in Liverpool led to the adoption of arbitration in London, first by the large commodity dealers (corn, oil seed, cotton, and coffee), followed by stock dealers and produce merchants, and then by professional associations of architects, engineers, estate agents, and auctioneers. "By 1883 a correspondent of the *London Times* could write that 'whole trades and professions have virtually turned their back on the courts.' . . . Once 'private courts' were tried their advantages quickly became apparent, and the London mercantile community, which only a few years before had been making tentative inquiries about Liverpool's experience with arbitration, now found itself the object of an American investigation."[66]

The Philadelphia Bar Society sent an investigator to London to learn about the arbitration process and his report may have been partly responsible for the re-emergence of commercial arbitration in the United States at the end of the nineteenth century. More significantly, however,

> its revival was nourished by the convergence of business organization and government regulation during the early years of the twentieth century. . .the stronger the regulatory state, the stronger the desire for spheres of voluntary activity beyond its control. The growth of the regulatory state unsettled advocates of commercial autonomy who turned to arbitration as a shield against government intrusion. Arbitration. . .permitted businessmen to solve their own problems "in their own way—without resorting to the clumsy and heavy hand of government."[67]

Commercial law began to return to private hands.

The main area of rapid redevelopment of commercial arbitration was in the trade associations. By the end of World War I, arbitration had become the preferred practice among many of these groups, and it has since "grown to proportions that make the courts secondary recourse in many areas and completely superfluous in others."[68] By 1977, insurance companies were arbitrating over fifty thousand claims.[69] The American Arbitration Association (AAA), the largest single group of arbitrators with 25 regional offices and 23,000 associates around the country in 1970, helped settle some 22,000 disputes that year. In 1978, the AAA settled 48,000 disputes, an increase of 118.2 percent in only eight years.[70] Since the association's founding in 1926, entire classes of legal disputes have been removed from the courts altogether.[71] Even so, a study conducted in the mid-1950s found that the AAA conducted only 27 percent of all commercial arbitration.[72]

One way to get an idea of the extent of the use of arbitration is to examine some of the disputes that are being arbitrated. Commercial arbitration is widespread, for example, and many business agreements have an arbitration clause built into their contracts. The AAA has a standard clause that is inserted into virtually every agreement, bill of sale, or contract in many industries. It reads:

> Any controversy or claim arising out of or relating to this contract, or breach thereof, shall be settled by arbitration in accordance with the Rules of the American Arbitration Association, and judgment upon the award rendering by the arbitrators may be entered in any court having jurisdiction thereof.[73]

In addition, Construction Industry Arbitration Rules have been adopted by national associations of architects, engineers, contractors, and subcontractors. About 2,800 cases per year are filed with the AAA under these rules, mostly involving disputes between contractors or subcontractors and building owners. The National Association of Home Builders has begun a Home Owners Warranty program that offers arbitration of buyers' complaints against the association's builders. The warranty had been applied to roughly 950,000 homes by 1981, and the AAA resolved 1,800 cases in 1980.[74]

Many industries and trade associations have established their own arbitration clauses and proceedings. Industries that require close continuing relationships among members (e.g., the New York Stock Exchange) typically adopt arbitration. Similarly, industries in which product quality is a matter of interpretation—such as the textile industry, and the Association of Food Distributors—use arbitration. Several associations have even established appeals boards (e.g., the Spice Trade Association and the American Cotton Shippers Association). Most associations testify to the increasing acceptability of arbitration and a decrease in their members' use of public courts.[75]

Consumer disputes are increasingly handled through arbitration. The Council of Better Business Bureaus operates arbitration programs for consumers in many parts of the country and encourages businesses to precommit to arbitration of customer complaints.[76] Typically, the BBB attempts informal conciliation in such cases; if that fails, the customer and business are given the choice of an arbitrator from a pool of volunteers. In many cases, the arbitration hearing is held in the consumer's home so the defective merchandise can be examined. Several automobile manufacturers have contracts with the Council of BBB to arbitrate car owners' complaints. In addition, the AAA arbitrates over 15,000 auto insurance cases per year.[77]

Arbitration is being used in other consumer disputes as well. For example, medical malpractice arbitration, begun in 1929, is on the rise as malpractice litigation has become more costly and widespread. Prior agreement is important in this case. For example, subscribers to the Kaiser Foundation of health plans in California, the nation's largest prepaid medical care system, agree to arbitrate any claims when they sign up. The hospital and medical associations in California sponsor a 200-hospital arbitration system, and the AAA also offers medical malpractice arbitration.[78]

Some countries have formal "labor courts," but the United States relies principally on arbitration of labor/management disputes. Most collective bargaining agreements now have arbitration clauses for employee grievances, and tens of thousands of labor-management cases are decided every year. Some industries appoint "permanent umpires" who hear all cases that arise. Others incorporate a list of arbitrators in the collective bargaining agreement, and still others choose arbitrators on a case-by-case basis from lists supplied by neutral agencies. The AAA, for example, had a list of around 3,000 labor arbitrators in 1983 and administered some 17,000 labor cases a year.[79] Similarly, the Federal Mediation and Conciliation Service had a roster of about 1,400 arbitrators for labor disputes and reported that around 14,000 arbitration appointments were made.

During the 1970s and early 1980s, the AAA became increasingly involved in minor criminal and civil disputes, such as neighborhood fights and juvenile offenses,[80] through its Community Disputes Division. Similar arrangements with local courts also exist. Of course, some of the same qualifications made above about some neighborhood dispute resolution systems apply.

Government Influence on the Evolution of Arbitration.   Arbitration, and particularly commercial arbitration, is undeniably a private sector process of dispute resolution, but it is in competition with government institutions that may attempt to suppress it. After the turn of the century, lawyers began to recognize this threat to the government's adversarial dispute resolution process, which they had come to dominate. In 1915, the New York Bar Association established a committee to examine ways to alleviate the pressure on the court docket. "Arbitration captured the committee's attention but lawyers and businessmen wanted different results from it. Lawyers, defensive about criticism, were eager to improve their public image, without losing clients, while retaining control over dispute resolution."[81] Businessmen wanted speedy, inexpensive dispute resolution based on business custom and practice but the New York Bar and the Chamber of Commerce joined forces to pass a 1920 New York statute that made arbitration agreements binding under New York law and enforceable in New York courts. Since then, all the other states have passed similar laws.

Many observers contend that these laws make arbitration viable. Landes and Posner, for example, argued that the arbitration clauses in contracts are "effective, in a major part anyway only because the public courts enforce such contracts; if they did not, there would often be no effective sanction against the party who simply breaches the contract to arbitrate."[82] In other words, private arbitration is a viable option to public courts, because it is backed by those public courts. This claim is demonstrably false. The historic development of the Law Merchant demonstrates that a significant boycott sanction can be produced by the commercial community. In fact, the international Law Merchant continues to survive and flourish without the backing of a coercive government authority. Beyond that, however, it was during the years prior to 1920 that arbitration began to catch on, particularly among trade associations, so the process was well established before government coercion was available. The merchant community backed the rulings with sanctions similar to those that evolved under the medieval law merchant. Anyone who refused to accept an arbiter's decision found access to his trade association's arbitration tribunal withdrawn or saw his name released to the association's membership: "these penalties were far more fearsome than the cost of the award with which he disagreed. Voluntary and private adjudications were voluntarily and privately adhered to if not out of honor, out of self interest."[83] This does not mean, however, that the New York statute and all those that followed have not had an impact on arbitration. In fact, the effect is precisely the opposite of that suggested by Landes and Posner: *Arbitration became a less attractive alternative to the public courts than it would have otherwise been in the absence of these laws.*

How can this be? The problem is that what statute law protected, government also controlled.[84] An enormous number of court cases were filed after the New York statute was passed, for instance, as businessmen tried to determine what characteristics of arbitration would be considered "legal" by the courts. Cases involved such issues as the appropriate way to select arbitrators, whether lawyers had to be present (lawyers became active in arbitration because of these statutes), whether stenographic notes of the proceedings should be taken, and so on. One case involved courts in two states, led to two appeals before a circuit court of appeals, produced five court opinions—three on jurisdictional issues—and took more than five years to resolve. Businessmen, forced to pay attention to the prospect of judicial review, had to make their arbitration processes compatible with statute and precedent law, including public court procedure.

Some of the most attractive aspects of the arbitration alternative were substantially weakened as a direct result of the statutory legalization of the process. In particular, arbitration has taken a much more complex "legalistic" character, arbitration is less a summary proceeding, concern for government-imposed laws is relatively more significant, and arbitration is costlier. The government has not eliminated arbitration as a competitor, but the arbitration statutes have limited its competitiveness. A Harvard business law professor who observed the period immediately following passage of the arbitration statutes suggested as much when he wrote: "There is irony in the fate of one who takes precautions to avoid litigation by submitting to arbitration, and who, as a reward for his pain, finds himself in court fighting not on the merits of his case but on the merits of arbitration . . . [this] monumental tragicomedy [demonstrates the success of the government legal process at] thwarting legitimate efforts to escape its tortuous procedure."[85]

Commercial arbitration has continued to face attacks from the legal establishment since the 1920s. During the 1930s, for example, many saw it as a way for business to avoid the rule of government law. But the advantages of commercial arbitration are simply too significant, and private arbitration continues to grow at the expense of the public court system. While the character of private arbitration has been substantially influenced by the efforts of government to subjugate it, by the 1950s almost 75 percent of all commercial disputes were being adjudicated before arbitrators rather than public courts.[86] The same factors explain the recent phenomenon of private for-profit dispute resolution firms and "rent-a-judge" systems.

Rent-a-Judge Justice. In 1976, two California lawyers discovered an 1872 statute that states that individuals in a dispute have the right to a full court hearing before any referee they choose.[87] At that time, California had a 70,000 case public court backlog, with a median pre-trial delay of 50 and one-half months.[88] The two lawyers, who wanted a complex case settled quickly, found a retired judge with expertise in the area of the dispute, paid him at attorney's fee rates, and saved their clients a tremendous amount of time and expense.[89]

The California law (and similar laws in several other states) allows opposing parties to choose a referee to "try any or all of the issues in an action or proceeding, whether of fact or of law, and to report a finding and judgment thereon."[90] The findings will "stand as the findings of the court." Anyone who meets the requirements for jury duty can serve as a private judge, although virtually all have been retired public court judges. There is no count of the number of rent-a-judge cases tried since 1976, but the civil court coordinator of the Los Angeles County Superior Court estimated that several hundred disputes had been so settled during the first five years. Most of the cases involve complex business disputes that litigants "feel the public courts cannot quickly and adequately" try.[91]

Private for-profit firms have entered the justice market during the last few years in virtually every state. Civicourt in Phoenix and Judicate in Philadelphia have offered quick and inexpensive dispute resolution since 1983.[92] As of March 1987, Judicate employed 308 judges in 45 states and has been called the "national private court." A typical hearing at Judicate takes one or two days. Charges for simple cases are $600 per court session, while more complex suits involving multiple parties cost $1,000 a session.[93] Half the money is paid to the judge. Judicate's procedures are streamlined adaptations of government court procedures, allowing pretrial conferences, discovery process, settlement conferences, and so on. At Civicourt, three hours of judge time costs each litigant $250; thereafter, each additional hour costs $75. Most trials are completed quickly, with no juries to contend with, and the trials are held at the convenience of the parties in the dispute.

Similar systems are developing elsewhere. The Washington Arbitration Services, Inc., established in 1981, has four franchised offices around the state. Judicial Mediation, Inc., of Santa Ana, California, and Resolution, Inc., of Connecticut are more recent entrants into the private judicial market. One of the earliest for-profit dispute resolution firms was EnDispute, Inc., which opened in Washington, D.C., and Los Angeles in 1982 and offers "mini-trials." The firm has since added offices in Chicago, Cambridge, Massachusetts, and Santa Ana, California. One of their successes involved a $61 million suit between American Can Co. and Wisconsin Electric Power Co., which was expected to last at least 75 days in the public court. EnDispute arranged a tribunal made up of an executive from each company and a neutral advisor. All lawsuits were dropped, and a solution to the problem was found.[94] Mini-trials are now considered an attractive option for companies involved in what are expected to be large, time-consuming, and expensive litigations.

Private sector adjudication is likely to continue to increase in importance. As Denenberg and Denenberg point out, private "[d]ispute resolution is a method whose potential applications are limited only by the ingenuity of the potential users. It satisfies a widely felt need for flexible, accessible justice."[95]

CUSTOMARY LAW

The Re-emergence of the Law Merchant.   In 1606, when Lord Edward Coke ruled that the decisions of private courts could be reversed by royal courts, the common law courts gained a substantial advantage in competing for commercial cases. In essence, Coke's ruling asserted that the Law Merchant was not a separate, identifiable system of law but a part of the common law. The use of private courts for commercial disputes virtually disappeared. But the Law Merchant did not die. During the sixteenth and seventeenth centuries, the Law Merchant became less universal and more localized and began to reflect the policies, interest, and procedures of the various nation states. Merchant custom remained the underlying source of much of commercial law in Europe, in the United States, and to a lesser degree in England, but it differed from place to place. "National states inevitably *required* that their indigenous policies and concerns be given direct consideration in the regulation of commerce. As a result, distinctly domestic systems of law evolved as the official regulators of both domestic and international business."[96] As commercial cases were taken over by government courts dominated by domestic lawyers rather than merchant judges, localized procedures and national laws were naturally applied.

The changes were most striking in England, where the courts rejected many of the underpinnings of the Law Merchant. But even in England, the Law Merchant survived. England was a great trading nation, and custom still prevailed in international trade. English judges had to compete with other national courts for the attention of international merchants' disputes, so they had to recognize commercial custom in cases involving international trade if they hoped to attract such cases. One important reason for this was that the European countries' civil law had been much more receptive to the Law Merchant than had English common law. "On the Continent the Law Merchant suffered to a limited extent. Merchant practices were often codified within commercial codes which bore a strong resemblance to the medieval Law Merchant. Consequently, the commercial laws of European states often embodied trade practices within their legal frameworks."[97] There was some fragmentation in the form of the Law Merchant across Europe, but there was little difference in its substance. Trade between these geographically contiguous countries had become vital, and there was substantial benefit associated with "free trade unimpeded by needless legal restraint."[98] Thus, continental codes were a much more direct reflection of the Law Merchant than was English common law.

The trend toward increasing subjugation of the Law Merchant began to change in the nineteenth century when "the decisions of Lord Holt and Lord Mansfield introduced into English common law most of the customs and usages of English merchants, and the Law Merchant became an integral part of the common law realm, and the common law courts."[99] Some legal historians call Mansfield the "founder of commercial law" in England, but "Mansfield pioneered the reception into English law of an international Law Merchant based on practices of the merchants of both the continent and Britain."[100] Mansfield argued quite forcefully that England's commercial law had to develop as business practice developed and that it had to recognize business custom and usage. The primary impetus for recognizing merchant's law at this time, however, was the *significant competitive threat* to the common law court's hold on commercial law. International competition by national courts for the attention of merchants was apparently getting more intense, and as England's relative position in world trade began to decline, common law courts began to lose international business disputes to other nations' courts. In addition, the Liverpool Cotton Traders Association adopted arbitration clauses in their contracts during the early 1860s. Common law courts witnessed a rapid loss of jurisdiction and had little alternative but to respond to the competitive threat by recognizing the Law Merchant. At roughly the same time, many of the various competitive jurisdictions (e.g., common law, equity) were being combined so the intensity of inter-jurisdictional competition between government courts was declining. This may have contributed to the impetus for turning to private arbitration, as the combined courts would clearly face even weaker incentives than the more competitive courts in recognizing the law as the merchant community desired. The merchants, therefore, had to create another source of competitive pressure to induce the public courts to recognize their laws. As it turned out, this new source became a much more significant competitive threat than the alternative public courts.

The long period of subjugation was not without its costs, however. "The fact that the Law Merchant lost some of its identifying characteristics in English law, in effect, reduces the function of the Law Merchant to an uncertain role in our common law system. It becomes unclear in what circumstances the English courts will have recourse to the institutions of the Law Merchant in deciding commercial cases."[101] Furthermore, as common law developed through judicial precedent, particularly before Mansfield's influence, the evolution of Merchant custom and practice was altered from what it might have been. "Customs of the Law Merchant which were adopted in the early common law have sometimes been so rigidified in legal content that they have varied from their merchant origins."[102] The rigid definition of custom and the requirement that it be consistent with the law remain an integral part of British common law as it applies to commercial disputes. Numerous conflicts between common law and the international Law Merchant remain.

The end result is that the common law courts took over the adjudication of business law through successful competition with other court systems. Once they gained a substantial share of this market they began acting more like coercive monopolists, dictating or administering law rather than recognizing the more important body of customary law. When the situation got sufficiently out of line with the Law Merchant, common law courts once again began to feel competitive pressures with commercial arbitration and with other nations' tribunals in international trade. The courts responded to the pressure but did not welcome the Law Merchant with open arms. The long period of subjugation had so altered business practices in England that merchants had become used to functioning under common law rigidities. Trakman concluded that "English courts have paid lip service to the precepts of the Law Merchant, while in reality undermining the flexible foundations of Law Merchant principles."[103] But this was not the case in the United States.

American judges have been somewhat more receptive of the Law Merchant than their English counterparts. This probably reflects competition due to the widespread acceptance of commercial arbitration in the country prior to 1800 and its revitalization since 1900. In addition, many litigants can choose among different jurisdictions, and competition for hearing disputes may be much more significant than in England. Thus, "American courts have revitalized the medieval Law Merchant in a number of respects." In fact, the Uniform Commercial Code indicates that business practices and customs have served as the primary source of substantive business law, as "the positive law of the realm was forced to conform to the mandate of the merchants, not vice versa."[104]

Trakman suggested that the uniformity of commercial law might be undermined because of separate state court systems and regional specific federal court jurisdictions, if local custom supersedes more uniform national or international business practices.[105] The potential for the same kind of breakdown in the universality of the Law Merchant that occurred with the rising power of royal law in England may be present in the United States. In fact, substantial differences in business practices across local American communities are rare, so uniformity of the law has generally prevailed in the American legal system.[106] Given the open nature of the U.S. economy, the potential for competition between geographically separated court systems remains significant. If judges were only interested in monopolized local disputes, then state precedents might differ significantly; but interstate competition for business disputes is likely to reduce the tendency to favor local merchants and customs. Furthermore, commercial arbitration has re-emerged as a viable option for business disputes and its competitive influence has been substantial.

Creation of Customary Law.   U.S. courts enforce business practice and custom as law. Therefore, if businessmen develop a new practice, it is likely to take on the force of government-backed law. More importantly, the private sector continues to develop an expanding base of customary law. For example, enforceable rights and duties derive from a contract just as they do from the provisions of a statute.[107] Thus, contracts negotiated and voluntarily entered into by private individuals provide one form of privately created law. If the contract is a standard one reflecting long-standing tradition, then it reflects customary commercial law. If the contract develops a new business practice in the face of a new situation, then it is likely to add to customary law, just as a new court precedent adds to common law. Because commerce operates in a dynamic environment, new contractual arrangements are always being developed.

The contracting process involves a mediation element, so it follows that private mediation often creates law. As Fuller explained, *"mediation is commonly directed,* not toward achieving conformity to norms, but *toward the creation of the relevant norms themselves."*[108] Arbitrators (like government judges) also may create precedents that become part of customary law (as opposed to common law). This contradicts Landes and Posner's contention that commercial arbitration does not set precedents but simply applies laws established by the public sector.[109] That they are wrong can be superficially demonstrated. When individuals make an agreement in a contract that may not stand up in government courts, they frequently write an arbitration clause into the contract.[110] Private commercial arbitrators will consider the contractual agreement valid.

More fundamentally, when a dispute arises because a contract did not anticipate a change in the business environment, the arbitrator must determine what business practice should be under the new conditions based on custom and practice under related circumstances. When this occurs then "even in the absence of any formalized doctrine of state decisis or res judicata, an adjudicative determination will normally enter in some degree into the litigants' future relations and into the future relations of other parties who see themselves as possible litigants before the same [type of] tribunal. Even if there is no statement by the tribunal of the reasons for its decision, some reason will be perceived or guessed at, and the parties will tend to govern their conduct accordingly."[111] In other words, a new law has been created that begins to "govern" the behavior of parties entering into similar circumstances in the future. Such a law is likely to be recognized quickly when the arbitration is internal to a trade association; it may take longer to spread through the entire population if the relevant group is more diverse. But if the law is an effective remedy to a frequent potential conflict, then it will become part of customary law—the "language of interaction." The law-making consequences of private arbitration led Wooldridge to suggest that its substantial growth in this century has involved a "silent displacement of not only the judiciary but even the legislature."[112] Actually, it simply reflects the evolution of commercial law as business practices develop and change.

It is often difficult to see the important role that customary law plays in determining the social order, since so much of custom has been codified or co-opted by common law courts and claimed as state law. One instance of social order through customary law does remain relatively free of government interference, however. International trade is still largely ruled by customary commercial law as it has evolved from the medieval Law Merchant.

The International Law Merchant.   International commercial law is a universal law. It has moved away from the restrictions of national law, thus overcoming the difference in the political and authoritarian legal systems of the world. "Moreover, the demand for uniform principles of international trade law, acceptable to the international community of merchants at large, looms ever larger in a world dominated by an uncertain balance of political-economical power."[113] The merchants themselves are the only potential source of such uniformity, of course, and their agreements have to produce that uniformity since agreements between governments are unlikely.

Arbitration and mediation are the means of resolving disputes in international trade. The decisions and agreements that arise are not backed by government, but by the reciprocal arrangements of the international commercial community. Many international trade associations have their own conflict resolution procedures. Other traders rely on the International Chamber of Commerce (ICC), which has established a substantial arbitration institution. Experts in international commerce, ICC arbitrators are typically chosen from a different national origin than those of the parties in the dispute. ICC procedures are speedy and flexible reflections of commercial interest.

The Law Merchant has certainly changed substantially since its medieval beginnings, but it is still firmly in place governing international trade. It has also proven to be a very effective source of order:

> Continuing experience in world trade provides a tested environment in which merchants can interact freely, choosing their trade partners and contract terms with an expanding awareness of both the marketplace and of one another. Together, market, agreement and time allow business instruments to evolve into uniform codes and documents, comprehensive in their terms and farsighted in their application to an ever-changing business world. . . .
>
> Studies of industry usage reveal the sophistication of the international merchants to adapt their trade agreement to meet the demands of interdisciplinary change.[114]

The international Law Merchant, free from the dominant influences of governments and localized politics, has developed and grown much more easily and effectively than has the intra-national commercial law of most nation-states.

The General Impact of Customary Law.   Even some legal scholars of the positivist school have been forced to recognize the role of customary law in international trade. However, as Fuller noted, the prevailing tendency to regard social order as imposed from above has led to a general neglect of the phenomenon of customary law in modern legal scholarship. Outside the field of international law and that of commercial dealings legal theorists have been uncomfortable about the use of the word law to describe the obligatory force of expectations that arise tacitly out of human interaction. The most common escape from this dilemma is to downgrade the significance of customary law and to assert that it has largely lost the significance it once had in human affairs. Another and more radical way out was. . .to assert that what is called customary law becomes truly law only after it has been adopted by a court as a standard of decision and thus received the imprimatur of the state. This linguistic expedient, it should be noted, would deny the designation law to a custom so firmly rooted and so plainly just and useful that no one would waste his time taking it to court to be tested for its right to be called law.[115]

Customary law continues to govern a tremendous amount of social interactions, from family relations to commercial exchanges to international relations between governments. It is difficult to visualize this for a number of reasons. First, many customary laws are not adopted and "enacted" by a state authority and are not necessarily written down. Second, customary law "owes its force to the fact that it has found direct expression in the conduct of men toward one another."[116] Third, customary law requires voluntary acceptance in recognition of reciprocal benefits, so it is much less likely to be violated than enacted authoritarian law. Customary law, therefore, is less likely to require adjudication, and its role and impact are less likely to be noticed as a consequence. Nonetheless, customary law flourishes and promotes order in many facets of modern society.

ENDNOTES

1. Truett A. Ricks, Bill G. Tillett, and Clifford W. Van Meter, *Principles of Security* (Cincinnati: Criminal Justice Studies, Anderson Publishing Co., 1981), p. 11.
2. Lawrence W. Sherman, "Patrol Strategies for Police," in *Crime and Public Policy*, ed. James Q. Wilson (San Francisco: Institute for Contemporary Studies, 1983), pp. 145–149.
3. Charles T. Clotfelter, "Public Services, Private Substitutes, and the Demand for Protection Against Crime," *American Economic Review* 67 (December 1977): 868.
4. Sherman, "Patrol Strategies for Police," p. 145.
5. Research and Forecasts, Inc., *America Afraid: How Fear of Crime Changes the Way We Live, Based on the Widely Publicized Figgie Report* (New York: New America Library, 1983), p. 68.

6. Ibid., pp. 70, 71, 72, 76.
7. Ibid., p. 73.
8. Ibid., p. 91. Emphasis added. Also see pp. 79, 81.
9. California Department of Justice, *Homicide in California, 1981* (Sacramento: Bureau of Criminal Statistics and Special Services, 1981); "Shootings by Civilians Rise Sharply in Houston," *New York Times,* November 21, 1982.
10. Research and Forecasts, Inc., *America Afraid,* p. 109.
11. Ibid., p. 110.
12. Ibid., pp. 118, 110.
13. Christopher Dobson and Ronald Payne, "Private Enterprise Takes on Terrorism," *Reason* 14 (January 1983): 36.
14. Ibid., pp. 34–41.
15. Sherman, "Patrol Strategies for Police," p. 145.
16. Aaron Podolefsky and Fredric Dubow, *Strategies for Community Crime Prevention: Collective Responses to Crime in Urban America* (Springfield, Ill.: Charles C. Thomas, Publisher, 1981), p. 44.
17. Ibid., p. 45.
18. Ibid., p. 48.
19. Ibid., pp. 53–54.
20. Ibid., p. 64.
21. Roger D. McGrath, *Gunfighters, Highwaymen and Vigilantes: Violence on the Frontier* (Berkeley: University of California Press, 1984), p. 266.
22. See Podolefsky and Dubow, *Strategies for Community Crime Prevention,* p. 71.
23. Wesley Skogan and Michael Maxfield, *Coping with Crime: Victimization, Fear and Reaction to Crime in Three American Cities* (Evanston, Ill.: Center for Urban Studies, Northwestern University, 1979).
24. Podolefsky and Dubow, *Strategies for Community Crime Prevention,* p. 73.
25. Ibid., p. 76.
26. Robert K. Yin, Mary E. Vogel, Jan N. Chaiken, and Deborah R. Both, *Citizen Patrol Projects* (Washington, D.C.: National Institute of Law Enforcement and Criminal Justice, Law Enforcement Assistance Administration, U.S. Department of Justice, 1977), p. 13; Neal R. Pierce, "Justice Demonstration Successful for Country," *Washington Post,* April 23, 1984.
27. Robert W. Poole, Jr., *Cutting Back City Hall* (New York: The Free Press, 1978), p. 38.
28. Podolefsky and Dubow, *Strategies for Community Crime Prevention,* p. 84.
29. Ibid., p. 84.
30. Poole, *Cutting Back City Hall,* p. 38.
31. Gary T. Marx and Dane Archer, "Citizen Involvement in the Law Enforcement Process: The Case of Community Police Patrols," *American Behavioral Scientist* 15 (1971): 52–72.

32. Podolefsky and Dubow, *Strategies for Community Crime Prevention*, p. 81.
33. William C. Wooldridge, *Uncle Sam, the Monopoly Man* (New Rochelle, N.Y.: Arlington House, 1970), p. 115.
34. Oscar Newman, *Community of Interest* (Garden City, N.Y.: Anchor Press, 1980), p. 124. Emphasis added.
35. Theodore J. Gage, "Getting Street-Wise in St. Louis," *Reason*, August 1981, p. 18.
36. Ibid., p. 19. For a more detailed examination of the history of private streets in St. Louis, see David T. Beito, "The Private Places of St. Louis: The Formation of Urban Infrastructure through Non-Governmental Planning, 1869-1920," Institute for Humane Studies Working Paper, May 20, 1988.
37. Newman, *Community of Interest*, p. 131.
38. Ibid., pp. 137, 140.
39. Ibid., p. 133.
40. Ibid., p. 142.
41. "Rich Towns Walling Themselves Off for Security, Privacy," *Daily Commerce*, July 4, 1983.
42. James S. Kakalik and Sorrel Wildhorn, *Private Police in the United States: Findings and Recommendations* (Santa Monica, Calif.: The Rand Corporation, 1971), p. 1.
43. "Police Outnumbered by Security Guards," *Billings Gazette*, December 10, 1984.
44. Edward Iwata, "Rent-a-Cops on Trial," *This World*, March 18, 1984, p. 10.
45. "Police Outnumbered by Security Guards."
46. Ricks, et al., *Principles of Security*, p. 13.
47. Quoted in "Police Outnumbered by Security Guards."
48. Poole, *Cutting Back City Hall*, p. 39.
49. For a brief discussion, see Tai Schneider Denenberg and R. V. Denenberg, *Dispute Resolution: Settling Conflicts Without Legal Action*, Public Affairs Pamphlet No. 597 (New York: Public Affairs Committee, Inc., 1981), p. 2. For more detailed analysis, see Lon L. Fuller, *The Principles of Social Order* (Durham, N.C.: Duke University Press, 1981).
50. Denenberg and Denenberg, *Dispute Resolution*, p. 3.
51. Edmund Burke, "An Appeal from the New to the Old Whigs (1791)" in *The Writings and Speeches of Edmund Burke*, vol. 4 (Boston: Little, Brown, 1901), pp. 189-190.
52. Fuller, *The Principles of Social Order*, pp. 179-180.
53. Ibid., p. 142.
54. Ibid., p. 136.
55. Denenberg and Denenberg, *Dispute Resolution*, p. 19.
56. Ibid., p. 20. Emphasis added.
57. Ibid., p. 21.

58. Ibid.
59. Ibid., p. 15.
60. Ibid., p. 18.
61. Jerold S. Auerbach, *Justice Without Law?* (New York: Oxford University Press, 1983), p. 131.
62. Roger F. Cook, et al., *Neighborhood Justice Centers Field Test—Final Evaluation Report* (Washington, D.C.: U.S. Department of Justice, 1980), pp. 4–6.
63. D. I. Sheppard, J. A. Roche, and R. F. Cook, *National Evaluation of the Neighborhood Justice Centers Field Test: Interim Report* (Washington, D.C.: U.S. Department of Justice, 1979), p. 56.
64. Wooldridge, *Uncle Sam, the Monopoly Man,* p. 99.
65. Ibid., p. 99.
66. Ibid.
67. Auerbach, *Justice Without Law,* p. 101.
68. Wooldridge, *Uncle Sam, the Monopoly Man,* p. 101.
69. Ibid., p. 101.
70. Poole, *Cutting Back City Hall,* p. 54.
71. Ibid., p. 54.
72. Soia Mentschikoff, "Commercial Arbitration," *Columbia Law Review* 61 (1961): 857.
73. Denenberg and Denenberg, *Dispute Resolution,* p. 5.
74. Ibid.
75. Steven Lazarus, et al., *Resolving Business Disputes: The Potential of Commercial Arbitration* (New York: American Management Association, 1965), p. 28.
76. Denenberg and Denenberg, *Dispute Resolution: Settling Conflicts Without Legal Action,* p. 6.
77. Ibid., p. 8.
78. Ibid., p. 10.
79. Poole, *Cutting Back City Hall,* p. 55.
80. Ibid., p. 55.
81. Auerbach, *Justice Without Law?* pp. 103–104.
82. William M. Landes and Richard A. Posner, "Adjudication as a Private Good," *Journal of Legal Studies* 8 (March 1979), p. 247.
83. Wooldridge, *Uncle Sam, the Monopoly Man,* pp. 100–101.
84. Auerbach, *Justice Without Law?* p. 109.
85. Nathan Isaacs, "Review of Wesley Stugess, *Treatise on Commercial Arbitration and Awards,*" *Yale Law Journal* 40 (1930): 149–151.
86. Auerbach, *Justice Without Law?* p. 113.
87. Robert W. Poole, Jr., "Can Justice Be Privatized?" *Fiscal Watchdog* 49 (November 1980): 2; James S. Granelli, "Got a Spat? Go Rent a Judge,"

National Law Journal, June 8, 1981, p. 1; Gary Pruitt, "California's Rent-a-Judge Justice," *Journal of Contemporary Studies* 5 (Spring 1982): 49–57.

88. Poole, "Can Justice Be Privatized?" p. 2.
89. Granelli, "Got a Spat?" pp. 1–2.
90. Pruitt, "California's Rent-a-Judge Justice," p. 50.
91. Ibid., p. 51.
92. Richard Koenig, "More Firms Turn to Private Courts to Avoid Expensive Legal Fights," *Wall Street Journal,* January 4, 1984; Josh Meyer, "Judicate, Others Provide Novel Alternative," *The Legal Intelligencer,* March 17, 1987; Kerry Hannon, "Turnstile Justice," *Forbes,* December 15, 1986, pp. 174–175.
93. Ray Holton, "With the New Private Court System, You Can Shop Around for a Judge," *Philadelphia Inquirer,* November 11, 1983.
94. Koenig, "More Firms Turn to Private Courts"; Meyer, "Judicate, Others Provide Novel Alternatives"; Hannon, "Turnstile Justice."
95. Denenberg and Denenberg, *Dispute Resolution,* p. 26.
96. Leon E. Trakman, *The Law Merchant: The Evolution of Commercial Law* (Littleton, Colo.: Fred B. Rothman and Co., 1983), p. 24.
97. Ibid.
98. Ibid., p. 25.
99. W. Mitchell, *Essays on the Early History of the Law Merchant* (New York: Burt Franklin, 1904), pp. 77–78.
100. Trakman, *The Law Merchant,* p. 27.
101. Ibid., pp. 29–30.
102. Ibid., p. 30.
103. Ibid.
104. Ibid., p. 34.
105. Ibid., pp. 34–35.
106. Ibid., p. 35.
107. Fuller, *The Principles of Social Order,* p. 175.
108. Ibid., p. 128.
109. Landes and Posner, "Adjudication as a Private Good," pp. 257–258.
110. Wooldridge, *Uncle Sam, the Monopoly Man,* p. 104.
111. Fuller, *The Principles of Social Order,* p. 90.
112. Wooldridge, *Uncle Sam, the Monopoly Man,* p. 104.
113. Trakman, *The Law Merchant,* p. 43.
114. Ibid., pp. 2–3.
115. Fuller, *The Principles of Social Order,* p. 177.
116. Ibid., p. 212.

10

BENEFITS OF PRIVATIZATION

The increase in private sector efforts to prevent crimes and adjudicate disputes reflects more than a negative response to certain aspects of public sector performance. Benefits of private production are substantial, and they apply to crime control and dispute resolution just as they do in other areas of production. Several aspects of privatization in the enterprise of law shall be considered here, including the potential for avoiding the congestion and resource misallocation that arise from the commons problem of public provision, the benefits of specialization that characterize private sector crime control, the relative production costs in private and public production, and the impact that privatization has on the effectiveness of the public sector.

EFFICIENCY GAINS AND RATIONING OF LAW ENFORCEMENT

Judge Learned Hand contended that the "chief judicial commandment" should be "Thou shalt not ration justice."[1] But justice is rationed—it must be because it involves limited supplies of scarce resources. Due to court congestion, justice is rationed by waiting. Those willing to wait *might* get a trial. The court also terminates a large number of cases without trial (*91 percent* of all federal civil cases in 1978) because they are seen as "weak" cases. This usually means that they are difficult cases that would be time consuming because the merits of the arguments are not obvious and

235

compelling. The courts choose instead to try the easiest cases. In Person's view: "Such patterns occur particularly when a judge is under pressure. . .to produce a large number of case terminations without costly time-consuming trials. Government courts and judges have no choice but to violate Judge Hand's injunction against the rationing of justice."[2]

Similar rationing techniques have been adopted by prosecutors and even the police. In order to build up conviction records, prosecutors pursue the easiest cases and ration through plea bargaining. Police build up arrest records by pursuing relatively easy cases and ignoring many others that are difficult to solve.

In contrast, a market system allocates scarce resources on the basis of willingness to pay. This method of allocation results in scarce goods and services being allocated to the highest valued uses, because those who are willing to pay the market clearing price clearly value the right to consume the purchase more than those who are unwilling to pay. As a result, resources are guided toward their most efficient uses. If a resource is scarce, then the potential competitive uses of the resource will vie for its attention. In a price system, this competition for the use of resources means that the winner must pay a price at least equal to, if not greater than, the price someone else is willing to pay. The individual who gets the greatest benefit from using the resource will be willing to pay the most for it. Those who would get lesser benefits are outbid and cannot use the resource.

There is a market-like structure to the criminal justice process and those with the greatest ability and willingness to pay often get the most out of the system. Superficially, this appears to imply the possibility of efficiency, and some have suggested that at least some aspects of the criminal justice system may be efficient because the wealthy are able to influence decisions.[3] But most police, court, and other law enforcement resources are not allocated according to willingness to pay; first-come, first-served or some other discriminatory criteria apply. These rationing systems do not guarantee that resources go to their highest valued use. One advantage of privatization, then, is that allocation by price replaces less efficient rationing techniques.[4] Individuals turn to the private sector when they are unable to benefit from the services of the public criminal justice system because the public sector has misallocated resources to lower valued uses. For instance, the American Banking Association and the American Hotel-Motel Association retain the William J. Burns International Detective Agency to *investigate* crimes committed against their members. A bank security director pointed out why: "[I]t was necessary to employ private investigators because the public police and investigative forces were too busy to devote the amount of effort required by [banks]."⁵ Private investigators generally perform tasks that public police do not, such as pre-employment background checks or undercover work to detect employee dishonesty or customer shoplifting.

Private guards and patrolmen also perform tasks that the public police cannot or will not do, such as making routine checks on buildings for residents or businesses and "watching to prevent" crime. Private courts also take cases that the public sector has been unwilling to handle. The inability of government to provide the types of security measures and adjudicative services that individuals required has historically produced a demand for private alternatives. Private sector alternatives must provide benefits, of course, or they would not be purchased. One of these benefits is that privately employed resources tend to specialize.

GAINS FROM SPECIALIZATION

One reason that the private sector might be expected to do well what the government criminal justice system does badly is that consumers generally have narrowly focused concerns. Thus, when they pay a private firm to alleviate those concerns, they can hire someone with expertise. Both the evidence and economic theory tell us that when resources *specialize* in their area of comparative advantage, economic efficiency is enhanced. More is produced with the same resources, or fewer resources are needed to produce the same level of output.

Specialization in Private Courts.   Justice William O. Douglas once observed that "the labor arbitrator is usually chosen because of the parties' confidence in his knowledge of the common law of the shop."⁶ Because disputants can pick the judge who hears their case in private court, they pick a judge with expertise in the matter at hand. "Perhaps the most important advantage" of private courts, Poole reported, "is specialized expertise. Since a referee does not even have to be a judge. . .cases involving complex technical matters can be handled by someone skilled in the field."⁷ The private sector has responded to the demand for specialized judges. The American Arbitration Association's list of arbitrators includes attorneys, professors, engineers, and numerous other types of professionals, as well as many manufacturing and trade association executives.

How does this specialization generate benefits? Disputes can be settled more quickly, thus tying up resources for shorter periods of time. Private judges have expertise and need no "education" in technical issues of a particular case, which saves considerable time.[8]

Specialization in Private Crime Prevention and Protection. Security personnel range from minimum wage guards who work on a temporary basis, to full-time guards with relatively few skills, to highly trained professionals. Security equipment ranges from the simplest locks to the most complex alarm and monitoring equipment. Naturally, relatively few private resources will be used to police victimless crimes (although neighborhood groups may choose to exclude prostitutes or addicts); they will be concentrated on prevention of and protection against violent crimes and property crimes. This concentration of effort can be very effective. Consider, for example, the success of the railroad police.

At the end of World War I, railroad police were established as complete and autonomous police forces. They compiled what must be considered a "remarkable" record of effectiveness, particularly relative to public police forces. Between the end of World War I and 1929, for instance, freight claim payments for robberies fell by 92.7 percent, from $12,726,947 to $704,262.[9] Furthermore, arrests by railroad police produced a substantially higher percentage of convictions than that achieved by public police: a five-year sample from the Pennsylvania Railroad, for instance, resulted in conviction of 83.4 percent of those arrested; a thirteen-year sample from another line showed a 97.47 percent conviction rate.[10] The overall conviction rate of railroad police arrests has been maintained at close to 98 percent over the years, with an average of 60,000 arrests per year.[11] Wooldridge observed that the primary reason for this success is that the railroad police specialized in one area of enforcement, developing "an expertise not realistically within the grasp of public forces."[12] This specialization and the consequent gain in proficiency and efficiency often characterize private sector police firms.

Specialization in crime prevention has two major benefits. First, specialization makes it less likely that a criminal will succeed in his attempt at theft or violence. That is, increasing levels of private protection increase the potential cost to the criminal by increasing the probability of capture (or, in the case of guns for protection, the probability of personal injury or death). Second, as the potential cost of committing crime rises, potential criminals are less likely to become actual criminals. In other words, there is a deterrent effect.

Unfortunately, most studies of crime deterrence have examined the effects of public sector efforts. There is some evidence, however, that private sector production of protection does deter crime. Using a Tobit maximum likelihood statistical procedure, Timothy Hannan found that the presence of guards in banks "significantly reduce[s] the risk of robbery. Accepting point estimates, the magnitude of this reduction is approximately one robbery attempt a year for those offices which would have otherwise suffered a positive number of robbery attempts."[13] This result supports the findings of G. M. Camp whose interviews of imprisoned bank robbers revealed that 77 percent of them found out whether the bank had a guard before committing the robbery.[14] Only 6 percent of those interviewed bothered to learn the police routine in the area before the robbery. One implication is that these criminals were more concerned with the private protection measure than with public enforcement (although another is that information about police routine is both more costly to obtain and less valuable because police change their routines).

Charles Clotfelter considered the impact of private and public security services on the manufacturing, wholesaling, finance, insurance, and real estate sectors. His empirical results "appear to indicate that private protective firms are more effective than public police at protecting firms in these industries."[15] He also found that private protection is more effective and more readily responsive in areas experiencing rapid population growth. Thus, there is some support for the expectation that these specialized private services should generate benefits in terms of reduced criminal activity, at least for those who employ private police. Indeed, "few would argue that ceterus paribus, if private security services were drastically reduced or eliminated, reported crime, fear of crime, and prices of retail merchandise would rise."[16] But beyond that, what little evidence exists implies that the private sector is more effective than the public sector in meeting needs such as those of some large industrial groups and in areas of rapid population growth.

EXAMPLES OF INDIVIDUAL SPECIALIZATION

Firearm ownership is a specialized form of protection that generates the benefit of deterring crime and preventing successful completion of crimes. Many private citizens keep guns in their homes to address potential situations where relatively delayed actions by public or private police are likely to fail.[17] There is some evidence that the immediate response of gun owners can be effective. Although information on the relative success of the private use of firearms to interrupt crime and apprehend criminals is scarce, it appears that such private efforts are at least as successful as police efforts. Kates compared the success rates of police and private citizens by examining every story in 42 of the nation's largest newspapers between January and June 1975 and May and July 1976 that reported the use of firearms for protection or prevention of crime. He estimated that police successfully prevented a crime or apprehended a criminal 68 percent of the time when they used firearms, while private citizen firearm use resulted in an 83 percent success rate.[18] It is true that firearms are a relatively risky means of protection, but Carol Silver and Don Kates found that benefits from using handguns for protection may be very high relative to the risk from criminal handgun use. They concluded that it "appears that the number of instances in which handguns were used for defense exceeds the number in which they were misused to kill (between 1960 and 1975) by a factor of 15–1."[19] If handgun use for defense outstrips handgun use to kill by anything close to that amount, then the risk of death associated with handgun use for defense is quite small.

The deterrent effect of private handgun ownership cannot be accurately measured, of course, but there is some powerful evidence that gun ownership deters crime. Philip Cook used cross-section data to examine the relationship between armed robbery rates and the strength of gun control laws.[20] He found that areas with strong gun controls have higher levels of armed robbery than areas with weaker controls. This could mean that when individuals' ability to defend themselves with guns is limited, they become more vulnerable to crime and are more likely to become victims. That is, gun ownership is a deterrent. There is a danger in such an interpretation because correlation does not necessarily imply causation. In this case, the correlation may arise because the strictest gun controls have been established in high crime areas in an unsuccessful effort to reduce crime, based on the mistaken but widely held belief that guns cause crime.[21]

There is more persuasive evidence. For example, surveys of prisoners "uniformly find felons stating that, whenever possible, they avoid victims who are thought to be armed, and that they know of planned crimes that were abandoned when it was discovered that the prospective victim was armed."[22] Based on data from Atlanta, Georgia, Cook concluded that a robber doubles his chances of dying by committing only seven robberies, because of the risk of being attacked by a victim.[23]

Some of the best evidence of the deterrent effect of gun ownership for protection comes from publicized programs to provide firearms training for potential victims. Between October 1966 and March 1967, the Orlando police department sponsored a program designed to train women in the safe use of firearms because of the increase in rapes in the city during 1966. The program was widely publicized in Orlando newspapers. Kleck and Bordua found that the rape rate in Orlando fell from a 1966 level of 35.91 per 100,000 inhabitants to only 4.18 in 1967.[24] This was not a part of any general downward trend, since the national rate was increasing, and rates in surrounding metropolitan areas and Florida were either constant or increasing. Furthermore, this decrease did not reflect a continual downward trend for Orlando, since the trend had been erratic but upward for several years. It seems obvious that the knowledge that potential rape victims might be carrying a gun and might know how to use it was a significant deterrent.

The Orlando example is not unique. Publicized training programs in the use of firearms have led to a reduction in armed robberies in Highland Park, Michigan, drug store robberies in New Orleans, and grocery store robberies in Detroit. When potential criminals become aware that potential victims might be ready to protect themselves with a gun, the increased perceived risk of committing a crime can lead to the abandonment of the crime. Of course, it may also lead to the choice of another victim, perhaps in an area where guns for protection are less likely. As a consequence, location-specific gun control could easily lead to higher crime rates in that area, as the Cook results imply.

This brings up an important point. Wealthy individuals typically have many options for protecting themselves.[25] They often live in high income communities where the tax base allows for a well-financed public police department. The number of police per crime committed is probably very high in these communities, relative to most intercity low income neighborhoods. In addition, wealthy individuals can buy alarms, guard dogs, and bulletproof cars, and can hire private police for protection. No gun control advocate has contended that private police should have their rights to carry firearms limited, so gun control laws will not be very limiting as far as the wealthy's self-protection efforts are concerned. The effect could be significant for middle and lower income individuals, however, because they typically are not as well protected by the public police and have far fewer self-protection options available. As evidence of the relative importance of guns for protection for lower income individuals, of the 120 justifiable homicides by private citizens in California during 1981, 28.6 percent were committed by Hispanics, 47.6 percent by blacks, and 21.4 percent by whites.[26] There is no reason to expect that particular races are more likely to be crime victims or to kill criminals than other races. But a much larger percentage of blacks and Hispanics are in the lower income classes in California than are whites, so we might conclude that lower income individuals tend to turn to firearms for protection more often than higher income individuals, simply because their choices are more limited. In addition, they are more likely to be the victims of crimes, so they are more likely to seek some means of self-protection. If strict gun control laws are passed, many lower income individuals will be forced to choose between giving up their primary tool for protecting their persons and property or becoming criminals themselves by disobeying the gun control laws (evidence is that they will choose the latter; an estimated one million illegal guns are held in New York City despite its gun control statute).

Other evidence must be noted here. The city council of Kennesaw, Georgia, passed a highly publicized ordinance on March 15, 1982, that required each household to keep a firearm. The publicity surrounding the passage of this ordinance apparently provided potential criminals in the area with the knowledge that many Kennesaw residents owned firearms and were willing to use them for protection. Consequently, crime in Kennesaw dropped at a dramatic rate. Serious crime dropped by 74.4 percent from 1981 to 1982.[27] Residential burglaries fell from 55 in 1981 to 19 in 1982; aggravated assault declined from nine to two, rapes fell from three to zero, armed robbery declined from four to zero, and homicide from one to zero. In the seven months immediately following the passage of the ordinance, there were only five burglaries as compared to 45 during the same seven-month period in 1981.[28] Reviewing the evidence from Orlando, Kennesaw and other sources led Kleck and Bordua to conclude:

> it is a perfectly plausible hypothesis that private gun ownership currently exerts as much or more deterrent effect on criminals as do the activities of the criminal justice system. . .there is the distinct possibility that although gun ownership among the crime-prone may tend to increase crime, gun ownership among the noncriminal majority may tend to depress crime rates below the levels they otherwise would achieve.[29]

Other protection equipment has also proven effective in detecting and preventing crime. In Cedar Rapids, Iowa, for example, a fairly inexpensive alarm system was installed in 350 businesses that had been frequent targets of burglars.[30] The system cost $100,000 during the first year, $185 per business to buy and install the equipment plus $185 a year for phone line charges and maintenance. Forty burglars were caught during the first year and a half after the system was in place, more than had been caught in the previous four years combined. All forty were convicted.

Other actions also appear to be successful. A National Institute of Law Enforcement and Criminal Justice study of four cities, for example, found that households that engrave identification numbers on their property appear to reduce their chances of being burglarized.[31] Surveys of people involved in similar projects in 78 other communities indicated similar results.

Another study, conducted by the Western Behavioral Science Institute with Southland Corporation's 7-Eleven stores, worked with former armed robbers to rate a large number of stores according to their attractiveness as robbery targets.[32] Using a sample of 120 stores of similar attractiveness, 60 were used as a control group and experimental changes were tested on the other 60. The changes were quite inexpensive (about $100 per store) and included stripping store windows of ad banners after dark and posting signs reading "Clerk cannot open this safe." The result was a 30 percent lower robbery rate in the test stores than in the control stores during the first eight months of the study. Prior to the study, Southland was experiencing an average of one robbery per store per year.

Patrols and neighborhood watches are also desirable crime prevention alternatives because of their low cost.[33] In fact, because volunteer and paid private security patrols are effective watchers, Sherman suggested that for cost-effectiveness reasons public police should *not* be the primary providers of crime prevention through watching. According to Sherman, public police should assist in the organization and use of both private voluntary watch organizations *and* private police, rather than viewing these other watchers as threats.[34]

One final privatization effort deserves attention—the private streets of St. Louis, as discussed in Chapter 9. Some observers have argued that the lower crime rates on these streets are the result of limiting access, not privatization. Certainly limited access might be expected to have been a major factor, but closures of public streets have been tried elsewhere with little success. A Department of Justice experiment in Hartford, Connecticut, for example, closed streets and assigned police teams to the neighborhood. But "to the disappointment of the project directors, police statistics did not show any dramatic drop in crime."[35] Private streets have two advantages that simple street closures and even neighborhood associations do not. First, "ownership gives the neighborhood a high degree of cohesiveness." Second, all residents sign a contract agreeing to property use and maintenance. The resulting incentives for cooperative crime control are apparently very strong.

Although empirical evidence is scarce, there are indications that the specialized uses of private resources are effective—and in many cases more effective than public resources. Of course, the fact that private resources that are substituted for public resources (or for which public resources could be substituted) are effective at crime deterrence is not necessarily sufficient justification for their use. The same resources might be used more efficiently by the public bureaucracy.

EFFICIENCIES GAINS IN ENFORCEMENT

Private sector production of protection or dispute resolution is likely to be relatively efficient when compared to public sector production. One reason is that private firms that produce protection services or adjudication can only survive if they make a profit. In an effort to be profitable, the private entrepreneur attempts to produce the level of service demanded at the lowest possible cost. If he is successful, he reaps the benefits. But citizens do not expect a public police department or court to make a profit. Taxes cover costs, and police departments and courts survive regardless of costs. Because police chiefs and judges do not have to make profits to survive, they have weaker incentives for concern about production costs. Furthermore, they reap no special reward by successfully producing at the lowest possible cost. This does not imply that police chiefs and judges will be completely ambivalent to the costs a department or court generates; it means that they are likely to make a relatively smaller effort at monitoring employees to check on wasted time and resources.

But the differences go beyond the incentives of public bureau managers. Even a manager who ignores his incentives and acts like a profit maximizer (cost minimizer) would not be effective, given bureaucratic rigidities. A study of public production versus contracting out by New York City's Office of Administration found:

> It is clear that municipal enterprises function under handicaps. Labor productivity is influenced by civil service rules and a union-management situation entirely different from that in private industry. A municipal worker costs more per unit of work. Other handicaps result from the prevailing attitude that

watchdog systems are not needed to prevent municipal officials from stealing public funds.

The point is basically that the rules of the game handicap productivity in municipal enterprise. A good manager will be able to do better than a poor manager, but it will be nearly impossible for him to do as well as he could in private industry, playing under a different set of rules.[36]

The organizational inflexibility inherent in the civil service system prevents management from disciplining inefficient employees unless their behavior is extreme. Lateral movement to adjust manpower needs in the face of changing demands is virtually impossible, as is hiring at any but the lowest grades. "Such dysfunctional qualities of civil service systems commonly reflect employee pressure which tends to emphasize continuity and seniority over competence as qualifications for higher-level positions, and by employee unions which emphasize the traditional union goals of more pay, less work, and job security."[37]

The profit motive provides strong incentives to produce at low costs. Because consumers are free to choose among private protection options, the only way that a private firm can legally obtain customers is by *persuading* people that it offers a quality service at a reasonable price. Government producers of protection (or even governments contracting out for protection services) have another option: they can use the government's power of *coercion* to collect taxes and produce protection whether it is valued at the price paid or not.

Resources are most efficiently used when they are guided to the use that generates the greatest benefit to members of society. Competitive markets tend to guide resources to their highest and best uses, because the price consumers are willing to pay for a good or service reflects the benefits they expect to obtain from its consumption. Public police departments do not take advantage of price signals in deciding how to allocate resources, while private providers of protection service and equipment *are forced* to pay attention to price signals. As Gustave de Molinari, a nineteenth-century French economist, wrote, the "option the consumer retains of being able to buy security wherever he pleases brings about a constant emulation among all producers, each producer striving to maintain or augment his clientele with the attraction of cheapness or of faster, more complete and better [services]."[38]

The importance of price signals and competition for clientele should not be overlooked in a discussion of efficiency. Most police departments have not perceived the pressures of competition (except in terms of competition for a share of the budget that other bureaucracies are also seeking) because their clientele is guaranteed. In the private sector, however, firms must compete for consumer dollars, and consumers choose among the options available. Under these circumstances, if a consumer buys a gun, installs an alarm, or hires a guard for protection, then the decision implies a rational, efficient allocation of protection resources. Such a decision reflects the fact that these are specialized resources for protection that provide benefits the public police cannot provide.

The Relative Efficiency of Private Courts.   Private police are relatively cost-effective, but what about private courts? Robert McLucas, director for casualty property claims at Travelers Insurance explained: "There are two reasons to use [private courts]. One, they're cheap. And two, they're inexpensive."[39] For example, a small Virginia wholesale supplier had a disagreement with a large computer company over problems it was having with a recently purchased computer. A court dispute would have cost them at least $25,000 each,[40] so they arranged a mini-trial with EnDispute. The issue was settled in a day and a half at a total cost of $4,500 each. A major reason for the savings is that mini-trials operate under extremely simplified procedures and rules relative to those set up by the public court bureaucracy.

Simplification of rules and procedures characterizes arbitration, and businessmen who choose arbitration typically recognize the desirable relationship between informality and speed.[41] Arbitration avoids the time-consuming procedural aspects of public litigation and offers considerable flexibility due to its simpler proceedings. In fact, there is still a relatively widespread rejection of lawyers as arbitrators, reflecting a desire to maintain the informality that distinguishes it from public courts (see Chapter 2).[42]

Consider this example. Suing one's neighbor is one of the simplest procedures in the law, but what is involved in just filing such a suit? First, a lawyer is engaged and the problem is explained. A retainer is paid. Then the lawyer draws up a complaint—a formal, legal document that explains the grounds on which the court's jurisdiction rests, details why the suit is being filed, and outlines what the plaintiff wants the defendant to do. Numerous copies of this complaint are made for the court and the person being sued. "Certificates of service" are drawn up to inform the plaintiff that the defendant has received the complaint. Once the papers have gotten to the defendant, after passing through the Clerk of Court and the sheriff and then back to the plaintiff (again through the sheriff and the Clerk of Court), the suit has officially commenced, "with as few papers and as few lawyer-hours and as little complexity as almost any process known to the law."[43]

What if the same dispute had gone to arbitration? The complaining party can obtain a one-page form from the AAA and briefly describe his complaint. The form is mailed to the other party and a copy is deposited at the nearest regional office of the AAA. "That commences the arbitration, at the cost of five minutes and a few postage stamps."[44] Wooldridge concluded: "The process for bringing an argument before a private court is. . .infinitely more speedy and economical than that for bringing an identical dispute before an official court. . . . Whatever the historical, theoretical and practical reasons for the painstaking, measured pace of the courts, that pace also entails an abundance of two increasingly expensive commodities, paper and lawyers."[45] Wooldridge predicted that the complexity of the public sector legal process might push people to greater uses of private means of dispute resolution even if court congestion does not.

INFORMATION AS A SOURCE OF EFFICIENCY

Allocative decisions made in private markets are typically based on better information for both demanders and suppliers than allocative decisions made in the public sector. David Friedman provided an interesting analogy that emphasizes a reason why buyers have better information in markets. Consumers making purchases in a market can compare substitutes. Consumer information is clearly not perfect, nor is the information needed to make most decisions, so mistakes can be made. But alternatives actually *exist* and can be compared on the basis of past performance records. On the other hand,

when you elect a politician, you buy nothing but promises. You may know how one politician ran the country for the past four years, but not how his competitor might have run it. You can compare 1968 Fords, Chryslers, and Volkswagens, but nobody will ever be able to compare the Nixon administration of 1968 with the Humphrey and Wallace administrations of the same year. It is as if we had only Fords from 1920 to 1928, Chryslers from 1928 to 1936, and had to decide what firm would make a better car for the next four years. Perhaps an expert automotive engineer could make an educated guess as to whether Ford had used the technology of 1920 to satisfy the demands of 1920 better than Chrysler had used the technology of 1928 to satisfy the demands of 1928. The rest of us might just as well flip a coin. If you threw in Volkswagen or American Motors, which had not made any cars in America but wanted to, the situation gets ridiculous. Each of us would have to know every firm unlimitedly in order to have any reasonable basis for deciding.[46]

Consumers buying goods or services in competitive markets have *relatively* good bases for comparison, so they have a better idea of the quality available.

Consumers in private markets have relatively strong incentives to use information that is available, because when they make a purchase decision, they consume the good or service. They *benefit directly* from any time, effort, and expenses invested. Consumers of publicly produced goods have relatively weak incentives to obtain information, however, because after obtaining information and making a choice the individual has no guarantee that government will respond in the desired fashion. Indeed, in representative politics, there is no guarantee that the individual's choice, after seeking information, will matter at all. As Friedman suggested,

> Imagine buying cars the way we buy governments. Ten thousand people would get together and agree to vote, each for the car he preferred. Whichever car won each of the ten thousand would have to buy it. It would not pay any of us to make any serious effort to find out which car was best; whatever I decide, my car is being picked for me by the other members of the group. Under such institutions the quality of cars would quickly decline.
>
> That is how I must buy products on the political marketplace. I not only cannot compare alternative products, it would not be worth my while to do so even if I could. This may have something to do with the quality of the goods sold on that market. *Caveat emptor.*[47]

Indeed it does have something to do with the quality of government output, because it clearly affects the incentives of those in government who produce goods and services.

Individual voters and taxpayers have little incentive to inform themselves regarding the workings of their government. That is, they have few incentives to *monitor* the performance of those who produce government goods and services. This generates the possibilities for interest groups to influence government decisions, for bureaucrats to produce inefficiently, and for corruption to flourish. Producers in competitive markets, on the other hand, must provide what consumers want in order to survive and prosper.

DISCIPLINE FROM COMPETITION

Neighborhood watches and patrols generally involve private cooperative actions to deter crime. When a crime is observed, the private individual on patrol calls the public police. Because crimes are more likely to be solved if observed in progress than if discovered after completion, the police are more likely to apprehend and successfully prosecute a criminal. So neighborhood watches are likely to reduce crime because of the deterrent effect of the visible patrol, and they are also likely to increase the probability of the police solving crimes actually committed. Thus, it is not surprising that police departments actively support neighborhood watch organizations and aid in their formation. There is similar support for Operation ID, which involves marking property so it can be easily identified when stolen.

There are other examples. Gun ownership allows individuals to respond much more quickly to a crime in progress than the response time of most public police efforts. A relatively quick response by a gun owner increases the likelihood of apprehending the criminal. It is not surprising, then, to find an overwhelming majority of police officers opposing gun control. The Second Amendment Foundation found in 1977 that approximately 64 percent of the 34,000 police officers surveyed believed that an armed citizenry serves as a deterrent to crime; 86 percent indicated that even if they were not police officers they would keep a gun for protection; and more than 83 percent indicated that banning handguns would benefit criminals rather than citizens.[48] A 1976 survey conducted by the Planning and Research Division of the Boston Police Department found that over 66 percent of the nation's leading police administrators favored possession of handguns by the citizenry; 80 percent approved of possession of handguns in homes and business places.[49]

Kakalik and Wildhorn pointed out that "private police often act as extended eyes and ears for the public police; they occasionally assist in serving warrants and citations on private property, or in traffic control around private property; they report suspicious persons and circumstances to public police; they may make preliminary investigations; they may make, or assist in making, arrests; they may apprise police of impending unusual situations, such as strikes; and so on."[50] When private police work with public police, law enforcement appears to be enhanced.

Public and Private Crime Control: Substitutes or Complements?   If public and private services are complements, then the growth of the private sector will clearly enhance the performance of the public sector. If they are substitutes, however, then the apparent impact on public sector performance is likely to be mostly illusory. Kakalik and Wildhorn argued that public and private security services are largely complementary: "with very few exceptions, [private] guards perform work that the regular public police cannot or will not perform. . . . Typically, private guards perform functions that *complement* those of public police." They also maintained that the private sector does very little investigation work and those investigations that are performed by private firms occur where public police are unable or unwilling to investigate. So, "the vast majority of private investigative effort is *complementary* to the public police." Private patrolmen on private property patrol where police rarely do, so their role is said to be "primarily *complementary* to police." In addition, "the intrusion alarm systems *complement* the functions of public police because they are intended to prevent crime (if the alarm system is conspicuous), to detect crime, and to report crimes that occur on the premises where alarms are located." Finally, "armored delivery service personnel. . .provide security during transit of items between locations. . .[where] the public police will generally take no preventative action. Thus, the typical roles of public police and private armored delivery personnel are *complementary*."[51] In fact, virtually all of these activities "complement" public police only in the sense that they have taken up potential crime protection and prevention functions that the police are either unable or unwilling to perform. In other words, they are *substituting* for public police.

There are probably private crime control actions that really are complements to public police in the economic sense. By definition, two goods are complements if a price reduction for one leads to increased purchases of both. The relationship holds in the opposite direction as well; price increase of one good leads to reduced purchases of both. So, for example, more public and private police services should be purchased because of a lower price for public police. But the increasing privatization has occurred in the face of *rising prices* for public police services. The economic definition of a substitute is that the purchase of one good or service increases as a consequence of rising prices of another.[52]

Most private security efforts *appear* to be complements to public police because as private sector crime control efforts increase crimes are deterred and criminals are caught; that is, the output of the *entire* system (private and public) that is attributed solely to the public police, increases as measured by arrests and relatively less crime. What actually occurs, however, is that private security efforts are substituted for some of the duties that public police might perform, partially relieving the public police of congestion problems. Public police *appear* to become more effective as a consequence.

There is, however, one way that the availability of substitutes could actually enhance public performance. As more citizens turn to the private sector to supplement public protection or dispute resolution, they should come to realize the advantages of privatization. Private sector services will become specialized, and consequently, relatively more effective than the public sector. Furthermore, private sector efforts will generally be available at relatively low costs, and citizens will become increasingly reluctant to pay taxes for public police and courts. The threat of loss of budgets and jobs may be great enough for public bureaucrats to have stronger cost monitoring incentives and for public employees to modify their wage and working condition demands. In this way, some of the benefits of private sector competition may spill over into public sector production.

The same occurs with the growth of private courts. As Pruitt observed, the shift from public to private courts tends to alleviate some of the problems in the public courts that created the incentives for shifting to private courts in the first place.[53] In particular, court congestion might be eased both because a number of cases are diverted from the docket *and* because those cases tend to be relatively complex and time consuming. Consequently, availability of private courts may make public courts *appear* to be more efficient. But private courts are substituting for public courts, not complementing them. Again, privatization of protection and dispute resolution can have positive spillover effects on the public sector criminal justice system if public producers perceive private substitutes as a real competitive threat to their budgets.

CONCLUSIONS

How much privatization should be allowed? There are conflicting views as to the answer to this question. Consider, for example, the study by Marshall Clinnard that contrasted crime rates in Switzerland and Sweden and attempted to explain observed differences in crime rates by noting differences in the social and political makeup of the two countries.[54] Clinnard's explanation for the relatively low crime rate in Switzerland stressed the different degrees of government control. Sweden has a strong central government that has tended to inhibit individual initiative and responsibility in all areas, including crime. The Swiss have relied more on individual efforts with a much weaker central government. In fact, private sector provision of police services is common in Switzerland, with more than 30 Swiss villages and townships currently purchasing protection at what the Swiss Association of Towns and Townships describes as "substantial savings."[55] Clinnard concluded: "Communities or cities that wish to prevent crime should encourage greater political decentralization by developing small government units and encouraging citizen responsibility for obedience to the law and crime control. The increased delegation and responsibility for crime control to the police and to governmental agencies. . .should be reversed."[56] Clinnard's findings clearly support greater privatization.

A growing number of scholars contend that government should have no role whatever in crime protection or dispute resolution.[57] Their argument is an appealing one, stressing the advantages of freedom of choice and competition, the cost-minimizing incentives of profit-seekers, the avoidance of the commons problem, and the benefits of specialization. This point of view stresses the efficiency and effectiveness of *supply* by private producers *relative* to supply by public producers. Some would contend, however, that it tends to overlook certain problems that may emanate from the demand side of the market. These arguments are considered in the next chapter.

APPENDIX TO CHAPTER 10

THE ECONOMIC THEORY OF CRIME AND PRIVATIZATION

The economic theory of crime approaches criminal activity in a manner that differs significantly from other paradigms. This theory does not try to specify the ultimate causes of crime; instead, it attempts to identify variables that structure the costs of and returns to criminal activity in order to predict the incidence of crime. In other words, the economic theory of crime attempts to explain crime rates directly through examination of social and economic variables rather than indirectly as a result of the psychological makeup of potential criminals. The underlying rationale is that criminals respond consistently to incentives. Thus, crime is explained as a problem of constrained utility maximization. Individuals maximize expected utility by choosing between legal and illegal activities after considering the expected gains and costs associated with each alternative. Many reasons for the significant trend toward privatization can be visualized by adding the private sector to Gary Becker's path-breaking model.[58]

THE ECONOMIC THEORY OF CRIME WITHOUT PRIVATE ENFORCEMENT

Following Becker and Ehrlich,[59] consider a supply of offenses in which per capita crimes are related to the probability and severity of punishment for that type of crime, the expected income from the criminal activity, and returns from alternative legal activities (and perhaps other environmental factors). The first two factors represent the potential criminal's assessments of the costs he might bear if he commits the crime. If the probability of punishment rises, an individual is less likely to commit the crime, and the supply of offenses should diminish. Similarly, if the severity of punishment increases, then the number of offenses can be expected to fall. On the other hand, if the gains from committing this crime rise, then more such crimes should occur. Finally, if the opportunities for or level of legitimate income generation increase, then criminal activity should decline. Some might point out that "crimes of passion" do not generate monetary rewards. As Sedgwick observed, however, "the economic model can be applied to any situation where an individual is seeking to maximize his subjective utility: Thus, the fact that crimes of passion often do not involve transfers of money does not mean that they cannot be explained by the economic model."[60]

Becker, Ehrlich, and others have pointed out that the supply of offenses is determined simultaneously with the demand for criminal enforcement services. But they generally only consider the public sector's contribution to enforcement. Thus, production of enforcement affecting the probability of punishment depends on such factors as the number of police per capita or for a geographic area, the level of a suspect's rights, and characteristics of the community in which the crimes are carried out. Similarly, the production of enforcement services affecting the severity of punishment depends on factors such as the length of prison terms, the rights of prisoners, the prison environment, and perhaps the potential for capital punishment.

Given these relationships, Ehrlich and others have developed predictions regarding the allocation of and demand for enforcement. For instance, a community's demand for such services depends on the crime rate, the level of income or wealth of the community, the opportunity costs of using the community's resources for criminal enforcement, and other community characteristics.

So, the economic theory of crime envisions an interdependent (or simultaneous) system in which the supply of offenses cannot be determined without simultaneously determining the community's demand for enforcement services. But the demand for enforcement services is a much more complex issue than has typically been assumed. First, let us consider the evidence supporting this theory and then see whether the economic theory can explain the growth in demand for private enforcement services.

EMPIRICAL SUPPORT FOR THE ECONOMIC THEORY OF CRIME

Because the economic theory of crime hypothesizes that criminal activity can increase with a reduction in the cost of committing crime or an increase in its benefits, two empirical questions have been examined: Do crime rates rise with a reduction in the opportunity costs of crime? Do crime rates rise with a decline in the expected cost of crime due to reduction in the probability of and severity of punishment? A large amount of literature indicates that a fall in the opportunity costs of crime either in terms of a reduction of wages or an increase in unemployment leads to an increase in crime.[61] These findings are not unique to economics; virtually all social scientists agree on this point. Thus, one explanation for the rapidly rising (through the 1960s) and then relatively stable but high crime rates (during the 1970s and early 1980s) has to be the long and deep recessions and the uncertainty of legal opportunities arising from continual high inflation and high unemployment. Similarly, the slight drops in crime rates may be due to improving economic conditions. In fact, a general conclusion of the empirical literature on the economic theory of crime may be that the best way to reduce crime is to increase legitimate opportunities.[62] There is evidence to support the hypothesis that crime rates rise with reductions in the probability of and severity of punishment, however, and this hypothesis is of particular interest.

Tests of this "deterrence hypothesis" are widespread in the economics, sociology, and criminology literatures. As Palmer noted: "It is probably safe to say that many economists have concluded that an increase in the expected punishment does reduce crime, while many sociologists have concluded such an increase does not deter crime or has too small an effect to be considered a useful instrument of society."[63] The economic theory essentially contends that criminals are *about* like anyone else in that they rationally maximize utility given their estimates and evaluations of the potential costs and benefits of alternative criminal and legal activities. Criminals may have different preferences than non-criminals, but they *do respond to incentives,* so punishment can deter crime.[64]

In his examination of the deterrent impact of the likelihood (and severity) of punishment on all seven of the FBI index crimes, Isaac Ehrlich found that "the rate of specific crime categories, with virtually no exception, varies inversely with estimates of the probability of apprehension and punishment by imprisonment."[65] Perhaps the most important result of his findings is that so-called crimes of passion (murder, rape, assault) respond just as strongly to the expected costs of punishment as do the property crimes.[66] This provides strong support for the economic theory of crime, which assumes that even potential criminals who may have different preferences respond to incentives.

To sum up, we might conclude that: 1) relatively poor legal income generating opportunity will result in more crime; and 2) crime rates are reduced by higher probabilities of punishment.[67] Some critics may not agree with these conclusions, pointing out that the data and at least some of the econometric techniques used to obtain the results were poor. As Elliot observed, however, "these problems do not appear to make existing crime data unsuitable for empirical tests of the economic theory of crime" since, when the biases of under-reporting are eliminated, it appears that the effect of sanctions is greater.[68] In addition, "the econometric problems associated with recent studies of crime are not noticeably more serious than in other areas of applied econometrics—especially when one 'seasonally adjusts' for its relatively late development—and, moreover, that the findings are in agreement with a priori theoretical expectations and are robust across widely different geographic cross-sections."[69] Thus, it seems reasonable to conclude that if there are noticeable trends in the direction of reduced certainty (and perhaps severity) of punishment, this would provide at least a partial explanation for increasing crime rates.

TRENDS IN THE PROBABILITY OF PUNISHMENT

If crime rates are negatively related to chances of punishment, when the probability of punishment declines, crime rates will rise. Such a decline is easily documented, at least in part. For example, criminals are increasingly likely to get away with their crimes, and over the 1960–1980 period the percentages of reported crimes cleared have diminished considerably (see Table 10.1). Additional indicators of expected chances of punishment include conviction and dismissal rates. David Jones reported that total conviction rates in federal courts peaked and dismissal rates bottomed out in 1952; after that, conviction rates declined while dismissal rates increased gradually through 1970. Jones also examined states' conviction and dismissal rates and found that in many states the chances of punishment have declined. One possible reason for declining conviction rates may be the general constriction in the willingness of many courts to admit evidence against criminal defendants, especially when it has been obtained by means of police

Table 10.1 Percentage of Offenses Known Cleared by Arrest.

Year	Total Crime*	Violent Crimes**	Murder and Nonnegligible Manslaughter	Forcible Rape	Robbery	Aggravated Assault
1980	19.2	43.6	72.3	48.8	23.8	58.7
1975	21.0	44.7	70.3	51.3	27.0	63.5
1970	21.0	47.6	86.5	56.4	29.1	64.9
1965	24.6		90.5	64.0	37.6	72.9
1960	26.1		92.3	72.5	38.5	75.8
1955			92.7	78.6	42.8	77.4
1950			93.8	80.3	43.5	76.6

SOURCE: U.S. Department of Justice, Uniform Crime Reports, Federal Bureau of Investigation, for various years.
*The values for the Aggregated Crime Index were not reported for 1950 and 1955.
**The Aggregated Violent Crime Index was not reported for 1950, 1955, 1960, and 1965.

search and seizure.[70] David Jones reported that "lower court judges and prosecutors have complained that the 'criminal law revolution' and its aftermath have shackled their ability to bring the guilty to justice, forcing them to stay out of the courtroom and to rely upon the willingness of many defendants to admit their guilt in consideration of promises for lenience in punishment."[71] The National Advisory Commission on Criminal Justice Standards and Goals found that a major factor contributing to increases in serious crime is that courts have applied more stringent standards for admitting evidence without adequately explaining their reasoning for doing so and often without providing sufficient guidelines for obtaining sufficiently admissible evidence.[72]

One reason for the reduced probability of arrest is an increasing trend to criminalize activities. Discussion of this trend and its consequences can be found in Chapters 4, 5, and 6.

David Jones observed trends in plea bargaining that also indicate that the severity of punishment is on the decline. Increasingly, criminals are able to have their charges reduced if they are willing to plead guilty; defendants charged with multiple crimes can get most of the charges dropped if they plead guilty to one or two; and charges against the use of a weapon in commission of a crime are routinely dismissed in exchange for a guilty plea to another charge. It is clear that reductions in the probability of punishment are far more widespread than the measurable statistical evidence indicates.[73]

With the changes in the expected costs of committing criminal acts, it is not surprising to see rising and then continually high crime rates. As the potential costs of crime to the potential criminal fall, it becomes increasingly likely that crime will pay.

When compared to legal options, crime is an attractive source of income for large numbers of people. Clearly, the relative gains from criminal activity play a major role in determining the number of crimes committed. The most effective way to reduce crime appears to be to increase legitimate opportunities through economic and, therefore, income and employment growth, thereby making the returns to crime relatively less attractive.

Explanations offered by many observers for the sharp rise in crime rates through the 1960s and the continuing high rates through the 1970s and early 1980s may appear to conflict with the economic theory of crime. For instance, there is a strong statistical correlation between crime rates and the portion of the population in the teenage and early twenties age group. The post-war "baby boom" began moving into this age group in the early 1960s, expanded rapidly through the 1960s and more slowly during the

1970s, peaked in the early 1980s, and has declined since. Thus, the crime rates rose rapidly through the 1960s, stabilized in the 1970s, and fluctuated only slightly for the last few years because of changes in this "crime-prone" age group. This would seem to deny the claims made in this appendix. But this argument fails to address the more fundamental question of why this age group is more prone to commit crimes. The answer comes directly from Becker's economic theory of crime. Virtually any proxy measure for the opportunity costs that members of this group face as an alternative to crime indicate that crime should be relatively attractive. Wages for young people are low, and their unemployment is always substantially higher than for the older population. In addition, punishment for young criminals tends to be less severe, particularly for those under eighteen who are prosecuted as juveniles. Even for those over 18, punishment may be less severe in a relative sense. A fifteen-year prison sentence is, in all likelihood, considerably less frightening for a 20-year-old who expects to live 50 or 60 more years than for someone who is 50 and expects to live only 20 more years.

The economic theory of crime predicts that crime rates among young people should be relatively high and an increase in the number of young people should raise overall crime rates. Does this deny that the reductions in the likelihood of punishment have also led to higher crime rates? Not at all. It simply says that there are also other forces at work—forces that cannot be directly influenced by the criminal justice system. In one sense, it even reinforces the contentions made here. If the citizenry wants government to control crime with the resources and techniques available while at the same time a growing portion of the population finds crime to be a relatively attractive option, then trends in the probability and severity of punishment are precisely the opposite of what they should be.

This discussion should not be interpreted as an advocation of more severe criminal sanctions or an expansion of the public sector's law enforcement bureaucracy in order to increase the probability of punishment. As Tullock noted, "The fact that we can deter a crime by a particular punishment is not a sufficient argument for that punishment."[74] Similarly, Ehrlich pointed out that "the results of the empirical investigation indicate that the rate of murder and other related crimes may also be reduced through increased employment and earning opportunities. The range of effective methods for defense against murder thus extends beyond conventional means of law enforcement and crime prevention."[75] These arguments stress a significant shortcoming in viewing crime with an emphasis on publicly produced enforcement efforts, ignoring the role of the private sector. Indeed, many of the reasons for the current level of privatization in the criminal justice arena and the significant trends toward increased privatization can be visualized by adding the private sector to Becker's model of crime.

THE ECONOMIC THEORY OF CRIME WITH PRIVATIZATION

Becker's model recognizes that the probability and severity of punishment are affected by public law enforcement activities, but there is no mention of how private sector efforts affect crime protection and prevention.[76] Yet, such private efforts are likely to have a major effect, particularly on the probability of punishment. In Becker's model, the demand for public enforcement services applied to a crime was a function of the wealth of the community, the opportunity cost of the community's tax dollars used for publicly produced criminal law enforcement, the level of criminal activity, and other community characteristics. Private sector crime control efforts should be added to these factors.

An additional relationship can also be added to the Becker model of crime. What determines the demand for various private crime control activities? In this case, demand functions are true "market demands." Each is a function of the price of the activity that individuals must pay—in money or in terms of individual commitments of time and effort. The aggregate demand for each of the private sector's crime control activities is a function of the price of that crime control activity, the prices of the other private crime control goods and services (substitutes and complements), the levels of wealth and crimes in the community, and the nature of public investments and punishments.

Increasing Demand for Privately Provided Crime Control.   Kakalik and Wildhorn asked: "What are the forces spurring the growth of private security?" They answered by pointing out that most observers would list at least some of the following factors:

- The high level of and rate of increase in reported crime of all types and in all regions.
- Increasing public awareness and fear of crime.
- The federal government's need for security in its space and defense activities during the past decade and, more recently, for security against violent demonstration, bombings, and hijackings.

- The basic trend toward specialization of all services.
- Rising claims to fire and casualty insurance losses.
- Withdrawal of some insurers from the market.
- Insurers raising rates and/or requiring use of certain private security systems.
- Insurers offering premium discounts when certain private security measures are used.
- The nation's growth and advancing state of the art in electronics and other scientific areas, which has sparked new and distinct manufacturing branches of several companies, providing greatly improved security devices, especially for intrusion detection.
- The general increase in corporate and private income; this means there is more property to protect and, at the same time, more income to pay for protection.
- A feeling in some quarters that the regular police are overburdened and have not been able to stem the tide of rising crime, and therefore, that private security measures are needed to supplement regular police protection in some situations.[20]

Many of these forces have already been well documented in this book, such as the increase in crime rates, the fear of crime, and the failure of government's crime control efforts. Some of the other factors listed above have not been discussed, but their consequences are straightforward when considered in terms of the current discussion. Growing income will normally lead to increasing purchases of most private protection equipment and services. Economic growth has occurred through virtually all the 1960s, 1970s, and 1980s. This has led to a growing demand for private (and perhaps public) crime prevention and protection.

Most of the other factors listed by Kakalik and Wildhorn enter our analysis through consideration of the prices of substitutes and complements. For instance, insurance is obviously a substitute for property protection equipment and services. As insurance has become increasingly expensive, individuals and firms have switched to relatively more protection and less insurance. Much of the electronic security equipment, on the other hand, apparently is complementary to other protection services, particularly the use of guards to monitor the equipment and respond to its signals. Because of technological advances, the price of this kind of security has fallen—

more security can be obtained for the same level of outlay for equipment, or the same level of security could be obtained with a smaller expenditure. This lower price has two implications. First, as the price of effective security through the use of advanced security equipment falls, more of that equipment is purchased. Thus, it is not surprising that "the progression from vacuum tubes to transistors to integrated circuit technology has played a major role in the growth of the security industry. Today, electronic security products and services comprise a sizable portion of the security market."[78] Second, as the price of security produced with this equipment has fallen, the demand for complementary security services (e.g., guards) has increased.

Substitution of Private for Public Crime Control. Because most private and public crime control goods and services are substitutes in an economic sense, as the price of one source of crime control rises *relative* to the price of another, demand for the now relatively low priced good or service will increase. Table 10.2 details the rising price (proxied by average monthly payroll) for public police for 1970–1979. This trend existed throughout the 1950s and 1960s as well. Of course, the price of private police has also been rising, as Table 10.2 indicates. During the decade of the 1960s, however, the wages of public police increased much faster. During the 1970s, public police monthly payroll per police officer increased by 87.7 percent over the ten-year period, while private police payroll per employee rose by only 68.1 percent. Thus, as the ratio of public police payroll per officer to private police payroll per employee in Table 10.2 indicates, the relative prices of the two services have changed. Public police cost 2.5 times as much as private police in 1970, but this ratio had risen to 2.79 by 1979. Other conditions (e.g., income) might lead to increasing purchases of both public and private police even though prices are rising (and, in fact, explain in part why the prices are rising), but given the changes in relative prices, consumers should substitute private police (and other private security services and equipment) for public police to the degree that they can. As Clotfelter concluded: "Substitution may well provide one explanation for recent growth of private means of protection in the United States."[79]

There are legal opportunities for substitution, such as surveillance, guarding, and some maintenance of order; and Clotfelter found evidence that communities' demands for public and private protection are quite sensitive to relative wage rates. Clotfelter's point estimate for the elasticity of substitution was 2.47, implying that expenditures for private sector protection should be rising more than proportionally for public police, given

Table 10.2   Average and Relative Average Monthly Wages for Public Police and Employees in Private Detective Agencies and Protective Services, 1970–1979.*

Year	Public Police**	Private Police***	Ratio of Public Police Payroll to Private Police Payroll
1970	793	317	2.50
1971	842	331	2.54
1972	915	353	2.59
1973	993	363	2.74
1974	1,062	384	2.77
1975	1,134	422	2.69
1976	1,230	456	2.70
1977	1,312	458	2.86
1978	1,385	492	2.82
1979	1,489	533	2.79
% Change 1970–79	87.7%	68.1%	11.6%

*Average monthly salaries for public police are calculated from data provided in Tables 5.1 and 5.2 while data for private employment in detective agencies and protective services is from Table 9.3. Payroll data for these employees is from the same source as the data in 9.3.

**Calculated as payroll for the month of October (from Table 5.2) divided by police employment (Table 5.1).

***Calculated as payroll for the first quarter of the year divided by 3, and then divided by employment from Table 9.3.

the relative prices in Table 10.2. But the implications go beyond just public police versus private police. During 1967–1973, the average salary for public police rose by 56 percent, while the average salary of employees of private protective and detective agencies rose by 34 percent. In addition, however, the average price of door locks and other locking equipment rose by 15 to 35 percent and the price of small arms rose by only 23 percent. Many private sector protection options appear to be getting increasingly attractive *relative* to public police.[80]

CONCLUSIONS

Can private citizens really substitute private protection for increasingly expensive public police, given that interest group politics determine the budgets for public police and citizens have no choice but to pay the resulting taxes? This question is addressed in more detail in Chapter 13, but for now let us recognize that if voters get sufficiently disillusioned with public police or become more aware of the relative advantages of private protection, they may refuse to pay those taxes. Sherman noted that as dissatisfaction with increasingly expensive public police has risen, voters have turned to private sources of watching (volunteer groups and private police).[81] The same is true of other private crime control services and equipment. In fact, three cities have recently rejected taxes explicitly designated to pay for additional police.[82] Thus, an obvious explanation for the rapid privatization we are observing is the inadequacy of publicly provided services. This clearly goes a long way towards accounting for the phenomenon.[83]

ENDNOTES

1. Carl Person, "Justice, Inc.," *Juris Doctor* 8 (March 1978), p. 32.
2. Ibid.
3. See for example, John R. Lott, Jr., "Should the Wealthy Be Able to 'Buy Justice'?" *Journal of Political Economy* 95 (December 1987): 1307–1316.
4. There may be an equity issue, of course. The poor may be excluded while the wealthy command all the best (private) security services. This issue is examined in Chapter 14.
5. James S. Kakalik and Sorrel Wildhorn, *The Private Police Industry: Its Nature and Extent* (Santa Monica, Calif.: The Rand Corporation, 1971), pp. 112–113.
6. Quoted in Tai Schneider Denenberg and R. V. Denenberg, *Dispute Resolution: Settling Conflicts Without Legal Action*, Public Affairs Pamphlet No. 597 (New York: Public Affairs Committee, Inc., 1981), p. 11.
7. Robert W. Poole, Jr., "Can Justice Be Privatized?" *Fiscal Watchdog* 49 (November 1980): 2; Richard Koenig, "More Firms Turn to Private Courts to Avoid Expensive Legal Fights," *Wall Street Journal,* January 4, 1984.
8. Gary Pruitt, "California Rent-a-Judge Justice," *Journal of Contemporary Studies* (Spring 1982), p. 50.
9. William C. Wooldridge, *Uncle Sam, the Monopoly Man* (New Rochelle, N.Y.: Arlington House, 1970), p. 116.
10. Ibid.
11. H. S. Dewhurst, *The Railroad Police,* Springfield, Ill.: Charles C. Thomas, Publishers, 1955), p. 4.
12. Wooldridge, *Uncle Sam, the Monopoly Man,* p. 117.
13. Timothy Hanna, "Bank Robberies and Bank Security Precautions," *Journal of Legal Studies* 11 (January 1982), p. 91.
14. G. M. Camp, "Nothing to Lose: A Study of Bank Robbery in America" (Ph.D. diss., Yale University, New Haven, Conn., 1968).

15. Charles T. Clotfelter, "Public Services, Private Substitutes, and the Demand for Protection Against Crime," *American Economic Review* 67 (December 1977): 874.
16. Kakalik and Wildhorn, *Private Police in the United States,* p. vii.
17. John Sneed, "Order Without Law: Where Will the Anarchists Keep the Madman?" *Journal of Libertarian Studies* 1 (1977), p. 17.
18. Don Kates, Jr., unpublished tables, no date.
19. Carol Silver and Don Kates, Jr., "Self-Defense, Handgun Ownership and the Independence of Women in a Violent, Sexist Society," in *Restricting Handguns: The Liberal Skeptics Speak Out,* ed. Don Kates, Jr. (New York: North River Press, 1977), p. 158.
20. Philip Cook, "The Effect of Gun Availability on Robbery and Robbery Murder: A Cross-section Study of 50 Cities," in *Policy Studies Review Annual* (1979): 743–781.
21. Bruce L. Benson, "Guns for Protection and Other Private Sector Responses to the Fear of Rising Crime," in *Firearms and Violence: Issues of Regulation,* Don Kates, Jr., ed. (Cambridge, Mass.: Ballinger Press, 1984), pp. 329–356.
22. Silver and Kates, "Self-Defense," p. 151. See also Van den Haag, "Banning Handguns: Helping the Criminal Hurt You," *New Woman* (November–December 1975): 80.
23. Cook, "The Effect of Gun Availability," p. 755.
24. Gary Kleck and David Bordua, "The Factual Foundation for Certain Key Assumptions of Gun Control," *Law and Policy Quarterly* 5 (Spring 1983): 271–298.
25. This is as it should be, given that an efficient allocation of resources is desired, since a wealthy individual's time typically has higher valued alternative uses than a relatively poor individual's time. See for example, Lott, "Should the Wealthy Be Able to 'Buy Justice'?"
26. California Department of Justice, *Homicide in California,* 1981, p. 74.
27. "Kennesaw's Crime Down 74 Percent," *Gun Week,* January 28, 1983, p. 3.
28. Kleck and Bordua, "The Factual Foundation for Certain Key Assumptions of Gun Control."
29. Ibid.
30. "To Catch a Thief: Antiburglar System Works in Iowa Town," *Wall Street Journal,* November 24, 1970.
31. "Operation Ident Seen Helpful in Reducing Burglary Chances," *Crime Control Digest,* September 29, 1975, p. 1.
32. "Holding Down Holdups," *Business Week,* March 8, 1976.
33. Robert K. Yin, Mary E. Vogel, Jan N. Chaiken, and Deborah R. Both, *Citizen Patrol Projects* (Washington, D.C.: National Institute of Law Enforcement and Criminal Justice, Law Enforcement Assistance Administration, Department of Justice, 1977), p. 30.

34. Lawrence W. Sherman, "Patrol Strategies for Police," in *Crime and Public Policy*, ed. James Q. Wilson (San Francisco: Institute for Contemporary Studies, 1983), p. 158.

35. Theodore J. Gage, "Getting Street-Wise in St. Louis," *Reason* 13 (August 1981): 20.

36. Quoted in E. S. Savas, "Municipal Monopolies Versus Competition in Delivering Urban Services," in *Improving the Quality of Urban Management*, ed. Willis D. Hawley and David Rogers, *Urban Affairs Annual Review*, vol. 8 (Beverly Hills: Sage Publications, 1974), p. 492.

37. Lyle C. Fitch, "Increasing the Role of the Private Sector in Providing Public Services," in *Improving the Quality of Urban Management*, ed. Willis D. Hawley and David Rogers, *Urban Affairs Annual Review*, vol. 8 (Beverly Hills: Sage Publications, 1974), p. 507.

38. Gustave de Molinari, "De la Production de la Sécurité," *Journal des Economistes* (February 1849): 277–290. This article has been translated into English and published as *The Production of Security*, tr. J. Huston McCullock (New York: The Center for Libertarian Studies, 1977). This citation is from p. 13 of the translation.

39. Quoted in "Private Court Systems: Discount Decision," *Inc.* (August 1984), p. 34.

40. Ibid., p. 34.

41. See for example, Poole, "Can Justice Be Privatized?" p. 3.

42. Steven Lazarus, et al., *Resolving Business Disputes: The Potential of Commercial Arbitration* (New York: American Management Association, 1965),
pp. 28, 54–55.

43. Wooldridge, *Uncle Sam, the Monopoly Man*, p. 108. More complex litigation involves even greater costs. A complex business case, for instance, leads "down a path of motions, counterclaims, discovery, depositions, and a variety of pretrial maneuvers that can last for years." See James F. Henry, "Minitrials: Scaling Down the Cost of Justice," *Across the Board* (October 1984), p. 45.

44. Ibid.

45. Ibid., p. 109.

46. David Friedman, *The Machinery of Freedom: Guide to a Radical Capitalism* (New York: Harper and Row, 1973), pp. 179–180.

47. Ibid., pp. 180–181.

48. Nassad F. Ayoob, *The Experts Speak Out: The Police View of Gun Control* (Bellevue, Wash.: Second Amendment Foundation, 1981), p. 7.

49. Ibid., pp. 7–8.

50. Kakalik and Wildhorn, *The Private Police Industry*, p. 117.

51. Ibid., pp. 111, 113, 114, 115–117.

52. See Clotfelter, "Public Services," p. 876.

53. Pruitt, "California's Rent-a-Judge Justice," p. 54. A similar point is made in James Granelli, "Got a Spat? Go Rent a Judge," *National Law Journal* (June 8, 1981), p. 30.

54. Marshall Clinnard, *Cities With Little Crime: The Case of Switzerland* (Cambridge: Cambridge University Press, 1978).

55. Theodore J. Gage, "Cops, Inc.," *Reason* 14 (March 1982): 26.

56. Clinnard, *Cities With Little Crime*, p. 156. See also Elinor Ostrom, William Baugh, Richard Guarasci, Roger Parks, and Gordon Whitaker, "Community Organization and the Provision of Police Services," *Administrative and Policy Studies Series* 1 (1973): 668; Ostrom and Parks, "Suburban Police Departments: Too Many and Too Small?" *Urban Affairs Annual Review* 7 (1973); Ostrom and Whitaker, "Does Local Community Control of Police Make a Difference? Some Preliminary Findings," *Midwest Journal of Political Science* 17 (1973).

57. See for example, Murray Rothbard, *For a New Liberty* (New York: Macmillan, 1973); Friedman, *The Machinery of Freedom: Guide to a Radical Capitalism;* Sneed, "Order Without Law"; George Smith, "Justice Entrepreneurship in a Free Market," *Journal of Libertarian Studies* 3 (Winter 1979): 405–426; Randy Barnett, "Justice Entrepreneurship in a Free Market: Comment," *Journal of Libertarian Studies* 3 (Winter 1979): 439–451; Wooldridge, *Uncle Sam, the Monopoly Man.*

58. Gary Becker, "Crime and Punishment: An Economic Analysis," *Journal of Political Economy* 78 (March/April 1968): 526–536.

59. Isaac Ehrlich, "Participation in Illegitimate Activities: A Theoretical and Empirical Investigation," *Journal of Political Economy* 81 (May/June 1973): 521–565.

60. Jeffrey Sedgwick, *Deterring Criminals: Policy Making and the American Political Tradition* (Washington, D.C.: American Enterprise Institute, 1980), pp. 20–21.

61. See for example, John Allison, "Economic Factors and the Crime Rate," *Land Economics* 48 (May 1972): 193–196; Belton Fleisher, "The Effects of Income on Delinquency," *American Economic Review* 56 (March 1966): 118–137; Fleisher, *The Economics of Delinquency* (Chicago: Quadrangle, 1966); Llad Phillips, Harold Votey, and Donald Maxwell, "Crime, Youth and the Labor Market," *Journal of Political Economy* 80 (June 1972): 491–501; Danny M. Leipziger, "The Economics of Burglary: A Note," in *Readings in Correctional Economics,* ed. The Correctional Economics Center (Washington, D.C.: Correctional Economics Center of the American Bar Association, 1975), pp. 29–34.

62. Jan Palmer, "Economic Analyses of the Deterrent Effect of Punishment: A Review," *Journal of Research in Crime and Delinquency* 12 (January 1977): 15.

63. Ibid., p. 9.

64. See Isaac Ehrlich, "The Deterrent Effect of Capital Punishment: A Question
     of Life and Death," *American Economic Review* 65 (June 1975): 397–417;
     Ehrlich, "Capital Punishment and Deterrence: Some Further Thoughts and
     Evidence," *Journal of Political Economy* (August 1977): 741–788; and Ehrlich
     and Joel C. Gibbons, "On the Measurement of the Deterrent Effect of Capital
     Punishment and the Theory of Deterrence," *Journal of Legal Studies* 6
     (January 1977): 35–50. For a different perspective, see Peter Passell and John
     Taylor, "The Deterrent Effect of Capital Punishment: Another View,"
     American Economic Review (June 1977): 445–451; David Baldus and James
     Cole, "A Comparison of the Work of Thorstein Sellin and Isaac Ehrlich on
     the Deterrent Effect of Capital Punishment," *Yale Law Review* 85 (December
     1975): 164–186; William Bowers and Glenn Pierce, "The Illusion of Deterrence
     in Isaac Ehrlich's Research on Capital Punishment," *Yale Law Review* 85
     (December 1975): 187–208; Jon Peck, "The Deterrence Effect of Capital
     Punishment: Ehrlich and His Critics," *Yale Law Journal* 85 (January 1976):
     359–367; Peter Passell, "The Deterrent Effect of the Death Penalty: A
     Statistical Test," *Stanford Law Review* 28 (November 1975): 61–80; William
     Bailey, "Capital Punishment and Lethal Assault Against Police," *Criminology*
     19 (February 1982): 608–625; Richard McGahey, "Dr. Ehrlich's Magic Bullet:
     Econometric Theory, Econometrics, and the Death Penalty," *Crime and
     Delinquency* 26 (October 1980): 485–502.
65. Ehrlich, "Participation in Illegitimacies," p. 545.
66. Ibid., p. 560. Ehrlich has considerable empirical support for these results.
     See Jack Gibbs, "Crime, Punishment and Deterrence," *Southwest Social
     Science Quarterly* 48 (March 1968): 515–530; Charles Tittle, "Crime Rates
     and Legal Sanctions," *Social Science* 16 (Spring 1969): 409–423; Theodore
     Chiricos and Gordon Waldo, "Punishment and Crime: An Examination of
     Some Empirical Evidence," *Social Problems* 18 (Fall 1970): 200–217; Charles
     Logan, "General Deterrent Effects of Imprisonment," *Social Forces* 51
     (September 1972): 64–73; George Antunes and A. Lee Hunt, "The Impact
     of Certainty and Severity of Punishment on Levels of Crime in American
     States: An Extended Analysis," *Journal of Criminal Law and Criminology*
     64 (December 1973): 486–493; William Bailey, J. David Martin, and Louis
     Gray, "Crime and Deterrence: A Correlation Analysis," *Journal of Research
     in Crime and Delinquency* 11 (July 1974): 124–143; Robert Chauncey, "Deter-
     rence: Certainty, Severity, and Skyjacking," *Criminology* 12 (February 1975):
     447–473; Samuel Myers, Jr., "Crime in Urban Areas: New Evidence and
     Results," *Journal of Urban Economics* 11 (March 1982): 148–158; Llad
     Phillips and Harold Votey, "Crime Control in California," *Journal of Legal
     Studies* 4 (June 1975): 327–350; David Sjoquist, "Property Crime and
     Economic Behavior: Some Empirical Results," *American Economic Review*
     83 (June 1973): 439–446; William Chambliss, "The Deterrent Influence
     of Punishment," *Crime and Delinquency* 12 (January 1966): 70–75; Shlomo
     Shinnar and Reuel Shinnar, "The Effects of the Criminal Justice System

on the Control of Crime: A Quantitative Approach," *Law and Society Review* 9 (Summer 1975): 581–611; K. L. Avio and C. S. Clark, *Property Crime in Canada: An Econometric Study* (Toronto: University of Toronto, 1976).

67. For similar conclusions see: Nicholas Elliot, "Economic Analysis of Crime and the Criminal Justice System," in *Public Law and Public Policy,* ed. John Gardiner (New York: Praeger, 1977), pp. 68–89; M. Silver, *Punishment, Deterrence, and Police Effectiveness: A Survey and Critical Interpretation of Recent Econometric Literature* (New York: Crime Deterrence and Offender Career Project, 1974).

68. Elliot, "Economic Analysis of Crime and the Criminal Justice System," pp. 82, 85.

69. John Taylor, "Econometric Models of Criminal Behavior: A Review," in *Economic Models of Criminal Behavior,* ed. J. M. Heineke (Amsterdam: North Holland, 1978), p. 81.

70. David Jones, *Crime Without Punishment* (Lexington, Mass.: Lexington Books, 1979), pp. 73–75, 83.

71. Ibid., pp. 2–3.

72. National Advisory Commission on Criminal Justice Standards and Goals, *Report on Police* (Cincinnati: Anderson Publishing Co., 1973), p. 206. Also see Fred Graham, *The Self-Inflicted Wound* (New York: Macmillan, 1970); Richard Seeburger and R. Stanley Wettick, Jr., "Miranda in Pittsburgh—A Statistical Study," *University of Pittsburgh Law Review* 29 (1967): 2–12.

73. These non-quantifiable changes generally cannot be examined statistically so the empirical research noted above clearly has not been able to control for all changes.

74. Gordon Tullock, "Does Punishment Deter Crime?" *The Public Interest* 36 (Summer 1974): 108.

75. Ehrlich, "The Deterrent Effect of Capital Punishment," pp. 416–417.

76. Goran Skogh and Charles Stewart, "An Economic Analysis of Crime Rates, Punishment, and the Social Consequences of Crime," *Public Choice* 38 (1982): 178.

77. Kakalik and Wildhorn, *The Private Police Industry: Its Nature and Extent,* pp. 7–8.

78. Truett A. Ricks, Bill G. Tillett, and Clifford W. Van Meter, *Principles of Security* (Cincinnati: Criminal Justice Studies, Anderson Publishing Co., 1981), p. 12.

79. Clotfelter, "Public Services," p. 876.

80. Ibid., p. 875.

81. Lawrence W. Sherman, "Patrol Strategies for Police," in *Crime and Public Policy,* ed. James Q. Wilson (San Francisco: Institute for Contemporary Studies, 1983), p. 149.

82. Ibid.

83. William C. Wooldridge, *Uncle Sam, the Monopoly Man* (New Rochelle, N.Y.: Arlington House, 1970), p. 112.

PART IV

RATIONALIZING AUTHORITARIAN LAW

11

MARKET FAILURE IN LAW AND JUSTICE

The arguments for public provision of law and its enforcement are largely "market failure" arguments, which imply that the private sector will not efficiently produce law and order. The implicit assumption underlying such justifications for public production is that when the market fails, government can do better. But even if the market failure arguments are correct, it does not necessarily follow that government production of law and order is justified. As Tullock explained: "In every case, the problem that we face when deciding whether some activity shall be market or government is. . .the maximization of the [net] benefit. Clearly, neither method is perfect, and clearly, we are choosing between two techniques that will produce less than if we lived in a perfect world."[1] The evidence presented thus far suggests that market imperfection may not be nearly as severe as many advocates of public law and law enforcement have suggested. Let us now bring the relevant historical and current facts to bear on each of the arguments for public (against private) provision of law and order. Some are simply unsubstantiated, while others may have some validity in our modern enterprise of law.

There are two basic types of market failure: 1) externality or spillover costs and benefits (including public good externalities), whereby the private sector is presumably unable to internalize either some of the costs or the benefits associated with production or consumption of a particular good or service; and 2) monopoly power, whereby the forces of competition are

271

presumably not sufficient to guarantee efficient production. Both types of market failure have been suggested as likely if law and law enforcement are not publicly produced. The first is addressed in this chapter, and the second is examined in Chapter 12.

EXTERNALITIES AND PUBLIC GOODS

The externality argument for public provision of law and order might be characterized this way. Private sector production of law and law enforcement generates external benefits for which private suppliers may be unable to charge. Suppose that a few individuals hire a private security firm to patrol their neighborhood. The patrol deters criminals, both for those who pay the firm and those who do not. Thus, there are strong *free-rider* incentives at work here. If everyone paid for the benefits received, the firm would patrol more often and prevent more crime; but because individuals can reap benefits without paying, they have strong incentives not to enter into the neighborhood group that hired the firm. Even many strong free market advocates have accepted the validity of this argument.[2]

If there is a significant free-rider problem, it means that *too little* private sector protection is purchased and produced. The problem arises because individuals cannot be persuaded to cooperate in buying the good or service in question, not because the private sector would not produce it if producers were fully compensated for the benefits they provide. When free riding is prevalent, people have to be *coerced into paying* for a service, and government is the only entity that is widely recognized to have the power to coerce. Professor Richard Epstein concluded:

> In essence the entire system of governance presupposes that in a state of nature there are two, and only two, failures of the system of private rights. The first is the inability to control private aggression, to which the police power is the proper response. The second is that voluntary transactions cannot generate the centralized power needed to combat private aggression. There are transactions costs, holdout and free-rider problems that are almost insurmountable when the conduct of a large number of individuals must be organized. To this problem, the proper response is the power to force exchanges upon payment for public use.[3]

This argument has been used to a greater or lesser degree to justify the historical trend of increasing government production of such services to supplement or replace private sector protection efforts.

A similar rationale has been made to justify the public provision of courts.[4] Perhaps the most widely claimed external benefit of court decisions is the body of law or precedents that court decisions generate. Mabry, et al., for instance, wrote that "the continuous creation of a collection of decisions, interpretations, opinions, and precedents is the production of a collectively consumed service. ... Since they are available to others at no additional cost, precedents are externalities. Indeed the entire set of law known as common law has developed as an external benefit of past adjudication."[5] While individuals would be willing to pay for the private benefits they obtain from a private court (e.g., dispute resolution, restitution), they would be the only benefits considered. The failure to recognize and capture payment for the additional benefits accruing to the community at large implies that suppliers in a private market would be unwilling to provide enough judicial services to maximize the net benefits of adjudication.[6]

A similar but perhaps even more fundamental externality argument is put forth by even the staunchest supporters of the market economy. F. A. Hayek, for instance, argued that "government becomes indispensable...in order to see that the mechanism which regulates the production of...goods and services is kept in working order...it provides an essential condition for preservation of...overall order."[7] Clearly defined property rights are critical requirements for the operation of a market system, so some system of defining and then protecting and enforcing property rights is needed before a market economy can develop. Enforcement of property rights, it is suggested, requires coercion, and only government is widely viewed to have coercive powers. The establishment of laws and a mechanism for their enforcement, therefore, has the beneficial external effect of allowing the market economy to develop and function. Because no private individual who might benefit from laws and their enforcement would be able to charge for all the benefits generated, too few laws and too little enforcement would develop without government. Besides, individuals would not freely grant other individuals the power to coerce.

It could be contended that the existence of nonexclusionary external benefits makes laws and law enforcement "public goods." And they are, given Samuelson's delineation of the domain of public goods: "A public good is one that enters two or more persons' utility. What are we left with? With a knife-edge pole of the private good case, and with all the rest of the world in the public good domain by virtue of involving some consumption externality."[8] As Goldin pointed out, however, the theory of public goods "is a dangerous and misleading theory if it suggests to the unwary that government services should be handled *as if* they were public goods."⁹ The efficient provision of goods that generate external benefits requires cooperation, but cooperation does not always require government. Whenever external benefits exist, there are tremendous incentives to internalize them. Consequently, voluntary cooperation occurs daily in the private sector. Every market transaction involves cooperation between the buyer and seller, every good or service produced requires the voluntary cooperation of input suppliers, and every contract is a formal agreement to cooperate. A major distinction between government and the private sector is the means used to induce cooperation.

POLICE

Let us consider the policing stage of law and order. First, note that some aspects of the policing function clearly do *not* generate large external benefits. Investigation of crimes already committed, arrests, and the presentation of evidence involve specific crimes with specific victims, so there is typically an identifiable primary benefactor from these police activities. There are scale economies and gains from specialization, so enforcement functions have been performed by family units or villages in primitive societies; by voluntary associations under surety arrangements; by temporary organizations of individuals with common concerns such as vigilante organizations in the American West and medieval merchant fairs; by more permanent arrangements such as cattlemen's associations and merchant organizations; and by individuals and firms specializing in solving crimes.¹⁰ During the mid-1800s, public police began to expand and broaden their investigation/prosecution roles in the United States, primarily for political reasons. The police proved useful for politicians and powerful interest groups, and, of course, police bureaucrats were seeking expanded budgets and power.¹¹

There can be a deterrent effect from the successful apprehension and prosecution of criminals, but this deterrence is not likely to be an *external* benefit. It should be internal to the group or organization that successfully solves crimes. Members of an especially effective private surety organization or subscribers to a particularly efficient enforcement agency's services would be the primary benefactors of the deterrent effects. As Friedman pointed out:

> If "enforcers" contract in advance to pursue those who perpetrate crimes against particular people, and so notify the criminals (by a notice on the door of their

customers), the deterrent effect of catching criminals is internalized; the enforcers can charge the customers for the service. Such arrangements are used by private guard firms and the American Automobile Association, among others. . . . Under medieval Icelandic institutions, who was protected by whom was to a considerable degree known in advance.[12]

Similar arrangements characterized other primitive and medieval legal systems, but these surety groups no longer exist. What is stopping the private sector from organizing and internalizing the scale economies as it once did?

Free Riding or Common Pool Underinvestment? Government has effectively created a different type of externality problem by significantly altering the property rights structure. If property rights are clearly defined and assigned to private individuals, then no externalities need arise.[13] That is precisely what customary law did before European kings began to concentrate and centralize power.[14] One consequence of the development of monarchical government was the creation of criminal law as a way to generate revenues and power for the kings. Criminalization took away the right to restitution, along with the incentives to voluntarily cooperate in law enforcement. The result is not a public good externality but a common pool problem. When property rights are assigned to the "public" rather than to private individuals, people not only have incentives to overuse the common pool service, they do not have incentives to invest in inputs as replacements for the services they consume. Underinvestment is a result of free riding, of course, but it also occurs in common pool situations. The same incentives apply to other policing functions as well.

Consider crime prevention. First, note that the benefits of many crime prevention efforts are internal as individuals use burglar alarms, locks, and other devices to protect themselves and their property. The preventive action of visibly patrolling and watching, however, are often cited as sources of positive externalities. That the benefits are localized is important. The individual tendencies to underinvest in patrolling to prevent *crime* (with emphasis on the fact that we are referring to offenses *defined* to be against society at large, or the state, rather than against individuals) are clearly of different orders of magnitude than the same characteristics of, say, national defense. Far fewer people are involved, so the likelihood of a private sector contractual arrangement for patrolling is far greater. This does not mean that underinvestment will be avoided, of course. There are hundreds of neighborhood watch and patrol groups around the country, and many suffer from incomplete cooperation.

Stigler relabeled the free-rider problem the "cheap rider problem."[15] When the potential cost of free riding is large or the benefits of not free riding are significant, then free riding is considerably less likely. Free riding is still possible, of course, but we can expect that contractual arrangements will evolve that exclude free riders from the benefits of reciprocally organized protection arrangements, as they did in Anglo-Saxon England. Residential neighborhoods and business districts will develop where individuals will be unable to buy property without contracting to support the crime prevention system. Such communities already exist, but developers would find it profitable to provide similar arrangements for a much wider range of income groups.

Government Failure in Policing.   Appropriate *private* assignments of property rights (e.g., recognition that crimes are torts and that victims should have rights to restitution) would eliminate many of the underinvestment incentives. In the absence of such changes, there is another question that should be asked when arguments are made that the private sector inefficiently produces police services: Do the public police allocate resources more efficiently than private police? The allocation of resources by the public police is far from efficient. The commons problem is pronounced in the system due to the incentives associated with non-price rationing of police services. Because police resources are limited and fees are not charged for services rendered, there is an excess demand for services. Under these circumstances, there is no guarantee that the services will be allocated to their highest and best use. Similarly, special interest groups influence the allocation of investigative resources. Because costs are shifted onto others, the benefits that interest groups receive may be considerably less than the total cost of production.

Another significant factor in the inefficient allocation of police resources is the incentives the public police face. The aspect of policing that is most likely to generate external benefits, *given existing rights structures,* is that of watching and patrolling to prevent crimes. But rewards and prestige come when police solve crimes *after* they occur. Thus, *public police have incentives to concentrate their efforts on police functions other than those which may have "public good" characteristics.* Even if free riding leads the private sector to produce too little patrolling, it is not clear that the public sector does a more efficient job. When we add the other aspects of bureaucratic incentives to produce inefficiently (see Chapters 4 and 6) and the advantages of private sector incentives to produce efficiently (see Chapter 10), the external benefits argument against private sector law enforcement appears pretty weak.

COURTS

A typical "efficiency" argument for courts has been stated by Landes and Posner:

> because of the difficulty of establishing property rights in a precedent, private judges may have little incentive to produce precedents. They will strive for a fair result between the parties in order to preserve a reputation for impartiality, but why should they make any effort to explain the result in a way that would provide guidance for future parties? To do so would confer an external, an uncompensated benefit, not only on future parties but also on competing judges. If anything, judges might deliberately avoid explaining their results because the demand for their services would be reduced by rules that, by clarifying the meaning of the law, reduce the incidence of disputes.[16]

As Friedman commented, this argument "shows insufficient ingenuity" in envisioning the system of private courts that would probably arise.[17] Indeed, Landes and Posner cited evidence contradicting their own arguments. For instance, they contended that "a problem is that a system of voluntary adjudication is strongly biased against the creation of precise rules of any sort," but then observed that "precise rules are familiar features of primitive legal systems."[18] As explained in Chapter 2, primitive law was privately adjudicated customary law. Landes and Posner also criticized private law for being too precise, preferring what they perceived to be the flexibility and potential for setting precedents of modern common law to the inflexible precision of primitive law. Such inflexibility, they predicted, would probably characterize private law today. Of course, this is simply not the case. If a primitive society was characterized by very few and very slow changes, then the benefits of precision would far outweigh any advantage of extreme flexibility.[19] But when flexibility and growth in the law are vital to facilitate growth and change, then customary law—including primitive law—has been characterized by such flexibility.[20] Witness the rapid development of privately produced mercantile law, for example. The number of important precedents set in a relatively short span of time is phenomenal. The foundation of today's commercial law was established by this customary system of law within a few centuries.[21] Furthermore, after common law courts absorbed the medieval Law Merchant it lost a good deal of flexibility, became relatively rigid, and its development slowed.[22]

Landes and Posner also explained that commercial arbitration does not set precedents but simply applies the laws established by the public sector. I have already shown the fallacy of this in Chapter 9. More significantly, however, consider that the Law Merchant was developed by the merchant community and disputes were handled in private merchant courts until, as Landes and Posner report,

> gradually, the doctrines developed by the merchant courts to deal with contract and commercial matters were absorbed into common law and official courts began winning business from merchant courts. Conceivably the financial self-interest of the English judges, who. . .were paid in part out of litigation fees during the period was a factor in the absorption of the law merchant into the common law. In similar vein, English procedural reform in the nineteenth century has been attributed in part to the competition from private arbitration.[23]

A more complete explanation recognizes that only *part* of the cost of litigation arose from user fees when mercantile law was absorbed; therefore, part of the costs were being shifted from the merchants to others. The merchants certainly would find this to be an attractive arrangement, *given* that the public courts enforced the law as the merchants had developed it. When the common law or public court procedures departed too far from what merchants desired and began to generate costs to merchants that exceeded the benefits associated with the costs, commercial arbitration surfaced again (see Chapter 9).[24] It follows that under these circumstances, commercial arbitration should enforce virtually the same laws recognized by the public sector, but the causation actually flows in the opposite direction. Public courts enforce virtually the same laws as commercial arbitrators do. If they did not, the public court bureaucracy would lose its commercial business because businessmen would use their own courts (as they are).

Even if this argument were not true, it cannot be denied that privately produced mercantile law in the medieval period and the modern international Law Merchant have both generated substantial numbers of significant precedents. The merchants have internalized the benefits of the precedents and jointly supported *their* judicial system. Similar arrangements would arise in a more extensive system of customary law. In fact, many international (and intranational) industrial and trade groups have their own arbitration systems today. Landes and Posner recognized that the benefits of precedents could be internalized if the parties "agree on the judge (or on the method of selecting him) before the dispute arises, as is done in contracts with arbitration clauses."[25] Nonetheless, they went on to argue that "this solution is available, however, only where the dispute arises from a preexisting voluntary relationship between the parties; the typical tort or crime does not."[26] They are largely correct, of course. Under existing incentives and institutions, such arrangements may not provide for judgments of torts or crimes. However, the current system is far from the historic norm. The claim that a modern free-market judicial system would not produce contractual arrangements to cope with the complexities of modern society has no basis in historical fact. We may not be able to visualize the arrangements that would arise, but there is little doubt that what we see today in a system dominated by public courts *and criminal law* does not correspond with what would arise in the process of privatizing law and order.

Landes and Posner argued that in a private judicial system judges are likely to "deliberately avoid explaining their results" in order to create demand for their services, although

> private judges just might produce precedents. . .competitive private judges would strive for a reputation for competence and impartiality. One method of obtaining such a reputation is to give reasons for a decision that convince the disputants and the public that the judge is competent and impartial. Competition could lead private judges to issue formal or informal "opinions" declaring their interpretation of the law, and these opinions—though intended simply as advertising —would function as precedents, under a public judicial system.[27]

Landes and Posner contended that this is an unlikely scenario because, in an effort to reduce costs, other methods of advertising would be sought. As with the policing function, however, contractual organizations and surety arrangements that would characterize a privatized legal system would internalize the benefits of precedents. These organizations would either have their own judges or contract with judges who applied a clear set of rules and provided clear rulings that would reduce future disputes. Under such an arrangement, maximizing profit does not involve maximizing the number of cases decided. A judge who provided clear rules and opinions would command a relatively high price for *contracts* with various organizations. Once under contract, the judge would actually have incentives to minimize the number of disputes that go to trial by making his rules clear—that is, by setting precedents. Under this scenario, private judges have precisely the opposite incentives to those predicted by Landes and Posner. Those judges who "tend to promulgate vague standards which give each party to a dispute a fighting chance"[28] would actually do less business. The point is not that these internalization procedures arise in all private adjudication arrangements, but that institutions can be envisioned that produce incentives to write clear opinions and set precedents. Furthermore, such institutions are likely to arise if they generate substantial benefits. Thus, Fuller contended that private arbitrators' incentives are diametrically opposed to those proposed by Landes and Posner. He proposed: "Being unbacked by state power...the arbitrator must concern himself directly with the acceptability of his award. He may be at greater pains than a judge to get his facts straight, to state accurately the arguments of the parties, and generally to display in his award a full understanding of the case."[29]

In the area of medical care, some have argued that physicians have incentives to "create demand" for their services by advising uninformed consumers that they need more medical care than they actually do. This is quite similar to the argument Landes and Posner made regarding private judges. But new institutional arrangements have been created during recent years in the face of rapidly rising costs of medical care. Consumers can now pay a flat fee for services at HMOs and PPOs, reversing the physicians' incentives. Physicians have incentives to keep their patients healthy with preventive medicine that avoids more costly treatments after an illness arises. Similar arrangements are certainly possible in the provision of judicial services.[30]

Of course, none of the preceding arguments are intended to imply that the external benefits of the judicial process must be entirely internalized by private court systems. They suggest that the misallocation of resources under private adjudication may not be tremendous. On the other hand, the misallocation of resources by the public courts already documented in this book is demonstrably substantial. The public inputs to the process play significant roles in determining what cases come to trial and which rules are clarified or overturned.

Assume, for example, that private judges have incentives to promulgate vague and confusing rules that create uncertainty and thereby maximize demand for their services, but also consider what occurs with the public courts. The vice president of Control Data, after a privately arbitrated construction dispute stated, "We will use these contractors and architects again. I guarantee that if we had gone to court, there would have been no further business relationships with them."[31] Such an outcome is *relatively* unlikely in a publicly settled dispute because the public court process is designed to be adversarial. It "isolates disputants, sets them against adversaries, consigns them to professional specialists [lawyers], and resolves their dispute according to rules and procedures that are remote and inaccessible."[32] In addition, a government court ruling may be made on procedural grounds that have nothing to do with the essentials of the dispute itself so the parties remain adversaries and future conflicts in similar circumstances remain possible. In other words, the public courts are more likely to create uncertainty and additional litigation than are private courts. The uncertainty generated by the public court system's myriad of confusing procedural rules is undeniable.

LAW-MAKING

Jeremy Bentham may have had as much to do with the way legal scholars think about law as anyone. Property and state-made law, he wrote, "are born and must die together."[33] Without state law, he contended, there would be no property. But does government have to assign property rights to establish the basis for a market economy? Rothbard argued that

> the principles of a free society do imply a very definite theory of property rights, namely, self-ownership and the ownership of natural resources found and transformed by one's labor. Therefore, no State or similar agency contrary to the market is needed to define or allocate property rights. This can and will be done by the use of reason and through market processes themselves; any other allocation or definition would be completely arbitrary and contrary to the principles of the free society.[34]

As Fuller noted, "it is clear that property and contract were. . . functioning social institutions before state-made laws existed or were even conceived of."[35] Examples of private creation of private property rights range from the complex system of water rights among the primitive Ifugao, to the allocation of mining rights in the western territories of the United States during the 1800s, to development of a system of mercantile law in the tenth and eleventh centuries.[36]

Government Legislation Versus Evolutionary Customary Law. Laws that are legislatively created generally are not designed for some "public interest" goal like maximizing social welfare by supporting a market economy. Much of common law was simply a codification of the basic norms common to Anglo-Saxon society (that is, from customary law). But common law was also royal law; therefore, even during its earliest periods of development some aspects of it were legislated by kings. The basic character of much common law can be traced back to such royal legislation, which was designed to either enhance the power of the kingship or to increase government revenues. Of course, the legislated portion of the law that has been growing in relative importance in our representative democracy is one of the most striking features of recent history.[37] But legislation in a representative democracy is generally designed to meet the demands of special interest groups, not to establish and maintain property rights.

Furthermore, it must be recognized that the judicial system is also part of the political market (see Chapters 4 and 6). When courts make new law through "creative interpretation" of legislation or by setting a new precedent, it is frequently as a consequence of a political dispute between interest groups rather than a dispute arising out of the need for clarifying private property rights. Court time is increasingly being taken up by political issues or by disputes involving conflicting interest groups' efforts to influence government. As Neely explained, "There are certain classes of cases on the frontier of the law where there are real disputes, but these are political disputes between interest groups where the battleground is a lawsuit. Efforts to change existing laws can be characterized as 'disputes,' but they are political disputes rather than the factual disputes that courts are theoretically in business to resolve."[38] There is no reason to expect that the resulting precedents are desirable in the sense that they produce important external benefits. Benefits are likely to accrue to the interest group involved, but others can bear substantial costs.

Politically dictated rules are not designed to support the market process; in fact, government-made law is likely to do precisely the opposite. As Leoni explained: "Even those economists who have brilliantly defended the free market against the interference of the authorities have usually neglected the parallel consideration that no free market is really compatible with a law-making process centralized by authorities."[39] Indeed, it appears that the increasing centralization of law-making has been associated with increasing transfers of property rights from private individuals to government or perhaps, more accurately, to interest groups.[40] In other words, public production of law undermines the private property arrangements that support a free market system.

Beyond that, the continual and growing process of taking private rights creates considerable uncertainty about the future value of those private rights that have not yet been taken.[41] When resource owners are relatively uncertain about their continued ownership of those resources, they tend to use them up relatively rapidly. When producers of resources (or those who may improve resources to enhance future production) are relatively uncertain about their ability to retain control of those resources, they will produce less (or expend less on improvements). Thus, the government process of taking private rights creates negative externalities for society since resources will be overused and underproduced.

This does not mean that the law should be rigid. Law has to grow in the face of changing technology and social norms, which is precisely the characteristic of common law that Landes and Posner, Leoni, and others have found desirable.[42] They attribute this characteristic to the fact that common law is judge-made law. But *assuming away legislature interference by non-judges* (e.g., kings, legislators, and bureaucrats) and outright authoritarian legislation imposed at the discretion of judges, common law would grow gradually. It would grow and develop in the same way that all customary law grows and develops, particularly as a consequence of the mutual consent of parties entering into reciprocal arrangements. For example, two parties may enter into a contract, but something then occurs that the contract did not clearly account for. The parties *agree* to call upon an arbitrator or mediator to help lead them to a solution. The solution affects only those parties in the dispute, but if it turns out to be effective and the same potential conflict arises again, it may be *voluntarily* adopted by others. In this way, the solution becomes a part of customary law.[43] In effect, then, private arbitrators/mediators have no authority beyond what individuals *voluntarily* give them.

The basic substantive principles underlying the law are not likely to change, nor should they.[44] University of Chicago Law Professor Richard Epstein suggested an example of evolving contract law:

the merits of freedom of contract in no way depend upon the accidents of time and place. Acceptance of that basic principle will not however put an end to all contractual disputes. It remains to discover the terms of given contracts, usually gathered from language itself, and the circumstances of its formation and performance. Even with these aids, many contractual gaps will remain, and the [private or public] courts will be obliged, especially with partially executed contracts, to fashion the terms which the parties have not fashioned themselves. To fill the gaps, the courts have looked often to the custom or industry practice. The judicial practice makes good sense and for our purposes introduces an element of dynamism into the system. . . . But it by no means follows that conduct in conformity with the custom of one generation is acceptable conduct in the next. The principles for the implication of terms, I believe, remain constant over generations. Yet the specific rules of conduct so implied will vary with time and with place. At one level therefore, the major part of the thesis is secure. At another level, it is subject to sensible modification.[45]

The basic rules of private property and freedom of contract characterize all primitive law systems. As such systems evolve, the need for extensions of these basic principles to cover unanticipated circumstances always arises, however, and customary law adapts, building on the existing base of substantive principles.

Hayek pointed out that the articulation of pre-existing customary law often produces changes in the law, but the process should be regarded as one of discovering the law rather than creating it. As a consequence, however, something new is sometimes created: "In this sense, a rule not yet existing in any sense may yet appear to be 'implicit' in the body of the existing rules, not in the sense that it is logically derivable from them, but in the sense that if the other rules are to achieve their aim, an additional rule is required."[46]

The Negative Externalities of Legislation.   When authoritarian legislation makes major changes in property rights assignments that affect many parties, then negative externalities are generated. Leoni explained it well when he noted that

> legislation may have and actually has in many cases today a negative effect on the very efficacy of the rules and on the homogeneity of the feelings and convictions *already prevailing* in a given society. For legislation may also deliberately or accidentally disrupt homogeneity by destroying established rules and by nullifying existing conventions and agreements that have hitherto been voluntarily accepted and kept. Even more disruptive is the fact that the very possibility of nullifying agreements and conventions through supervening legislation tends in the long run to induce people to fail to rely on any existing conventions or to keep any accepted agreements. On the other hand, the continual change of rules brought about by inflated legislation prevents it from replacing successfully and enduringly the set of nonlegislative rules (usages, conventions, agreements) that happen to be destroyed in the process.[47]

When negative externalities arise in the process of producing some good or service, too much of the good or service is being produced. This is the case with government production of laws through legislation.

Some of the founding fathers of the United States recognized this potential misuse of legislation and its resulting uncertainty. James Madison wrote:

"The sober people of America are weary of the fluctuating policy which has directed the public councils. They have seen with regret and indignation that sudden changes and legislative inferences...become...snares to the more industrious and less informed part of the community. They have seen, too, that one legislative inference is but the first link of a long chain of repetitions."[48] The division of power dictated in the Constitution between the three branches of the federal government and between federal and state government was clearly an effort to limit the government's ability and authority to legislate. One legal scholar has even suggested that "the better the society the less law there will be. In Heaven there will be no law...in Hell there will be nothing but law, and due process will be meticulously observed."[49] "Law" here refers to government-imposed law, of course, rather than customary law. But Auerbach observed that both government laws and lawyers have proliferated so rapidly in the United States that our society is burdened by "legal pollution so that American citizens in general suffer from the malady of hyperlexis."[50] The Constitution has clearly not accomplished what Madison hoped it would.

Coercive power in the hands of judges also produces legislative externalities. Leoni, despite his strong support for court-created law as opposed to legislation, noted that judicial law may acquire the characteristics of legislation, including all its undesirable ones, whenever judges have the discretion to decide "ultimately" on a case.[51] In particular, when "supreme courts" are established, the members of these courts can impose law on all citizens concerned. Thus, according to Leoni, establishment of a supreme court actually introduces the legislative process into the judiciary.

Any government court is in a sense "supreme" if its rulings are backed by coercive power. Thus, the tendency for "legal pollution" arises whether legislation comes from a legislature or from a public court. Furthermore, given the allocation mechanism for court time, it would appear that many of the issues that should get court attention never get through the system. So, not only are there too many legislated laws by courts, they are not necessarily the laws that the court should be making. As Neely reported: "The mass of precedent in law is so enormous that nothing is open-and-shut once it hits the courts."[52] Tremendous uncertainty results from rapid legislative change, whether the legislation comes from a king, a judge, or a representative body. In this regard, it is especially relevant to note with Epstein that in property, contract, and tort law matters, law performs its essential function best only if it remains constant: "Social dynamism is not an undesirable feature. To the contrary, it is wholly desirable, but not best implemented by Judicial decision. The desired initiatives come best from private sources, who should be spared the burden of planning their affairs in an environment filled with unwanted legal uncertainties."[53]

One other negative externality arises with legislation. Fuller pinpointed the problem when he noted that much of legislated law does *not* facilitate interaction. As an example, he cited those criminal law statutes that are often characterized as victimless crimes. Indeed, given that participants are of sound mind and that there is no deception involved, laws against gambling, prostitution, marijuana use, and so on are intended to prevent forms of interaction. And as Fuller stressed, it is precisely with this kind of law that "the grossest failures of law have everywhere occurred."[54] Such laws lead to selective enforcement, corruption, *and* open tolerance of illegal acts. Clearly a negative externality is created as respect for and fidelity to all law is harmed when large numbers of such largely unenforceable laws are openly defied. As Fuller concluded: "Legal morality is seriously affected. There is no way to quarantine this contagion against a spread to other parts of the legal system."[55]

Once again, such negative externalities imply government produces *too much* law. Thus, even if the private sector would produce too little law, as is implied by the public good externality argument for government provision of law, it does not follow that the public sector does a better job. Neither system is likely to be perfect. The question is: Which creates the most significant imperfections? This discussion implies that private sector failures have been substantially exaggerated by government law advocates while significant government failure arguments have been overlooked.

ENDNOTES

1. Gordon Tullock, *Private Wants, Public Means: An Economic Analysis of the Desirable Scope of Government* (New York: Basic Books, 1970), pp. 127-128. Also see Randy E. Barnett, "Pursuing Justice in a Free Society, Part Two: Crime Prevention and the Legal Order," *Criminal Justice Ethics* 4 (Summer/Fall 1985): 50-72.

2. See for example, Tullock, *Private Wants,* pp. 83-84.

3. Richard A. Epstein, *Takings: Private Property and the Power of Eminent Domain* (Cambridge, Mass.: Harvard University Press, 1985), p. 5.

4. See Burton Weisbrod, "Collective-Consumption Services of Individual Consumption Goods," *Quarterly Journal of Economics* 78 (August 1964): 471-477; Rodney H. Mabry, Holly H. Ulbrich, Hugh H. Macauley, Jr., and Michael T. Maloney, *An Economic Investigation of State and Local Judiciary Services*

(Washington, D.C.: National Institute of Law Enforcement and Criminal Justice, Law Enforcement Assistance Administration, Department of Justice, 1977), p. 81.

5. Mabry, et al., *An Economic Investigation of State and Local Judiciary Services,* p. 80.

6. William M. Landes and Richard A. Posner, "Adjudication as a Private Good," *Journal of Legal Studies* 8 (March 1979): 235–284; James N. Buchanan, *The Bases for Collective Action* (New York: General Learning Press, 1971), p. 2.

7. F. A. Hayek, *Law, Legislation and Liberty,* vol. 1 (Chicago: University of Chicago Press, 1973), pp. 47–48. See also James Buchanan, "Before Public Choice," in *Explorations in the Theory of Anarchy,* ed. Gordon Tullock (Blacksburg, Va.: Center of the Study of Public Choice, 1972); *Freedom in Constitutional Contract* (College Station, Tx.: Texas A & M University Press, 1972).

8. Paul A. Samuelson, "Pure Theory of Public Expenditures and Taxation," in *Public Economics: An Analysis of Public Production and Consumption and Their Relations to the Private Sectors: Proceedings of a Conference Held by the International Economics Association,* ed. J. Margolis and H. Guitton (London: Macmillan, 1969).

9. Kenneth D. Goldin, "Equal Access vs. Selective Access: A Critique of Public Goods Theory," *Public Choice* 79 (Spring 1977): 53.

10. See for example, Bruce L. Benson, "Enforcement of Private Property Rights in Primitive Societies: Law Without Government," *Journal of Libertarian Studies* 9 (Winter 1989); Leopold Popisil, *Anthropology of Law: A Comparative Theory* (New York: Harper and Row, 1971); E. Adamson Hoebel, *The Law of Primitive Man* (Cambridge, Mass.: Harvard University Press, 1954); Walter Goldsmidt, "Ethics and the Structure of Society: An Ethnological Contribution to the Sociology of Knowledge," *American Anthropologist* 53 (October/December 1951); R. F. Barton, "Procedure Among the Ifugao," in *Law and Warfare,* ed. Paul Bohannan (Garden City, N.Y.: The Natural History Press, 1967); David Friedman, "Private Creation and Enforcement of Law: A Historical Case," *Journal of Legal Studies* 8 (March 1979); and Joseph R. Peden, "Property Rights in Celtic Irish Law," *Journal of Libertarian Studies* 1 (1977): 81–95; Terry Anderson and P. J. Hill, "An American Experiment in Anarcho-Capitalism: The *Not* So Wild, Wild West," *Journal of Libertarian Studies* 3 (1979): 9–29; John R. Umbeck, *A Theory of Property Rights With Application to the California Gold Rush* (Ames: Iowa State University, 1981); Roger D. McGrath, *Gunfighters, Highwaymen and Vigilantes: Violence on the Frontier* (Berkeley: University of California Press, 1984); Bruce L. Benson, "The Spontaneous Evolution of Commercial Law," *Southern Economic Journal* 55 (January 1989): 644–661; Harold J. Berman,

Law and Revolution: The Formation of Western Legal Tradition (Cambridge, Mass.: Harvard University Press, 1983); Leon E. Trakman, *The Law Merchant: The Evolution of Commercial Law* (Littleton, Colo.: Fred B. Rothman and Co., 1983); W. Mitchell, *Essay on the Early History of the Law Merchant* (New York: Burt Franklin, 1904); Truett A. Ricks, Bill G. Tillett and Clifford W. Van Meter, *Principles of Security* (Cincinnati: Criminal Justice Studies, Anderson Publishing Company, 1981), p. 8; Bruce L. Benson, "The Evolution of Law: Custom Versus Authority" (manuscript, Florida State University, Tallahassee, Fl., 1990); Frank Morn, *The Eye that Never Sleeps* (Bloomington: Indiana University Press, 1982), p. 14.

11.   Ricks, et al., *Principles of Security,* p. 8; Morn, *The Eye that Never Sleeps,* p. 12.

12.   Friedman, "Private Creation and Enforcement of Law," p. 403.

13.   Ronald Coase, "The Problem of Social Cost," *Journal of Law and Economics* 1 (October 1961): 1–44.

14.   Benson, "The Evolution of Law."

15.   George J. Stigler, "Free Riders and Collective Action: An Appendix to Theories of Economic Regulation," *Bell Journal of Economics and Management Science* 5 (Autumn 1974): 359–365.

16.   Landes and Posner, "Adjudication as a Private Good," p. 238. Also see Mabry, et al., *Economic Investigation of Judicial Services,* p. 82.

17.   Friedman, "Private Creation and Enforcement of Law," p. 402.

18.   Landes and Posner, "Adjudication as a Private Good," pp. 239, 245.

19.   But see Bruce L. Benson, "Legal Evolution in Primitive Societies," *Journal of Institutional and Theoretical Economics* 144 (December 1989): 772–788.

20.   See Popisil, *Anthropology of Law: A Comparative Theory.*

21.   Berman, *Law and Revolution,* p. 530. Also see Benson, "The Spontaneous Evolution of Commercial Law."

22.   Trakman, *The Law Merchant,* pp. 25–26.

23.   Landes and Posner, "Adjudication as a Private Good," pp. 257–258.

24.   Also see Benson, "The Spontaneous Evolution of Commercial Law."

25.   Landes and Posner, "Adjudication as a Private Good," p. 237.

26.   Ibid.

27.   Ibid., p. 238.

28.   Ibid., p. 240.

29.   Lon L. Fuller, *The Principles of Social Order* (Durham, N.C.: Duke University Press, 1981), pp. 110–111.

30.   In a related argument, Mabry, et al. pointed out that citizen requirements for court services are uncertain and infrequent, and that the cost of expanding production is high. Given these characteristics, "the public at large will have an effective demand for current output (whether or not they ever actually consume the good) because they desire the option of consumption in the

future." This, they concluded, is a reason for public provision of court and police services. But they explicitly stated that the conclusion required the assumption "that a system of law *requires* a judicial system, [and] in its absence anarchy would prevail." A legal structure does arise in the absence of government, however, so the assumption that only government can meet this particular option demand does not hold. See *An Economic Investigation of State and Local Judiciary Services,* pp. 81–82.

31. James F. Henry, "Minitrials: Scaling Down the Costs of Justice to Business," *Across the Board* (October 1984), p. 47.
32. Jerold S. Auerbach, *Justice Without Law* (New York: Oxford University Press, 1983), p. 12. Also see Gordon Tullock, *The Logic of the Law* (New York: Basic Books, Inc., 1971); Tullock, *Trials on Trial;* John H. Langbein, "The Criminal Trial Before Lawyers," *University of Chicago Law Review* 45 (Winter 1978): 307–316.
33. Jeremy Bentham, *Works,* ed. John Bowring, vol. 1 (Edinburgh: W. Tait, 1838), p. 309.
34. Murray N. Rothbard, *Power and Market: Government and the Economy* (Kansas City: Sheed Andrews and McMeel, Inc., 1970), p. 3.
35. Fuller, *The Principles of Social Order,* p. 174.
36. See Benson, "Enforcement of Private Property Rights in Primitive Societies"; Bruce L. Benson, "The Lost Victim and Other Failures of the Public Law Experiment," *Harvard Journal of Law and Public Policy* 9 (Spring 1986): 399–427; Hoebel, *The Law of Primitive Man;* Barton, "Procedure Among the Ifugao"; Anderson and Hill, "An American Experiment in Anarcho-Capitalism"; Umbeck, *A Theory of Property Rights With Application to the California Gold Rush;* Benson, "The Spontaneous Evolution of Commercial Law"; Berman, *Law and Revolution;* Trakman, *The Law Merchant.*
37. Bruno Leoni, *Freedom and the Law* (Los Angeles: Nash Publishing, 1961), p. 4. Also see Auerbach, *Justice Without Law;* Berman, *Law and Revolution.*
38. Neely, *Why Courts Don't Work,* pp. 166–167.
39. Leoni, *Freedom and the Law,* p. 90.
40. See Terry Anderson and Peter J. Hill, *The Birth of the Transfer Society* (Stanford, Calif.: Hoover Institute Press, 1970); Tullock, *Private Wants, Public Means;* Bruce L. Benson, "Land Use Regulation: A Supply and Demand Analysis of Changing Property Rights," *Journal of Libertarian Studies* 5 (Fall 1981); Berman, *Law and Revolution.*
41. Benson, "Land Use Regulation"; Leoni, *Freedom and the Law;* Hayek, *Law, Legislation and Liberty.*
42. In addition, see Paul H. Rubin, "Why Is the Common Law Efficient?" *Journal of Legal Studies* 6 (January 1977): 51–64; Rubin, *Business Firms and the Common Law: The Evolution of Efficient Rules* (New York: Praeger

Publishers, 1983); Rubin, "Predictability and the Economic Approach to Law: A Comment on Rizzo," *Journal of Legal Studies* 9 (March 1980): 319–334; Rubin, "Common Law and Statute Law," *Journal of Legal Studies* 11 (June 1982): 203–224; George L. Priest, "The Common Law Process and the Selection of Efficient Rules," *Journal of Legal Studies* 50 (January 1977): 65–82; and Hayek, *Law, Legislation and Liberty*, vol. 1, pp. 94–103.

43.   Benson, "Legal Evolution in Primitive Societies."
44.   Richard A. Epstein, "The Static Concept of the Common Law," *Journal of Legal Studies* 9 (March 1980): 254. For additional arguments against judge-made law, see Tullock, *Trials on Trial;* Tullock, *The Logic of the Law.*
45.   Epstein, "The Static Concept of the Common Law," p. 266.
46.   Hayek, *Law, Legislation and Liberty*, vol. 1, p. 78.
47.   Leoni, *Freedom and the Law*, p. 17.
48.   James Madison, "The Federalist No. 44," in Alexander Hamilton, John Jay, and James Madison, *The Federalist: A Commentary on the Constitution of the United States* (New York: The Modern Library, 1937), pp. 289–298.
49.   Grant Gilmore, *The Age of American Law* (New Haven: Yale University Press, 1950), p. iii.
50.   Auerbach, *Justice Without Law?* p. 9.
51.   Leoni, *Freedom and the Law*, pp. 23–24.
52.   Neely, *Why Courts Don't Work*, p. 110.
53.   Epstein, "The Static Concept of the Common Law," p. 254.
54.   Fuller, *The Principles of Social Order*, pp. 232–233.
55.   Lon L. Fuller, *The Morality of Law* (New Haven: Yale University Press, 1964), p. 153.

12

THE LEGAL MONOPOLY ON COERCION

Two conflicting monopoly arguments are presented to justify state provision of police, courts, and law. First, a single law-and-order firm will naturally emerge to monopolize the entire industry, which means that this firm will be able to dictate citizens' behavior. A benevolent government monopoly, therefore, is presumably necessary to preserve freedom. Second, there *must* be a single centralized authority of last resort (e.g., a supreme court) to prevent the development of the conflicting (competing) systems of law and the inefficient duplication of services that privatization would generate. If one argument is correct, then the other cannot be—privatized law and order either leads to a monopoly or to a competitive arrangement. But in fact, neither argument is valid.

THE POLICE MONOPOLY

The primary reason given for fearing monopolized private policing is that the agencies could become organized criminal firms that would use threats of violence to coerce "protection money" from citizens and to force their will on the rest of the population. Innocent people or people simply "guilty" of resistance will be killed or driven out without receiving fair trials, or without trials at all. After all, government systems of law and order have been misused in this way throughout modern history. It is doubtful that the political dissidents in eighteenth-century Ireland, nineteenth-century

France, or twentieth-century Russia and China were justly treated before they were killed, banished, or imprisoned. It is doubtful that the Jews sent to death by the German government during the 1930s and 1940s or the Cambodians slaughtered by their government during the 1970s and 1980s felt they had received justice.

Before you say, "but that cannot happen in a democracy," consider the lives ruined by Joe McCarthy and the U.S. Congress or the racial discrimination that flourished in the United States as a consequence of interest group manipulation of government and government-produced law and order.[1] And consider the use of force to extract taxes (protection money) and impose the will of some people on others by every government in history. The American Revolution was, in a large part, a tax revolt against what was supposedly one of the most advanced liberal and enlightened governments of the day. Hitler hoped to impose his will on the entire world in the 1930s and 1940s, as did Napoleon, the Romans before that, and countless other governments through recorded history. Clearly, we have reason to fear that government will misuse force and summarily "punish" citizens without trial.

Of course, the fact that government has misused power does not address the question of whether or not the private sector would do the same thing. In the absence of public police, what would prevent an armed private police from setting themselves up as a government? Friedman responded to this concern by noting that nothing can completely prevent such an abuse of power, except perhaps an armed populace willing to use those arms. He stressed, however, that "we must ask, not whether [a society where the private sector produces law and law enforcement] would be safe from a power grab by the men with guns (safety is not an available option), but whether it would be safer than our society is from a comparable seizure of power by the men with guns. I think the answer is yes."[2]

Friedman summed up the basic argument for private protection. First, he wrote:

> in our society the men who must engineer such a coup are politicians, military officers, and policemen, men selected precisely for the characteristics of desiring power and being good at using it. They are men who already believe that they have a right to push other men around—that is their job. They are particularly well qualified for the job of seizing power. Under [a private system of law and law enforcement] the men in control of protection agencies are "selected" for their ability to run an efficient business and please their customers. It is always possible that some will turn out to be secret power freaks as well, but it is

less likely than under our system where corresponding jobs are labeled "non-power freaks" need not apply.[3]

The institutional framework is different under the two systems. Under the present system, power has been accumulated and concentrated in the hands of a relatively small number. When one political power broker goes out of business, the power simply passes to another and continues to build. In a private system, a seller of protection services has to *convince* customers that he is going to protect them before he even can begin amassing power. If he suddenly turns on his customers, they can hire another protection firm and the power dissipates.

This brings us to Friedman's second point:

> In addition to the temperament [and incentives] of potential conspirators, there is another relevant factor: the number of protection agencies. If there are only two or three agencies in the entire area now covered by the United States, a conspiracy among them may be practical. If there are 10,000, then when any group of them start acting like a government, their customers will hire someone else to protect them against their protectors.
>
> How many agencies there are depends on what size agency does the most efficient job protecting its clients. My own guess is that there will be nearer 10,000 agencies than 3. If the performance of present-day police forces is any indication, a protection agency protecting as many as one million people is far above optimum size.[4]

Friedman's guess is probably fairly accurate, although it may err on the low side. The number of private protection and detective agencies in the United States is probably approaching 10,000; if all police were private, the number could easily be twice that. In other words, competition would probably be fierce.[5] Let us review the facts of the case. From 1964 to 1981, employment in the detective agency and protective services industry in the United States grew by 432.9 percent. Privatization would certainly generate similar or even greater growth. There is also no evidence that the industry would be monopolized since the number of firms offering such services grew from 1,988 to 7,126 during 1964–1981. Some of these firms are very large, of course, and, interestingly, many of the largest owe their success to government contracts. The Pinkerton Agency, clearly the biggest detective agency during the nineteenth century, earned a large portion of its income from the federal government.[6] Today, large companies like Wackenhut contract with government units to protect everything from airports to Cape Kennedy. But just because these companies are large under current institutional arrangements does not imply that they would be large without government contracts. Beyond that, with more than seven thousand competitors, even large companies are not likely to have monopoly power; they are only large in terms of the dollar value of their business, not relative to the size of the market. And if competitive firms become large because they are efficient, then they are desirable; big is not synonymous with bad.

There is one more point to be considered here. In a free market arrangement, protection firms have only those rights that each individual has. Thus, they "cannot engage in *legitimized* coercion" as they can under a system of government law and order.[7] Public police and military have the right to coerce; private firms would have to take that power before they would be in the position to use it. As Rothbard explained,

> in a stateless society there would be no regular, *legalized* channel for crime and aggression, no government apparatus the control of which provides a secure monopoly for invasion of person and property. When a state exists, there does exist such a built-in channel, namely the coercive taxation power, and the compulsory monopoly of forcible protection. In the purely free market society the would-be criminal police or judiciary would find it very difficult to take power, since there would be no organized State apparatus to seize and use as the instrumentality of command. To create such an instrumentality *de novo* is very difficult, and, indeed, almost impossible; historically, it took State rulers centuries to establish a functioning State apparatus.[8]

What are the sources of the persistent belief that without government, terror would reign? One source is popular fiction, which has given us stories of outlaw bands seizing control of a frontier town, big ranchers and their hired guns running roughshod over meek sodbusters, or vigilantes hanging innocent citizens. Certainly such things may have happened on occasion; but the shopkeepers, peasants, and sodbusters were not as meek as the movies have made them out to be, and vigilantes were organizations of concerned individuals attempting to quell violence and establish order. Good usually triumphs over evil in the movies, but in reality evil rarely amassed enough power to force its will on entire communities. "Shane" or the "Magnificent Seven" were not needed to triumph, nor were situations such as that depicted in the "Ox-Bow Incident" likely to arise. In fact, virtually every instance of temporary reigns of terror involved the power of some centralized government authority (see appendix).[9]

THE NECESSITY FOR COERCIVE POWER

If laws cannot be enforced without the government's power to coerce, it is irrelevant whether or not public officials are relatively likely to misuse power. It has been argued that "public" intervention may be required 1) to ensure compliance with a (private) judge's decision and 2) to compel submission of the dispute to adjudication.[10] While it is certainly true that a credible threat is needed to create sufficient incentives to submit to and then to comply with a court's judgment, this threat does not have to come from government.

Even today, as Fuller explained, rules of duty and entitlements established by government cannot regulate complex, interdependent relationships; but that does not mean that such relationships cannot be established and maintained: they "receive an effective ordering by silent processes, which, manifested in a primitive society, would be called customary law."[11] Indeed, while it is often assumed that our society functions because of individuals' moral control (typically attributed to a Judeo-Christian upbringing) combined with sanctions established by state-made law, Fuller argued, "we constantly orient our actions toward one another by sign-posts that are set neither by morals, in any ordinary sense, nor by words in law books."[12]

Most laws require some threat of sanction, of course. Umbeck explained that the threat of violence underlies any system of exclusive property rights:

> Whenever a group of individuals agrees to some system by which exclusive rights to scarce resources will be rationed, they are implicitly agreeing not to use violence. Yet this contract must provide for the use of violence to punish any member who does not follow the rules and maintain the rights of members against attacks from nonmembers. If the group is not willing or able to use violence in either of these two situations their property rights will be lost to those who are. *Ultimately, all exclusive rights are based on the threat or the use of violence.*[13]

Two points should be noted here. First, government enforcement of property rights is based on the threat of violence in the same way that a customary property rights system is (e.g., as in primitive societies, or gold camps). If someone refuses to comply with government's rules, he is declared an outlaw. Outlaws may be killed if they refuse to submit to arrest, trial, or punishment. So, even though Umbeck's study was of the customary systems of law established during the California gold rush, his argument is general.

Second, just because the threat of violence "ultimately" underlies any system of laws, whether privately or publicly enforced, violence need not be threatened to induce *most* people to comply with laws. In many cases a sufficient threat can take some form of nonviolent ostracism or boycott sanction.

In basketball, for example, a player is allowed to commit up to four fouls and still continue to play, but a fifth foul results in ejection from the game. Most players try not to commit five fouls before the end of a game, and a large majority are successful. This is an effective form of ostracism that creates incentives to comply with a rule but does not require government coercion or a threat of violence. Some might argue that 1) this is not an effective mechanism because players still foul out, or 2) this is not a relevant example because crimes are far more serious violations than fouling out of a basketball game. The first objection is simply not valid, because no system that citizens would find acceptable would prevent all violations of laws. The second objection is also not relevant. There are thousands of cooperative arrangements that enforce their rules through the threat of ostracism, including contracts between firms from different countries and between firms in producer organizations that have their own arbitration systems. In fact, throughout history, international commercial law has been enforced through threat of boycott,[14] and anyone who violated a contract under the medieval Law Merchant and refused to submit to the judgment by a commercial arbitrator was boycotted by other merchants.[15]

For some types of offenses, of course, the nature of the ostracism or boycott sanction would have to be severe. When the potential punishment is severe or costly, the threat must be severe to create sufficient incentives to comply. For many breaches of another individual's rights in primitive and medieval societies with private law and order, a violator was considered an outlaw or outcast if he or she refused to submit to arbitration (or, in some cases, mediation) and could be killed by anyone without fear of punishment.[16] This is similar to the threat used by government law enforcers today, and there is little doubt that similar sanctions would arise under modern privatization of law and law enforcement.

Should the power to coerce ever be exclusively granted? Should the state be able to monopolize policing? Even in the absence of clear misuses of police power, as Gustave de Molinari predicted in 1849, if "the consumer is not free to buy security wherever he pleases, you forthwith see open up a large profession dedicated to arbitrariness and bad management. Justice becomes slow and costly, the police vexatious, individual liberty is no longer respected, the price of security is abusively inflated and inequitably apportioned, according to the power and influence of this or that class of consumers."[17] De Molinari could be describing current public provision of police services (see Chapters 5, 6, and 7). In other words, there is every reason to fear and avoid monopolization of police coercion; *but* it is not the private sector that is likely to monopolize and abuse the police power—it is the public sector.

Without a doubt, most public law enforcement officials are good people with good intentions. But the discretion and power they are given create almost irresistible incentives to use the position for personal or political gain. Of course, there are those who argue that people are inherently bad so government must have the power to prevent such a monopoly. If this is true, then there is even more reason to avoid a public monopoly by encouraging private sector competition. As Barnett suggested, when it is assumed that people are either essentially corrupt or that they will try to gain an unfair advantage over others, then advocates of granting government coercive powers are immediately faced with a difficult question: Who should get the power?[18] Whoever gets power must, by assumption, be essentially corrupt or try to take unfair advantage over others. What we must recognize is that coercive power, whether we assume that people are inherently good or bad, is neither necessary nor desirable in law enforcement.

WOULD THERE BE A SINGLE LEGAL SYSTEM?

There appear to be significant economies of size (or standardization) for some *systems* of law. Still, it is likely that several specialized systems would arise under private enforcement arrangements. These systems may have a functional basis and be extensive geographically (e.g., the international Law Merchant), or have a geographic basis and be extensive in terms of subject area (see Chapter 14), but it is doubtful that there would be one monopoly system.

The development of our present Western legal system involved several separate law systems. In fact, as Berman explained, "perhaps the most distinctive characteristic of the Western legal tradition is the coexistence and competition within the same community of diverse jurisdictions and legal systems."[19] During the early middle ages, there was canon law and several secular legal systems, including mercantile, urban, manorial, feudal, and royal law. Only royal law was truly centralized law, but the other systems did not emulate this government law. In fact, "all the various secular legal systems. . .adapted to their own uses many basic ideas and techniques of canon law, if only because the canon law was more highly developed and was available for imitation. . . . At the same time, the secular authorities resisted the encroachments of the ecclesiastical authorities upon the secular jurisdiction; and for that reason, too, they sought to achieve for secular law the cohesion and sophistication of the canon law."[20] A significant difference from most of the secular legal systems was that canon law was more directly connected with and influenced by political events and less directly influenced by social and economic developments.

Competing systems of law are not unique to periods when legal systems are developing or to privately produced law, of course. Every country has its own legal system and there are competing systems within countries as well. For instance, "each of the fifty-three separate court systems in the United States, including the federal court system, has its own substantive and procedural rules that are often in conflict with one another. Each side of any quarrel rushes to get the case started in that jurisdiction that has the laws most favorable to its side."[21] There are legal systems for the fifty states and the District of Columbia in addition to the federal system. There are municipal and county systems, military systems, and customary systems with arbitration and mediation arrangements. When we define law as Fuller did as "the enterprise of subjecting human conduct to the governance of rules," then "this enterprise is being conducted, not on two or three fronts, but on thousands. Engaged in this enterprise are those who draft and administer rules governing the internal affairs of clubs, churches, schools, labor unions, trade associations, agricultural fairs, and a hundred and one other forms of human association. . .there are in this country alone 'systems of law' numbering in the hundreds of thousands."[22]

It might be argued that there is a hierarchical arrangement of law in the United States, with federal law at the pinnacle. Government law backed by powers to coerce can forcefully overrule the customary systems, and state systems are subject to federal control. These government systems, including the federal system, have their constitutional limitations, of course. In fact, appeal to the U.S. Supreme Court requires the consideration of a constitutional issue, so many court cases are outside its jurisdiction. Berman contended, however, that "the plurality of legal jurisdictions and legal systems within the same legal order is threatened in the twentieth century by the tendency within each country to swallow up all the diverse jurisdictions and systems in a single central program of legislation and administrative regulation. . . . In federal systems such as that of the United

States, the opportunity to escape from one set of courts to another has radically diminished."[23]

SHOULD THERE BE A SINGLE LEGAL SYSTEM?

Is this trend toward monopolization under government law necessary or even desirable? Many argue that it is, and Landes and Posner put the case as clearly as any: "There would appear to be tremendous economies of standardization in [law], akin to those that have given us standard dimensions for electrical sockets and railroad gauges. While many industries have achieved standardization without monopoly, it is unclear how the requisite standardization of commonality could be achieved in the [law] without a single source for [law]—without, that is to say, a monopoly."[24] This is especially true, they argue, with today's highly mobile population where lawbreakers can leave the jurisdiction of "regional monopolies" in law.[25] Rothbard offered an obvious counter argument, however, by noting that those who assume that there must be a monopoly in coercion and decision-making (e.g., one Supreme Court to hand down unquestioned decisions) have failed to recognize that

> the Argentinean, for example, lives in a state of "anarchy" of nongovernment, in relation to the citizen of Uruguay. . .and yet the private citizens of these and other countries live and trade together without getting into insoluble legal conflicts. . . . Although it is true that the separate nation-states have warred interminably against each other, the private citizens of the various countries . . .have managed to live together in harmony without having a single government over them. If the citizens of northern Montana and of Saskatchewan across the border can live and trade together in harmony without a common government, so can the citizens of northern and of southern Montana. In short, the present-day boundaries of nations are purely historical and arbitrary, and there is no more need for a monopoly government over the citizens of one country than there is for one between the citizens of two countries.[26]

Rothbard could have gone even further. It took privately produced and adjudicated mercantile law to *overcome* the limitations of political boundaries and localized protectionism, paving the way for the commercial revolution and development of international trade (see Chapter 2). In fact, modern international commerce still relies on private customary law and arbitration to adjudicate disputes. The International Chamber of Commerce Court of Arbitration, established in 1923, is just one of at least 120 arbitration organizations concerned with international trade disputes.[27] Where the "tremendous economies of standardization" that Landes and Posner alluded to exist, the private sector will take advantage of them. Government typically cannot respond because of the artificial constraints of political boundaries. There is no reason to believe that any national government is of the ideal size to take full advantage of the economies of standardization in law. In some areas of law (e.g., commercial law), these economies appear to be greater than any existing nation can encompass. In other areas, such economies may be considerably more limited so that existing political entities are too large. A private system of law would generate efficiently sized "market areas" for the various aspects of law, and perhaps many would be smaller than most nations while others would overlap many of today's political jurisdictions. The existence of economies of standardization really provides a justification for private law, then, in order to break away from the inefficient artificial political restrictions.

Finally, consider the desirability of a diversified legal arrangement consisting of several specialized but competing jurisdictions and legal systems. As Berman explained,

> It is this plurality of jurisdictions and legal systems that makes the supremacy of law both necessary and possible. ... The very complexity of a common legal *order* containing diverse legal *systems* contributes to legal sophistication. Which court has jurisdiction? Which law is applicable? How are legal differences to be reconciled? Behind the technical questions lay important political and economic considerations: church versus crown, crown versus town, town versus lord, lord versus merchant, and so on. Law was a way of resolving the political and economic conflicts. ... The pluralism of Western law, which both reflected and reinforced the pluralism of Western political and economic life, has been, or once was, a source of development, or growth—legal growth as well as political and economic growth. It also has been, or once was, a source of freedom. A serf might run to the town court for protection against his master. A vassal might run to the king's court for protection against his lord. A cleric might run to the ecclesiastical court for protection against the king.[28]

In contrast to those who believe that the entire system of law must be monopolized, there appears to be substantial benefit from not having monopoly, just as there is for the production of all other goods and services.

OTHER "MONOPOLY" CRITICISMS OF PRIVATIZATION

A number of arguments against privatization of law enforcement are not couched in terms of monopoly power. These arguments are commonly raised against market processes in general by people who either do not understand the way competitive markets work or refuse to believe that they work as they do. These critics anticipate abuses that cannot arise in a competitive environment. We shall consider these arguments to illustrate that they are simply incorrect when applied to markets and that they would be correct if applied to government production.

Self-interest Motives Lead to Cost Cutting, Poor Service Quality, and Abuses of Power. Private police are often criticized for being undertrained, too old, and often abusive of their authority.[29] This view is particularly strong among public police and is frequently expressed by the media: "Most law enforcement officers view [private police] as that minimum-wage, overaged, overweight, half-asleep, rent-a-cop nodding against the wall at a mall or retail store. Scarcely better is the earlier image of the elderly night watchman asleep in a chair with a time clock on the floor beside him."[30] The reason for expecting low quality private police, so the argument goes, is that security firms cut corners in order to cut costs and raise profits.

The same sort of argument has been applied to other aspects of law enforcement. Mark Conniff, director of the National Association of Criminal Justice Planners, for instance, predicted that firms that provide prisons on contract will cut costs by cutting back on services and the quality of staff. The American Civil Liberties Union brought suit in federal court in an attempt to ban private contracting of prisons, "contending that private agencies are not adequately equipped and trained to do a humane job of incarceration, and that a profit motive is likely to generate cost-cutting measures not in the interest of the prisoners or the public."[31] Private courts have been similarly maligned.[32] Ira Glasser, executive director of the ACLU, expressed the fear that private, for-profit courts, such as Judicate, will take shortcuts and ignore procedures that guarantee fairness in public courts.[33]

There are several problems with using these arguments to justify public production of law enforcement and adjudication services. First, it is doubtful that sellers in private markets are motivated in the way these arguments assume. Second, even if the private producers of such services were so motivated, market forces would probably prevent such behavior. Third, even if these predictions are born out, it does not follow that government does a better job; in fact, the evidence indicates that government provision of such services is far more likely to involve abuses and poor quality than private production. Let us expand on each of these points in turn.

Are private producers motivated to increase profits by cutting costs and reducing quality? There is no question that they have incentives to minimize production costs and there are clearly products that vary in quality, but neither of these circumstances implies an incentive to cut corners and reduce quality below the level that consumers desire. The only way the arguments can be valid is if cutting costs by reducing quality does not generate an offsetting reduction in revenues. But that is precisely what happens in a *competitive* market.

Consider the ACLU's argument about private contract prisons. If a firm wants only one contract for a relatively short period of time, it may provide unsatisfactory services; but there are not many firms that have such narrow goals. If a firm acquires a reputation for doing unsatisfactory work, it will not survive for very long in a competitive market. As Tom Beasley, president of Corrections Corporation of America, explained: "The great incentive for us. . .is that [we] will be judged on performance. . .we want that contract renewed next year and the year after."[34] William MacQueen of Judicate noted that "if we can't guarantee fair and impartial justice we're a failure. We would put ourselves out of business."[35] In a competitive environment where sellers have long-range profit goals, the incentives are to offer the same quality of service at lower prices (and, therefore, cost) than competitors or to offer a superior quality product than competitors but at a comparable price.

A free market for law enforcement generates precisely the opposite incentives to those ascribed to it by its critics. The only circumstances under which this would not be the case is if the market were to result in monopoly (which we have already discounted) or if sellers had only short-term profit goals. There are con men and hucksters who move into an area, defraud a number of consumers, and move on; but no matter how ignorant consumers might be, it is unlikely that many of them would buy security or adjudicative services from such fly-by-night operations. A sense of permanence and a reputation for quality services would clearly be much more important criteria for consumers choosing such services than the "quality cutting" argument assumes.

What about the obvious lack of training and skills and the age of so many guards and watchmen? It would be foolish for someone who simply wants a night watchman to check I.D.s and set off an alarm in the event of trouble to pay $20,000 or $30,000 to hire a person with the training of an urban police officer. On the other hand, it would be foolish for a large corporation that wants a large-scale security system installed to hire someone to design and initiate that system who only has the training and skills of an urban police officer. The market does provide minimum-wage watchmen to those consumers who demand them, but "virtually ignored [by the critics of private security] are the many thousands of well-qualified proprietary loss control personnel earning salaries of $18,000 to $100,000 and earning it in supervisory, management, and consultant roles."[36] The current trend in private security is toward more training and an upgrading of personnel, practices, and procedure, which is not surprising given the increased demand for private protection against property and violent crimes (see Chapter 9).

Other Abuses.   Abuses by private police supposedly go beyond their cost-cutting efforts. Landes and Posner contended that

> the private enforcer is paid per offender convicted, regardless of the actual guilt or innocence of the accused. There are several ways in which the enforcer can increase his "catch" and hence his income, by augmenting the supply of "offenders." (1) He can fabricate an offense. (2) He can prosecute an innocent person for an offense that in fact occurred. (3) He can encourage an individual to commit an offense that he would not have committed without encouragement, and then prosecute him for the offense; this is the practice known as "entrapment." (4) Knowing that an individual is about to attempt the commission of a crime, the enforcer can wait until the crime has been committed and then prosecute him for a criminal attempt. The incentive for waiting is to obtain greater compensation, since the penalty for the completed crime will presumably be heavier than the penalty for the attempt.
>
> These abuses would doubtless occur under any system of private enforcement, but how frequently?[37]

But a security firm whose employees abuse the rights of citizens is not going to attract much business. An enforcer who fabricates offenses, intentionally prosecutes innocent people, practices entrapment, or waits for crimes to be committed is not going to receive many contracts once consumers of enforcement services catch on. After all, even though such actions may initially generate more work and profit for the enforcer, they also generate higher costs and poorer quality services for the purchasers of enforcement. Thus, competitors should easily be able to offer better services at a lower cost. Once again, competition instills incentives to offer quality services at competitive prices. As Smith noted, "Its own public reputation. . .demands that it shun fabricated or poorly founded accusations."[38] Furthermore, a prerequisite for the incentives to commit abuses listed is that the enforcer is paid on a per offender convicted basis. But it is easy to envision contractual arrangements that include flat fees for services over a period of time, thus creating incentives to prevent crime and minimize the number of offenses prosecuted.

Quality Cutting and Other Abuses by Government.   The final point to be considered here is evidence of the actual level of abuses resulting from cost cutting or other incentives in private sector production of law enforcement, *relative* to similar occurrences in the public provision of those services. My argument is that firms in private competitive markets are not nearly as likely to offer poor quality services and abuse their powers as is frequently claimed. On the other hand, government bureaus often provide poor services and bureaucrats can be abusive.

Consider the incident that triggered an ACLU suit to ban private prisons. The Immigration and Naturalization Service had placed some illegal aliens in a private Texas security firm's detention facilities. There had been no competitive bidding for this job, and no contract with the firm existed. When an alien was killed and two were wounded during an escape attempt, the ACLU concluded that the private sector provides prisons of poor quality. But what about the public prison system's performance? An AP story in October 1984 reported the nineteenth inmate killing of the year in the Texas prison system.[39] At the time that the ACLU suit was initiated, at least 32 states were under federal court orders to remedy what federal judges considered to be unconstitutionally cruel conditions in state prisons. As of April 1984, some 150 county governments and 39 states were in litigation or under court order to improve their prisons, with entire prison systems in some states declared unconstitutional.[40] In the mid-1980s, investigators discovered that prisoners' medical needs in the Florida state prison system were so neglected that between April 1983 and April 1984 "17 inmates died preventable deaths" at the system's Medical Center Hospital. A review team, appointed by a federal judge, "found medical care in the department shot through with incompetence, negligence and indifference toward inmates' health. It found doctors who could not speak English, medical technicians who were untrained and unsupervised, and a medical administration with little authority in an unresponsive prison hierarchy."[41] Deaths in prison will occur under any system. Does one death in a private detention facility warrant a claim that private prisons produce poorer quality and greater abuse than the public system?

Critics of private sector police frequently cite violent acts by those police as evidence of their poor training and lack of skills. Edward Iwata reported that in 1983 twenty-two people in California were killed in shooting incidents involving private security personnel, "including both guards and suspects (or victims)."[42] The report failed to point out, however, that there are probably twice as many private police as public police in California and that public police kill more people than private police do. In 1981, for instance, 68 "justifiable homicides" were committed by public police in California.[43] This figure does not include police killed or unjustified homicides by police; the figure for killings involving private police encompasses all these categories.

In 1970, a study of complaints filed against licensed private security firms was conducted under the auspices of the National Institute of Law Enforcement and Criminal Justice.[44] Of the 17 state licensing authorities contacted, five apparently did not believe the problem was sufficient to warrant compiling data; three states—Delaware, Iowa, and Minnesota—collected data but had no complaints to report for 1970. Similarly, 24 local licensing agencies were contacted, with seven not compiling data and three reporting no complaints. The average complaint rate was 6 percent of the private firms for state regulators and 4.3 percent for local regulators. Private firms may abuse their power, and they may make mistakes. But there are strong reasons to expect that public police will be much more abusive than private police.

First, an individual who is not fully responsible for the consequences of his actions is likely to be *relatively* unconcerned about those consequences. A civil suit brought against a private security firm for abuse of an individual's rights can be costly, and could destroy the business. In a suit against a public law enforcement agency, taxpayers pick up the tab, so the cost to the manager of that bureau is relatively small. Furthermore, the incentives under a private system where individuals can be held fully liable for their mistakes or their abuses (see Chapter 14) are quite different from those of a governmental system where a police officer (or a judge) has only limited liability. A policeman cannot be sued for false arrest, for example, unless it can be proven that the individual arrested is innocent *and* that the police officer had no reason to suspect that individual. No legal claim against the government or its officials can be made by an innocent person who is wrongly imprisoned. It might be recognized that the government has made an error, but government officials have the *right* to make such errors and are not liable for them; private citizens, of course, generally are liable. As Friedman explained:

> Such special rights allow a government to kill off its opponents and then apologize for the mistake. Unless the evidence of criminal intent is very clear,

the murderers are immune from punishment. Even when the evidence is over-whelming, as in the case of the Chicago Black Panther raid of a few years ago, there is no question of trying those responsible for their actual crime. Hannahan, the Cook County district attorney responsible for the raid, is being charged, not with conspiracy to commit murder, but with the obstruction of justice—not, in other words, with arranging to have people he disliked killed, but with lying about it afterward. This is not an isolated instance of the miscarriage of justice, it is the inevitable result of a system under which the government has certain special rights, above and beyond the rights of ordinary individuals —among them the right not to be held responsible for its mistakes [or abuses]. When these rights are taken away, when the agent of government is reduced to the status of a private citizen and has the same rights and responsibilities as his neighbors, what remains is no longer government.[45]

Judge Neely wrote that in order to understand why judges act the way they do we must consider the interaction of judges with the structure of the courts, for it is the institutional setting that generates much of the behavior we observe. "Certain personal vices are not remarkable in people employed outside the judiciary (immediately arrogance and indolence spring to mind)," Neely observed. "And if the people appointed to the bench exhibited various qualities to excess before their appointments, they would not have been selected. It is the nature of the judiciary, with its life tenure, or long elected terms, that it can encourage arrogance and indolence as the occupation of salesperson tends to mask them."[46] This is a very important point. Many individuals would abuse their positions by cutting costs, doing poor quality work, and bullying *if they could*. The institutional arrange-ments within which people perform their tasks determine whether or not such abuses can be carried out, and competitive markets are one of the best (if not *the* best) institutional arrangements designed to discourage abusive, inefficient behavior. A public judge can abuse every party in every dispute he adjudicates without fear of losing his job. But a private judge "needs" litigants to stay in business, and he must treat litigants with respect.

The differences between public institutions and competitive private institutions go well beyond the difficulty in firing public officials who do poor jobs. The premise underlying the predictions of much of the abusive behavior that many expect from private judges is that private judges will be rewarded according to the *number* of cases tried. In fact, private producers are rewarded for providing what consumers want—clear, quick resolution of disputes with opinions based on the commonly held norms of society. Public bureaucrats obtained their rewards through the political process, where rewards are frequently tied to some measurable representation of the *size* of the bureaucracies' operations. Thus, public employees who provide law enforcement and adjudication face the same incentives that some have attributed to private police and judges, but they are not regulated by the threat of competition at anything close to the level that exists in private markets. Consequently, public producers are far more likely to react to those incentives than private producers.

Markets Favor the Rich.   Mabry, et al. argued that "if the rendering of verdicts is to be independent of the relative wealth of the litigants, then the provision of judicial services naturally requires separation of the decision-maker's gain from that of each litigant. This fact either requires heavy regulation or it requires public provision of the judge directly."[47] This presumably occurs because of the "possible corruption in a private payment system"[48]—that is, the wealthy can pay a judge more so they will be favored. Private justice will not be impartial justice.[49] This argument has also been applied to the privatization of police. Are such arguments valid?

After arguing that competitive courts should produce biased opinions, Landes and Posner admitted some difficulty with the argument: "Left unexplained by this analysis is the actual pattern of competition in the English courts during the centuries when judges were paid out of litigant fees and plaintiffs frequently had a choice among competitive courts. . .none (of which we are aware) of the kind of blatant favoritism that our economic analysis predicts. . .emerge[d] in such a competitive setting. Why it did not emerge (assuming it has not simply been overlooked by legal historians) presents an interesting question."[50] Similar evidence can be found in many primitive and medieval systems of private law. The Comanche and the medieval Icelanders had private institutional arrangements to ensure that there was no bias against the poor, and the medieval Irish system was noted for its development and protection of the rights of women.[51] In his analysis of private Icelandic law and order, Friedman explained that victims were given a *transferable* property right, the right to restitution, which meant that "a man who did not have sufficient resources to prosecute a case or enforce a verdict could sell it to another who did and who expected to make a profit in both money and reputation by winning the case and collecting the fine. This meant that an attack on even the poorest victim could lead to eventual punishment."[52] In addition, the wealthy in Iceland were not immune from prosecution. *Anyone* refusing to pay restitution was outlawed, and an outlaw who defended himself by force was liable to pay for every injury inflicted on those trying to bring him to justice. The point here is that the private sector will produce some arrangement to prevent favoring one group over another in the justice process. In a private system, where no state power to coerce exists, a plaintiff cannot force a defendant to submit to trial before a *particular* judge. The defendant must be persuaded that participation is in his best interest. That persuasion may come from some form of ostracism that is strong enough to convince him to submit to a fair trial.[53] But a defendant is not likely to agree to appear before a judge who is biased against him, particularly if other judges are available. Arbitrators and mediators who have successfully stayed in business have done so by providing fair, impartial judgments.

What guarantees this impartiality? Might not all the private judges have the same biases because it is the wealthy who can afford to pay the most? In a private system where the wealthy are not protected by the government, it is doubtful that the wealthy as a group would want such a biased court system. First of all, one rich man may at some point have a dispute with an even richer man, so he would be reluctant to support a system where a decision goes to the highest bidder. But more importantly, the poor would simply opt out of such a system and establish their own. If the wealthy tried to force their brand of justice on the poor (e.g., form a government), there would be a violent confrontation, which in the long run typically costs the rich more than it does the poor. As Smith pointed out, "The fear of governmentalists that free-market agencies will sell mock-justice to the highest bidder without regard for justice, objectivity and reliable procedures is without foundation. . . . For an agency to use (allegedly) restitutive force without public verification is to brand itself an outlaw in the public eye."[54]

One might respond that the poor will not be able to afford privately provided justice, so it is irrelevant that private courts are not biased against them—the system is. But we have seen that arrangements can be and have been made to ensure that attacks against poor victims are brought to justice. Beyond that, privatization does not just mean private firms *selling* law enforcement and adjudication. It means private citizens freely choosing among competitive options, one of which is the arbitration or mediation of disputes between some people in a group (e.g., in a neighborhood) by others in the same group.

Consider an even more important question. Is access to the public court system "free" to the poor, or is it biased in favor of the rich? Supreme Court Justice William Rehnquist explained that a great deal of time and money typically must be spent before trial and in appealing cases afterward.

"The result is a system ideally suited to a lawsuit by General Motors against IBM—both of which have the resources to accommodate the delay. But how well suited is it for the countless other litigants who are not in that class?"[55] Under the current public system, it frequently seems that only the wealthy can afford to use the public courts. This, Rehnquist pointed out, is forcing more and more people to turn to private alternatives to get their disputes resolved.

Although a private dispute resolution system would provide the poor with access to an arbitrator or mediator that is unavailable from the public courts, some observers maintain that availability of such private arrangements is unjust. Laura Nader argued that "one of the worries is that you're creating a two-tiered system, one for the poor and one for the rich. The courts become for important problems of the rich and the poor use the mediation."[56] Such criticisms are irrelevant, of course, because the choice is not between public courts freely and equally available to everyone and a "two-tiered system"; for many of the poor, the choice is between private justice and no justice.

An interesting twist is that some have argued that privatization favors the rich because they can opt out of the public system, leaving only the poor. When this happens, the argument goes, "public services deprived of their most influential customers inevitably decline."[57] Another critic argued that private adjudication should be illegal, because "so long as there are two systems of justice, one of which is readily accessible, relatively inexpensive, and efficient, the major defects of our legal system as a whole will remain uncorrected, thereby making permanent exclusion of the majority of middle class and poor persons from effective use of our legal system."[58] In other words, there is alot wrong with the public courts including their tendency to exclude the poor and middle class from justice, and the private adjudication system is more efficient, relatively inexpensive, and readily accessible. The solution, then, is to outlaw private adjudication to force the wealthy back to the public courts so they will demand that the public system be improved. Clearly, however, if private adjudication is "relatively inexpensive," it is not justice for the rich—it is justice of *relatively* easy access to everyone. A much better solution would eliminate the public courts (or at least let them compete with private alternatives) so the poor, and the middle class, and the wealthy all have access to adjudication.

The argument that privatization would favor the rich has also been applied against the use of private police. Only the wealthy will be able to afford to have their neighborhoods patrolled and crimes against them investigated, it is said. Again, institutional and contractual arrangements may arise that insure that even the poor have private police protection. Beyond that, under privatization a whole array of options would be available to the poor, including voluntary neighborhood watches and patrols.

Under the current system, the cost of crime is disproportionately borne by the poor. They are victims of the largest portion of crimes committed and receive a disproportionately small portion of the benefits of public expenditures on both preventing and solving crime cases. The probability that a woman from a family making under $3,000 a year will be raped is almost four times the probability that a woman from a family that makes $25,000 or more will be raped; the same is true for other violent crimes.[59] The government's performance in providing the poor with law and order is, to say the least, bleak. For the poor, privatization means switching from a system to which they currently contribute but from which they feel alienated to a system where they get the protection and justice they pay for.

Some might retort that the poor often do not pay taxes and that whatever public law enforcement they get is more than they would get in a private arrangement. But their rent includes the capitalized taxes of landlords and the prices they pay for other goods and services cover taxes paid by producers, so that argument is not valid. Furthermore, as Neely explained: "In terms of tax revenues, the release of dangerous felons is very cheap. The cost of the sanction is then shifted from the government treasury [that is, from the middle and upper classes who pay taxes] to the lower socio-economic class because that is the class that disproportionately bears the brunt of crime."[60] If privatization leads to greater concern for preventing offenses against persons and property and for recovering victims' losses, then many costs currently shifted onto the poor in lieu of taxes will decline and more resources may be available to purchase protection should they *choose* to.

The current publicly dominated system of justice also appears to favor the relatively wealthy *criminal*.[61] For instance, the punishment of some crimes involves a criminal choosing between paying a fine or spending time in prison. Becker explained that many laws in the United States that permit either fines or imprisonment place a very low value on time in prison: For example, Class A misdemeanors in New York State can be punished by a prison term as long as one year or a fine no larger than $1,000; Class B misdemeanors are punished by a term as long as three months or a fine no larger than $500. "These statutes permit excessive prison sentences relative to fines, which may explain why imprisonment in lieu of fines is considered unfair to poor offenders, who often must 'choose' the prison alternative."[62]

The preceding discussion does not imply that under a private system the rich and poor alike will have access to precisely the same enforcement and adjudicative resources. As Lott stressed, efficiency requires that different resources be employed by relatively wealthy individuals.[63] Someone who earns a high wage, for example, should have the option of employing security services rather than producing them himself, because his own time has valuable alternative uses. Thus, an array of policing and adjudicative *options* would be available in a privatized system, and different options would be used by individuals according to *their own* choices, based on willingness and ability to pay. In our current politicized common pool system of justice, individuals are excluded from considering some options because other individuals have the power to make decisions for them; taxpayers are forced to pay for public services and mistakes whether they want to or not. As a consequence, the poor are much worse off under the current system than they would be under privatized law enforcement.

CONCLUSIONS

Some of the arguments against privatization of law and order may have some validity, but the answer to the question of whether or not to privatize must involve an examination of the *relative* performance of private and public systems of law and order. Neither system will be perfect. Neely noted: "Perfect justice under ideal conditions is illusory. To ask perfect justice of a court system is like asking a skilled surgeon to perform brain surgery with a meat ax. He might be able to do it 5 percent of the time if he is really skilled, but smart money does not bet on it."[64] The "meat ax" that must be used under the public system of law and order consists of the institutional arrangements that have arisen in the public sector and the incentives that those institutions create. A competitive private sector involves a very different set of institutions and incentives that are far less cumbersome. They probably should not be likened to a perfect scalpel, but rather, to a set of cutlery consisting of several well-sharpened knives with specialized functions and uses. The surgeon still will not perform perfectly 100 percent of the time, but the patient's chances of survival are a lot better than when a meat ax is used.

APPENDIX TO CHAPTER 12:

VIOLENCE AND VIGILANTE JUSTICE
IN THE AMERICAN WEST

The eighteenth-century American West is widely cited as an example of a lawless society dominated by violence, where the strong and ruthless ruled by force. It is true that miners, farmers, ranchers, and other individuals moved westward much more rapidly than the U.S. government could expand its law enforcement system, particularly from 1830 to 1900. But this does not mean that the frontier was lawless. While government law enforcement may have been the norm in the original thirteen states (and even this is questionable[65]), order for virtually the entire westward expansion was based to a large extent on private sector production of law and law enforcement.[66] In most cases, there was no alternative. But a private sector enterprise of law was chosen mainly because it worked. As Anderson and Hill concluded after considering several of these non-governmental systems, "the western frontier was not as wild as legend would have us believe. The market did provide protection and arbitration agencies that functioned very effectively, either as a complete replacement for formal government or as a supplement to that government."[67] Similarly, historian Roger McGrath concluded that "some long-cherished notions about violence, lawlessness, and justice in the Old West...are nothing more than myth."[68] Let us briefly examine the historical evidence regarding the violent, lawless frontier.

Violence in the West: Myth or Reality?[69]   According to Mabel Elliott, the American frontier was a place "where a man could exist without tribute to tax collectors, or law makers, and if he moved fast enough he did not need to defer even to his neighbor's opinion."[70] This lack of effective government, Elliot suggested, encouraged a sense of individualism that *supposedly* produced frequent violent confrontations, particularly in the mining and cattle frontier. R. W. Mondy noted that men found no stable social order waiting for them as they moved westward.[71] This lack of social order *presumably* forced frontiersmen to act independently and to establish social relationships without the framework of an existing order. The resulting lack of law and order, Mondy concluded, led to frequent violent confrontations and deaths. Mondy also cited the physical and cultural isolation of the frontier communities as contributing factors to the problem of violence.

Interestingly, Elliott and Mondy provided *no proof* of widespread violence on the frontier. They simply *assumed* (or *asserted*) that violence was prevalent and then proceeded to explain why that should be the case. In this same vein, Gilbert Geis wrote: "We can report with some assurance that, compared to frontier days, there has been a significant decrease in [crimes of violence]."[72] But Geis cited no evidence. Joe Frantz even suggested that American violence today reflects our frontier heritage.[73]

Is there any real evidence of relatively violent behavior in the West? H. S. Drago found cases where violence broke out over the use of range lands, but he pointed out that such confrontations were not very common.[74] A number of authors have written about gunfighters in the West, and it is true that some gunfighters were involved in a number of killings.[75] The reasons for such violent behavior, according to some historians, are the nonexistence of government institutions of law and order, the isolation of communities and the need for individuals to defend themselves and pursue attackers themselves or in conjunction with vigilante committees, who generally contributed more to violence than to order. Beyond these problems with law enforcement, there were supposedly many sources of confrontations, such as scarce land and large numbers of saloons, gambling, and prostitution establishments.

Some writers have focused on vigilante activity as a source of violence. Historian Richard Maxwell Brown cited at least 300 historical vigilante movements in the United States and its western territories.[76] These occurrences began as early as 1767 in South Carolina, but they have been particularly prominent in the western frontier because private citizens had to enforce their own laws. These vigilante movements were frequently effective at establishing social order and deterring offenses, but in doing so they often resorted to capital or corporal punishment.

Some historical accounts have focused on regions that have contained a particularly notorious event or individual, so there may be a selection bias problem in trying to characterize the entire West on the basis of their conclusions. Interestingly, however, these studies discover a good deal of social order. W. C. Holden studied the Texas frontier from 1875–1890 and found that many kinds of offenses were simply nonexistent.[77] Burglaries and robberies of homes and businesses (except for banks) simply did not occur. Doors were not locked, and hospitality was widespread, indicating that citizens had relatively little fear of invasive violent offenses. Shootings did occur, but they typically involved what the citizenry considered to be "fair fights." Stage and train robberies occurred, but these incidents were isolated from most citizens and caused them little or no concern.[78]

The conclusion that the western frontier was a lawless, violent place comes from one of two sources: 1) it is simply *assumed* that since the West had no effective government law enforcement apparatus, it *must* have been lawless and violent; or 2) violent individuals or events have been *assumed* to represent the general character of the western frontier. UCLA historian Roger McGrath concluded that

> the frontier-was-violent authors are not, for the most part, attempting to prove that the frontier was violent. Rather, they assume that it was violent and then proffer explanations for that alleged violence. These explanations are based on conditions that the authors think were peculiar to or exaggerated on the frontier and to the personality traits of the frontiersman himself. The authors reason that it must have been the unique frontier conditions and the frontiersman's personality that caused the violence.
>
> Their conclusions are not based on a thorough investigation of *all* forms of violence and lawlessness in the West or even in a particular town or region. . . . These authors provide a less than complete—in some cases a highly selective and perhaps unrepresentative—picture of frontier violence and lawlessness.[79]

There is a growing literature that concludes that the West was not very violent. W. Eugene Hollon found that the western frontier "was a far more civilized, more peaceful and safer place than American society today."[80] According to Hollon, violence became a problem in the West only *after* urban development. Frank Prassel concluded: "It would appear that, in the American West, crime may have been more closely related to the developing urban environment than the former existence of a frontier" and that in general a westerner "probably enjoyed greater security in both person and property than did his contemporary in the urban centers of the east."[81] Both Hollon and Prassel provided reasonable explanations for the impression that the West was a violent place. Prassel pointed out that, in part because of the general *absence of disorder,* the notorious actions of a few individuals received undue attention. He emphasized that western fiction, movies, and television have all created inaccurate perceptions of the West. Hollon made similar arguments, suggesting that the western frontier has a poetic image where its extremes have been exaggerated.

Both Hollon and Prassel were surprised to find that the West was really quite orderly. Prassel wrote, "Considering the factors present it is surprising that even more murders, assaults, and robberies did not occur [in the western frontier]."[82] Hollon concluded that "it is miraculous that the last and largest frontier region in the United States was settled in as orderly a fashion as it was."[83]

Hollon and Prassel are not the only scholars who have begun to recognize that the frontier West was not the lawless society of popular fiction or of academic assumption.[84] Their inability to explain the social order that was the norm in the West, however, is typical of much of this literature. McGrath concluded that

> the frontier-was-not-especially-violent authors, while contending that there was relatively little violence on the frontier, nevertheless indicate that the unique frontier conditions which the frontier-was-violent authors enumerate were present, and they believe that those conditions *should* have caused violence. That those conditions did not do so suggests that they might have actually promoted peacefulness—though none of the frontier-was-not-so-violent authors proposes such a connection.[85]

But this is not quite accurate. As economic historians Terry Anderson and P. J. Hill explained:

> The West during this time often is perceived as a place of great chaos, with little respect for property or life. Our research indicates that this was not the case; property rights were protected and civil order prevailed. Private agencies provided the necessary basis for an orderly society in which property was protected and conflicts were resolved. These agencies often did not qualify as governments because they did not have a legal monopoly on "keeping order." They soon discovered that "warfare" was a costly way of resolving disputes and lower cost methods of settlement (arbitration, courts, etc.) resulted. In summary. . .a characterization of the American West as chaotic would appear to be incorrect.[86]

Anderson and Hill illustrated the role of private arrangements in making and enforcing law in the American West by examining the historical literature on and records of the law established by land claim clubs, cattlemen's associations, wagon trains, and mining camps. Their analysis is consistent with the brief discussion of customary law systems in Chapter 2.

Vigilante Justice in Response to the Failure of Government Law.   Local governments were established to replace privately produced law fairly rapidly in some places in the western frontier, and public police (e.g., sheriffs) were appointed. State and federal officials also appeared on the scene. But in several instances this government law enforcement was so ineffective or corrupt that private citizens had to re-establish law and order. As Alan Valentine wrote, "If the people had the right to make their own laws and to elect their own officials, then it followed in pioneer logic that the people had the right to change or overrule them. When they were sufficiently aroused to do so, they were not inclined to waste time on fine points of procedure or to show much deference to a protesting officer of the law."[87] Perhaps the best known cases of this kind occurred in San Francisco.

Most of San Francisco's laws during the late 1840s and early 1850s were developed through popular assemblies of citizens.[88] Governmental law enforcement was instituted early, however, so anyone accused of a crime had to be arrested by the publicly employed sheriff and waited for a trial in the next Court of Sessions, which met every two months at the county seat. Lawyers often got trials delayed, and because jail facilities were scarce or nonexistent "postponements almost always meant that the accused would be discharged if he had not escaped first."[89] Witnesses had to pay their own expenses; and given the delays, many did not wait for the trial. With the swelling of San Francisco's population during the gold rush, things began to get out of hand. In Valentine's words:

> As they became increasingly harassed by crime and arson, San Franciscans became more and more ready to sacrifice legal procedure for elementary justice and security. The situation was becoming worse, not better, as new criminals moved in and more and larger fires swept across the city. The better citizens were torn between two fears: fear that nothing short of popular tribunals could cope with crime and fear that popular tribunals would degenerate into lynching mobs, led by the worst elements in town. . . .
>
> Many of the most respectable citizens believed that the only compromise between rampant crime and rampant lynching was an organized, stable popular tribunal that could be controlled by the better elements in the city. . . .
>
> San Franciscans wanted something better than slapdash justice, whether legal or popular, but above all they wanted crime reduced.[90]

The city's press was urging drastic action by early 1849, but the citizens of San Francisco held back until February of 1851.

On February 19, 1851, the owner of a San Francisco clothing store was robbed and beaten. The sheriff arrested two men and charged them. A large number of people gathered the next day before the city offices, demanding quick action against the accused. Some speakers advocated an immediate hanging, but one, William T. Coleman, prevailed. He told public officials,

> We will *not* leave it to the courts. The people here have no confidence in your promises, and unfortunately they have no confidence in the execution of the law by its officers. Matters have gone too far! I propose that the people here present form themselves into a court. . .that the prisoners be brought before it. That testimony be taken, counsel on each side allotted. . .if the prisoners

be found innocent let them be discharged, but if guilty let them be hung. . . .
We don't want a mob! We won't have a mob! Let us organize as becomes men![81]

A committee of fourteen prominent citizens, including Coleman, was chosen to take charge of the case. The legal authorities were invited to participate but declined, although they raised no resistance and handed over the prisoners. The committee impaneled a jury and appointed three judges and a clerk. Two "highly regarded" lawyers were appointed to represent the prisoners; Coleman acted as prosecutor. After hearing the case, the jury voted nine guilty and three for acquittal. The prisoners were turned back over to the authorities. The impetus for a vigilante organization was in place, however.

In May 1851, a volunteer force was organized to "assist" city officers in discovering and apprehending criminals, with the "reluctant" cooperation of the sheriff. Some 3,000 citizens gathered in early June during the trial of a suspected arsonist, and during the next few days small groups of businessmen began meeting and discussing the possibility of forming a "committee of vigilance." Finally, a "selected group of responsible citizens" was called together, and a committee was formed on June 10, 1851. The June 13 San Francisco *Alta* printed a statement from the committee:

Whereas, It has become apparent to the citizens of San Francisco that there is no security to life and property, either under the regulations of society as it at present exists, or under the laws as now administered, therefore, the citizens whose names are hereunto attached, do unite themselves into an association, for the maintenance of the peace and good order of society and the preservation of the lives and property of the citizens of San Francisco, and do bind themselves each unto the others, to do and perform every lawful act for the maintenance of law and order, and to sustain the laws when faithfully and properly administered. But we are determined that no thief, burglar, incendiary or assassin shall escape punishment either by the quibbles of the law, the insecurity of prisons, or laxity of those who PRETEND to administer justice.[82]

The committee took its first action even before the statement appeared. On the night after the group had organized, John Jenkins was caught stealing a safe from an office. Two vigilantes assisted in the capture and took the prisoner to their headquarters. A trial was immediately organized, and Jenkins was easily convicted. The statutory penalty under California law for grand larceny was death, and Jenkins was hanged. There was only token resistance by public officials. A coroner's jury ruled that Jenkins died as a consequence of violent means and that the committee was guilty of the crime, but no steps were taken by San Francisco's public officials to act on the jury's verdict.

The Jenkins case was only the vigilantes' first step in their drive to eliminate crime from San Francisco. One source of criminals to California was the British penal colonies in Australia. The vigilantes, apparently with permission from federal authorities, began boarding every ship that entered the port from Australia to examine the papers of anyone wishing to disembark. If someone did not have a permit issued by the U.S. consul in Sydney, he was not allowed to enter San Francisco. The committee also invoked an old Mexican law that forbade admission to the territory of anyone previously convicted of a crime in another country. Many city residents were examined by the committee and expelled from the city. Many others simply left to avoid the process. "There was no question," Valentine concluded, "that the Vigilantes had become the most powerful force in the city and had the support of most of the citizens."[93]

On August 21, the vigilance committee was preparing to hang two convicted criminals when the sheriff and a small group of police arrived with a warrant of *habeas corpus* procured at the request of the governor.[94] The prisoners were turned over to the sheriff's authority but no action was taken. Two days later, an organized group of thirty-six vigilantes went to the jail, removed the two prisoners, and hanged them.

This double hanging was the committee's last major act. It had hanged four men, banished several others from the city, and frightened off still more.[95] The committee officially made 91 arrests during their hundred days.[96] In addition to the four who were hanged, one was whipped, fourteen were deported to Australia, and fourteen were informally ordered to leave California. Fifteen were handed over to public authorities, and forty-one were discharged (two others for whom no decision is recorded were apparently discharged). George Stewart concluded:

> The record is eloquent in itself. It speaks of moderation and of the attempt to render justice. There were no mass hangings, no men shot down in the street. There was none of the grim nonsense, "Give him a fair trial and then hang him!" To be arrested did not mean that a man was already condemned, but only that he stood trial, with a half-and-half chance of being cleanly acquitted.[97]

But this "moderation" was evidently more effective than the public law enforcement system had been. "Crime had declined so rapidly that for a few months, at least, San Francisco was a city of normal order and safety."[98]

The committee announced that it was suspending action as of September 16, 1851. An executive committee was appointed to act as a "watchdog of public order," but it took only two actions and both were in support of city officials. The deterrent impact of vigilante actions in 1851 was short-lived. "By the spring of 1855 the city administration had become so corrupt and crime so prevalent again that the *Herald* called for a return of the good and vigorous days of the vigilance committee."[99]

Between November 1855 and May 1856, more than one hundred murders were committed in San Francisco. One such incident occurred on November 17, 1855, when a machine politician named Charles Cora shot and killed U.S. Marshall William Richardson. Cora was arrested, but he was not very concerned. The sheriff was one of his "cronies," and the best lawyers in the city had been retained to defend him. James King of William, publisher of the *Bulletin* and former vigilante, reported that $40,000 had been spent to get Cora acquitted. The trial was held on January 3, 1856, but "the jury was fixed, the witnesses were rehearsed in perjury, and the proceedings were a farce. On the seventeenth the jury reported disagreement, as planned by Cora, and was discharged."[100]

On May 14, 1856, the *Bulletin* reported that James Casey, a city supervisor, had been a convict in Sing Sing. When Casey went to the *Bulletin*'s office and confronted the publisher, King ordered him out of the office and told him never to come back. That evening, Casey shot the publisher as King was walking home, and that night the committee on vigilance was revived as some ten thousand citizens gathered in the streets demanding action. William Coleman was chosen to head the new committee and within two days 5,500 members were enrolled.[101] Casey had been arrested and was being held at the city jail. On May 18, 500 vigilantes marched to the jail armed with rifles and bayonets. Coleman threatened to destroy the jail with cannon fire if both Casey and Cora were not turned over to the committee.

Cora went on trial on May 20 before the vigilante court for the murder of Richardson. James King of William died that afternoon and Casey also went on trial. Both politicians were found guilty of murder and sentenced to be hanged. But, "this was no judicial farce or lynching mob."[102] The defendants had chosen their own counsel, and the jury had reached a unanimous verdict. The two men were hanged within a few hours of King's funeral. The committee remained active for another three months, its membership growing to 8,000 (during those three months there were two murders in San Francisco).

On August 18, 1856, the committee on vigilance disbanded. The leadership was extremely popular and William Coleman was urged to accept a senatorial nomination. The *London Times* observed: "It is seldom that self-constituted authorities retire with grace and dignity, but it is due to the vigilance committee to say that they have done so."[103] Perhaps Stewart's observation about the 1851 committee is even more appropriate for the 1856 committee. He concluded that the committee was "remarkable, not so much for what it did as for what it did not do. Against the background of all the executions and killings of history, the hanging of four rascals is insignificant. We should rather remember that the Committee did *not* yield to the temptations of power, and did *not* carry its revolution to a logical conclusion."[104]

Similar stories could be told about other communities in the American West. Henry Plummer, the sheriff of Bannack, Montana, in 1863, was also the organizer of "an intricate network of bandits, agents, and hideouts in southwestern Montana."[105] Plummer participated in numerous robberies and was responsible for several deaths. When the citizens finally organized their vigilante justice, they hanged Plummer and twenty-one of his gang, banished several others from the area, and frightened most of the rest off. The Montana vigilante courts were less formal than those in San Francisco, but "they had good leadership and seldom acted except in extreme cases. Usually they gave the defendant an opportunity to clear himself if he could...the [Montana] vigilance committees were called into existence by frontier necessity. When the need for them passed, they quietly and quickly faded away."[106]

Generally, vigilante movements involved law-abiding citizens enforcing the law and *re-establishing order.* Those who view a vigilante movement under any circumstances as an example of lawlessness are victims of one of the most serious flaws in the argument that law and its enforcement must be monopolized by government. When law is only what government says it is, then vigilantes are always lawless and deserve to be "put down by force." This implies the law-must-be-monopolized contention, wherein there seems to be "no recognition that...a single source of legal power...may be so ineptly or corruptly exercised that an effective legal system is not achieved."[107] But government officials have a reciprocal obligation to duty, just as do citizens. As Lon Fuller explained,

If we accept the view that the central purpose of law is to furnish baselines for human interaction, it then becomes apparent why the existence of enacted law as an effectively functioning system depends upon the establishment of stable interactional expectancies between lawgiver and subject. On the one hand, the lawgiver must be able to anticipate what the citizenry as a whole will accept as law and generally observe the body of rules he has promulgated. On the other hand, *the legal subject must be able to anticipate that government will itself abide by its own declared rules.* ... A gross failure in the realization of either of these anticipations—of government toward citizens and of citizens toward government—can have the result that the most carefully drafted code will fail to become a functioning system of law.[108]

Furthermore, recognition of a system of law breaks down when reciprocities are not maintained, whether those reciprocities were established through kinship, contract, or legislation. A sufficient breakdown "must—if we are to judge the matter with any rationality at all—release men from those duties that had as their only reason for being, maintaining a pattern of social interaction that has now been destroyed."[109] Such a breakdown in the governmentally backed legal system occurred in San Francisco and most other places where vigilante action was taken. Importantly, however, this did not result in lawlessness. Customary law still prevailed, and private arrangements arose to enforce that law.

CONCLUSIONS: CUSTOMARY LAW AS AN IMPLICIT CONSTITUTION

The widely held perception that government must establish and enforce law is a recent phenomenon. When government law was unavailable or undesirable to a particular community, private options filled the void. The vigilante movements that were so common in the American West and the decisions by many to establish and enforce their own custom-based laws illustrate an important point about a valid legal system. Vigilantes re-established law when government officials were ineffective or corrupt and, therefore, in violation of the law. The power of law is not absolute, even when it is in the hands of a government authority. As Hayek observed, "the allegiance on which this [rules established by a legislature, or government] sovereignty rests depends on the sovereign's satisfying certain expectations concerning the general character of those rules, and will vanish when this expectation is disappointed. In this sense all power rests on, and is limited by, opinion."[110]

Government law is not paramount, and there is some implicit constraint on power or authority. This fact is probably not widely perceived today; it is a firmly established force in American culture and clearly part of our customary law. During the American Revolution, revolutionaries chose to establish their own law, and similar "vigilantism" has been a common occurrence ever since. As with Fuller,

> every kind of social power, whether designated as formal or real, is subject to an implicit constitution limiting its exercise. . . . When we speak of power as an aspect of social relations, we mean the power holder, A . . . has the capacity to control B's actions in certain respects. In other words, A is in a position to take advantage of B's capacity for self-direction and to shape B's exercise of that capacity for purposes of his own, which may of course include that of benefiting B. The fact that A must leave in the address of his power some remnant at least of his [B's] capacity of self-direction introduces into every power relationship an element of reciprocity, though the reciprocity may be most unwelcome to A. . . . Nevertheless, this element of reciprocity is always present and may under changing conditions grow in force.[111]

Thus, the "implicit constitution" emanates from reciprocity, as does the recognition of duty (and, therefore, law) in general.

Customary law reflects the norms of those who choose to function in the particular social order "governed" by those laws. In a very real sense, then, such customary law is a unanimously adopted "social contract" or "constitution." It establishes the rules that are the basis for spontaneous social order. This social contract evolves and adapts to changing social conditions. Even when people *consent* to live under the authority of a government, reciprocity requires that certain duties be effectively performed by that government.

Our government has a primary role in making law and keeping order. But that does not mean that individuals *consented* to the development of government legal institutions and increasing domination of the private sector, or that government was better than the private institutions and their customary law. Furthermore, it should be noted that authority can be *granted* as part of a reciprocally beneficial arrangement, wherein such authority is implicitly or explicitly limited, or it can be *taken* through coercion and force. As Fuller suggested, those with power often prefer not to recognize any reciprocal duty on their part; and as more and more power is taken, government's reciprocal duties are reduced—the social contract is weakened. But "even the lawmaking of a dictator commonly undergoes some accommodation to demands tacitly expressed in rumbling discontent."[112] If even a very powerful government fails to fulfill its duties or takes more than citizens are ready to give, revolution (or vigilantism) occurs. In fact, the rise of government law in England and the United States reflected a gradual but almost continuous striving for greater power by those in government in the face of continual but gradually weakening resistance by citizens.[113]

ENDNOTES

1. See for instance, Gary S. Becker, *The Economics of Discrimination* (Chicago: University of Chicago Press, 1957); Jennifer Roback, "Southern Labor Law in the Jim Crow Era: Exploitive or Competitive?" *University of Chicago Law Review* 51 (Fall 1984): 1161–1192.

2. David Friedman, *The Machinery of Freedom: Guide to Radical Capitalism* (New York: Harper and Row, 1973), pp. 168–169.

3. Ibid., p. 169.

4. Ibid., pp. 169–170.

5. See Harold Demsetz, "Two Systems of Belief About Monopoly," in *Industrial Concentration: The New Learning*, ed. H. J. Goldschmid, H. M. Mann, and J. F. Weston (Boston: Little, Brown and Co., 1974).

6. Truett A. Ricks, Bill G. Tillett, and Clifford W. Van Meter, *Principles of Security* (Cincinnati: Criminal Justice Studies, Anderson Publishing Co., 1981); Frank Morn, *The Eye that Never Sleeps* (Bloomington: Indiana University Press, 1982).

7. Friedman, *The Machinery of Freedom*, p. 170.

8. Murray N. Rothbard, *Power and Market: Government and the Economy* (Kansas City: Sheed Anderson and McMeel, Inc., 1970), p. 6.

9. A similar argument against privatization is that without government there would be no law and order. For views on this, see E. Adamson Hoebel, *The Law of Primitive Man* (Cambridge, Mass.: Harvard University Press, 1954), p. 294; Walter Goldsmidt, "Ethics and the Structure of Society: An Ethnological Contribution to the Sociology of Knowledge," *American Anthropologist* 53 (October/December 1951): 506–524; Bruce L. Benson, "Enforcement of Private Property Rights in Primitive Societies: Law Without Government," *Journal of Libertarian Studies* 9 (Winter 1989): 1–26; R. F. Barton, "Procedure Among the Ifugao," in *Law and Warfare*, ed. Paul Bohannan (Garden City, N.Y.: The Natural History Press, 1967); David Friedman, "Private Creation and Enforcement of Law: A Historical Case," *Journal of Legal Studies* 8 (March 1979): 399–415; Joseph R. Peden, "Property Rights in Celtic Irish Law," *Journal of Libertarian Studies* 1 (1977): 81–95; Leon E. Trakman, *The Law Merchant: The Evolution of Commercial Law* (Littleton, Colo.: Fred B. Rothman and Co., 1983); Bruce L. Benson, "The Spontaneous Evolution of Commercial Law," *Southern Economic Journal* 55 (January 1989): 644–661; Robert K. Yin, Mary E. Vogel, Jan N. Chaiken and Deborah R. Both, *Citizen Patrol Projects* (Washington, D.C.: National Institute of Law Enforcement and Criminal

Justice, Law Enforcement Assistance Administration, U.S. Department of Justice, 1977), p. iii.
10. William M. Landes and Richard A. Posner, "Adjudication as a Private Good," *Journal of Legal Studies* 8 (March 1979): 237.
11. Lon L. Fuller, *The Principles of Social Order* (Durham, N.C.: Duke University Press, 1981), p. 246.
12. Ibid., p. 246.
13. John R. Umbeck, *A Theory of Property Rights: With Application to the California Gold Rush* (Ames: Iowa State University, 1981), p. 9.
14. Trakman, *The Law Merchant.*
15. Ibid., p. 10; William C. Wooldridge, *Uncle Sam, the Monopoly Man* (New Rochelle, N.Y.: Arlington House, 1970), p. 96.
16. See Friedman, "Private Creation and Enforcement of Law"; Peden, "Property Rights in Celtic Irish Law."
17. Gustave de Molinari, "De la Production de la Sécurité," *Journal des Economistes* (February 1849): 277–290, translated as *The Production of Security,* trans. J. Huston McCullock (New York: Center for Libertarian Studies, 1977), pp. 13–14.
18. Randy Barnett, "Pursuing Justice in a Free Society, Part One: Power vs. Liberty," *Criminal Justice Ethics* 4 (Winter/Spring 1985).
19. Harold J. Berman, *Law and Revolution: The Formation of Western Legal Tradition* (Cambridge, Mass.: Harvard University Press, 1983), p. 10.
20. Ibid., p. 274.
21. Richard Neely, *Why Courts Don't Work* (New York: McGraw-Hill, 1982), pp. 56–57.
22. Lon L. Fuller, *The Morality of Law* (New Haven: Yale University Press, 1964), pp. 124–125. Also see Leopold Popisil, *Anthropology of Law: A Comparative Theory* (New York: Harper and Row, 1971), pp. 125–126.
23. Berman, *Law and Revolution,* pp. 38–39.
24. Landes and Posner, "Adjudication as a Private Good," p. 239.
25. Ibid., p. 259.
26. Rothbard, *Power and Market,* p. 4.
27. Steven Lazarus, et al., *Resolving Business Disputes: The Potential for Commercial Arbitration* (New York: American Management Association, 1965), p. 29.
28. Berman, *Law and Revolution,* p. 10.
29. See for example, "Private Police Forces in Growing Demand," *U.S. News and World Report,* January 29, 1983, pp. 54–56.
30. Norman K. Bottom and John Kostanoski, *Security and Loss Control* (New York: Macmillan Publishing Co., 1983), p. 31.
31. Philip E. Fixler, Jr., "Can Privatization Solve the Prison Crisis?" *Fiscal Watchdog* 9 (April 1984): 3.

32. See Landes and Posner, "Adjudication as a Private Good," p. 241.
33. Martin Tolchin, "Private Courts with Binding Rulings Draw Interest and Some Challenges," *The New York Times,* May 12, 1985, p. 38; Bob de Sando, "Rented Scales of Justice Ends Wait for Day in Court," *The Asbury Park Press,* June 23, 1986, p. A2.
34. "Crime Pays," *60 Minutes,* vol. 16, no. 11 (CBS Television Network, November 25, 1984), p. 12.
35. De Sando, "Rented Scales of Justice," p. A2.
36. Bottom and Kostanoski, *Security and Loss Control,* p. 31.
37. Landes and Posner, "The Private Enforcement of Law," pp. 26–27.
38. George Smith, "Justice Entrepreneurship in a Free Market," *Journal of Libertarian Studies* 3 (Winter 1979): 413.
39. "Inmate Killed in Texas Prison Violence," *Billings Gazette,* October 14, 1984, p. A3.
40. Fixler, "Can Privatization Solve the Prison Crisis?" p. 1.
41. Kirk Spitzer, "Care Crumbles Behind Prison Walls, Report Finds," *Tallahassee Democrat,* June 9, 1985, 1A.
42. Edward Iwata, "Rent-a-Cops on Trial," *This World,* March 18, 1984, p. 10.
43. California Department of Justice, *Homicide in California, 1981* (Sacramento: Bureau of Criminal Statistics and Special Services, 1981).
44. James S. Kakalik and Sorrel Wildhorn, *Current Regulation of Private Police: Regulatory Agency Experience and Views* (Santa Monica, Calif.: The Rand Corporation, 1971).
45. Friedman, *The Machinery of Freedom,* pp. 171–172.
46. Neely, *Why Courts Don't Work,* p. 35.
47. Rodney H. Mabry, Holly H. Ulbrich, Hugh H. Macauley, and Michael T. Maloney, *An Economic Investigation of State and Local Judiciary Services* (Washington, D.C.: National Institute of Law Enforcement and Criminal Justice, Law Enforcement Assistance Administration, Department of Justice, 1977), p. 83.
48. Ibid.
49. For a slight twist on this argument see Landes and Posner, "Adjudication as a Private Good," p. 254.
50. Ibid., p. 255.
51. E. Adamson Hoebel, "Law-Ways of the Comanche Indians," in *Law and Warfare,* ed. Paul Bohannan (Garden City, N.Y.: The Natural History Press, 1967); Friedman, "Private Creation and Enforcement of Law"; Peden, "Property Rights in Celtic Irish Law."
52. Friedman, "Private Creation and Enforcement of Law," p. 406.
53. See for example, Peden, "Property Rights in Celtic Irish Law"; Barton, "Procedure Among the Ifugao"; Benson, "Enforcement of Private Property Rights in Primitive Societies."
54. Smith, "Justice Entrepreneurship in a Free Market," pp. 413–414.

55. See for example, Benson, "The Spontaneous Evolution of Commercial Law"; Trakman, *The Law Merchant.*

56. Quoted from *Justice Without Law,* a production of the KQED Current Affairs Department, Channel 9, San Francisco, December 19, 1984, p. 26.

57. "Private Everything," *New York Times,* October 20, 1980, p. D3.

58. Kenneth Jost, "Renting Judges in California," *Los Angeles Daily Journal,* July 12, 1981.

59. Neely, *Why Courts Don't Work,* p. 140.

60. Ibid.

61. John R. Lott, Jr., "Should the Wealthy Be Able to 'Buy Justice'?" *Journal of Political Economy* 95 (December 1987).

62. Gary Becker, "Crime and Punishment: An Economic Approach," *Journal of Political Economy* 78 (March/April 1968): 198.

63. Lott, "Should the Wealthy Be Able to 'Buy Justice'?"

64. Neely, *Why Courts Don't Work,* p. 122.

65. See Bruce L. Benson, "The Evolution of Law: Custom Versus Authority" (manuscript, Florida State University, Tallahassee, Fl.); Jerold S. Auerbach, *Justice Without Law* (New York: Oxford University Press, 1983).

66. See Alan Valentine, *Vigilante Justice* (New York: Reynal and Co., 1956), p. 10.

67. Terry Anderson and P. J. Hill, "An American Experiment in Anarcho-Capitalism: The *Not* So Wild, Wild West," *Journal of Libertarian Studies* 3 (1979): 27.

68. Roger D. McGrath, *Gunfighters, Highwaymen and Vigilantes: Violence on the Frontier* (Berkeley: University of California Press, 1984), p. 259.

69. See ibid., pp. 201–227, for a more detailed review of much of the literature discussed in this section.

70. Mabel A. Elliot, "Crime on the Frontier Mores," *American Sociological Review* 9 (April 1944): 189.

71. R. W. Mondy, "Analysis of Frontier Social Instability," *Southwestern Social Science Quarterly* 24 (September 1943): 167–177.

72. Gilbert Geis, "Violence in American Society," *Current History* 52 (June 1967): 357.

73. Joe B. Frantz, "The Frontier Tradition: An Invitation to Violence," in *The History of Violence in America,* ed. Hugh D. Graham and Ted R. Gurr (New York: New York Times Books, 1969), pp. 127–154.

74. Henry S. Drago, *The Great Range Wars: Violence and the Grasslands* (New York: Dodd, 1970).

75. See McGrath, *Gunfighters, Highwaymen and Vigilantes,* p. 264; Walter N. Burns, *The Saga of Billy the Kid* (Garden City, N.Y.: Doubleday, 1926); Stuart N. Lake, *Wyatt Earp: Frontier Marshall* (Boston: Houghton Mifflin, 1931); William E. Connelley, *Wild Bill and His Era* (New York: The Press of the Pioneers, 1933).

76. Richard Maxwell Brown, *Strain of Violence: Historical Studies of American Violence and Vigilantism* (New York: Oxford University Press, 1975).

77. William C. Holden, "Law and Lawlessness on the Texas Frontier 1875–1890," *Southwestern Historical Quarterly* 44 (October 1940): 188–203.

78. Ibid., p. 196.

79. McGrath, *Gunfighters, Highwaymen and Vigilantes,* pp. 270–271.

80. W. Eugene Hollon, *Frontier Violence: Another Look* (New York: Oxford University Press, 1974), p. x.

81. Frank R. Prassel, *The Western Peace Officer* (Norman: University of Oklahoma Press, 1972), p. 22.

82. Ibid., p. 23.

83. Hollon, *Frontier Violence,* p. 125.

84. See Lynn I. Perrigo, "Law and Order in Early Colorado Mining Camps," *Mississippi Valley Historical Review* 28 (1941): 41–62; Robert R. Dykstra, *The Cattle Towns* (New York: Knopf, 1968).

85. McGrath, *Gunfighters, Highwaymen and Vigilantes,* pp. 270–271.

86. Anderson and Hill, "An American Experiment in Anarcho-Capitalism," p. 9.

87. Valentine, *Vigilante Justice,* p. 13.

88. See also Anderson and Hill, "An American Experiment in Anarcho-Capitalism"; John R. Umbeck, *A Theory of Property Rights With Application to the California Gold Rush* (Ames, Iowa: Iowa State University Press, 1981); Benson, "The Evolution of Law." Laws were enforced and adjudicated in the same manner in the mining camps, but San Francisco established a governmental law enforcement system.

89. Valentine, *Vigilante Justice,* p. 28.

90. Ibid., pp. 28–29.

91. Quoted in ibid., p. 48.

92. Quoted in ibid., p. 68.

93. Ibid., p. 74.

94. Ibid.

95. Ibid., p. 75.

96. George R. Stewart, *Committee of Vigilance: Revolution in San Francisco, 1851* (Boston: Houghton Mifflin Company, 1964), p. 319.

97. Ibid.

98. Valentine, *Vigilante Justice,* p. 78.

99. Wayne Gard, *Frontier Justice* (Norman, Oklahoma: University of Oklahoma Press, 1949), p. 161, quoting from the San Francisco *Herald,* April 22, 1855.

100. Ibid., p. 162.

101. Ibid., p. 163.
Valentine, *Vigilante Justice,* p. 131.

102. Quoted in Gard, *Frontier Justice,* p. 166.

103. Stewart, *Committee of Vigilance,* p. 316.

104. Gard, *Frontier Justice,* p. 171.

106.   Ibid., p. 188.
107.   Lon L. Fuller, *The Morality of Law* (New Haven: Yale University Press, 1964), p. 157.
108.   Lon L. Fuller, *Principles of Social Order* (Durham, N.C.: Duke University Press, 1981), pp. 235–236. Emphasis added.
109.   Fuller, *The Morality of Law*, p. 22.
110.   F. A. Hayek, *Law, Legislation and Liberty*, vol. 1 (Chicago: University of Chicago Press, 1973), p. 92.
111.   Fuller, *The Principles of Social Order*, p. 195.
112.   Ibid., p. 172.
113.   For more detail, see Chapter 3 and Benson, "The Evolution of Law."

PART V

FROM AUTHORITARIAN
TO PRIVATE LAW

13

POLITICAL BARRIERS TO PRIVATIZATION

I have argued that the market failure justifications for government involvement in the enterprise of law are not valid, particularly when compared to the tremendous level of government failure in law-making and enforcement. Furthermore, there are substantial benefits to be gained from privatization in law and order. While the resulting system of justice may not be perfect, it would be considerably more effective, efficient, and equitable than the current system. Realistically, however, theoretical justifications for privatization and even examples of private sector successes do not go far toward reducing public sector involvement in the justice process. The political barriers to privatization must be recognized before substantial progress can be made.

Privatization in law and order involves two separate processes: 1) increases in the privately owned and allocated resources devoted to the protection of persons and property, including the establishment and clarification of property rights through rule-making and adjudication; and 2) decreases in publicly controlled resources devoted to the same purposes. There may be resistance to both of these processes, but given the ingenuity of the private sector for innovating means of getting around legislated barriers, fairly significant strides are likely to be made in increasing the private resources allocated to law and order. Some components of this process will probably occur much more rapidly than others. Privately provided equipment and services for protection against violent and property crimes should continue

331

to increase. Private dispute resolution should continue to be a rapid growth industry. Privately produced customary laws will also play a significant role, arising in part through private dispute resolution processes. But barriers to rapid reductions in publicly controlled resources used in law enforcement, law-making, and corrections appear to be more substantial. In other words, the shrinking of the public sector is likely to face strong resistance.

OPPOSITION TO REDUCING THE GOVERNMENT'S ROLE

The primary forces that will resist a shrinking public sector role in law and order are the same as those that generated its rapid growth. Interest groups that have demanded an ever-increasing government role will resist any reduction in that role. At the same time, much of the cost arising from government expansion have been borne by unorganized and politically ineffective individuals; the same people remain relatively ineffective politically in pressing demands for a smaller government. The groups with the largest stake in government's law and its enforcement will provide the strongest opposition to its dismantling.

Public Employees. The major growth area for unionization now is the public sector. Between 1960 and 1970, government worker union membership doubled while total union membership increased by only 14 percent.[1] During the 1970s, *total* union membership declined in the U.S., and membership as a percentage of employees declined dramatically, from 30 percent in 1970 to 24.7 percent in 1980.[2] At the same time, membership in public employee unions has risen sharply. In 1960, about one-third of all federal employees were unionized; by 1979, 60 percent of non-postal workers and 74 percent of postal workers belonged to unions. More significantly, there were roughly one million union members at the state and local levels in 1960.[3] This number rose to over five million in 1979, when about 40 percent of all state and local government employees were organized. During that period, total government employment almost doubled.

One of the most rapidly growing areas of public sector unionization has been police. As of 1976, 55 percent of all police had been organized, with some 255,000 members in several unions.[4] Correctional institution personnel have also unionized in increasing numbers. In 1978, the American Federation of State, County, and Municipal Employees had 20,000 members out of the nation's 75,000 state corrections employees; by 1986, the figure had risen to 50,000.[5] Beyond that, other unions have actively recruited and attracted membership from corrections employees, including the Service Employment International Union and the Teamsters.[6] In addition, police and corrections personnel have organized associations (e.g., Policemen's Benevolent Associations, various state police associations) that are politically active.

Public sector labor-management relationships were institutionalized during the 1970s, and unions and their representatives now have a legal right to voice their demands and confer in the shaping of political decisions. The rapid organization of public sector unions has allowed the accumulation of large amounts of funds that have been used to press union demands. The unions are strong, active, and effective in the political arena, and they will attempt to prevent or at least delay any programs that might reduce their members' wages, job security, or number of positions. Even partial privatization through contracting out runs into opposition from unions. In Lyle Fitch's words, "once a public employee union has gotten a firm hold on a government function, any attempt to escape by resorting to private contracts will be considered union-busting and dealt with accordingly."[7]

Funds collected through dues mean that the tactics available to all organized interest groups—lobbying, publicity campaigns, political contributions and support, and lawsuits—are available to and are actively employed by public sector unions and associations. But beyond the political tactics that can be used by any interest group, public employees have additional strength. They can threaten or take job actions to force their demands on political decision makers. Police have "blue-flu" and corrections workers have "sick-outs" and "lock-ins," even though such actions are illegal in most states.[8] For example, during the spring of 1975, New York state proposed to close one prison, transfer 380 prison inmates to another facility, and lay off a number of corrections employees. The union representative called a press conference and reported that "the announced closing, transfer of inmates, and the proposed layoffs of employees represent total fiscal irresponsibility and this union will not be a party to it."[9] The union membership refused to do the work necessary for transferring the prisoners and threatened that if the employees were replaced by "scabs" the union would *prevent* the transfer. As a result, the facility was *not* closed.[10] In 1975, illegally striking corrections officers in Ohio stopped delivery trucks from entering the prisons, forcing the state to use national guard helicopters to send in needed supplies.[11] Similar stories can be told about police strikes and job actions.

The threat posed by police and corrections employee unions is often even more substantial because of cooperation with other unionized public employees. For example, Massachusetts fired striking correctional officers in 1973, but the officers were reinstated after the president of the state's American Federation of State, County and Municipal Employees threatened to declare a strike of all state employees.[12]

The majority of the political activity and job actions by police and corrections unions have been economic in nature, with demands for higher wages, earlier retirement, disability pay, sick leave, shorter hours, and so on. Other factors can also play a role, but as Wynne reported: "The chief causes [for strikes by correctional institution employees] appear to be (1) economic issues and (2) issues pertaining to safety and security, a matter made particularly complex by the presence of covert motives."[13] For instance, a prison employees union may try to prevent community-based programs and deinstitutionalization (e.g., halfway houses) out of an expressed concern for "public safety," but the fact is that such programs result in relatively reduced needs for prison facilities and institutional jobs. Perhaps all such demands represent true concerns for public safety, but one has to at least recognize the potential self-interest motives.

Contracting out in corrections is a recent threat to prison employees, but their unions expressed opposition as early as 1976.[14] Corrections unions have actively opposed virtually any new program that reduces the traditional custodial role of public correctional institutions, so strong opposition to contracting out (particularly for existing facilities) can be anticipated. And *any* move toward eliminating public facilities in favor of a fully private system will run up against violent opposition.

The perceived threat to public police of contracting out is probably much less than for corrections officers. Nonetheless, public police organizations have reacted to contracting efforts in both Arizona and Ohio (see Chapter 8). The threat of contracting is much more obvious in the area of fire protection, and some idea of the options available to and the likely reactions by public police can be gained by looking at what happens when communities with public fire departments try to contract out.

During 1982–1983, Willimantic, Connecticut, and Dover, New Hampshire, attempted to contract out for fire protection services. The International Association of Fire Fighters (IAFF) actively opposed both efforts, for fear that "this apparent threat to their members' job security could spread rapidly, leaping across state boundaries" throughout New England.[15] Willimantic was considering a 1983 cost for fire protection of about $900,000, one-fourth of the city's budget and approximately $180 per household per year. At that time, private subscription fire services charged between $30 and

$50 per household per year, so early in 1982 the city announced it was receiving bids for fire services. Three companies responded, and the city council began negotiations with one: Wackenhut Services, Inc. Wackenhut's offer would have generated savings of $1.4 million for the city over five years, primarily by economizing on personnel.

The union denounced the bids, accused the city of "union busting," and predicted that contract fire fighting could "like a cancer, spread all the way through the state of Connecticut."[16] The union campaigned hard for the city-county consolidation referendum that was on the ballot in December 1982; if the referendum passed, a new city government would be elected and they hoped to influence that vote. The referendum passed, but the consolidation was not to take place until six months later. The city council decided to vote on the proposed contract in February. The union packed the city hall, and "when the meeting was called to order, Deputy Fire Marshal Joseph Beaulieu announced the hall was overcrowded. The meeting would have to be closed down, he said, or moved elsewhere, because fire regulations were being violated."[17] When the Wackenhut representative went out to his car, he found his tires slashed.

Once the meeting resumed, the IAFF claimed that the union had submitted an alternative proposal that was competitive with Wackenhut's. No city officials had seen the proposal, but the council agreed to postpone its vote. A week later, the council again postponed its vote because the union representative wanted additional time to "prepare the proposal that he previously claimed had already been submitted."[18] The union was also working on the state legislature to pass a bill that would ban private fire services. The bill did not pass.

The union finally produced its proposal for fire protection services. It offered concessions on overtime and fire engine manning, which would reduce the city's costs by $340,000 over five years. The city council accepted the union's proposal by a 4 to 3 vote. According to one council member, a majority of the council favored the Wackenhut contract, "but the common knowledge that the fire fighters would have called successfully for a referendum on the issue—which the city might lose—had a strong deterrent effect. 'If the fire fighters were successful in the referendum, it would severely damage the concessions [the union had otherwise agreed to],' council member Rita Cantor told local newspapers. And so the city settled on a sure $340,000 rather than pushing for $1.4 million."[19] The union had won.

Dover, New Hampshire, began looking into contract fire fighting in May of 1982. Once again Wackenhut made the most attractive bid for fire services, resulting in a net savings over three years of $350,000. The IAFF began its fight in the state legislature by having a bill introduced to ban private fire services. The bill was defeated, but another was introduced requiring private fire companies to be certified by the state fire marshal.

The IAFF's regional vice-president and other union officials began a media campaign in Dover with advertisements in the local paper asking, "Should the City Gamble with Your Life and Property?" and urging, "DON'T PERMIT A PRIVATE FIRE SERVICE INTO DOVER."[20] Union officials were quoted as saying: "History has proven that when profit is considered, safety takes a back seat"; and "You can't make a profit and protect private property at the same time. If profit isn't high enough, the people of Dover will suffer."[21]

Finally, the union announced: "It is the unanimous decision of Local 1312 that we would not work for a profit-making company. We are concerned with life and property. We have no interest in working with a company working to make a profit, with no interest in life or property."[22] The threat did not work. Council members accepted the Wackenhut contract by a 5 to 3 vote.

Within two days, lawsuits were filed claiming the contract was illegal and requesting an injunction to stop its implementation. The county superior court denied the request, and another suit was filed claiming that fire protection was a "police power" so state law prevented it from being delegated to a private company. The superior court granted a temporary restraining order, and the question was referred to the state supreme court. Attorneys for Wackenhut and the city were confident of winning the case, but they suspected that the real purpose was to delay implementation. The contract stipulated a 90-day trial period, so substantial delay would result in a new election before the 90-day period had passed. Regional union representatives made regular trips to Dover, and the IAFF sent in a full-time political organizer. A petition drive was started to amend the city charter through a referendum to prohibit contracting out for police and fire services. The political pressure was effective. One council member who voted against the contract conceded that he voted that way to avoid losing his job, and another believed contracting was best for the city but admitted voting against contracting because of the union's campaign.[23]

Dover was the first city with a unionized fire department to actually sign a contract with a private firm. But the fight is far from over. Similar confrontations can be expected in any effort to contract policing. Such resistance may be extremely costly to overcome, both in terms of monetary outlays (e.g., legal fees) and political concerns. In order to overcome the unions' political clout, given elected officials' incentives to ensure their re-election, there must be sufficient organized support for public sector cost-cutting and privatization.

Other Public Sector Opposition.   Public employee unions and associations will not be the only source of resistance to privatization. Bureau managers who enjoy the income, power, and prestige of their positions should resist the loss of these sources of utility. Consider the implications of the following example.

A privatized system would require a market for convicted offenders' labor and in prison work programs to generate restitution and fines. At the Maine State Prison, inmates were given access to the prison's shop equipment to produce novelties. Other prisons have done the same thing, but Maine's program differed from others in some significant ways. First, there is a strong market for novelties because the prison is located on a major tourist route. Second, inmates were allowed to hire one another, thus allowing for specialization and the division of labor. The prisoners could not use dollars for these transactions so the currency used was canteen coupons, which could be spent in the prison's canteen or banked in the prison's business office.

After Warden Richard Oliver was appointed in 1976, prisoners were allowed to "patent" their novelty designs so they had incentives to innovate and expand their production. More significantly, Oliver lifted the limit on inmates' economic activity, and by 1978, the cap of $5,000 and 5 novelty patterns that existed in 1976 was tripled.[24] A "miniature economy" developed inside the prison, with two-thirds of the inmates participating as employers, employees, or both. Some entrepreneurs were extremely successful. One took over the prison's canteen and turned it into a profit-making operation. This prisoner also had 30 to 50 employees in novelty production, and had diversified into other areas (e.g., he owned and rented about 100 TV sets to inmates). One prison administrator considered him to be the "most brilliant businessman I've ever seen."[25] He is now out of prison running a novelty firm that employs former prisoners. As Shedd concluded, "It wasn't called that, but Maine State Prison had a rehabilitation program that was *working.*"[26]

Despite the program's significant benefits, on April 16, 1980, a lockdown of the Maine State Prison began. Inmates were confined to their cells 24 hours a day for 10 weeks. An extensive search and seizure operation

FROM AUTHORITARIAN TO PRIVATE LAW

destroyed the prisoners' businesses. After the lockdown, substantial reductions in economic rights and incentives were implemented that destroyed any potential for reviving the program. Why? One explanation may be political. For several years, the Maine Corrections Bureau had tried unsuccessfully to obtain larger budgets and to have the bureau elevated to cabinet level. Following the lockdown, budget increases were approved, and the Bureau of Corrections was elevated to cabinet-level status. Key legislators had switched their position on both issues because of the lockdown. Another explanation may simply be bureaucratic rigidity and resistance to change. Prison authorities wanted complete control over prisoners, not "ambitious and talented individuals finding a way around bureaucratic restrictions on their activities."[27]

These situations are not unique. As Poole explained, "one characteristic that's most typical of local government is adherence to tradition. . . . [E]xamples of real innovation. . .are hardly typical. . . . [D]epartment heads, mayors, councils, and city managers are far more likely to tell you why, say, private contracting of fire protection may work in Scottsdale but would *never* work in your town than they are to take a serious look at it as a way of providing more services for less money."[28]

There are other reasons to expect government officials to resist reductions in public sector involvement in the enterprise of law. For example, 5,523 of the 25,589 civil cases concluded in New York City public courts during the first forty weeks of the 1979–1980 fiscal year were brought *against* New York City. There are billions of dollars in potential liabilities facing the city from civil suits now waiting for trial. Judge Neely concluded: "New York City cannot afford an efficient court system because it would be bankrupt beyond bail-out if all those suits got to trial in one or two years."[29] Suits challenging conditions in public mental hospitals, prisons, schools, and other state and local facilities threaten governments with billions in unbudgeted expenditures. The longer such suits can be delayed, the smaller will be their political impact on current office-holders.

Private Sector Benefactors of Public Law and Order. Every special interest group that benefits from the current public laws and their enforcement will fight to protect its benefits. Consider the public court system. Judge Neely noted that "the current antiquated and overloaded structure is a political advantage to many groups."[30] If courts become more efficient, then there will be many losers. For example, if court delay keeps a case against an insurance company from being settled for several years, then the company can invest its money during that period for a substantial return. Because billions of dollars change hands through litigation, the interest payments on money that can be retained for several years is enormous. On top of that, long delays encourage early settlement for relatively low amounts. The non-price rationing that generates the court congestion and delay also benefits lawyers. A proposal to charge for the use of courts, as privatization would require, attracts intense, organized resistance from lawyers.

Private interests are also opposed to other changes that would accompany privatization. Consider this example. In Montana, the "production and distribution of wood furniture by state prison inmates has angered office furniture dealers, who say it represents a threat to the free enterprise system."[31] A substantial political and publicity campaign was mounted to destroy this modest project that employed twelve prisoners being paid 31 to 58 cents an hour in a small prison factory.

The production and sale of goods is not restricted by statute in Montana as it is in many other states. In most states, political pressure has resulted in laws or constitutional provisions that prevent the sale of all but a few prison-made items (e.g., license plates). New York passed the first of these laws in 1801 in the face of business pressure to eliminate competition from the then self-supporting prisons.[32] The federal government also restricts the sale of prison-made goods, prohibiting interstate commerce in prison-made products when the receiving state has laws against the marketing of such goods. Private contractors are also prohibited from using prison labor to meet government contracts. "The effect of all these statutes was virtually to wipe out the market for prisoner labor and for prisoner-made goods," Shedd reported; "in virtually every prison the only work opportunities are in the traditional prison industries—the making of license plates being, of course, the classic example—and in prison maintenance and custodial work. In almost every case these positions are low-paying, and in spite of that the industries involved are almost everywhere money losers."[33]

Another source of opposition to more complete privatization is likely to be the firms and industries that contract to produce for the public sector. Private industry sees "a large, essentially untapped market for business. . .in the local government sector."[34] Firms currently contracting to provide services could provide similar services in private markets, but doing business with government may be more profitable than doing business in competitive private markets. One reason that private firms can have a corrections facility built for less money is that they can get a better price from construction contractors than public bureaus can. The implication is that government ends up paying more than a private firm even when it uses competitive bidding processes. And when competitive bidding breaks down due to political influence, corruption, or bureaucratic interference, the result is likely to be quite profitable. Government officials even admit that price and reputation (e.g., documented past performance) are not the only criteria for awarding contracts: political considerations also influence contract decisions.[35]

Resistance to eliminating the public legal system will also come from those who believe that law and order *must* be produced by the public sector and that the private sector will be ineffective, inefficient, and abusive. Many "experts" and "public interest" advocates consistently oppose policies that might lead to greater privatization. As Savas noted: "Unfortunately, politicians campaigning on an economy platform, aided and abetted by students of public administration and management consultants, have devoted their energies to reducing and eliminating competitive behavior among government units, on the erroneous assumption that such competition was invariably, by definition, a wasteful duplication of effort."[36] They fail to consider that competition is the key to effective law and its enforcement.

Political Barriers to Privatization. The consequence of the political pressures brought on by self-interest or mistaken public-interest motives is that government-imposed laws now stand in the way of reducing the government's role in law and order and in instituting policies that might move us toward greater privatization. Most states ban private ownership of maximum security prisons, for example, and many states have statutes against private individuals making arrests.[37] In fact, the power to take a person into custody is frequently *vested* in local government employees. Other laws set maximum and minimum wages that can be paid to individuals producing contracted "public services." Legislated restrictions on victim participation in criminal prosecution are even more substantial. Repeal of all such barriers will not take place without sufficient political pressure to *dominate* the existing groups who demanded and now benefit from the laws.

There have been organized demands for court reform, better government, and tax cutting, and some of these efforts could lead to a smaller public legal system. "Reform" advocates are not likely to have a government reducing effect, at least given their current demands. Most see corruption and inefficiencies and call for new personnel, perhaps for more laws to regulate these personnel, and ultimately for a larger government sector. And in general, it would appear that tax cuts are likely to have larger impacts on public services other than law-making and enforcement. Law and order seems to be viewed as a necessary function of government by even the most avid tax-cutters (e.g., many political conservatives want greater expenditures for crime control and lower taxes). Nonetheless, at least three communities have refused to pass levies specifically designated for expansion of their police departments.[38] It is possible that the "tax revolt" may ultimately reach police, courts, and corrections.

The problem is that there is no organized political interest group advocating a smaller public legal system to be supplanted by the private sector. "Succinctly stated, in the legislative process the squeaky wheel gets the oil, and there is no organized squeaking lobby for [privatization]."[39] No privatization group with any size or resources is making campaign contributions, mailing out newsletters describing public performance in law and order, or bargaining in the back rooms of legislatures. Even if interest groups were to form, the changes advocated here would not be implemented. The full self-interested force of those opposed to privatization would coalesce and apply all its political power to prevent the process.

Are there reasons to expect politically effective groups to begin pressing for changes that might ultimately lead to privatization? We should not rule out such a possibility. For example, the increasing militancy of police and corrections unions may eventually work against them. Already, "in most strikes in the public sector, the outrage over the resulting inconvenience to the public helps to bring about an early settlement."[40] Early settlement may involve giving in to the unions now, but in the future it may mean refusal to deal with a union. President Reagan obviously believed he had sufficient political support to fire striking air traffic controllers, and Ohio successfully fired thirty correctional officers in 1975 for participating in a strike.[41]

The best way to convince people of something is to show them that it works. If the private sector crime control and adjudication industries continue to grow and provide superior services to those coming from the government, increasing numbers of citizens may recognize the benefits of privatization. The question is: Will these industries continue to grow?

PROSPECTS FOR GROWTH OF PRIVATE SECTOR LAW

The same groups that oppose the decline of the public system for law and order probably have incentives to resist growth of the private sector's provision of those services, but the resistance is likely to be substantially weaker. For instance, public police unions have referred to private police as "scab labor,"[42] and police executives, in response to a recent survey, also indicated considerable "distaste" for private police.[43] Yet private police and other private crime control efforts often cooperate with public police in ways that make the police *appear* more effective. Thus, the police often support these private sector activities. These conflicting incentives can substantially weaken and perhaps even eliminate opposition to privatization. Similarly, many judges favor diverting some cases to private arbitration to help relieve court congestion,[44] and perhaps citizens' discontent with the court system.

Many private sector interest groups face similar conflicts. For example, while "marketing. . . private courts presents a major challenge because lawyers stand to lose enormous fees by referring their cases," it was lawyers who rediscovered the law in California that started its now thriving rent-a-judge business.[45] In a competitive market for legal services, it is ultimately the lawyers who best serve their clients that get the bulk of the legal business and income. As a reflection of these conflicting incentives, many bar association committees have spoken in favor of private forums for dispute resolution.[46]

Legislated barriers to private police and private courts do exist, however. Commercial arbitration is a "legal" option all over the country, with state recognition of arbitrated decisions, but the California rent-a-judge system can be legally reproduced in very few states. Seven states have similar statutes (Idaho, Nebraska, New York, Oregon, Rhode Island, Utah, and Washington), but Washington's law limits a private judge's pay to no higher than what a public judge receives, and Utah's law can only be invoked when a public judge is not available.[47] Furthermore, while arbitration is possible in all states, arbitrators cannot legally issue rulings on state-made "legal" issues. Litigation increasingly reflects legislated rules rather than customary law. For instance, workplace disputes that require settlement involve claimed violations of federal and state statutes such as anti-discrimination legislation, health and safety regulations, and laws regulating pensions and welfare funds. As a result, "such cases may gravitate away from the arena of arbitration and towards the courts."[48]

Another governmentally erected barrier to the use of private arbitration and dispute resolution has been established by the public courts. Recall from Chapter 12 that a system of private dispute resolution that does not have government's power to coerce people into accepting a judgment must rely on threat of expulsion, ostracism, and other forms of boycotting. For example, if a businessman refuses to accept an arbitration decision, other businessmen may refuse to enter into a contract with him in the future. But in *Paramount Lasky Corporation* v. *United States,* the Supreme Court ruled that it was illegal for a group of motion picture producers to boycott any motion picture exhibitor who refused arbitration or refused to accept an arbitration ruling, even though arbitration clauses were in all contracts between producers and exhibitors.[49] What may appear to be a liberalization of *Paramount Lasky* was rendered in *Silver vs. New York Stock Exchange.*[50] The court held that enforcement of stock exchange rules by boycott was not in violation of the antitrust laws, *given* that adequate procedural safeguards existed in the exchange's procedures. "Yet before *Silver* it was generally assumed that the antitrust laws had no application to the private self-government scheme of the regulated exchanges."[51] The courts maintain the power to make rulings that could undercut the move toward more arbitration. In fact, "the result in *Paramount Lasky* is sometimes explained on the basis of hostility to private government."[52]

Government-erected barriers to privatization exist in non-adjudication areas as well. For instance, private police and citizens in general cannot take people into custody in many states. Gun control statutes limit the availability of guns for protection. Licensing and regulatory restrictions, often supervised by public police, limit entry into private police markets and prevent existing firms from providing many services. The same situation characterizes the potential legislative repeal of such statutes as characterizes the repeal of government laws supporting public sector law enforcement institutions. There are simply not enough effective political interest groups actively pursuing repeal.

Private individuals can often effectively "repeal" a government-produced law, however, if they feel it is unjust or inappropriate. Consider the huge underground economy that exists as citizens avoid tax laws, for example, or the utter failure of the constitutional amendment that attempted to outlaw alcoholic beverages. Or examine Umbeck's discussion of privately produced mineral laws during the California gold rush.[53] But in many cases the private sector does not have to violate a government-imposed law to repeal it. If incentives exist to subvert the law, innovative individuals can often find an unanticipated and "legal" way to do so. Thus, for instance, some have viewed arbitration as a "silent displacement of not only the judiciary but even the legislature."[54]

Consider an example. The public courts consistently rule that the aggrieved party in a breach-of-contract suit can *only collect the losses actually suffered* or a reasonable advance estimate of such losses. Thus, even if a contract stipulates the payment of damages plus a penalty, the courts would not award the penalty. If the contract contains an arbitration clause, however, arbitrators can and consistently do award the penalty despite its presumed illegality.[55] The fact is that whenever a law appears inappropriate or too complicated, arbitration abandons the enacted law for other standards of judgment.[56] But this phenomenon goes well beyond arbitration. There are many government laws for which "we see apparently paradoxical instances of nonlegislated [customary] law prevailing over legislated law, as a sort of unrecognized, but still effective, 'common law.' "[57]

In the case of enforcement of criminal laws, as an increasing share of the resources devoted to crime control is shifted to the private sector, we can anticipate that victimless crime laws will be "repealed" simply through neglect, as private resources are devoted to prevention of or recovery from violent and property crimes (see Chapter 14). In effect, then, the privatization process "passes" laws or, more accurately, enforces property rights assignments that are important to citizens and ignores those that are not. Laws against property crimes may be codified but they are meaningless if they are not effectively enforced. Privatization would make these laws meaningful.

CONCLUSIONS

We cannot expect to see reductions in the size of the public law enforcement sector in the immediate future. Why, then, go to all the trouble of detailing the shortcomings of publicly provided law and order and the benefits of privatization? As Friedman pointed out, the "fundamental task" for those of us who envision substantial benefits from reductions in government power "is one of education."[58] If this book convinces a few people that the components of the process of law and order do not have to be produced by government, it will have served its purpose. Political reality dictates the effect these arguments can have on the current system, of course, but when the role of customary law and the benefits of the growing markets for private crime prevention and dispute resolution become more obvious, advocates of privatization can support their political demands with arguments such as those put forth here and elsewhere (e.g., by Barnett, Friedman, Rothbard, Wooldridge, de Molinari, Leoni, Becker, and Stigler).

The fact remains, however, that "the most effective way to demonstrate that these things can be done privately is to do them."[59] It is not the "academic scribblers" who will convince people of the benefits of customary law and privatized police, courts, and corrections; it is Wackenhut, Judicate,

RCA, international merchants, and all the other providers of private police, courts, and corrections. George Zoley of Wackenhut foresees a "gradual building process in which the private sector will establish a good track record and prove it can do the job."[60] As this process continues, citizens should begin to see the shortcomings of the public sector. Then, perhaps political coalitions supported by academic research will begin to develop and demand less government in the area of law and order.[62] Perhaps a political coalition will not even be needed. Perhaps the private sector will have effectively "repealed" all the laws barring privatization by innovating ways around them and taxpayers will have "revolted" to such a degree that the public law production and enforcement system is eliminated. Friedman contended: "There is no reason for us to accept politics as a way of running the conspiracy to abolish politics. If this society is made freer, it will be done by a large number of people working individually or in small groups."[62] He may be right.

ENDNOTES

1. Sumner M. Rosen, "Public Service Unions and Public Service," in *Improving the Quality of Urban Management,* ed. Willis D. Hawley and David Rogers, vol. 8 of *Urban Affairs Annual Review* (Beverly Hills, Calif.: Sage Publications, 1974), p. 563.
2. Ray Marshall, Vernon M. Briggs, Jr., and Allan G. King, *Labor Economics,* 5th ed. (Homewood, Ill.: Richard D. Irwin, Inc., 1984), p. 113.
3. Ibid., p. 123.
4. Lloyd G. Reynolds, *Labor Economics and Labor Relations,* 8th ed. (Englewood Cliffs, N.J.: Prentice-Hall, Inc., 1982), pp. 574–575.
5. John M. Wynne, Jr., *Prison Employee Unionism: The Impact on Correctional Administration and Programs* (Washington, D.C.: National Institute of Law Enforcement and Criminal Justice, January 1978), p. 70; Warren I. Cikens, "Privatization of the American Prison System: An Idea Whose Time Has Come?" *Notre Dame Journal of Law, Ethics and Public Policy* 2 (1986): 455.
6. Ibid., p. 66.
7. Lyle C. Fitch, "Increasing the Role of the Private Sector in Providing Public Services," in *Improving the Quality of Urban Management,* ed. Willis D. Hawley and David Rogers, vol. 8 of *Urban Affairs Annual Review* (Beverly Hills, Calif.: Sage Publishing, 1974), p. 508. See also Chapter 8.
8. Wynne, *Prison Employee Unionism,* p. 202.
9. Ibid., p. 198.
10. Ibid.
11. Ibid., p. 219.
12. Ibid., p. 204.

13. Ibid., p. 218.
14. Ibid., p. 228.
15. Jim Peron, "Blazing Battles," *Reason* 15 (November 1983): 39.
16. Ibid., p. 40.
17. Ibid.
18. Ibid.
19. Ibid., p. 41.
20. Ibid., p. 42.
21. Ibid.
22. Ibid.
23. Ibid., p. 43.
24. Jeffrey Shedd, "Making Good[s] Behind Bars," *Reason* 13 (March 1982): 25.
25. Ibid., p. 26.
26. Ibid., p. 24.
27. Ibid., p. 9.
28. Robert W. Poole, Jr., *Cutting Back City Hall* (New York: Universe Books, 1978), p. 194.
29. Richard Neely, *Why Courts Don't Work* (New York: McGraw-Hill Book Co., 1982), p. 17.
30. Ibid., p. 9.
31. Tom Cook, "Retailers See Prison Made Products as a Threat," *Billings Gazette,* August 12, 1984, p. 1.
32. Shedd, "Making Good[s] Behind Bars," p. 27.
33. Ibid., pp. 27–28.
34. Donald Fisk, Herbert Kiesling, and Thomas Muller, *Private Provision of Public Services: An Overview* (Washington, D.C.: Urban Institute, 1978), p. 3.
35. Patricia S. Florestano and Stephen B. Gordon, "Public vs. Private: Small Government Contracting with the Private Sector," *Public Administration Review* 46 (January/February 1980): 32.
36. E. S. Savas, "Municipal Monopolies Versus Competition in Delivering Urban Services," in *Improving the Quality of Urban Management,* ed. Willis D. Hawley and David Rogers, vol. 8 of *Urban Affairs Annual Review* (Beverly Hills, Calif.: Sage Publishing, 1974), p. 495.
37. Fisk, et al., *Private Provision of Public Services,* p. 5.
38. Lawrence W. Sherman, "Patrol Strategies for Police," in *Crime and Public Policy,* ed. James Q. Wilson (San Francisco: Institute for Contemporary Studies, 1983), p. 149.
39. Neely, *Why Courts Don't Work,* p. 62.
40. Wynne, *Prison Employee Unionism,* pp. 222–223.
41. Ibid., p. 204.
42. Sherman, "Patrol Strategies for Police," p. 151.
43. Ibid., p. 150.

44. Tai Schneider Denenberg and R. V. Denenberg, *Dispute Resolution: Settling Conflicts Without Legal Action*, Public Affairs Pamphlet No. 597 (New York: Public Affairs Committee, Inc., 1981), p. 2.
45. "Private Court Systems: Discount Decisions," *Inc.* 5 (August 1984): 34.
46. Denenberg and Denenberg, *Dispute Resolution*, p. 2.
47. James S. Granelli, "Got a Spat? Go Rent a Judge," *National Law Journal*, June 8, 1981, p. 31.
48. Denenberg and Denenberg, *Dispute Resolution*, p. 13.
49. 282 U.S. 30 (1930).
50. Landes and Posner, "Adjudication as a Private Good," *Journal of Legal Studies* 8 (March 1979): 256–257; 373 U.S. 341 (1963).
51. Landes and Posner, "Adjudication as a Private Good," p. 257.
52. Ibid.
53. John R. Umbeck, *A Theory of Property Rights With Application to the California Gold Rush* (Ames, Iowa: Iowa State University Press, 1981).
54. William C. Wooldridge, *Uncle Sam, the Monopoly Man* (New Rochelle, N.Y.: Arlington House, 1970), p. 104.
55. Ibid.
56. Bruno Leoni, *Freedom and the Law* (Los Angeles: Nash Publishing, 1961), p. 179.
57. Ibid., p. 180.
58. David Friedman, *The Machinery of Freedom: Guide to a Radical Capitalism* (New York: Harper and Row, 1973), p. 219.
59. Ibid.
60. Quoted in Robert W. Poole, Jr., "Why Not Contract Policing?" *Reason* 15 (September/October 1983): 11.
61. Now that contracting out of many kinds of government services is becoming fairly widespread, for example, several academic studies have been widely publicized and used by advocates of contracting. See Fisk, et al., *Private Provision of Public Services*, p. 2.
62. Friedman, *The Machinery of Freedom*, p. 221.

14

ENVISIONING A PRIVATE SYSTEM

It is impossible to describe what a fully privatized enterprise of law would look like in our complex society. One cannot describe what does not exist, and guesses based on historic privatized systems and current trends may miss the mark substantially. The sophisticated equipment and the level of training possessed by many crime prevention specialists today may be archaic compared to what would emerge from the incentives created by full privatization. Today's contractual arrangements may be considered as simple and as inefficient as businessmen today would consider thirteenth-century Irish contract law or eleventh-century mercantile systems. Who but the "wildest, most fantastic" science fiction writers at the turn of the century could have predicted a revolution in communications and computer technology? Who but the most fantastic dreamers in the tenth century could have envisioned the commercial revolution that was made possible by the innovations in contractual arrangements and dispute resolution that we now call the international Law Merchant.

Some may consider the arguments in this book to fit in the category of science fiction as well. But it is important to take the final step and describe how a modern society *might* function under a system of customarily produced and privately enforced and adjudicated laws. Some of the following "predictions" are made with considerable confidence, but some are no more than "educated guesses." It should also be acknowledged that this is not the first attempt to visualize such a system and that the following discussion draws heavily from analysts including Barnett, Friedman, Rothbard, Tucker, Smith, Sneed, Becker, and Stigler.

THE UNWRITTEN SOCIAL CONTRACT

Without a centralized state government, how do laws emerge and command respect?[1] Some analysts contend that collective action is necessary to devise a "social contract" or "constitution" designed to define the rights of the people and to establish a limited government to enforce them.[2] But customary law emerges spontaneously as a consequence of cooperation induced by reciprocities, and reciprocity provides the basis for recognition of duty or obligation.[3] Cooperation does not require collective action. Furthermore, systems of customary law have always defined individual rights, including the right to private property.[4] Such law no more requires a written constitution than it requires legislative authority. As Hayek suggested, "Individual freedom, wherever it has existed, has been largely the product of a prevailing respect for such principles which, however, have never been fully articulated in constitutional documents. Freedom has been preserved for prolonged periods because such principles, vaguely and dimly perceived, have governed public opinion."[5]

Lon Fuller maintained that modern aspects of customary law are appropriately viewed as

> a branch of constitutional law, largely and properly developed outside the framework of our written constitutions. It is constitutional law in that it involves the allocation among various institutions of our society (e.g., churches, social clubs, labor unions, trade associations, etc.) of legal power, that is, the authority to enact rules and to reach decisions that will be regarded as properly binding on those affected by them. That this body of constitutional law should have grown outside our written constitution should not be a source of concern. It would have been impossible to have anticipated the rich institutional growth that has occurred since their time. Furthermore, the intellectual climate of the late eighteenth century was such to obscure a recognition of the centers of authority created when men form voluntary associations.[6]

Today's intellectual climate apparently obscures recognition of the potential for voluntary law creation even more than it did in the eighteenth century.

CHARACTERISTICS OF CUSTOMARY LAW

Individual rights were the basis of customary law in primitive societies, through the Middle Ages, and for all the remnants of such law that exist today.[7] As Tucker pointed out, in a free society without government imposition or enforcement of laws, "man's only duty is to respect others' rights...[and] man's only right over others is to enforce that duty."[8] Exceptions to this general rule may arise, but such occurrences should be rare under a system of customary law. Individuals will pay for protection (and investing in an effort to recover losses if an offense occurs), and will be willing to make payments when their own rights are at stake. This does not mean that there will be no cooperative efforts to protect everyone's private rights. It means that because individuals are paying directly for law enforcement, either with their own time and effort or with money, there will be a strong tendency to protect those individuals and their property and considerably less willingness to support (or interest in) the enforcement of other types of laws.

Epstein noted that when the purpose of law is to facilitate interaction and minimize conflict, three functions or branches of law are important: 1) determining individuals' property holdings (property law); 2) governing cooperative exchanges of property (contract law, including conveyancing); and 3) protecting persons and their property, including methods of property transfer, from third-party aggression (tort law).[9] Customary law has always defined private property rights while stipulating rules for reciprocal interaction through custom *and* contract and treating all offenses as torts.[10] Privatized law would fulfill all three functions.

One function of modern law is conspicuously absent from Epstein's analysis: criminal law. Offenses in a customary legal system with private law enforcement would be treated as torts—offenses against victims rather than against society—so there would be no criminal law. Many "crimes" would still be illegal, particularly if there are victims. But certain types of activities that are currently defined as "criminal" will probably be allowed. Because black market activities—such as gambling, prostitution, the use and sale of marijuana and most other drugs—generally do not have identifiable victims, few people are likely to be willing to pay for their enforcement. It is possible, of course, that a group may *voluntarily* cooperate to enforce a law where no identifiable victim exists, but the allocation of enforcement resources will be determined by individuals' willingness to pay rather than by political strength or bureaucratic discretion over common pool resources. "People who want to control other people's lives are rarely eager to pay for the privilege. They usually expect to be paid for the 'service' they provide for their victims. And those on the receiving end—whether of laws against drugs, laws against pornography, or laws against sex—get a lot more pain out of the oppression than their oppressors get pleasure."[11] A private system of law enforcement will be strongly biased toward individual freedom when individual action does no harm to another's physical person or property. As Friedman suggested, "compulsory puritanism" should be much rarer under customary law than it is under politicized law.[12]

The possibility of a community having its own law that differs substantially from law in other communities brings up an important point. Friedman noted that one advantage of a private legal system "is its ability to tailor its product to its customers—geographically as well as in other ways. If the maximum return comes from having heroin illegal in some places and legal in others, that is what will happen."[13] But this does not mean that an irrational patchwork of entirely different law systems will exist (see Chapters 2 and 12). There may be relatively minor localized differences, perhaps as there are from state to state and even city to city under the current system, but standardization of many aspects of private law over large geographic areas will arise. Mercantile law was largely standardized over all of Europe during the Middle Ages even though political systems of the day differed sharply.[14] There is little doubt that the same would be true in many other aspects of privately produced and enforced law.

PUNISHMENT OF LAWBREAKERS

When the rights of individuals are paramount, there is no need for "criminal law." Under a system of customary law, aggressive acts against another's person or property will be analogous to the law of torts. When an offense is committed, the victim will seek restitution from the offender. A significant advantage of such a "victim oriented" system of law is "that specifying the victim has the practical function of giving someone an incentive to pursue the case."[15] These incentives arise because of the nature of the "punishment" that will exist under a system of private law and order.

Punishment will typically take the form of a "fine" payable to the victim of at least sufficient magnitude to compensate the victim for *all* losses *and* cover the full cost of bringing the offender to justice. All systems of privately produced law have been oriented toward restitution, with fines as the major form of punishment.[16] Robert Poole wrote of a recent revival of victim restitution experiments:

When "Fred Stone" broke into the Tucson house and stole the color TV, he had little idea that he would be caught. Still less did he expect to be confronted face-to-face by the victim, in the county prosecutor's office. In the course of the meeting, Stone learned that the TV set was the center of the elderly, invalid woman's life. With the approval of the Pima County, Arizona prosecutor, he agreed not only to return the TV, but also to paint her house, mow her lawn, and drive her to the doctor for her weekly checkup. By doing so he avoided a jail sentence, and saved Tucson area taxpayers several thousand dollars.

The Pima County program under which Fred Stone was handled is just one example of a promising *new concept in criminal justice*: restitution by offenders to victims.[17]

But this "promising new concept" is not new at all. It has been a benchmark of law and order through history.

Poole makes three valuable points, however. First, he raises another aspect of the current turn back to a private system of law and order, even though government officials are involved. One part of government's failure to adequately provide law and order has been the abandonment of concern for victims. Citizen reaction has forced the public sector to begin to consider victims again, however, thus experimentally adopting some characteristics of private systems of law and law enforcement. Several states have passed laws urging judges to sentence criminals to restitution, and the federal government began supporting some short-term restitution program experiments in 1978. Some of the restitution programs, even though sanctioned by public prosecutors and courts, produce private restitution contracts negotiated by the offender and the victim and sanctioned by the court.[18] In these cases, the prosecutor and court become an arbitrator-mediator.

The second point to be taken from Poole is that the payment of restitution need not be monetary. One criticism of fines as a means of punishment is that criminals may not be able to pay a fine large enough to either compensate the victim or to be an effective deterrent. It is likely, however, that a private system of justice would allow for working off the fine, either by working directly for the victim or by the offender selling his labor.

The third point is that fines are an efficient form of punishment. In 1977, when Poole wrote about the Pima County case, roughly 200,000 prisoners were in jails and prisons in the United States (today there are over 300,000) with an annual cost to taxpayers of three billion dollars. Imprisonment is an inefficient form of punishment. It uses up social resources like guards and other personnel, the capital and resources needed to build the prisons, *and* the prisoners' time. Fines require far fewer resources. Some offenders may require close supervision in prison-like work places to ensure payment, but the prisoners are working to produce goods and services that can be sold to pay off their debts. From a social perspective, "a fine is a [relatively] costless punishment: the cost to the payer is balanced by a benefit to the recipient. It is in this respect superior to punishments such as execution, which imposes cost but no corresponding benefit, or imprisonment, which imposes costs on both the criminal and the taxpayers."[19]

There are other advantages to imposing fines as the major form of punishment. Suppose that fines are set equal to the full cost to the victim plus the full cost of bringing the offender to justice, all divided by the probability that the offender will be brought to justice.[20] For example, the fine for stealing a car would be the value of the loss plus the cost of pursuit, court time and so on associated with solving and prosecuting the offense, all divided by the probability of successful solution and prosecution. If half the car thefts are solved, the long list of costs would be divided by .5, or, in effect, multiplied by two. The fine would be double the damages. The benefit to the offender is the value of the car. The expected cost is the probability of being brought to justice multiplied by the resulting fine; or, given that the offender and the judge perceive the same probability (.5), the full cost to the victim plus the cost of bringing the offender to justice. The expected cost of the crime is greater than the expected benefit, if the courts set the same probabilities that the offenders perceive. Offenders will probably have a different perception of risk than victims and, perhaps, judges, but the actual fine is still large relative to the gain. Private courts may not determine fines in precisely the manner discussed here,[21] but private citizens who contract with courts and enforcers will be attracted to firms that are effective at preventing offenses—that is, to enforcers who make significant efforts to recover for the victim and to judges whose fines are high enough to compensate the victim and the enforcer (naturally, a judge will be concerned about recovering his own costs as well).

The fine and victim restitution emphasis of privately produced law and order provides another reason to expect few laws against victimless crimes to arise and, even if they do, few resources to be devoted to their enforcement. It is certainly possible that fines could be dictated by the common will of some tightly knit community. Incentives could be created to enforce such laws as well if, for instance, a right to the collected fine is given to a successful enforcer. In other words, a successful enforcer could be treated as if he was the victim of a victimless crime.

One activity that will be subject to fines is offenses by private law enforcers against innocent citizens. Because falsifying violations, falsely charging innocent people of wrongdoing, and bullying citizens violate the rights of those who are innocent, a private, victim-oriented system of law will require full compensation from enforcers for anyone who is mistreated or acquitted of a charge. The loser in a court case would pay the full cost of the court appearance. Fines for restitution will not only deter the potential abuses of police, they will also deter frivolous and unfounded lawsuits. As Neely noted, "Placing the cost of frivolous litigation on the party who demands it will ultimately result in a dramatic reduction in frivolous litigation."[22]

Fines as a primary form of punishment will also create incentives for those who commit an offense to avoid unnecessary uses of court time. Because fines will include court costs, unsuccessful efforts by a guilty party to hide his guilt or to drag out a trial will result in higher fines. This encourages out-of-court settlements between offenders and victims. Unlike the plea bargaining used in the current system, however, victims will receive satisfactory restitution because the bargain will be between the victim and offender, not between the offender and a *public* prosecutor. Differential fines for those who admit guilt and those who try to hide it may become a formal part of the private law system. In Iceland, for instance, "the difference between two sorts of offenses provided a high 'differential punishment' for the 'offense' of concealing one's crime, an offense which imposed serious costs."[23]

There are advantages of fines as the primary form of punishment for the offender as well. Typically, three goals of punishment are cited: deterrence, preventing further crimes by the offender, and revenge.[24] As I have already argued, fines can serve as deterrents. In addition, optimal restitution will *fully* compensate victims so they are no worse off than before the offense occurred. Imprisonment not only fails to compensate victims, but it requires them to bear more costs (e.g., the cost of cooperating in prosecution, as discussed in Chapter 6). Under these circumstances, "it is not surprising, therefore, that the anger and fear felt toward ex-convicts who in fact have not 'paid their debt to society' have resulted in additional punishments, including legal restrictions on their political and economic opportunities and informal restrictions on their social acceptance."[25] But because fines for restitution do "restore" the victim, additional anger toward and demands for more punishment of the offender are less likely. Fines and restitution, particularly of a sufficient level to fully compensate the victim, eliminate incentives for further revenge. This also tends to minimize the potential for other forms of violence, such as feuds between families or other enforcement organizations.

Fines will be the primary type of punishment in a system of private law and order, but they may not be the only type of punishment. It is possible that the common will of members of a group may hold that some offenses, perhaps murder or rape, are so heinous that it is impossible to compensate for the harm inflicted.[26] Medieval Icelandic and primitive Kapauku systems of law considered capital punishment appropriate for some crimes (see Chapter 2). It is difficult to predict whether such punishment would arise in the private law system of a modern society. Possibly, the rest of an offender's life would be committed to working to pay the victim or the victim's family, even though full restitution could never be achieved.

Another characteristic of privately produced law can be predicted in light of its emphasis on individual rights. As with any private property right, the right to restitution is transferable in virtually all systems of privately produced law. Many primitive systems allowed an individual to join a group (e.g., a family, a religious congregation, a neighborhood) that would, in exchange for some portion of the settlement, back him in a dispute, providing the threat necessary to induce an offender to submit to nonviolent dispute resolution.[27] Friedman argued that a system of privately produced law and order would involve a marketable claim for a victim, such as in medieval Iceland, so that it can be sold to someone willing to pursue and prosecute the offender.[28] This, in turn, helps create arrangements under which those who violate the rights of the poor and the weak are pursued and prosecuted. Victims could offer bounties or rewards, but they might simply sell the right to collect a particular fine. Specialized firms (thief-takers, bounty hunters) could arise to pursue criminals and collect fines, or individuals might contract with firms that attempt to prevent aggression against clients, pay clients who are victimized as insurance companies do, and pursue offenders to recover the insurance payment.

If there is potential for external benefits of enforcement in the form of deterrence, then a private law enforcement system could involve a free-rider problem. Nonpurchasers of law enforcement services would benefit from the deterrence from enforcement activities purchased by others. As Landes and Posner recognized, however, "the free-rider problem does not arise under systems of private enforcement in which enforcers purchase rights from victims...or acquire rights by apprehending and convicting an offender. The reason is that in these systems the return to enforcement is a fine, whereas under a system in which enforcers are precluded from receiving fines the return to enforcement must come from those buying protection."[29] The one criticism of privatization of law and order that may have some validity is less of a problem under the rights structure that arises under privatization.

PRIVATE LAW ENFORCEMENT MECHANISMS

A variety of individual and cooperative arrangements can be anticipated under a privatized enterprise of law that will emphasize the protection of persons and property and the recovery of losses suffered by victims. Cooperative arrangements will involve everything from informal voluntary association to formal contractual exchanges. Sneed explained why such diversity is expected: "Once the State law-enforcement monopoly is destroyed, and the inadequate State protection of person and property is no longer forced upon us, each ex-citizen will have the opportunity to consume protection services according to his own tastes and preferences. . . . As in any other industry, there will be specialization on the basis of the economies to be derived from the division of labor. Each consumer will balance his purchases of protection services relative to self-supplied defense so as to maximize his utility."[30] Individuals may protect themselves and their property by owning guns, installing burglar alarms, building fences, or barring windows, much as they do today. These are private property rights that would be supported by customary law.

Cooperative arrangements would also arise. There would be strong incentives to share the watching and patrolling of geographic areas. In some communities or neighborhoods where individuals' budget constraints are more binding than their time constraints, residents will contribute their time to a voluntary patrol. Where budget constraints are less binding, people will contribute money to hire a private security firm that furnishes patrols, watchmen, guards, electronic watching devices, or whatever the community will pay for.

There may be free-rider incentives inherent in such localized watching arrangements (see Chapter 11). Over time, however, contractual arrangements will internalize the deterrent benefits of patrol systems, thus eliminating the free-rider problem. This might not take long in our highly mobile society, where people move an average of once every three years. Enterprising real estate developers would quickly see the benefit of establishing developments that offer, as part of the purchase price of a home or business location, a guarantee that everyone in the development will sign a legally binding contract to contribute to the community's security arrangements. As people move, these contractual arrangements will attract increasing numbers, because the communities are relatively safe from violations of property rights. Those least likely to free ride will find such contractual arrangements quite attractive, leaving relatively large numbers of free riders in noncontracting neighborhoods.

Voluntary arrangements without legally binding contracts will become relatively less effective, and these neighborhoods will face relatively greater threats to persons and property. As the threat increases, more people will move out or the cost of free riding will increase to such a level that more and more of those who remain will be willing to contract for protection. Free riders will face the increasing ire of their neighbors, ultimately backed by ostracism as they are prevented from consuming the benefits of living in the area. Communities that fail to internalize the benefits of group protection because of free riders will be at a competitive disadvantage with those that eliminate free riding. They will find it increasingly difficult to attract new residents and businesses, and property values will fall. Under privatization, the cost of free riding will rise tremendously.

Someone will undoubtedly argue that the contracting communities that internalize the deterrent benefits of group protection efforts will be havens for the rich. But this is not likely. Middle and lower income communities may employ different joint protection systems than some wealthy communities do (e.g., a combination of participatory and hired patrols, or simply participatory patrols), but contractual arrangements should still arise. They can also be part of rental contracts, so home ownership is not a prerequisite for entering into cooperative associations for the purpose of protection. Rothbard has reminded us that public "police service is not 'free'; it is paid for by the taxpayers, and the taxpayer is very often the poor person himself. He may very well be paying more in taxes for police now than he would in fees to private, and far more efficient, police companies. . . police protection would undoubtedly be much cheaper."[31] Subscribers to police services will no longer have to pay for enforcement of all the victimless crime laws; they will only pay for protection of their own person and property. None of this means that *all* free riding must be eliminated as *every* individual (or even every community) contracts to internalize the deterrent benefits of protection. Communities could survive without developing such security systems, although they would probably have "citizens" who choose very high levels of self-protection or have little they feel is worth protecting.

Security firms may offer protection services like patrols and guards, but they may also be vertically organized to offer recovery of losses as well. Some advocates of private law enforcement have theorized that the private security market will be organized much like a mutual insurance market. Under these arrangements, a firm or cooperative surety group organization insures individuals and their property against violations.[32] The firm or organization, therefore, would have strong incentives to prevent offenses by supplying police services with an emphasis on patrolling, watching, and other deterrents. If an offense does occur against a subscriber, then the insurance would pay the subscriber's claim unless all losses are recovered. In paying off the subscriber, the firm or organization purchases the right to collect at least some portion of the fine from the offender. Therefore, there are strong incentives to pursue offenders and gather evidence for court prosecution. This system guarantees recovery of losses for the victim or payment of claims, and it is much more likely that private insurance detectives will recover stolen property than that the public police will.[33] In fact, the insurance companies' approach would be quite different from the approach taken by public police. Public police are most concerned with making arrests; therefore, "restoring the stolen loot to the victim is strictly secondary. To the insurance company and its detectives, on the other hand, the prime concern is recovery of the loot, and apprehension and punishment of the criminal is secondary to the prime purpose of aiding the victim of crime. Here we see again the difference between a private firm impelled to serve the customer-victim of crime and the public police, which is under no such economic compulsion."[34]

Insurance arrangements with vertically organized firms providing both protection and investigative services may not arise. Individuals might buy protection from one company and contract with another to pursue the offender, or they might offer a reward to attract the attention of specialized thief-taking firms. Market forces of demand and supply will dictate the actual industrial organization that evolves, but there are strong reasons to suspect that insurance-like arrangements will emerge. Risk-averse individuals shift the risk of loss by purchasing insurance. Furthermore, such arrangements alleviate "a nightmare question of people who first hear about the idea of a totally private police: 'Why that means that if you're attacked or robbed you have to rush over to a policeman and start dickering on how much it will cost to defend you.' "[35] Obviously, many people will find it desirable to contract ahead of time for the potential need of investigative services, thus guaranteeing their availability should the need arise.

Numerous other contractual arrangements can be anticipated. The contract with a particular protection firm could include an arbitration clause so that disputes between clients of that firm can be settled internally. The company may provide an arbitrator or arbitrators (mediation may characterize some dispute resolutions as well) or contract with a particular dispute resolution firm. Under such arrangements, the benefits of precedent production are at least partially internalized. In addition, incentives are created to produce clear, impartial opinions and thereby minimize the number of disputes that require adjudication. An arbitration clause in a legal contract also means that refusal to submit to arbitration would be unlikely because it would probably result in ostracism, loss of protection services, and perhaps loss of ownership rights to property purchased under the contract (e.g., a residence or business location).

Similar contractual arrangements will probably arise *between* different communities and their protection agencies. Even if a formal contract does not exist, the desire to avoid violence will likely lead to submission to arbitration. Such arrangements might be likened to formal or informal extradition treaties among political entities. Because there are substantial economies of standardization in many areas of law, consider first an offense by a member of one group against a member of a different law enforcement organization where both law systems hold the act to be illegal. The organization whose member is alleged to be the offender has strong incentives to allow him to be arrested and to apply considerable pressure on him to submit to arbitration. Sneed noted that a protection organization that refused to allow the arrest of a member, given good cause, would suffer in several ways. First, other organizations will similarly resist attempts to arrest their clients in the future, so the organization's ability to protect its members will be reduced and the chances of violent confrontations will rise. Either violent confrontations or reciprocal impotence will result in a loss of membership. Second, reciprocal working relationships for the pursuit and capture of geographically mobile offenders would develop, but refusal to cooperate in other areas would jeopardize the chance to participate in such arrangements. Third, an organization that refused to turn over members who committed offenses would tend to attract members who intend to commit offenses, thus placing the organization in more confrontations.[36] These incentives apply whether the individual arrested is guilty or innocent. Indeed, "anticipation of such conflicts will generally lead to formal procedures agreed to by most companies in a given area concerning the limits of reciprocal powers of arrest. Similar 'treaties' will develop to define procedure in several other areas as well, assuming that companies have some degree of foresight, an assumption implicitly denied by most critics [of market provision of law enforcement]."[37] Above all, then, "such wars and conflicts would be bad—very bad—for business."[38] Thus, every policing organization would probably require that disputes between members of different organizations be decided by impartial private courts or arbitrators. Such reciprocal arrangements benefit both groups.

Sneed also suggested that bail bonds might be posted by an accused offender's protection company or organization.[39] Under the surety system in medieval Ireland, for example, a large fine levied against a member of a particular *tuath* might be paid by the group as a whole, and they could collect from the offender.[40] Such bonding or credit arrangements have some significant advantages. First, the victim's enforcement organization requires a bail sufficient to compensate the victim or his heirs and to cover the organization's cost associated with the case. Consequently, the victim and his organization will be relatively unconcerned if the accused fails to appear. The accused's own defense organization would be responsible for collecting from him if he is guilty.[41] Ostracism must play a predominant role in inducing someone to submit to arbitration, and this bail bonding arrangement makes ostracism possible. If the members of an accused offender's community or other mutual defense group have strong incentives to apply pressure on the accused to submit, then ostracism can be effective. Furthermore, in contracting with a particular organization or firm for the option of bail, the individual may voluntarily agree to submit to confinement or to yield a portion of his income to repay the bond, should he be found guilty. Whatever the arrangement, the onus is on the members of the accused's organization, not on the victim, to collect if the accused is guilty.

When the bail or credit arrangement is part of a contract with an organization, that organization has incentives to work on behalf of the accused to recover the bond (those acquitted of a violation will have the right to restitution of costs, including the cost of any investigation on his behalf). Thus, someone accused of an offense will "regularly have investigative agencies working on his behalf which wield powers of the same order as those of the arresting company. Deliberate as well as accidental conviction of the innocent would be far less feasible. Falsification of evidence would be considerably more risky."[42] This contrasts sharply with the current reliance on public police for investigations wherein the accused can mount an investigation of his own only if he hires a private firm—no firm or organization is already in place with incentives to perform an investigation.

Contractual arrangements have clear advantages for those who are guilty of an offense. The offender may be able to arrange for credit to pay the victim or his representative and then work off the debt in his own community, avoiding the consequences of an inability to pay a fine or of having to work off a debt in a relatively hostile environment. Of course, even if a guilty individual is held by the victim's organization, the likelihood of abuse is minimal, because

> if a company has a reputation for abusing prisoners, other companies will thus be provided with a legitimate ground for preventing the arrest of their clients, and will be able to thwart the offending company's enforcement efforts without the loss of respect and working relationships that non-co-operation would generally entail. The only sound position competitively is for the company to be able to point to its humane treatment of prisoners to prove to all that the innocent have nothing to fear from them, and therefore that any company refusing to allow them power to arrest must be harboring a man it knows to be guilty.[43]

No competitive private law enforcement firm could have the potential for abusing prisons that a government has. The torture, mutilation, experimentation, and elimination of prisoners that has characterized governments throughout history would be much less likely in a privatized system of law enforcement.[44]

My discussion of reciprocal arrangements between different law enforcement organizations was predicated on the assumption that the law that was violated was common to both communities and their enforcement organizations. But some differences in law could arise across communities or groups. Minor differences are quite likely and major differences are possible. (The same is true with governmentally produced law, of course, and perhaps to a greater degree because artificial political boundaries may prevent the most efficient level of standardization.) How could the private sector handle a situation in which a member of one legal organization violates a law unique to another legal organization? Several arrangements are possible. For instance, a risk-averse individual who expects to be in situations where he may inadvertently violate an unknown law could insure himself against that possibility. Thus, his protection company would pay his fine (or bail), and he would not suffer any exorbitant personal loss. Under this scenario, the relevant law is that of the group being violated.

A community's law could involve a fine that most of society considers unreasonable, or the law itself may be commonly held to be unreasonable. Imposition on outsiders of laws that are out of line with those that exist in most other communities certainly increases the chances of violence. If such a law is violated by someone from another community, however, both groups have strong incentives to avoid a violent confrontation. In most cases, a negotiated or arbitrated settlement would lower the cost to the accused and his insurers below that which would induce violence. A community that insists on strictly imposing its own morality and penalties on outsiders will initially face continual clashes, followed by boycott sanctions by other communities whose residents refuse to travel to or trade with them, or to enter into reciprocal arrangements to yield accused violators of their laws. A community that isolates itself will not survive in a competitive free market environment. Those who hold the norms the community wishes to impose, but relatively weakly, will leave first, and others will follow as property values and trade-generated incomes decline. If a community wishes to impose laws that differ substantially from the norm, its members have strong incentives to inform outsiders of the differences in order to avoid conflict and minimize the difficulty of maintaining non-standard laws. Part of the reciprocal agreements with other communities and enforcers for extradition may be the explicit recognition of differences in laws and procedures for treating conflicts.

This argument provides another reason for the tendency toward standardization of law under privatization. No community can effectively enforce its will on outsiders without the support of outsiders. Laws for members of a community may be relatively restrictive, but the laws that apply to outsiders will have to be moderated if the community is to survive. Sneed concluded that while laws will not be uniform, there is a strong tendency for them to standardize in the treatment of violence and of commerce "due to considerations of transactions costs and the costs of maintaining a stock of knowledge of other [laws]. Differences. . .would exist only in those areas where the demand for non-standard enforcement over-rides the economies of standardization. These areas would consist largely of enforcement demands based on moral and religious conviction."[45]

There undoubtedly will be individuals who will not join any cooperative law enforcement arrangement and who refuse to recognize any rules of law. After all, there are thousands of them in our society now and there is little reason to expect that privatization will somehow change all of them. How will these people be treated under privatization? First, they will be left alone unless they violate someone else's rights. Second, they will have to defend themselves and their property on their own. But what happens when they violate a law? Historically, all customary legal systems and the law of many more recent private legal systems had as a threat of last resort, the ultimate form of ostracism.[46] An individual who committed a major offense and then refused to yield to the legal justice system was declared an outlaw, and anyone was free to take any of that person's property and to take his life. Such actions were not illegal when committed against an outlaw, so the victim or the organization he belonged to had strong incentives to pursue the outlaw and take restitution (or revenge). Such a contingency would probably arise in a modern system of privatized law and order as well.

"Ah ha," the governmentalist might say, "private law ultimately does come down to no law, to rule by violence!" But, as I have stressed over and over, the private sector will establish laws and institutions that *minimize* the chances of turning to this last resort. More importantly, the same last resort already underlies the current system of publicly produced law. A criminal who resists arrest can be killed by the police and his property taken by the state. All systems break down when people refuse to participate in them. The question is: Which system is most likely to have to resort to that ultimate form of ostracism? The historical evidence is that privatized law and order has been *relatively* free of violence.[47]

PRIVATE COURTS

I have suggested that contractual arrangements for arbitration and mediation are likely to arise within the groups and communities that organize for joint security. These groups and communities may be geographically localized, but they may also be geographically dispersed and functionally "localized." For example, the "business community" will probably establish its own legal and adjudicative systems, given the historical evidence of the Law Merchant and the widespread modern-day use of arbitration by business groups, trade associations, and other industrial organizations.[48] Furthermore, if the reciprocal arrangements *between* communities should arise, then communities and agencies will have very strong incentives to seek out judges for both inter- and intra-community dispute resolutions who not only have reputations for impartiality but for issuing clear opinions that can be used as a guide in settling future disputes—that is, precedents. Judges who hand down such opinions will garner much more business (if not all the business) than judges who issue vague, uninterpretable, or secret opinions. Why? Disputes are costly and always raise the possibility of violence, and private sector law enforcers will avoid these costs if possible. Note that the concern for a security agency or community representing a victim is much stronger in this regard than the concern of *individual* disputants in our current system, since these firms or communities represent many potential victims and offenders and, therefore, many possible future confrontations.

There is another reason for demanding clear, well founded decisions. Smith referred to it as the "verification aspect."[49] In order to satisfactorily end a dispute, the decision must be acceptable—verifiable—not just to the victim and offender but also to the groups or firms representing these parties *and* to groups that might be drawn into a confrontation with one of the groups involved in the dispute. The willingness of other firms and organizations to enter into and honor reciprocal arrangements, such as extradition contracts, with those involved in the dispute depends in part on the way this and other disputes are handled. If an organization's disputes are submitted to judges whose opinions are not clear and well founded, then that organization will have problems influencing the choice of a judge and otherwise supporting their clientele in non-internal disputes.

Smith predicted that private courts would have to 1) allow citizen access to trials so third parties could observe proceedings (exceptions could arise if the parties in the suit had strong demands for privacy), 2) make details of that court's procedures accessible to any interested third party, and 3) make accurate records of a trial available to anyone who might want to review them.[50] These predictions certainly seem to be supported by most historical examples of private courts. Popisil's description of trial procedures among the primitive Kapauku, for instance, stressed the "public" nature of trials and the efforts that the *tonowi* took to firmly establish the legal precedent for their solution to a dispute.[51] Similarly, the medieval Icelandic, Anglo-Saxon, and Law Merchant courts were public forums.[52] Even though a well-publicized aspect of modern arbitration and rent-a-judge systems is their secrecy, this does not necessarily contradict Smith or the historical evidence that supports him. After all, what we see today is a relatively limited system of private courts. Those disputants who have a strong desire for privacy cannot get it from the public courts, so they may have the strongest incentives to employ private courts today. Under complete privatization, there will be many disputes that demand clear decisions for public scrutiny.

Private contractual arrangements can create a strong demand for clear, well-founded, impartial decisions—the types of decisions that serve as precedents whether that is their intent or not. In effect, given the contracts and agreements between diverse groups and protection firms, the benefits of precedents would be internalized. Internalization arises because of the reciprocal cooperation and competition between numerous identifiable groups rather than by merger of those groups into a single political entity (government).

Contractual arrangements between dispersed organizations to encourage arbitration of disputes between members also increases the likelihood of standardization of certain aspects of law. In effect, law will develop through dispute resolution to facilitate the interaction *between* groups—law based on common custom as reflected in previous judgments. Aspects of a particular group's law that prove to be efficient can be revealed to another group in the process, and they can also adopt it. This kind of process characterized the standardization of the Law Merchant throughout Western Europe.[53] Efficient rules adopted by one merchant community tended to spread to other communities quite rapidly. Furthermore, economies of standardization will become available as between-group judgments are made that might facilitate solution of (set precedents for) future within-group disputes.

Some have criticized private adjudication systems for lacking two institutional arrangements: trial by jury and courts of appeal. Under a private system, jury trials will be supplied if they are demanded, assuming that the demand is sufficiently strong to pay the full cost of the trial. Of course, jury trials would be relatively more expensive than judge-only trials, so they are relatively less likely under privatization than under a public system. But that is not necessarily bad. As Person noted, jury trials "are of great importance in the government courts as a means of protection from a hostile judge but of less importance when parties select their own judges."[54] Indeed, juries were developed by Norman kings for inquisitional purposes and were ultimately accepted as a desirable institution *because* they served as a counterforce to the judges of the king's courts.[55]

Courts of appeal will also be available if there is sufficient demand. There will be no monopolized "supreme court," of course, simply because there are not sufficient economies of standardization in adjudication to expect that. But there may be competitive appeals courts, just as there are competitive judges for the initial consideration of a dispute. Courts could serve as initial forums for some disputes and appeals courts for others, but there could also be a specialized group of judges who only consider appeals. Given the existence of appeals courts but no supreme court, what will prevent an offender from making a never-ending number of appeals? In all likelihood, the contractual arrangements for dispute settlement within a particular community or security organization will specify an appeals procedure and put a limit on the number of appeals. Rothbard suggested that a likely "cut off point. . .since there are two parties to any crime or dispute. . .[is that] a decision arrived at by any two courts shall be binding. This will cover the situation when both the plaintiff's and the defendant's [preferred] courts come to the same decision, as well as the situation when an appeals court decides on a disagreement between the two original courts."[56] This suggestion has an appealing logic and may be adopted in private contracting arrangements. Other arrangements may develop, of course (the Law Merchant allowed no appeals, for instance, because the costs in terms of delay and disruptions of commerce were considered to be too high).[57] Because formal and informal contracts will arise between groups to establish procedures for intergroup dispute resolution, appeals procedures may be established for those disputes as well. Alternatively, as part of the agreement to submit to arbitration, the parties may specify an appeals procedure and cut-off point.

It should be noted that the current system does not guarantee a *right* of appeal to the U.S. Supreme Court in all but the most unusual cases. A party must petition for review, generally on some constitutional issue, and the petition can be denied. The same is true of state supreme courts. In fact, then, our system has appellate courts of no resort.

OSTRACISM AND BOYCOTT SANCTIONS, PRIVATE PRISONS AND THE COLLECTION OF FINES

Once a dispute resolution has been reached, how does the winner collect from the loser? If the accused posted a bond and loses, then he and his insurers may simply forfeit the bond. But the insurers are faced with the same question: How are they reimbursed by the offender? Why would someone pay a fine or pay off a debt if the coercive power of the state does not exist to force payment? Ostracism and boycott sanctions will convince many to pay their debts. As Swartz suggested, "On account of the gregarious habits of human beings, to be put wholly beyond the pale of society would be more painful to many than to be incarcerated in a prison with others. To inflict such punishment has many advantages for the defensive organization that makes use of it. It is simple; it is easily and inexpensively applied; it involves, theoretically, none of the elements of physical force and, above all, it is not in itself an invasive act."[58] The potential effectiveness of ostracism/boycott threats is enhanced under the contractual arrangements predicted above. If part of the insurance arrangements entered into by a society is the provision of credit to pay bails or large fines, then the responsibility of collecting from the offender is shifted from the victim to the offender's security organization, and, therefore, to his community (whether it be localized geographically or functionally).

Some might argue that ostracism will not be effective in our modern, mobile society. An individual could leave his community and join another, obtaining the benefits of social interaction but avoiding payment of debt. But "nowadays, modern technology, computers, and credit ratings would make such. . .ostracism even more effective than it has ever been in the past."[59] This does not mean that some guilty offenders will not flee and attempt to hide. It means that the network of cooperative reciprocal contracts between various communities and their justice agencies are likely to prevent such an individual from obtaining the benefits of joining some other community. The incentives of members of a protection organization to exclude individuals who are likely to bring them into confrontational situations, thereby raising their costs (e.g., their insurance premiums), will be very strong under a privatized system. Thus, they will check any new entrant's background, much as a private bank checks on a loan applicant, through an established market arrangement that performs credit checks. The same technology would easily adapt to perform background checks before admitting someone into a protection organization.

A more relevant concern is that offenders may be unable to meet their financial obligations. If an offender cannot be appropriately fined, will the system break down? Friedman, in his examination of medieval Icelandic justice, suggested that a variation on the Icelandic debt-thralldom would solve the problem of judgment-proof offenders. He proposed: "An arrangement which protects the convicted criminal against the most obvious abuses would be for the. . .criminal. . .[to] have the choice of. . .accepting bids for his services. The employer making such a bid would offer the criminal some specified working conditions (possibly inside a private prison, possibly not) and a specified rate at which the employer would pay off the fine. In order to get custody of the criminal, the employer would obtain his consent and post bond with the court for the amount of the fine."[60] The offender would have a choice between ostracism or voluntarily working off the fine. Contracts between a debtor and a victim, or more likely the debtor's insurers, would specify the work conditions. If the insurers perceive little risk that a debtor will renege, they may allow him to continue in his current trade and make periodic payments. If the risk of reneging is perceived to be large, security and supervision may be provided for in the contract. For instance, in a restitution program called EARN-IT, in Quincy County, Massachusetts, forty local businessmen provided jobs to offenders who are unable to find work elsewhere.[61] The employers acted as supervisors during work hours, and offenders reported to probation officers. In other experimental restitution programs, offenders returned to jail or a "half-way house" at night.

If the risk of reneging is large enough, a "penal specialist" could be employed. Sneed predicted that a competitive penal system would arise wherein several firms would bid for employment of the convict under secure conditions.[62] Furthermore, the insurance company/convict would have the right to withdraw from the contract if the prison firm did not live up to its agreement, guaranteeing that the convict would make the highest possible wage so he could earn his way out of prison as quickly as possible. Whether this contractual arrangement arises or not, the private penal system will differ from current public prisons.

One important difference between prisons under a fully privatized system and current government prisons is that those who run private penal firms will have strong incentives to treat prisoners well. Such incentives are enhanced by an arrangement that insures prisoner mobility, as Sneed emphasized, but they exist even without a high degree of mobility. After all, a person's productivity and, therefore, the rate of debt repayment under such a system is likely to be significantly influenced by his treatment. A person who is brutalized will be unable or unwilling to perform well. The penal firm will either purchase a contract with the debtor from a victim or his insurer and assume the risk of debt payment, or contract to supervise the offender as he makes payments directly to the insurer (or perhaps victim) who wants the debt paid off as quickly as possible. A firm with a reputation for mistreating prisoners will not receive much business. Competitive forces work to preclude inhumane treatment of prisoners, then, even without prisoner mobility. This contrasts sharply with treatment of prisoners under our current penal system.[63]

Because a prisoner's effort is directly rewarded, he can predict and partially determine the length of his prison term. Prisoner morale would improve, making eventual rehabilitation easier.[64] There are a number of reasons to expect rehabilitation to be far more effective under such a system than it is with current efforts.[65]

In discussing work programs to generate restitution, Poole stressed that "by integrating the offender into the workforce and making him assume responsibility for his offense, restitution may just do more to rehabilitate offenders than all the fancy programs dreamed up by psychologists and sociologists over the past quarter century."[66] Because the purpose of prison in such a system is to allow the offender to work toward repayment of a debt, there are incentives to put the prisoner's time to its most productive use. This contrasts with current prison systems where prisoners are idle, put to work at menial labor to support the prison (e.g., in the prison laundry, kitchen, or shop), or engaged in make-work programs (e.g., making license plates). Productive use of inmate time will provide them with incentives to develop new or to strengthen existing marketable skills. It will teach them the discipline needed to hold a job in the marketplace after their release.[67] Prisoners will have incentives to cooperate with the program. But these incentives go beyond the potential for gaining a marketable skill. The self-determinative nature of a sentence means that the harder a prisoner works, the faster he obtains release. "He would be master of his fate and would have to face the responsibility. This would encourage useful, productive activity and instill a conception of reward for good behavior and hard work."[68] These incentives could have a significant rehabilitative impact.

Violence and drug abuse are significant problems in modern prisons.[69] Neither are as likely in a privatized system. Under current arrangements, an inmate sacrifices very little if he participates in violence or uses drugs; under a privatized system, he sacrifices much more because he is working toward his release. Drugs may reduce productivity and delay release and the risk of injury that significantly delays release is a substantial deterrent to violence. Under a private system, "the convict will have a direct incentive to exhibit good behavior. The better risk he appears to the penal agency, the more likely he is to be allowed parole or other freedoms in the interest of increasing his productivity."[70] Even under the Maine novelty program where greater freedoms were not likely to be available, the major novelty producers used their economic power to "counteract theft...and general thuggism" because it threatened their enterprises.[71]

Sneed concluded: "Our analog to prison would not be, as today, a brutal institution primarily functioning to teach brutes how to be more brutish, but would become almost a treatment center, a place to learn how to live peaceably in outside society. Our present system only teaches a person how to live in prison."[72] This is an important consideration for those who question the effectiveness of ostracism and boycott sanctions. The "prison" experience under privatization will not be comparable to what a convict faces in our "modern" public prisons. The offender will get something in return for his agreement to submit to a supervised work program: he will receive training and on-the-job experience with a marketable skill in a humane environment. The incentives to avoid such "punishment," therefore, are considerably weaker than under the current system, so the severity of threatened ostracism necessary to induce compliance will be considerably less than what might be expected given existing publicly produced punishment.

CONCLUSIONS

Some readers may find the proposals outlined here outlandish and even frightening. They may maintain that such a system could never work and that efforts to implement it would push us toward a lawless, violent society. For those who are so inclined, let me emphasize that the laws and institutions described in this chapter are simply predictions. Something far more sophisticated would probably emerge—something that even I cannot visualize. Certainly, any proposal to abandon a system that does work, no matter how imperfectly, must be treated with caution. The possibility of ending up with a system that does not work is definitely frightening. Of course, the movement toward a system like the one described here is likely to be a gradual one, so we need not fear an immediate disruption of life and law.

But consider the following question: Why do we entrust the decisions regarding the supplies of our food and clothing, two commodity groups that are more immediately vital to our survival than law and law enforcement, to private sector individuals operating in a market system that was created through a process of spontaneous evolution? Why do we allow government to interfere with and try to dominate the same kind of system that would efficiently and effectively produce law and its enforcement? If a government monopoly can do a better job producing law and distributing law enforcement resources, why can it not also do a better job of producing food and distributing it? American consumers are used to the efficient and effective way that they obtain food, and they would not stand for a "U.S. Food Service" patterned after the U.S. Postal Service with its lines and slow-moving clerks. Yet, we tolerate delays and slow-moving justice, perhaps because we do not have to obtain justice nearly as often as we need to obtain food and clothing and because we are not used to a more efficient arrangement.

Despite all the sophistication many observers attribute to it, our governmental legal system interrupted and slowed down the evolution of a superior legal system. Customary law still rules most of our interactions, but it is not recognized as law by most members of society. Recognition of customary law as a superior system may re-emerge, and the government institutions that impede its growth and application may be dismantled. I hope that the arguments presented in this book are sufficiently strong to convince readers that relying on customary law and private sector provision of law enforcement is not "outlandish" or "frightening." Some may even be convinced that the private sector could do a relatively good job of creating and protecting individual freedom and private property rights. Perhaps the process of privatization will accelerate a little as a consequence.

The time for significant change may be approaching. The last few decades have witnessed a substantial reduction in Americans' confidence in their government institutions and leaders.[73] From the late 1950s to the mid-1970s, self-reported trust in government fell from almost 80 percent of the population to roughly 33 percent.[74] Perhaps people will soon be ready to consider abandoning government institutions in favor of private sector alternatives, even in law and its enforcement. The rapid growth of private police and adjudicative industries attests to the fact that many Americans are already adopting such alternatives.

Many questions might remain, of course, even for those who find the arguments for privatization to be compelling. Some may accept the idea of partial privatization and a relatively limited government involvement in the production and enforcement of law to fully internalize external benefits. Possibly a limited government involvement would be even better than complete privatization. Friedman considers this possibility in the following way:

> Perhaps it would be—if the government stayed that way. . . . One cannot simply build any imaginable characteristics into a government; governments have their own internal dynamic. And the internal dynamic of limited governments is something with which we, to our sorrow, have a good deal of practical experience. It took 150 years, starting with a Bill of Rights that reserved to the states and the people all powers not explicitly delegated to the federal government to produce a Supreme Court willing to rule that growing corn to feed your own hogs is interstate commerce and can therefore be regulated by Congress.
>
> . . . [T]he logic of limited government is to grow. There are obvious reasons for that in the nature of government, and plenty of evidence. Constitutions provide, at the most, a modest and temporary restraint. As Murray Rothbard is supposed to have said, the idea of a limited government that stays limited is truly Utopian.[75]

Every aspect of government involvement in law and order started out to be *very* limited (or non-existent). English royal courts initially had very limited jurisdictions. Then they began competing with other courts in adjudicating more diverse laws. They had a "competitive" advantage in that part of the cost of using them was shifted onto taxpayers rather than being borne by litigants. Various interest groups were happy to shift their costs for protection services and the enforcement of their laws onto others by using government courts and later government watchmen, police, and prosecutors. Government entities were happy to oblige. The combination of power-seeking and bureaucratic growth by government officials and transfer (or rent) seeking by interest groups inevitably turns limited government into big government. Our founding fathers certainly could never have envisioned the pervasive government system we have today, given their clear and obvious efforts to limit its power. A customary system of law with private enforcement may not be perfect. An *ideal* and *permanently* limited government might be an improvement, but no government is going to be ideal nor can government be permanently limited. Within a relatively short time, government inefficiency would become significantly greater than the market inefficiencies a limited government might alleviate. And once government has grown, particularly to the level we currently experience, it is extremely difficult to shrink it back to its optimal limited size.

There is a problem with this argument, however. The enterprise of law described here assumes no coercive government. Such a system would require an insufficient concentration of power for any one group or organization to impose its will on others. Such diversification of power is certainly possible, and monopolization of internal security services in a private competitive market is very unlikely. But an *external* threat from a *foreign government* may *require* organization of military forces (consolidation of defense organizations, rather than competition).

Government law and coercive enforcement could arise for one of two reasons: 1) the external threat is so strong that it overcomes the internal population and subjugates that population to its government law, or 2) to resist the external threat, power becomes so concentrated internally that government formation cannot be resisted. Once that happens, the inevitable growth of government referred to by Friedman will follow, in part because those in government want more power and take it at every opportunity. If everyone were to resist such government growth, a truly limited government might be feasible, but many individuals will see the potential for personal gain through the use of governmental power. Government can take property from and restrict the rights of some individuals in order to *transfer* property or privileges to others. Thus, those in power can buy support from part of the population. Altering property rights requires legislation, of course, and the government law-making function is born.

Does this pessimistic outlook for the potential survival of a customary system of law and order mean that the arguments presented here are useless? Not at all. Privatization of many aspects of the enterprise of law are occurring, the benefits of privatization are substantial, and historical examples of successful customary law systems abound. Furthermore, the arguments for government production of law and order are generally false. Major resistance to privatization arises from the self-interest motives of those in government or those who gain transfers through the legal system, and government failure in providing law and order is significant. Finally, private arrangements for law production and enforcement can be visualized. Thus, government production of internal order is unnecessary, and there is justification for as much privatization as can be developed. If excuses for expanding government involvement in the enterprise of law are recognized as invalid, perhaps resistance to government growth will be a little stronger. Perhaps the trend can even be reversed. The fact that government may be inevitable for one society as long as an aggressive government exists someplace else is certainly no reason to accept the level of government involvement we have today or to discourage or prevent any of the privatization that is currently underway.

ENDNOTES

1. See James N. Buchanan, "Before Public Choice," in *Explorations in the Theory of Anarchy,* ed. Gordon Tullock (Blacksburg, Va.: Center for the Study of Public Choice, 1972), p. 37.
2. Ibid. See also James N. Buchanan, *Freedom in Costitutional Contract* (College Station: Texas A & M University Press, 1972).
3. Lon L. Fuller, *The Morality of Law* (New Haven: Yale University Press, 1964), pp. 23–24.
4. See for example, F. A. Hayek, *Law, Legislation and Liberty,* vol. 1 (Chicago: University of Chicago Press, 1973, p. 59; and Bruce L. Benson, "Enforcement of Private Property Rights in Primitive Societies: Law Without Government," *Journal of Libertarian Studies* 9 (Winter 1989): 1–26.
5. Hayek, *Law, Legislation and Liberty,* p. 55. Interestingly, Hayek also proposed that a limited government under a social contract was necessary for maintenance of order (see Chapter 11).
6. Fuller, *The Morality of Law,* pp. 128–129.
7. See for example, Benson, "Enforcement of Private Property Rights in Primitive Societies"; Leopold Popisil, *Anthropology of Law: A Comparative Theory* (New York: Harper and Row, 1971), p. 65; Joseph R. Peden, "Property Rights in Celtic Irish Law," *Journal of Libertarian Studies* 1 (1977): 82–94;

David Friedman, "Private Creation and Enforcement of Law: A Historical Case," *Journal of Legal Studies* 8 (March 1979): 399–415; Bruce L. Benson, "The Evolution of Law: Custom Versus Authority" (Manuscript, Florida State University, Tallahassee, Fl., 1990).

8. Benjamin R. Tucker, *Instead of a Book* (New York: Benj. R. Tucker, Publisher, 1893), p. 59.

9. Richard A. Epstein, "The Static Concept of Common Law," *Journal of Legal Studies* 9 (March 1980): 255.

10. Benson, "Enforcement of Private Property Rights in Primitive Societies"; Benson, "The Evolution of Law."

11. David Friedman, *The Machinery of Freedom: Guide to a Radical Capitalism* (New York: Harper and Row, 1973), pp. 173–174.

12. Ibid., p. 174.

13. Ibid., p. 175.

14. For example, see Benson, "The Spontaneous Evolution of Commercial Law."

15. Friedman, "Private Creation and Enforcement of Law," p. 414. Also see Randy E. Barnett, "Restitution: A New Paradigm of Criminal Justice," *Ethics* 87 (July 1977): 293.

16. See Friedman, "Private Creation and Enforcement of Law"; Peden, "Property Rights in Celtic Irish Law"; Benson, "Enforcement of Private Property Rights in Primitive Societies"; Benson, "The Evolution of Law"; Walter Goldsmidt, "Ethics and the Structure of Society: An Ethnological Contribution to the Sociology of Knowledge," *American Anthropologist* 53 (October/December 1951): 506–524; E. Adamson Hoebel, *The Law of Primitive Man* (Cambridge, Mass.: Harvard University Press, 1954); R. F. Barton, "Procedure Among the Ifugao," in *Law and Warfare,* ed. Paul Bohannan (Garden City, N.Y.: The Natural History Press, 1967).

17. Robert W. Poole, Jr., "More Justice—For Less Money," *Fiscal Watchdog* (July 1977), p. 1.

18. Poole, "More Justice—For Less Money," p. 1. See also David C. Anderson, "EARN-IT: A Key to the Prison Dilemma," *Across the Board* 20 (November 1983): 34–42.

19. Friedman, "Private Creation and Enforcement of Law," p. 408. Also see Barnett, "Restitution," p. 29.

20. See Gary S. Becker, "Crime and Punishment: An Economic Approach," *Journal of Political Economy* 76 (March/April 1969): 191–193; George J. Stigler, "The Optimum Enforcement of Laws," *Journal of Political Economy* 78 (May/June 1970): 531.

21. For other possibilities, see Barnett, "Restitution," p. 288.

22. Richard Neely, *Why Courts Don't Work* (New York: McGraw-Hill, 1982), p. 184.

23. Friedman, "Private Creation and Enforcement of Law," p. 409.

24. Neely, *Why Courts Don't Work*, p. 161.
25. Becker, "Crime and Punishment," p. 194.
26. Ibid., p. 196.
27. See for example, Benson, "Enforcement of Private Property Rights in Primitive Societies"; E. Adamson Hoebel, "Law-Ways of the Commanche," in *Law and Warfare*, ed. Paul Bohannan (Garden City, N.Y.: The Natural History Press, 1967).
28. Friedman, "Private Creation and Enforcement of Law," p. 414.
29. William M. Landes and Richard A. Posner, "The Private Enforcement of Law," *Journal of Legal Studies* 4 (January 1975): 29.
30. J. Sneed, "Order Without Law: Where Will Anarchists Keep the Madmen?" *Journal of Libertarian Studies* 1 (1977): 117.
31. Murray Rothbard, *For a New Liberty* (New York: Macmillan, 1973), p. 225.
32. See, for instance, Friedman, *The Machinery of Freedom;* Rothbard, *For a New Liberty,* pp. 222–228; Clarence L. Swartz, *What Is Mutualism?* (New York: Vanguard Press, 1927), pp. 155–166.
33. Rothbard, *For a New Liberty,* p. 222.
34. Ibid.
35. Ibid., p. 223.
36. Sneed, "Order Without Law," p. 119.
37. Ibid.
38. Rothbard, *For a New Liberty,* pp. 227–228.
39. Sneed, "Order Without Law," p. 119.
40. Peden, "Property Rights in Celtic Irish Law."
41. Sneed, "Order Without Law," p. 120.
42. Ibid.
43. Ibid., pp. 119–120.
44. See Benson, "The Evolution of Law."
45. Sneed, "Order Without Law," p. 121.
46. Benson, "The Evolution of Law"; Peden, "Property Rights in Celtic Irish Law"; Friedman, "Private Creation and Enforcement of Law"; John Umbeck, *A Theory of Property Rights With Application to the California Gold Rush* (Ames: Iowa State University Press, 1981); Terry Anderson and P. J. Hill, "An American Experiment in Anarcho-Capitalism: The *Not* So Wild, Wild West," *Journal of Libertarian Studies* 3 (1979): 9–29.
47. See, for instance, Benson, "Enforcement of Private Property Rights in Primitive Societies"; Friedman, "Private Creation and Enforcement of Law"; Peden, "Property Rights in Celtic Irish Law." Also see Chapter 2 and the appendix to Chapter 12.
48. Leon Trakman, *The Law Merchant: The Evolution of Commercial Law* (Littleton, Colo.: Fred B. Rothman and Co., 1983); Bruce L. Benson, "The

Spontaneous Evolution of Commercial Law," *Southern Economic Journal* 55 (January 1989): 644–661.

49. George Smith, "Justice Entrepreneurship in a Free Market," *Journal of Libertarian Studies* 3 (1979): 422–424.

50. Ibid., p. 422.

51. Popisil, *Anthropology of Law,* p. 36.

52. Friedman, "Private Creation and Enforcement of Law"; Benson, "The Evolution of Law"; Trakman, *The Law Merchant;* Benson, "The Spontaneous Evolution of Commercial Law."

53. Trakman, *The Law Merchant;* Harold J. Berman, *Law and Revolution: The Formation of Western Legal Tradition* (Cambridge, Mass.: Harvard University Press, 1983); Benson, "The Spontaneous Evolution of Commercial Law"; W. Mitchell, *Essay on the Early History of the Law Merchant* (New York: Burt Franklin, 1904).

54. Carl Person, "Justice, Inc.," *Juris Doctor* 8 (March 1978), p. 34.

55. See Benson, "The Evolution of Law," for more details.

56. Rothbard, *For a New Liberty,* p. 234.

57. Trakman, *The Law Merchant,* p. 16; Benson, "The Spontaneous Evolution of Law."

58. Swartz, *What Is Mutualism?* pp. 165–166.

59. Rothbard, *For a New Liberty,* p. 231.

60. Friedman, "Private Creation and Enforcement of Law," p. 415.

61. Anderson, "EARN-IT," p. 37.

62. Sneed, "Order Without Law," pp. 122–123.

63. In 1983, for example, 41 states and the District of Columbia were either under court order to remedy prison conditions or were subject to litigation. See U.S. Department of Justice, *Prisoners in 1983: Bulletin* (Washington, D.C.: Bureau of Justice Statistics, 1984).

64. Sneed, "Order Without Law," p. 123.

65. See Barnett, "Restitution," p. 293.

66. Poole, "More Justice—For Less Money," pp. 2–3.

67. In fact, Sneed logically suggested that since the penal firms will be producing marketable products they will probably offer offenders continued employment after they have retired their debts. This potential reduces the likelihood of a return to illegal activities by a released prisoner and adds to the superior rehabilitation under privatization, since many now return to crime out of virtual necessity. See Sneed, "Order Without Law," p. 123.

68. Barnett, "Restitution," p. 294.

69. Jeffrey Shedd, "Making Good[s] Behind Bars," *Reason* 13 (March 1982): 24–25.

70. Sneed, "Order Without Law," p. 123.

71. Shedd, "Making Good[s] Behind Bars," p. 27.
72. Sneed, "Order Without Law," p. 123.
73. Seymour Martin Lipset and William Schneider, *The Confidence Gap: Business, Labor and Government in the Public Mind* (New York: The Free Press, 1983).
74. E. S. Savas, *Privatizing the Public Sector: How to Shrink Government* (Catham, N.J.: Catham House Publishers, 1982), p. 1.
75. Friedman, *The Machinery of Freedom*, pp. 200–201.

INDEX

Pollock, Sir Frederick, 21, 29, 30, 47, 52, 62
Poole, Robert W., Jr.
  bureaucratic inefficiency, 338
  contracting out, 181–2, 184, 188
  corruption, 194
  privatization, 192
  restitution, 352–3, 369
  specialization, 192, 237
Poor, 71, 307–11
Popisil, Leopold, 15–21, 365
Posner, Richard
  arbitration, 221, 228, 278, 279
  common law, 283
  economic theory, 92
  free-rider problem, 356
  interest groups, 89, 91, 113
  precedent, 228, 278–80
  private institutions, 277, 303, 307
  standardization, 299, 300
Postal Service, U.S., 371
Prassel, Frank, 314
Precedent, 17, 142, 273, 278–81, 364
  arbitration, 360
  contractual arrangements, 365–6
  Kapauku Papuans, 18, 365
  primitive societies, 277
  property rights, 277
Predicasts, Inc., 204, 204 Table 9.1,
  205 Table 9.2
Primitive societies, 14, 275. See also Anglo-
  Saxons; Kapauku Papuans; Medieval
  systems
  characteristics, 5, 284
  customary law, 295, 350
  enforcement, 274, 296
  evolution, 284
  precedent, 277
  private judge, 307
  property rights, 281
  structures, 19
  trials, 365
Prisons
  drug abuse, 370
  private: ACLU, 189, 191, 301, 302, 304
  contracting out, 179, 180, 182–4, 187, 192,
    193–4, 195, 334
  evolution, 71–3, 304
  performance, 5, 190, 301, 369
  privatization, 345, 367, 368–70 (see also
    RCA; Wackenhut Services, Inc.;
    Weaversville)

public: abuse, 362
  commons problem, 143–4
  performance, 5, 187, 353, 369–70, 377n.63
  rationing, 143–4, 149
  reform, 73
  violence, 370
Prisons, Federal Bureau of, 182–3, 187
Pritchett, C. Herman, 114
Private investigators, 236–7
Private sector institutions, 2, 179–99
Private streets, 209–11, 243–4
Privatization. See also Arbitration;
  Bureaucracy, inefficiency; Courts, private;
  Crime, detection; Crime, prevention;
  Dispute resolution, community centers;
  Mediation; Protection; Security; Police,
  private; Vigilantism
  benefits of, 235–68, 331
  corporate security, 203–5
  courts, 355, 364–7
  definition, 192
  economic theory, 253–63, 307–11
  enforcement, 201, 342–4, 357–64
  evolution of law, 352–7, 363, 373, 371–4
  future implementation, 344–5, 349–78
  industry growth, 293, 341–4
  interest groups, 341
  judicial, 279
  law, 333, 336, 350–2
  lobbying, 335–6, 341
  level of, 351–2
  opposition, 300–11, 331–47
  performance, 291
  private streets, 209–11, 343–4
  process, 331–2
  punishment, 352–64
  resource allocation, 235–7, 331–2
  specialization, 237–44 (see also
    Specialization)
  standardization, 363 (see also
    Standardization)
  trends, current, 201–34
Profit, judicial. See Fines; Forfeiture
Profit motive, 185, 244–5
Property law, 285–6, 351
Property
  private, 284
  public, 76
Property rights. See also Rights assignment
  American West, 315

ABOUT THE AUTHOR

Bruce L. Benson is a Professor of Economics at Florida State University. He is also a research fellow of the Pacific Research Institute, on the advisory board of the James Madison Institute, and an associate of the Political Economy Research Center. He received his Ph.D. from Texas A&M University in 1978. Professor Benson was awarded an F. Leroy Hill Fellowship from the Institute for Humane Studies in 1985–86. He received the Georgscu-Roegen Prize in Economics for the best article in the *Southern Economic Journal* during 1988–89 for his paper, "The Spontaneous Evolution of Commercial Law," and his research in the areas of law and economics, public choice, regulation, and spatial pricing has also been published in the *American Economic Review,* the *Journal of Legal Studies, Economic Inquiry,* the *Journal of Urban Economics,* the *Joural on International Economics,* the *Journal of Industrial Economics,* the *American Journal of Agricultural Economics, Public Choice,* the *International Review of Law and Economics,* and several other journals. He coauthored *American Antitrust Law in Theory and Practice,* and has contributed chapters to several other books, including Pacific Research Institute volumes on *Firearms and Violence* and *Taxation and the Deficit Economy.*

PACIFIC RESEARCH INSTITUTE
FOR PUBLIC POLICY

The Pacific Research Institute produces studies that explore long-term solutions to difficult issues of public policy. The Institute seeks to facilitate a more active and enlightened discourse on these issues and to broaden understanding of market processes, government policy, and the rule of law. Through the publication of scholarly books and the sponsorship of conferences, the Institute serves as an established resource for ideas in the continuing public policy debate.

Institute books have been adopted for courses at colleges, universities, and graduate schools nationwide. More than 175 distinguished scholars have worked with the Institute to analyze the premises and consequences of existing public policy and to formulate possible solutions to seemingly intractable problems. Prestigious journals and major media regularly review and comment upon Institute work. In addition, the Board of Advisors consists of internationally recognized scholars, including two Nobel laureates.

The Pacific Research Institute is an independent, tax exempt, 501(c)(3) organization and as such is supported solely by the sale of its books and by the contributions from a wide variety of foundations, corporations, and individuals. This diverse funding base and the Institute's refusal to accept government funds enable it to remain independent.

OTHER STUDIES IN PUBLIC POLICY BY THE PACIFIC RESEARCH INSTITUTE

URBAN TRANSIT
The Private Challenge to Public Transportation
Edited by Charles A. Lave
Foreword by John Meyer

POLITICS, PRICES, AND PETROLEUM
The Political Economy of Energy
By David Glasner
Foreword by Paul W. MacAvoy

RIGHTS AND REGULATION
Ethical, Political, and Economic Issues
Edited by Tibor M. Machan and M. Bruce Johnson
Foreword by Aaron Wildavsky

FUGITIVE INDUSTRY
The Economics and Politics of Deindustrialization
By Richard B. McKenzie
Foreword by Finis Welch

MONEY IN CRISIS
The Federal Reserve, the Economy, and Monetary Reform
Edited by Barry N. Siegel
Foreword by Leland B. Yeager

NATURAL RESOURCES
Bureaucratic Myths and Environmental Management
By Richard Stroup and John Baden
Foreword by William Niskanen

FIREARMS AND VIOLENCE
Issues of Public Policy
Edited by Don B. Kates, Jr.
Foreword by John Kaplan

WATER RIGHTS
Scarce Resource Allocation, Bureaucracy, and the Environment
Edited by Terry L. Anderson
Foreword by Jack Hirshleifer

LOCKING UP THE RANGE
Federal Land Controls and Grazing
By Gary D. Libecap
Foreword by Jonathan R.T. Hughes

THE PUBLIC SCHOOL MONOPOLY
A Critical Analysis of Education and the State in American Society
Edited by Robert B. Everhart
Foreword by Clarence J. Karier

RESOLVING THE HOUSING CRISIS
Government Policy, Demand, Decontrol, and the Public Interest
Edited with an Introduction by M. Bruce Johnson

OFFSHORE LANDS
Oil and Gas Leasing and Conservation on the Outer Continental Shelf
By Walter J. Mead, et al.
Foreword by Stephen L. McDonald